APPROACHES TO THE HISTORY OF THE INTERPRETATION OF THE QUR'ĀN

Approaches to the History of the Interpretation of the Qur'ān

EDITED BY
Andrew Rippin

CLARENDON PRESS · OXFORD
1988

Oxford University Press, Walton Street, Oxford OX2 6DP
Oxford New York Toronto
Delhi Bombay Calcutta Madras Karachi
Petaling Jaya Singapore Hong Kong Tokyo
Nairobi Dar es Salaam Cape Town
Melbourne Auckland
and associated companies in
Berlin Ibadan

Oxford is a trade mark of Oxford University Press

Published in the United States
by Oxford University Press, New York

British Library Cataloguing in Publication Data
Approaches to the history of the
interpretation of the Qur'ān.
1. Koran—Hermeneutics
I. Rippin, Andrew
297'.1226 BP130.2
ISBN 0-19-826546-8

Library of Congress Cataloging in Publication Data
Approaches to the history of the interpretation
of the Qur'ān edited by Andrew Rippin.
Rev. and enlarged versions of papers originally
presented at a conference called The history of
the interpretation of the Qur'ān which was held
in April 1985 at the University of Calgary.
Includes index.
1. Koran—Criticism, interpretation, etc.—History—Congresses.
I. Rippin, Andrew, 1950– .
BP130.45.A66 1988 297'.1226'09—dc19 87-26275
ISBN 0-19-826546-8

Set by Hope Services
Printed and bound in Great Britain by
Biddles Ltd, Guildford and King's Lynn

ACKNOWLEDGEMENTS

IN the study of Islam, it can be said with some accuracy that the Qur'ān has come to the forefront in recent years, both in its role as scripture and as literature; this is true both outside and within the Muslim world. However, the traditional interpretation of the book, commonly termed *tafsīr* or more widely *'ulūm al-Qur'ān*, still remains a vast, virtually untapped field of investigation. Although the state of research has improved over the past twenty years, many modernist and revivalist Muslims tend to ignore the material, seeing it as a storehouse of traditional restraints, while Orientalists continue to gloss over its importance as a historical record of the Muslim community, as revealed in comments that declare the material to be 'dull and pettifogging' and the like.

The essays gathered here represent an attempt to expose and explore various aspects of the field of *tafsīr* and their potential for scholarly research. The papers have their origin, for the most part, in presentations given at a conference held at the University of Calgary in April 1985 called 'The History of the Interpretation of the Qur'ān'. The papers were invited from scholars, with contributions from within their own fields of specialization requested, with ultimate publication envisioned from the start. All the papers were revised, and often enlarged, by their authors, in light of the opportunities for discussion which the conference provided, in order to ready them for this volume and their subsequent presentation to a wider audience.

It is my pleasure as the convener of the conference to express thanks to the Social Sciences and Humanities Research Council of Canada and to the various branches of the University of Calgary—the Special Projects Fund, the International Activities Advisory Committee, the Research Grants Committee, the Faculty of Humanities, and the Department of Religious Studies, along with several other individual units of the University—for their financial support. A special note of appreciation is due to Dr Leslie Kawamura, Head of the Department of Religious Studies, for the extent of his contribution to all the facets of this conference; the

Department's support for such activities continues to play a major role in the effective teaching and research of its members.

In editing these papers, an attempt has been made to impose consistency upon the individual contributions, while, at the same time, making each paper stand on its own. In the citation of authors of texts, for example, the date of death is given on the first occasion of their citation in each chapter; the same holds true for bibliographical data. A uniform system of transliteration has been implemented; modern Indonesian orthography has been used where appropriate, however. The assistance of Mrs Vi Lake at the University of Calgary in preparing the essays for publication is most gratefully acknowledged. Floyd MacKay gave generously of his time in the preparation of the indexes.

A.R.

CONTENTS

III. SECTARIAN DIMENSIONS OF INTERPRETATION

IV. MODERN TRENDS IN *TAFSĪR*

CONTRIBUTORS

CHARLES J. ADAMS is Professor of Islamic Studies and former Director, Institute of Islamic Studies, McGill University. He has published widely on topics both within the general theory of the History of Religions and Islam. His major research interest is Islamic India, and he has been engaged for some time in the preparation of a book on Abū'l-A'lā Mawdūdī.

MAHMOUD AYOUB was educated at the American University of Beirut, University of Pennyslvania, and Harvard University, from where he received his Ph.D. in the History of Religion in 1975. He is presently Research Associate at the Centre for Religious Studies, University of Toronto. Among his publications are *Redemptive Suffering in Islam* (1978) and *The Qur'ān and its Interpreters* (1984)—the first volume of a projected 10-volume series—as well as many articles on Islam and Christology. Research in progress includes *Ja'far al-Ṣādiq, Life and Times* and *Towards an Islamic Christology: Studies in Muslim Views of Jesus*, the latter being sponsored by the United Church of Canada.

ISSA J. BOULLATA is Professor of Arabic at the Institute of Islamic Studies, McGill University. His main research interests are centred on Arabic poetry and poetics in both their classical and modern manifestations. Among his publications are *Modern Arabic Poets 1950–1975* (1976), the translation of Aḥmad Amīn, *My Life* (1978), and many journal articles.

ADRIAN BROCKETT is Lecturer in Islamic Civilization and Arabic Language in the Department of Modern Arabic Studies, University of Leeds. He has published 'Fragment of a Qur'ān, probably Spanish 15th century', *Codices Manuscript*, 10 (1984) and *The Spoken Arabic of Khābūra on the Oman Bāṭina* (*Journal of Semitic Studies*, monograph 7, 1985). His research interests include oral tradition and the transmission of the Qur'ān as well as teaching Arabic by computer.

FREDERICK M. DENNY has taught at Colby-Sawyer College, Yale, and the University of Virginia, and is currently on the faculty of

Religious Studies at the University of Colorado, Boulder. A specialist in Quranic studies and Islamic ritual, he is at work on a book about the place of the Qur'ān in the lives of Muslims in Egypt and Indonesia, based on field research in the two countries. Among his publications are the college-level text *An Introduction to Islam* (1985) and *The Holy Book in Comparative Perspective* (1985), co-edited with Rodney L. Taylor.

ANTHONY H. JOHNS is Professor and Head of the Southeast Asia Centre in the Faculty of Asian Studies at The Australian National University, Canberra. His research is focused on Indonesian Islam as well as the general field of Quranic exegesis, especially Fakhr al-Dīn al-Rāzī, and he has published widely in both fields, with recent articles appearing in *Abr-Nahrain*, *Islamo-christiana*, and the volume edited by A. H. Johns and R. Israeli, *Islam in Asia* (Jerusalem, 1984).

M. J. KISTER is Professor Emeritus of Arabic at the Hebrew University in Jerusalem. He has spent many years researching and writing about traditions on the pre-Islamic tribes, the *sīra* of Muḥammad, and early *ḥadīth* and its compilation. A number of his articles are collected in *Studies in Jāhiliyya and Early Islam* (Variorum, 1980). He has also edited volume 4a of al-Balādhurī, *Ansāb al-ashrāf* and al-Sulamī, *Kitāb ādāb al-suḥba*.

B. TODD LAWSON is Research Director with the Centre for Baha'i Studies, Ottawa. He has studied at the University of British Columbia and McGill University, from where he received his Ph.D. with a dissertation entitled 'The Qur'ān commentary of Sayyid 'Alī Muḥammad, the Bāb (1819–1850)'.

FRED LEEMHUIS is Associate Professor of Arabic at Groningen University and has written *The D and H Stems in Koranic Arabic: A Comparative Study of the Function and Meaning of the fa''ala and 'af'ala Forms in Koranic Usage* (Leiden, 1977) and, together with A. F. J. Klijn and G. J. H. van Gelder, *The Arabic Text of the Apocalypse of Baruch: Edited and Translated with a Parallel Translation of the Syriac Text* (Leiden, 1986). His major area of research is in philological aspects of early phases of Arabic and other Semitic languages.

JANE DAMMEN MCAULIFFE is Assistant Professor of the History of Religions and Islamic Studies at the Candler School of Theology, Emory University, Atlanta, Georgia. She has published in the areas of Quranic studies and Muslim-Christian relations. Her doctoral dissertation combined these emphases in a study entitled 'Perceptions of the Christians in Qur'ānic *tafsīr*' (University of Toronto, 1984). She is currently working on the issue of exegetical methodology with particular reference to Fakhr al-Dīn al-Rāzī.

Ismail K. Poonawala is Professor of Arabic and currently Chair, Islamic Studies Program, at the University of California, Los Angeles. His principle publications are *al-Sulṭān al-Khaṭṭāb: his Life and Poetry* (1967), *al-Urjūza al-mukhtāra by al-Qāḍī al-Nu'mān* (1970), *Biobibliography of Isma'īlī Literature* (1977), and *The Formation of the State: From the Ḥunayn Expedition to the Prophet's Death*, a part of the Ṭabarī Translation project (forthcoming). Presently he is working on Muḥammad 'Izzat Darwaza and his commentary on the Qur'ān.

David S. Powers is Associate Professor of Arabic and Islamics at Cornell University. He recently published *Studies in Qur'ān and* ḥadīth: *The Formation of the Islamic Law of Inheritance* (University of California Press, 1986). His annotated translation of the years 715 to 724 of al-Ṭabarī's *Ta'rīkh* will appear shortly as part of the Ṭabarī translation project from SUNY Press. At present, he is engaged in research on the practice of Islamic law in medieval Spain and North Africa.

Andrew Rippin is Associate Professor in the Department of Religious Studies, University of Calgary. He has published a number of articles on various aspects of the development of Quranic *tafsīr*, as well as *Textual Sources for the Study of Islam*, with J. Knappert (1986). His current research continues to be in the field of commentaries on the Qur'ān, especially those dealing with abrogation.

R. Marston Speight is Co-director of the Office on Christian–Muslim Relations of the National Council of the Churches of Christ and a member of the adjunct faculty of Hartford Seminary, Hartford, Connecticut. Among his publications are *Islam from Within: An Anthology of Texts*, with Kenneth Cragg (Wadsworth, 1980), as well as articles in *The Muslim World* and *Der Islam* on the Qur'ān and *ḥadīth*. He is presently undertaking a rhetorical analysis of *ḥadīth* literature.

ABBREVIATIONS

BSOAS	*Bulletin of the School of Oriental and African Studies*
EI^1	*Encyclopaedia of Islam* (Leiden, 1913–38)
EI^2	*Encyclopaedia of Islam*, new edn. (Leiden, 1960–)
GAL	C. Brockelmann, *Geschichte der arabischen Literatur* (Leiden, 1937–49)
GAS	F. Sezgin, *Geschichte des arabischen Schrifttums* (Leiden, 1968–)
GdQ	T. Nöldeke and F. Schwally, *Geschichte des Qorāns*, i–ii (Leipzig, 1909, 1919); G. Bergsträsser, O. Pretzl, *Geschichte des Qorāns*, iii (Leipzig, 1938)
Goldziher, *Richtungen*	I. Goldziher, *Die Richtungen der islamischen Koranauslegung* (Leiden, 1920)
IC	*Islamic Culture*
IJMES	*International Journal of Middle Eastern Studies*
IQ	*Islamic Quarterly*
IS	*Islamic Studies*
JAOS	*Journal of the American Oriental Society*
JMBRAS	*Journal of the Malaysia Branch of the Royal Asiatic Society*
JRAS	*Journal of the Royal Asiatic Society*
JSS	*Journal of Semitic Studies*
Lane, *Lexicon*	E. W. Lane, *An Arabic–English Lexicon* (London, 1863–93)
MW	*The Moslem World/The Muslim World*
QS	J. Wansbrough, *Quranic Studies: Sources and Methods of Scriptural Interpretation* (Oxford, 1977)
SI	*Studia Islamica*
ZDMG	*Zeitschrift der Deutschen Morgenländischen Gesellschaft*

Introduction

ANDREW RIPPIN

INVITED to give the Olaus-Petri Lectures at the University of Uppsala in Sweden in 1913, Ignaz Goldziher prepared his text (never to be delivered, as it happened) as *Die Richtungen der islamischen Koranauslegung.*[1] Published in 1920, these lectures provide a topical survey of the material of Muslim exegesis; in terms of their comprehensive overview of the subject, they have yet to be replaced in any European-language publication. While many authors have attempted to write short introductions to *tafsīr*, either as introductions to books[2] or as journal articles,[3] and other authors have attempted to supplement Goldziher's work with extended surveys of the more modern period,[4] little attempt has been made in scholarly circles towards updating, expanding, and ultimately replacing the now dated, although still stimulating, insights of Goldziher.[5]

Goldziher's work was not intended to be all-inclusive or truly comprehensive; his interest was only in sketching out the tendencies in the exegetical material. To this end, he composed his work in six major sections, covering the origins of the *tafsīr* material and then treating its development in its traditional, dogmatic, mystical, sectarian, and modern tendencies. As a basic approach, this division of the material still appears viable, so long as it is clear that

[1] Leiden, 1920.

[2] See, e.g., H. Gätje, *The Qur'ān and its Exegesis: Selected Texts with Classical and Modern Muslim Interpretations*, trans. A. T. Welch (Berkeley, 1976), 30–44; Mahmoud Ayoub, *The Qur'ān and its Interpreters*, i (Albany, 1984), 16–40.

[3] See, e.g., Ilse Lichtenstadler, 'Qur'ān and Qur'ān Exegesis', *Humaniora Islamica*, 2 (1974), 3–28; M. O. A. Abdul, 'The Historical Development of *tafsīr*', *IC* 50 (1976), 141–53; R. Ahmad, 'Qur'ānic Exegesis and Classical *tafsīr*', *IQ* 12 (1968), 71–119. For further bibliographical information on *tafsīr*, see A. Rippin, 'The Present Status of *tafsīr* Studies', *MW* 72 (1982), 224–38.

[4] See, e.g., J. M. S. Baljon, *Modern Muslim Koran Interpretation (1880–1960)* (Leiden, 1961); J. Jomier, *Le Commentaire coranique du Manār. Tendances modernes de l'exégèse coranique en Egypte* (Paris, 1954); J. J. G. Jansen, *The Interpretation of the Koran in Modern Egypt* (Leiden, 1974).

[5] See my call for such in 'Present Status', 238.

the division 'traditional' versus 'dogmatic' is one which reflects Muslim self-understanding of the enterprise, that is, the difference between *tafsīr bi'l-ma'thūr* ('interpretation following tradition') and *tafsīr bi'l-ra'y* ('interpretation by personal opinion'). How useful a separation this is for the critical scholar is certainly subject to debate.[6]

While no attempt has been made to replace Goldziher's work in recent years, the general field of study has by no means been inactive and has, in fact, been substantially stimulated in the last twenty years by three very significant publications. Nabia Abbott, *Studies in Arabic Literary Papyri*, ii. *Qur'ānic Commentary and Tradition* (1967),[7] Fuat Sezgin, *Geschichte des arabischen Schrifttums*, i (1968),[8] and John Wansbrough, *Quranic Studies: Sources and Methods of Scriptural Interpretation* (1979)[9] have all had a substantial impact upon various aspects of research in the field.[10] Most importantly, perhaps, all three of these works have made evident the truly vast quantity of texts which must be studied in order to achieve any sense of providing an overview of the Muslim exegetical enterprise.

Yet it would seem that today the challenge to produce a new survey must be taken up for a variety of reasons. The traditional historical-philological methods of analysing the Qur'ān as pursued in scholarly circles have been oriented towards re-establishing the 'original meaning' of the text or the 'author's intention' or the 'meaning of the text to the first hearers', however one wishes to express it. This latter way of expressing things has proven especially popular in the study of the Qur'ān, not because of a particular hermeneutical presupposition about the nature of the experience of texts, but rather for reasons which are closely aligned to an apologetic approach in Islamic studies: by putting things in terms of what the first hearers thought, we can avoid, it is suggested, talking about the author's intention or the original meaning—both concepts which might seem to imply an active participation in the creation of the text by Muḥammad.[11]

[6] See A. Rippin, 'Tafsīr', in *The Encyclopedia of Religion* (New York, 1987), xiv. 236–40.

[7] Chicago, 1967.

[8] Leiden, 1968.

[9] Oxford, 1977.

[10] See Rippin, 'Present Status', 226–8.

[11] See, e.g., A. T. Welch, 'Introduction: Qur'anic Studies—Problems and Prospects', in *Studies in Qur'ān and tafsīr*, issued as *Journal of the American*

Overall, this historical method has claimed that by establishing the historical context and the like at the time of the text's appearance, the original meaning can be ascertained—or at least, in the opinion of more cautious and more methodologically aware historians, the original meaning can be approximated. In many cases, too, this original meaning will be equated, sometimes explicitly, with the 'real meaning'.

The problems involved in this historical quest for truth are well known, especially within literary criticism circles,[12] but are probably worth restating here, however briefly. For one, doubts are often expressed about the possibilities of true historical knowledge, given the limitations imposed by the historian's own presuppositions. Crudely put, the scholar will never become a seventh-century Arabian townsperson but will remain forever a twentieth-century historian or philologian. Secondly, the problem of the lack of tangible evidence for a given reconstruction suggests that the scholarly historical answer will always remain speculative. Thirdly, one may raise the notion of so-called 'validity' in interpretation and question whether an 'original meaning' has any particular binding power upon the present-day researcher.[13]

It has been suggested that it is within the body of the exegetical texts that we find a way out of these kinds of hermeneutical dilemmas.[14] In exegetical works, we have evidence of 'reader

Academy of Religion, Thematic Issue, 47 (1979) supplement, 619–34, esp.626–7: 'The message of the Qur'ān is addressed initially to Muhammad and his contemporaries, and it is here that we must begin in seeking its meaning.'

[12] Among the vast quantity of literature which has appeared recently, the following may be suggested: D. C. Hoy, *The Critical Circle: Literature and History in Contemporary Hermeneutics* (Berkeley, 1978); F. Lentricchia, *After the New Criticism* (Chicago, 1980); B. Herrnstein Smith, *On the Margins of Discourse. The Relation of Literature to Language* (Chicago, 1978). Arguing the other point of view but useful for its summary of the argument is E. D. Hirsch, Jr., *Validity in Interpretation* (Chicago, 1967); on Hirsch see Robert Crossman, 'Do Readers Make Meaning?', in S. R. Suleiman and I. Crossman, eds., *The Reader in the Text: Essays on Audience and Interpretation* (Princeton, 1980), 149–64. The most immediate guide to the problems of interpretation is F. Kermode, *The Genesis of Secrecy: On the Interpretation of Narrative* (Cambridge, Mass., 1979).

[13] Some of these issues have also been raised in A. Rippin, 'Literary Analysis of Qur'ān, *tafsīr* and *sīra*: The Methodologies of John Wansbrough', in Richard C. Martin, ed., *Approaches to Islam in Religious Studies* (Tucson, 1985), 151–63.

[14] See A. Rippin, 'The Qur'ān as Literature: Perils, Pitfalls and Prospects', *British Society for Middle Eastern Studies Bulletin*, 10 (1983), 38–47; W. C. Smith, 'The True Meaning of Scripture: An Empirical Historian's Nonreductionist Interpretation of the Qur'ān', *IJMES* 11 (1980), 487–505.

reaction' to the text, and in that very concept of reader reaction may lie an answer. Gathering a great deal of popularity among literary critics today is the notion that a text does not exist in any real sense without a reader to react to and with the text.[15] And it is precisely through the exegetical works that we can establish a history of reader reaction to the Qur'ān and arrive at a meaningful construct and analysis of the Qur'ān, doubly meaningful, it would seem, because we have arrived at an intellectually satisfactory result and are at the same time actually studying what Muslims themselves have understood the Qur'ān to mean. One might wish to consider that a part of this overall literary-history reader reaction would be the twentieth-century historical-philological readings of the Qur'ān which modern scholarship has produced; these approaches may certainly be seen to have value in this sense, but little more than that. To re-create a history of the reaction to the Qur'ān in terms of what people have actually thought it means, through an analysis of exegetical texts, appears to be a most appropriate, intellectually convincing, and rewarding task for the modern scholar of the Qur'ān.[16]

Just how to go about the study of the historical reader reaction to the Qur'ān, is, of course, a problem which looms large. It is not just a simple matter of jumping in and doing the work. The field of *tafsīr* is a vast one with its own special language and concerns. The books available to the modern student and scholar as secondary sources to help in the comprehension of this material are, as has already been suggested, quite inadequate. To come to some sense of an overview of the subject would appear to be the first prerequisite for any serious study, and this is where the substance of Goldziher's *Richtungen* is appropriate but yet inadequate for today. A new history of *tafsīr* is needed. But the problem then becomes one of how to go about writing such a history. What form should such a work take? What approach should it take? Who would, in fact, be

[15] See Suleiman and Crossman, *The Reader in the Text*; Jane P. Tompkins, ed., *Reader-response Criticism: From Formalism to Post-structuralism* (Baltimore, 1980); Stanley Fish, *Is There a Text in This Class*? (Cambridge, Mass., 1980).

[16] Those who desire to construct a proper, theoretical basis for a historical reader-reception theory should consult the works of H. R. Jauss, e.g., his 'Literary History as a Challenge to Literary Theory', *New Literary History*, 2 (1970), 7–37. For the basic issue of how one interprets a commentary, James Holmes, 'Describing Literary Translations: Models and Methods', in his *Literature and Translation* (Leuven, 1978), provides a stimulating linguistic model.

qualified to undertake such a task? The essays that follow in this book are all attempts to answer these sorts of questions; one should harbour no illusions that these essays do, in themselves, comprise a 'rewritten Goldziher'. These essays are, rather, explorations in the field, each of which could undoubtedly be expanded into monograph form; indeed, it would seem that a likely conclusion to be drawn from these essays is that the eventual replacement for Goldziher must be a whole series of scholarly treatises rather than a single book. These essays are a modest start towards revealing the problems, the texts, the approaches, the principles, and the questions which underlie the field of study.

A fundamental notion which has been the topic of debate in scholarly circles since the time of Goldziher's work concerns the origins of *tafsīr* as a discipline. Recent studies by Birkeland, Sezgin, Abbott, and Wansbrough[17] have all brought this issue to the forefront as reflected in this book by the essay of Fred Leemhuis. At stake is the historical question of the rise of the formal discipline of exegesis. Is there evidence for Muḥammad's involvement in the activity or are reports of such to be treated with great scepticism, in a like manner to scholarship's attitude towards most *ḥadīth* reports? After discussing various issues surrounding the problem, Leemhuis makes the attempt to find tangible evidence for a date upon which one may peg the existence of *tafsīr* material. This he finds in a manuscript copy of a *tafsīr* ascribed by Mujāhid ibn Jabr (d. 104/722).

The separation between the text of scripture itself and its interpretation is an issue which likewise has been greatly discussed since the days of Goldziher.[18] Recently, Wansbrough has isolated the blurring which occurs in exegetical works between scripture and its interpretation by drawing attention to the various devices used for separation of the two and their presence or absence.[19] An aspect of this problem is contained also in the notion of variant readings to the text of the Qur'ān and the suggestion of their exegetical origin and intent, and the question of how their existence is to be understood in the light of a supposedly fixed text of scripture. Adrian Brockett argues a point of view in his essay not often heard in such discussions, suggesting that variants have no

[17] H. Birkeland, *Old Muslim Opposition to Interpretation of the Qur'ān* (Oslo, 1955); Sezgin, *GAS* i; Abbott, *Studies* ii; Wansbrough, *QS*.

[18] Goldziher, *Richtungen*, 4–32.

[19] *QS*, ch. 4.

significance for Muslims and have been misinterpreted by the scholarly community outside Islam. Brockett's argument rests on notions of lexicographical similarity and doctrinal insignificance as proof of individual variants having no particular value; such a position reveals that scholars may well need to go back to re-examine and reassess the variant issue.[20]

For Jane McAuliffe, it is the interpretational task itself which becomes the focus of attention. When *tafsīr* finds itself codified into books, it is not a simple matter of an author collecting together reports and presenting the material as a work of exegesis. Even those bastions of what is termed *tafsīr bi'l-ma'thūr*, al-Ṭabarī (d. 310/923) and Ibn Kathīr (d. 774/1373), are revealed in the essay to have brought to their task various exegetical principles, generally derived from the Qur'an's own separation of its content into *muḥkam* and *mutashābih*.

Likewise, it is the case that books of *ḥadīth*, apparently simple compilations, reveal a topical concern with *tafsīr* (when they have an interest in the subject at all). R. Marston Speight's examination of the body of *ḥadīth* material reveals the prime concerns of the *ḥadīth* collectors and raises, in vivid form, the differences between the *muḥaddith* and the *mufassir*. M. J. Kister attacks this same sort of problem in yet a different way. Compiling from a mass of sources—exegetical, historical, traditional, among others—all the traditions concerning Ādam as they are related (however tenuously) to certain Qur'ān texts, Kister reveals both the sources of the material and the pressures which such undergo in their eventual codification. Sectarian, theological, and moral debates are all revealed to have left their impact on the interpretational tradition.

Turning from the development of the *tafsīr* material itself to the emergence of various genres of exegetical material are the three essays of David S. Powers, Issa J. Boullata, and Andrew Rippin. Dealing with abrogation, inimitability, and lexicography respectively, each displays a different approach to the material. Powers takes a descriptive approach, analysing the genre of literature as a whole, its concerns and directions. He, like other writers on the topic such

[20] For attempts to see variants from a different perspective see A. Rippin, 'Qur'ān 21:95: "A Ban is Upon Any Town" ', *JSS* 24 (1979), 43–53; id., 'Qur'ān 7.40: "Until the Camel Passes Through the Eye of the Needle" ', *Arabica* 27 (1980), 107–13; id., 'Qur'ān 78/24: A Study in Arabic Lexicography', *JSS* 28 (1983), 311–20.

as Wansbrough and John Burton,[21] sees greater significance in the material than would seem to be immediately apparent, especially as it relates to the compilation of the Qur'ān. Boullata's essay on *i'jāz* takes essentially a historical approach, tracing the development and vicissitudes of various doctrines under the impact of a variety of influences on Muslim thought. Rippin, on the other hand, takes a topical approach, classifying various approaches to the lexicographical data of the Qur'ān, exploring their methods, and suggesting some modes of analysis. By isolating a genre of works (generally as defined within traditional *'ulūm al-Qur'ān*), each of these essays has a fairly clearly delineated group of texts to work with,[22] but the interrelationship between so many of the genres means that the boundaries are not quite as precise as one may in fact wish.

Focusing on doctrinal trends becomes the unifying element of the essays by Mahmoud Ayoub, Ismail K. Poonawala, and B. Todd Lawson. For both Ayoub and Poonawala, dealing with Ithnā 'asharī and Ismā'īlī *ta'wīl* respectively, the notion of authority becomes the matter of central concern. Both the role of the Imāms and the text of the Qur'ān itself are revealed to be the focus of speculation and dispute. But even more, the relationship between those two becomes crucial. If the Imām in one way or another represents an aspect of the Qur'ān here on earth, what is the nature of the connection between them and where does ultimate authority lie? What becomes the role of interpretation in such a circumstance?

Mystical *tafsīr* in general has a tendency, noted also in Ismā'īlī works, to raise the question of the connection between scripture and interpretation. The very use of key words as a stepping-off point for speculation means that 'interpretation' becomes a very broad term indeed, covering a vast array of possibilities. This tendency of mystical *tafsīr* reaches its pinnacle in the *tafsīr*s attributed to the Bāb (d. 1850) as explored in Lawson's essay. Here the Qur'ān serves as the basis of, as well as the model for, the interpretational text. Yet the link is always tenuous. Even more centrally the Bāb's *tafsīr* raises severe questions of authority in

[21] J. Burton, *The Collection of the Qur'ān* (Cambridge, 1977).

[22] See also A. Rippin, 'The Exegetical Genre *asbāb al-nuzūl*: A Bibliographical and Terminological Survey', *BSOAS* 48 (1985), 1–15; id., 'Al-Zarkashī and al-Suyūṭī on the "Occasion of Revelation" Material', *IC* 59 (1985), 243–58; id., 'The Function of *asbāb al-nuzūl* in Qur'anic Exegesis', *BSOAS* 51 (1988).

interpretation. Here the recourse is to the ultimate response: that the interpretation is revelation in itself. By no means is such a statement as audacious as it may at first seem when one considers the suggested midrashic origins of the New Testament gospels[23] or Qumranic *pesher* leading up to the 'revealed' Temple Scroll,[24] or, even more evidently, the status of the Mishnah as Oral Torah revealed to Moses.[25] In saying that, however, it should not be forgotten that there appears to be a unique relationship in the case of the Bāb's work *vis-à-vis* the Qur'ān; in virtually no other case did the tendency of Ṣūfī and Shī'ī *tafsīr* to locate a source of authority for their positions over against the majority Sunnī community (which vested its authority in the four *uṣūl*) reach the extent of a blatent claim to prophetic status.

Obviously the Bāb felt that the situation of his contemporaries required a radical re-evaluation of the sources of tradition and authority. This is a question faced by all Muslims at all times but it faces those in the outlying regions of the Muslim world, most especially in the modern world, most starkly. How the Qur'ān can be adapted and adopted outside its cultural, geographical, and historical origins is the question faced, once again in three different ways, in the essays by Anthony H. Johns, Frederick M. Denny, and Charles J. Adams. The Indonesian archipelago provides a stimulating test case of a country largely isolated from the Muslim heartlands and a relative newcomer to the Islamic fold, and its effect upon the Muslim sources. The enterprise of *tafsīr*, of course, provides a natural focal point for such an investigation and, at the same time, raises all sorts of crucial questions, for example, concerning the difference between translation and interpretation.

Johns's essay gives a historical summary of Indonesian involvement with the Qur'ān, specifically in the development of exegetical material. Pointing to the tradition of *diglossia*, his essay reveals the essentially conservative nature of the activity, at least until recent years. Studying the same geographical area and limited to the modern period, Denny's approach is genre-defined as related to the ritual process of Qur'ān recitation.

23 See, e.g., M. Goulder, *Midrash and Lection in Matthew* (London, 1974).

24 See, e.g., M. P. Horgan, *Pesharim: Qumran Interpretations of Biblical Books* (Washington, 1979), esp. 229–59; Y. Yadin, *The Temple Scroll: The Hidden Law of the Dead Sea Sect* (New York, 1985), esp. 78–80.

25 See Mishnah, Avot, i. 1.

The essay by Adams reveals the Indian subcontinent, by virtue of its longer history under Islam and its closer proximity to the Middle East, and also due to its unique situation of a Hindu majority under British rule, to be a place where Muslim sentiment became strongly expressed through *tafsīr*. While Mawdūdī's *Tafhīm al-Qur'ān* is far from a manifesto for revolution, it does manage to enunciate the principles which Mawdūdī felt Islam stood for and for which all Muslims should strive.

In combination, these essays reveal the scholarly field of the study of the history of interpretation of the Qur'ān to be a vibrant and bright one. Clearly there is much to be done in terms of examining and understanding the material itself. There are many approaches which need to be undertaken and developed. There are theoretical issues which must be confronted. The hope of the authors of all of these papers is, I believe, that this book will prove a stimulus to further developments in the field.

PART I

FORMATION AND DEVELOPMENT OF *TAFSĪR*

I

Origins and Early Development of the *tafsīr* Tradition

FRED LEEMHUIS

As tradition has it, even in the time of Muḥammad, the apostle and prophet of Islam, the revelation he had received needed exegesis.[1] Thus we find recorded in the tradition literature many instances of Muḥammad interpreting the meaning and implications of Quranic passages. Examples are well known; one widely recorded is the one 'Ā'isha told:

I heard the apostle of God say: 'Whoever is called to account (*man ḥūsiba*), will be punished.' She said: 'I said: "O Apostle of God, does not God say: 'His account will be easily settled' (Q. 84/8)." Whereupon the prophet [referring to Q. 69/18 ff.] answered: "O 'Ā'isha, that is the presentation (before God on Judgment Day), but anybody whose account is thoroughly examined (*man nūqisha al-ḥisāb*), will be punished." '[2]

Another well-known example is:

When the verse: 'those who believe, and have not confounded their belief with evildoing' (Q. 6/82) was sent down, it distressed the companions of God's apostle and they said: 'Which one of us does not confound his belief with evildoing?' Then the apostle of God said: 'It is not as you think, but it is what Luqmān said to his son: "Do not associate others with God; to associate others with God is serious evildoing (Q. 31/13)".'[3]

[1] Jalāl al-Dīn al-Suyūṭi, *al-Itqān fī 'ulūm al-Qur'ān* (Cairo, 1975), iv. 196–7. See also Muḥammad 'Abd al-'Aẓīm al-Zarqānī, *Manāhil al-'irfān fī 'ulūm al-Qur'ān* (Cairo, 1943), ii. 9–10, and Muḥammad Ḥusayn al-Dhahabī, *'Ilm al-tafsīr* (Cairo, 1977), 8, 10, 13–19.

[2] For the sources see A. J. Wensinck, J. P. Mensing, and J. Brugman, *Concordance et indices de la tradition musulmane* (Leiden, 1936–69), s.v. *n-q-sh*. The wording of this tradition often differs. I have followed the version that Ādam ibn Abī Iyās added to his redaction of *Tafsīr Warqā', ad* Q. 84/8, Ms Cairo Dār al-kutub, *tafsīr* 1075, fo. 89ᵛ; in the edition of 'Abd al-Raḥmān al-Ṭahīr al-Sūratī, *Tafsīr Mujāhid* (Islāmābād, n.d.), ii. 741, where however the words *yā rasūl Allāh* are omitted. See also al-Ṭabarī, *Tafsīr, ad* Q. 84/8.

[3] *Ṣaḥīḥ al-Bukhārī, kitāb al-tafsīr, ad* Q. 6/82 and 31/13. See also al-Ṭabarī, *Tafsīr, ad* Q. 6/82.

So *ẓulm*, at least in Q. 6/82, became equated with *shirk*.

The companions of Muḥammad transmitted his explanations and, because of their understanding of the language, their knowledge of the circumstances of revelation, and their insight into the religion, they supplemented them with their own explanations. All this was faithfully transmitted and complemented by the next generation, to be registered in writing by the following generation in the time of the dynastic change from the Umayyads to the ʿAbbasids.

According to a critical modern orthodox *sunnī* view, as expressed by Muḥammad Ḥusayn al-Dhahabī, we have to keep in mind that the material 'which was transmitted from the apostle on *tafsīr* was but little, as was that which was transmitted from his companions. This was only natural, because the people at that time were pure Arabs and where the verses of the Qur'ān were concerned only a small amount was unclear to them.'[4] In short, the more of the Qur'ān that became obscure in the course of time, the more of it became provided with an explanation.[5]

This is essentially a widely held Muslim view of the early history of *tafsīr*.[6] In accordance with it, we should take for granted that from the earliest times on, concern and/or disagreement about the precise meaning of God's word must have prompted exegetical activity. However, independent source material from this first phase of exegetical activity, that may verify or falsify that view, is virtually non-existent. All we know about the early period is from later ascriptions. Later works, from the middle of the second century AH at the earliest, claim to contain the exegesis of earlier authorities. But whether or not these claims are valid cannot be checked, because no objective criteria can be applied. Or to put it differently, original material, such as papyri from this early period that could substantiate these claims, has as yet not been found.

So reconstructions of the early history of *tafsīr* are all based on a preliminary assumption, which is the answer to the following question. Are the claims of the authors of the late second and the

[4] Al-Dhahabī, p. 30.
[5] Al-Dhahabī, p. 30.
[6] Cf. al-Zarqānī, ii. 1–32, and al-Dhahabī, pp. 12–46, both of whom rely on al-Suyūṭī, *al-Itqān*, but nevertheless clearly express their doubts on the reliability of much material that is transmitted from the *ṣaḥāba*. Cf. also the studies mentioned in A. Rippin, 'The Present State of *tafsīr* Studies', *MW* 72 (1982), 229 nn. 34, 35, 36.

third Islamic century, that they merely pass on the material of older authorities, historically correct?

The answer of Sezgin[7] is 'yes', and so much so that we may even believe that Ibn 'Abbās (d. 68/687),[8] 'the father of Quranic exegesis', is the author of a *Tafsīr*. The only problem is that 'it still has to be determined which of the commentaries on the Qur'ān, which his pupils transmitted from him, he wrote himself and which were recorded in writing by his pupils in accordance with his lectures.'[9] Apart from stating his perception that the lost early works may be partially or wholly reconstructed from our later sources on the basis of the technique of transmission,[10] Sezgin claims that we now have directly preserved commentaries on the Qur'ān of the pupils of Ibn 'Abbās.[11]

On the other hand Wansbrough's answer[12] is 'no', and so much so that he thinks that 'it must . . . be recognized that extant recensions of exegetical writing here designated haggadic, despite biographical information on its putative authors are not earlier than the date proposed to mark the beginnings of Arabic literature, namely, 200/815.'[13] And then haggadic or narrative exegesis is, according to Wansbrough, chronologically the earliest type of Quranic exegesis, to be followed successively by other exegetical types such as halakhic or legal and masoretical or textual exegesis.[14] Wansbrough arrived at his classification on the basis of extensive functional and stylistic analysis of an impressive number of early *tafsīr* works. In fact, he thus worked out a system of relative dating based on a literary development. It has to be noted that Wansbrough is strongly attracted to the view that 'a long period of oral composition and transmission, or possibly of oral delivery from notes is commonly supposed to have preceded the

[7] *GAS* i. 19 ff. Sezgin was able to make use of the results of analysis of *isnāds* in al-Ṭabarī's *Tafsīr* done by H. Horst, 'Zur Überlieferung im Korankommentar aṭ-Ṭabarīs', *ZDMG* 103 (1953), 290–307, who is, however, rather more cautious.

[8] I have refrained from giving references to biographical information. They may be found in the *GAS, EI*, Horst's study, etc. Only years of death are mentioned.

[9] *GAS*, i. 27 (cf. also 22). It is interesting to note Sezgin's solution for the problem that 'Alī ibn Abī Ṭalḥa did not hear *Tafsīr Ibn 'Abbās*. Whereas al-Suyūṭī had the problem resolved by quoting a tradition that Ibn Abi Ṭalḥa had learnt it from Mujāhid and Sa'īd ibn Jubayr as intermediaries (*al-Itqān*, iv. 238), Sezgin concludes that he must have received it written by Ibn 'Abbās himself, *because* he did not hear it from him!

[10] *GAS* i. 26.

[11] Ibid. 20–1, 25.

[12] Wansbrough, *QS* 119–246.

[13] Ibid. 144.

[14] Ibid. 119–21.

redaction of more or less fixed texts.' To this he adds: 'it is the chronology of that process which eludes satisfactory description.'[15]

Of course, the view that, because of the general untrustworthiness of *isnāds*,[16] the traditional Muslim view of the development of *tafsīr* in the first two centuries of Islam has to be considered—to put it mildly—more or less mythical had been eloquently voiced by Goldziher.[17] In his view he was followed by Birkeland,[18] who, however, differed from Goldziher's view that from the earliest times onward a strong opposition existed to certain kinds of *tafsīr*, namely mythological, subjective exegesis which was indicated as *tafsīr bi'l-ra'y*. Birkeland pointed out that during the greater part of the first century there was no such opposition; *ḥadīth* or *sunna*, ancient poems as well as sound reasoning (*ra'y*) were regarded as self-evident means of interpretation.[19] Only towards the end of the first century did opposition from ultra-pious circles to all interpretation of the Qur'ān arise, to fade away only around the year 200/815 when *tafsīr* was subjected to strict methods of transmission.[20] Against this view Abbott argued that when looking carefully at the story of Ṣabīgh ibn 'Isl,[21] Goldziher's point of departure for his views on early opposition,[22] the historicity of which was denied by Birkeland,[23] one could only conclude that already in early times a certain kind of *tafsīr* was frowned upon. It was, however, not *tafsīr bi'l-ra'y*, but *tafsīr al-mutashābihāt*. As was pointed out by Wansbrough, it remained unclear what precisely had to be understood in this early period by *mutashābihāt* as a technical term.[24] Apart from that, scrutiny of the respective reports on this Ṣabīgh ibn 'Isl[25] shows clearly enough that the

15 Ibid. 146.

16 See for a recent balanced view G. H. A. Juynboll, *Muslim Tradition* (Cambridge, 1983). Cf. also M. Cook, *Early Muslim Dogma: A Source-critical Study* (Cambridge, 1981), esp. ch. 11. In both works older European views, especially Schacht's, are presented and discussed.

17 Goldziher, *Richtungen*, 55–85, esp. 62–5, 81–3.

18 H. Birkeland, *Old Muslim Opposition Against Interpretation of the Koran* (Oslo, 1955).

19 A similar view is adopted by Al-Dhahabī, pp. 19–24.

20 Birkeland, p. 42.

21 N. Abbott, *Studies in Arabic Literary Papyri*, ii, *Qur'ānic Commentary and Tradition* (Chicago, 1967), 106–13.

22 Goldziher, *Richtungen*, 55–8.

23 Birkeland, pp. 13–14.

24 In his review of Abbott's book in *BSOAS* 31 (1968), 613–16 and *QS* 157–8. Cf. also A. Rippin, 'The Present Status', 226–7.

25 For the sources see Abbott, pp. 106–13; some additional sources will be mentioned below.

reasons for his punishment by 'Umar, if the story is historical, had nothing to do with *tafsīr* as such. The versions of what constituted Ṣabīgh's crime differ. He was:

(i) asking about matters from the Qur'ān among the armies of the Muslims;[26]
(ii) harassing people with difficult questions from the Qur'ān;[27]
(iii) asking about *mutashābih al-Qur'ān*;[28]
(iv) asking about *al-dhāriyāt*.[29]

Version (i) apparently shows a *taḥrīf*—*ashyā'* instead of *ashbāh*—and thus is synonymous with version (ii). How such a version later may develop into a version with the (by then) technical terms *mutashābih* with a totally different connotation is easily understood.[30] The overall impression that remains is clearly that Ṣabīgh was something of a rebellious agitator who was posing dubious questions. His brother Rabī'a showed the same rebellious nature. Ibn Durayd (d. 321/933) mentions that he took part in the battle of the camel on 'Ā'isha's side.[31] The nature of his questions may be guessed from the remark of Ibn 'Abbās quoted by al-Ṭabarī (d. 310/923) *ad* Q. 8/1 in the context of the question of what had to be considered *anfāl*,[32] and not, as may be pointed out, among the reports of those who forbade *tafsīr* or refrained from it. Ṣabīgh had probably been casting doubts on the nature and/or distribution of

26 Ibn 'Abd al-Ḥakam, *Kitāb futūḥ Miṣr wa-akhbārihā*, ed. C. C. Torrey (New Haven, 1922), 168: *anna Ṣabīgh^{an} al-'Irāqī ja'ala yas'alu ashyā' min al-Qur'ān fī ajnād al-muslimīn*.

27 Muḥammad ibn Aḥmad al-Azharī, *Tahdhīb al-lugha* (Cairo, *c.* 1967), viii. 27: *Ṣabīgh ism rajul kana yata'annatu al-nās bi-su'ūlāt mushkila min al-Qur'ān*.

28 Al-Dārimī, *Sunan*, i. 54, quoted by Abbott, . 108, n. 114. It is, among other versions, also quoted in Ibn Ḥajar al-'Asqalānī, *al-Iṣāba fī tamyīz al-ṣaḥāba* (Cairo, 1328), ii. 198, no. 4123: *qadama 'l-madīna rajul yuqālu lahu Ṣabīgh . . . fa-ja'ala yas'alu 'an mutashābih al-Qur'ān*.

29 Ibn Durayd, *al-Ishtiqāq* (Cairo, 1378/1958), 228: *wa-kāna Ṣabīgh hādhā atā 'Umar ibn al-Khaṭṭāb . . . fa-qāla ['Umar] lahu khabbirnī 'an al-dhāriyāt dharw^{an}*.

30 See, e.g., how al-Azharī's version is quoted in the *Lisān al-'Arab* by Ibn Manẓūr, s.v. *ṣ-b-gh*: *wa-Ṣabīgh ism rajul kāna yata'annatu al-nās bi-su'ūlāt fī mushkil al-Qur'ān*. It may be noted that Abbott (p. 108) tends to harmonize the different versions of Ṣabīgh's crime when she writes: 'Ṣabīgh, according to the earliest 'Irāqī and Egyptian sources . . . raised questions about the ambiguous (*mutashābih*) and difficult (*mushkilāt*) passages of the Qur'ān.'

31 Ibn Durayd, p. 228.

32 The version in 'Abd al-Razzāq's redaction of *Tafsīr Ma'mar*, MS Cairo Dār al-kutub, *tafsīr* 242 fos. 47^{v}-48^{v} is slightly different: the man who provoked Ibn 'Abbās's rebuke, 'You are like Ṣabīgh whom 'Umar flogged', is identified as an 'Irāqī, just like Ṣabīgh himself, cf. n. 26, above.

the spoils and, as such, was attacking political authority. It is clear that if the expression *mutashābih al-Qur'ān* from version (iii) is at all original it must be understood as a hint at Q. 3/7 in that Ṣabīgh was to be considered as belonging to *alladhīna fī qulūbihim zaygh^un^ fayattabi'ūna mā tashābaha minhu ibtighā'a'l-fitnati*, 'those in whose hearts is swerving, they follow the ambiguous part desiring dissension'. It is in this way that the suggestions that 'Umar suspected him to be a Kharijite probably have to be understood.[33] Being a Tamimite he may even have been suspected of still adhering to views of the false prophets of the *ridda*. Is it in this respect mere coincidence that we find among Musaylima's supposed imitations of the revelation: *wa'l-dhāriyāti qamḥ^an^*?[34]

Whatever may have been the precise nature of his inciting questions, Ṣabīgh was not explaining the Qur'ān, but casting doubt on its meaning and so undermining authority.[35] In short, he was a self-important[36] bumptious fool,[37] who, like his brother, later on, did not know his place and had to be taught a lesson by Mu'āwiya.[38] He was given a good lashing, was put under house arrest in Baṣra, and was not allowed to have contact with other people as long as he could not be expected to have mended his ways. Ṣabīgh's story probably reflects a historical event, but it has no connection with *tafsīr*, and the connection with *mutashābih al-Qur'ān* only arose secondarily. Thus, Birkeland's view about opposition to *tafsīr* only developing towards the end of the first century still stands. Although Abbott is somewhat more cautious than Sezgin as regards Ibn 'Abbās, she agrees with him in

[33] Ibn Durayd, p. 228, and Ibn Ḥajar, p. 199. The possible anachronism in this context is of course irrelevant.

[34] Among others, al-Ṭabarī, *Ta'rīkh al-rusul wa'l-mulūk* (Leiden, 1879–1901), Series i, p. 1934. Even much later, according to al-Ṭabarī (Series ii, p. 1287), Qutayba ibn Muslim in the year 96 abused the Tamimites (among others who refused to follow him in his rebellion) by addressing them as: 'You companions of Musaylima'.

[35] The title he claims for himself on 'Umar's question who he is: 'I am 'Abd Allāh Ṣabīgh', and 'Umar's answer: 'And I am 'Abd Allāh 'Umar' are indeed telling. See Abbott, p. 107.

[36] Ibn Ḥajar, p. 199, quotes a tradition that he was a *sayyid* among his people, which makes Ibn Ḥajar conclude that he was an important man in 'Umar's time.

[37] That is at least the opinion of Ibn Durayd, p. 228. Cf. al-Jāḥiẓ, *al-Bayān wa'l-tabyīn* (Cairo, 1968), ii. 259 f. and *Das biographische Lexikon des Ṣalāḥaddīn Ḫalīl Ibn Aibak aṣ-Ṣafadī*, ed. Wadād al-Qāḍī (Wiesbaden, 1982), xvi. 283.

[38] See esp. *The ansāb al-ashrāf of al-Balādhurī*, M. Schloessinger, ed. (Jerusalem, 1971), VI*a*. 35. From M. J. Kister's annotations we learn that Rabī'a was a *wālī* in Herat in the time of Mu'āwiya.

considering early ascriptions as being generally valid and also in asserting that, from early times on, the transmission of *tafsīr* was usually and widely connected with written documents.[39]

This presentation of approaches to the reconstruction of the early history of *tafsīr*[40] may have shown sufficiently that—to use the words of Michael Cook—the 'respective methods tend more to illustrate the indefinite tolerance of the source-material for radically different historical interpretations than to identify evidence which can confirm or refute the approaches in question.'[41] Recently, however, I came across a curious fact, which in my opinion constitutes a piece of such evidence which may enable us to draw somewhat more definitive conclusions about the early development of the *tafsīr* tradition. The clue is provided by a comparison of some of the transmissions of what is called *Tafsīr Mujāhid*. It was claimed by Sezgin that the Cairo Dār al-kutub manuscript *tafsīr* 1075 is one of the sources of al-Ṭabarī and thus proves his view that, by the method of *isnād* investigation, early written *tafsīr*s from the first century of Islam may be, as it were, excavated from later works.[42] Whereas for Sezgin this manuscript is a key external proof for the rightness of his views, Wansbrough did not make use of it, although he acknowledged its probable importance.[43]

As was pointed out by Stauth in his extended and careful analysis,[44] and by myself,[45] the manuscript contains in all probability just what it says it does: *Kitāb al-tafsīr 'an Warqā' ibn 'Umar* (d. 160/776) *'an Ibn Abī Najīḥ* (d. 131/749 or 132/750) *'an Mujāhid* (d. 104/722), which was transmitted by Ādam ibn Abī Iyās (d. 220/835).[46] It is, however, certainly not identical with one of al-Ṭabarī's sources, although it is clearly related to some of them, namely, the versions *'an* Ibn Abī Najīḥ *'an* Mujāhid of 'Īsā ibn Maymūn (d. *c.*170/785), Shibl ibn 'Ubād (d. 149/766), and

[39] Abbott, pp. 96–106.
[40] Cf. also Rippin, 'The Present Status', 226–30.
[41] Cook, p. 156. [42] *GAS* i. 19–21.
[43] Although mainly for other reasons, see *QS* 139.
[44] G. Stauth, *Die Überlieferung des Korankommentars Muğāhid b. Ğabrs. Zur Frage der Rekonstruktion der in den Sammelwerken des 3. Jh. d. H. benutzten frühislamischen Quellenwerke* (Giessen, 1969).
[45] F. Leemhuis, 'Ms. 1075 tafsīr of the Cairene Dār al-Kutub and Muğāhid's *Tafsīr*', in R. Peters, ed., *Proceedings of the Ninth Congress of the Union Européenne des Arabisants et Islamisants* (Leiden, 1981), 169–80.
[46] In his youth *mustamlī* of Shu'ba. Cf. 'Abd al-Karīm al-Sam'ānī, *Adab al-imlā' wa'l-istimlā'*, ed. M. Weisweiler (Leiden, 1952), 15, 89.

Warqā'.[47] A comparison of the independently transmitted text[48] with the versions from al-Ṭabarī shows that what may be called—not only for convenience's sake, as will become clear— *Tafsīr Warqā'*, *Tafsīr 'Īsā*, and *Tafsīr Shibl* must have been works of about the same length. They show, however, a difference in distribution of individual *tafsīrāt* and where they, as in the majority of cases, have *tafsīrāt* to the same passages, there is often a difference in wording, although mostly not in content.[49]

In the Cairo manuscript of *Tafsīr Warqā'*, or more accurately Ādam ibn Abī Iyās's redaction of it, a strange lacuna is found. From the beginning of *sūra* 68 until the beginning of *sūra* 77,[50] Ādam, with only one exception, adduces no *tafsīr* traditions from Warqā' *'an* Ibn Abī Najīḥ *'an* Mujāhid, whereas al-Ṭabarī quotes about a hundred, nearly all in the double-*isnād* from 'Īsā and Warqā' and so forth. Before *sūra* 68 and after the beginning of *sūra* 77, Ādam's traditions from Warqā' and his other sources and those quoted by al-Ṭabarī run largely parallel.

At first this did not strike me as peculiar, because Ādam filled up the gap with thirty-seven traditions that go back to a number of other authorities, such as 'Alī, Ibn 'Abbās, or Muḥammad himself, plus four with Mujāhid as the final authority through another chain of transmission. This lacuna is in all probability due to a very simple fact: Ādam, as a faithful transmitter,[51] simply did not transmit this material from Mujāhid via Warqā' except at one place, *sūra* 72/15, because he knew that the tradition he had from Shaybān *'an* 'Ikrima was the same as that from the Warqā' chain, namely *al-qāsiṭun* = *al-ẓālimūn*. Of course, many reasons could be suggested to explain the fact that Ādam could not transmit the missing part, but the obvious one is that it was already missing from the manuscript he transmitted. This is all the more likely because the amount of text that is missing must have been about the same as is provided by the respective *mutūn* that are found in *Tafsīr*

[47] Mainly in the redaction of al-Ḥasan al-Asyab, which is nearly always quoted in a double *isnād* with 'Īsā ibn Maymūn, to whose version it seems to have been assimilated; cf. Stauth, pp. 185–6.

[48] At least one copy, however, existed in Baghdad in al-Ṭabarī's time, cf. Leemhuis, 'Ms. 1075', 176.

[49] Stauth, pp. 148–91; Leemhuis, 'Ms. 1075', 170, 173.

[50] Fos. 83ʳ-85ʳ; in the printed edition, ii. 687–715.

[51] Cf. Stauth, pp. 73–6. It is interesting to note that Ādam in his redaction of *Tafsīr Warqā'* transmitted two traditions from 'Īsā ibn Maymūn, fo. 94ᵛ (ii. 790), but not *'an* Ibn Abī Najīḥ *'an* Mujāhid.

of al-Ṭabarī: about 950 words, which is the amount of text that the complete leaf of the papyrus fragment of *al-Wujūh wa'l-naẓa'ir* of Muqātil ibn Sulaymān (d. 150/767), which was published by Abbott, would have contained![52] The missing part must have had the same form, two joined folios which folded together formed four pages with a continuous text; in short, it would have been the middle leaf of a quire. This in itself is nothing extraordinary; it is precisely because of the fact that leaves get separated from books[53] that we are able to study such loose leaves as those from *al-Wujūh wa'l-naẓā'ir* or of Mālik's (d. 179/795) *al-Muwaṭṭa'* that were published by Abbott. That we are able to detect such a missing leaf from Ādam's direct source, however, confirms the reports on his trustworthiness and implies that there is no reason to doubt the *isnād*; it suggests that Ādam transmitted from Warqā' according to the rules which by then had become standardized. All this leads to the conclusion that Ādam's source must have been written before 160/776, the year of the death of Warqā'.[54]

This fact which may be considered as external independent evidence confirms the finding of Stauth and myself that the written fixation of the works that transmit *tafsīr* *'an* Ibn Abī Najiḥ *'an* Mujāhid must have taken place some time around the middle of the second century AH. These findings were based on *isnād*—as well as *matn*—analysis of the different Mujāhid transmissions.[55] The *mu'an'an* part of the *isnād*s, which practically always characterizes the transmission of the oldest authorities in *tafsīr isnād*s, may be regarded as reflecting the awareness of people from Ādam's generation that their masters had not had the material of their masters transmitted to them in the rigorously standardized way that had become the norm in their own time.[56] The fixation in writing of already existing variant versions of a *tafsīr* tradition that took place around 150/767 makes it impossible to reconstruct

[52] Abbott, pp. 92–5 and plates 1, 2.

[53] So, e.g., of the Arabic MS 589 of Mount Sinai, which contains the Arabic translation of the Syriac *Apocalypse of Baruch*, the outer leaf of the first quire is missing.

[54] Even if the leaf was missing not from a manuscript of Warqā', but from a rough copy Ādam had made upon dictation by Warqā', of which he later made a fair copy.

[55] Stauth, pp. 225–9; Leemhuis, 'Ms. 1075,' 175.

[56] Stauth, p. 225; Leemhuis, 'Ms. 1075', 174–5. The dispute about the inadmissability of *mu'an'an isnād*s is in this light, of course, quite understandable. See Juynboll, pp. 168 and 174.

original works from before that time, because we have no means of deciding to whom the variants are due, if they do not stem from those who fixed them. Whatever the role of writing in the transmission of *tafsīr* may have been before that time, such works, conceived as definitive and complete literary works, probably never existed.[57] A living tradition precludes them. On the other hand, the high degree of agreement in content of the variant versions shows that these are the deposit of exactly such a living tradition which must have existed for quite some time before its fixation.

The kind of exegetical activity that found its fixation in the works of Shibl, Warqā', and 'Īsā may easily be characterized. By far its most conspicuous characteristic is what may be called paraphrastic exegesis. The paraphrasis is mostly of a lexical nature of the following simple type:[58]

ad Q. 12/23 *fī qawlihi innahu rabbī ay sayyidī*: *rabb* = *sayyid*.
ad Q. 18/43 *wa-lam takun lahu fi'at*^{un} *qāla ya'nī 'ashīra*: *fi'a* = *'ashīra*.
ad Q. 42/15 *fī qawlihi lā ḥujjata baynanā wa-baynahum yaqūl lā khuṣūma baynanā wa-baynakum*: *ḥujja* = *khuṣūma*.
ad Q. 78/16 *wa-jannāt*^{in} *alfāf*^{an} *qāla yaqūl jannāt multaffa*: *alfāf* = *multaff*.

Also a somewhat more elaborate type is not uncommon:

ad Q. 6/19 *wa-ūḥiya ilayya hādhā'l-qur'ānu li-undhirakum wa-man balagha*; the *wa-man balagha* is paraphrased by: *ya'nī wa-man aslama min al-'ajam wa-ghayrihim*, 'those of the Persians and others who embrace Islam'.
ad Q. 7/57 *kadhālika nukhriju'l-mawtā* is paraphrased by: *ya'nī numṭir al-samā ḥattā tashaqqaqa 'anhum al-arḍ*, 'We shall cause the sky to rain so that the earth will split open for them.'
ad Q. 12/26 *wa-shahida shāhid*^{un} *min ahlihā* is paraphrased by *ya'nī qamīṣahu ay al-qamīṣ huwa al-shāhid in kān mashqūq*^{an} *min duburihi fa-tilka'l-shahāda*, 'his shirt, that is the shirt is the witness (or: piece of evidence) and the witness is: If his shirt is torn from behind then that is the evidence.'

[57] In this I disagree with Stauth's conclusion that all the variant versions of the Mujāhid *tafsīr* tradition quote an original work probably composed by al-Qāsim ibn Abī Bazza (see Stauth, pp. 226–7, cf. also Cook, p. 204 n. 39). It is a flaw in Stauth's reasoning, and in fact conflicts with his other conclusion that this original work cannot be reconstructed, and I doubt if Stauth would still stick to the first conclusion if his dissertation were to be made more widely available, as in my opinion it should be.

[58] Cf. Stauth, pp. 145–7.

ad Q. 66/6 *qū anfusakum wa-ahlīkum nār*^{an} is paraphrased by: *yaqūl ittaqū Allāha 'azza wa-jalla wa-awṣū ahlīkum bi-taqwā Allāhi wa-addibūhum*, 'fear God (powerful and exalted is He) and enjoin the fear of God on your families and discipline them'.

Sometimes additional information is supplied in the somewhat more expanded form of a short narrative. So, for example, *ad* Q. 17/4–7, where 'the servants of Ours, men of great might' are identified as having been an army from Persia among whom was Bukht Naṣar; they first came to spy on the Israelites and were destroyed by the Israelites the second time when the king of Persia sent them under Bukht Naṣar's command. This type of short narrative, which in fact only expands on the text of the Qur'ān, by identifying the name of the country where the men of great might came from together with the name of their commander, is in clear contrast with the very elaborate stories that are often recorded in connection with this passage in other works of *tafsīr* from a later period.[59]

What may be called real narrative does also occur. *Ad* Q. 12/19, the text of the Qur'ān is expanded upon by informing the reader that the brothers of Joseph followed the water-drawer and his fellow travellers, telling them to take care that he did not escape, and that Joseph, when offered for sale and wondering who would buy him, was bought by the king who was a Muslim. This type of narrative, however, is relatively rare in the *matn* of an *isnād* with Ibn Abi Najīḥ and Mujāhid as the oldest authorities.[60] In places which have traditionally called for such narratives, for instance, *sūra* 18 or the beginning of *sūra* 30, they are absent.[61]

It is not uncommon in Ādam's redaction of *tafsīr Warqā'*, however, to find this type of more extended narrative added by Warqā' from other authorities (for example, *ad* Q. 2/243), and especially by Ādam himself (as at *ad* Q. 6/12, 7/129, 7/175, 11/15, 12/101, 21/78, 21/100 etc.). Ādam even added very long stories (for example, *ad* Q. 28/6–11, 23–6, and 81).

Sometimes a narrative is found only in one of the versions *'an* Ibn Abī Najīḥ *'an* Mujāhid as, for example, in the case of 'Īsā's transmission regarding Q. 2/256,[62] where the story of the Jews who had fostered some men from the Aws is told, or in Shibl's *ad* Q.

[59] Cf. al-Ṭabarī, *Tafsīr, ad loc.*

[60] Cf. Stauth, pp. 141–3.

[61] *QS* 138.

[62] See al-Ṭabarī, *Tafsīr, ad loc.*

2/102,[63] where the story of Hārūt and Mārūt with al-Zuhra is mentioned.

Theologically, the three major versions of *tafsīr* in the Ibn Abī Najīḥ/Mujāhid tradition may be considered as rather neutral. They do not seem to belong to an identifiable school of thought.[64] There is, however, in accordance with the tendency to objectivism in the use of narrative, a slant to rationalism.[65] Nevertheless, it is striking that the rationalistic explanation, ascribed to Mujāhid by other sources, of Q. 75/23, *ilā rabbihim nāẓirat^un^*, 'gazing upon their Lord', amounting to a denial of the real seeing of God,[66] is not found in *Tafsīr al-Ṭabarī* as part of *Tafsīr 'Īsā* or *Tafsīr Warqā'*. In Ādam's redaction it is, of course, not present, but Ādam himself, who may be considered as continuing the Mujāhid tradition, has nevertheless explained it in the literal sense.[67]

The overall impression of the three major versions of *tafsīr* in the Ibn Abī Najīḥ/Mujāhid tradition is that they are primarily paraphrastic explications to which narrative elements serve as additional information. They are certainly not narrative *tafsīr* to which lexical and explicative paraphrasis was added; if anything, it is the other way round. The framework of the explications was apparently given by the text of the revelation.[68] They originated in all probability as oral glosses to a recited text. Not only is Mujāhid characterized by his epithet *al-Muqri'*, but it is precisely what may be gleaned from such traditions wherein *qirā'a* and *tafsīr* are coupled that appears to corroborate this conclusion.[69]

Another interesting fact of Ādam's redaction of *Tafsīr Warqā'* as regards the ascriptions to older authorities is that the *isnād*s of the additions of Warqā', quoting authorities other than Ibn Abī Najīḥ, and especially those of Ādam, quoting authorities other than Warqā', show a clear tendency to grow backwards.[70] Whereas

[63] See al-Ṭabarī, *Tafsīr*, *ad loc.*

[64] Although Ibn Abī Najīḥ became a Qadarite and Mujāhid had Murji'a connections. See Stauth, pp. 21–2, 28, 72.

[65] Stauth, pp. 144–5.

[66] Goldziher, *Richtungen*, 107.

[67] On the final authority of al-Ḥasan al-Baṣrī. However, on the question if Muḥammad saw God he quotes *ad* Q. 53/11 both a tradition from Ibn 'Abbās that the prophet saw his Lord with his heart and one from 'Ā'isha that anyone who claims that Muḥammad saw his Lord is lying.

[68] Cf. Stauth, p. 142.

[69] Cf. the introduction to al-Ṭabarī, *Jāmi' al-bayan fī ta'wīl āy al-Qur'ān*, ed. Shākir (Cairo, 1969), i. 80–2 and 90–1, *isnād* nos. 81–7, 89, and esp. 108, 112.

[70] Cf. Stauth, pp. 83–4.

*isnād*s ending with Ibn Abī Najīḥ and Mujāhid very rarely indeed go back any further, about twenty-five of the eighty or so additions of Warqā' go back to *ṣaḥāba*, mostly Ibn 'Abbās. Of the three hundred or so additions of Ādam, more than a hundred go back to *ṣaḥāba*, again with Ibn 'Abbās as the prominent authority.[71] The raising of *isnād*s to *ṣaḥāba* and especially to Ibn 'Abbās apparently started in the time of Warqā'.[72] Without implying too much, I would say that it is no real surprise that this happened in Iraq at about the time of the change of dynasty.[73] If, in agreement with the spirit of the times, one was able to raise a *tafsīr* tradition to one of the *aṣḥāb al-nabī* and especially to Ibn 'Abbās,[74] then this would enhance the respectability of *tafsīr*.

Doubts about the historicity of such ascriptions, that are expressed in remarks such as the one of al-Shāfi'ī quoted by al-Suyūṭī that only about a hundred traditions of Ibn 'Abbās in the field of *tafsīr* are authentic,[75] are nowadays amply corroborated by the research of Wansbrough[76] and Rippin[77] on the basis of literary and conceptual analysis of the text of works that are traditionally ascribed to him: *Gharīb al-Qur'ān*, *al-Lughāt fī'l-Qur'ān*, and *Masā'il Nāfi' ibn al-Azraq*. It may be clear that it is equally improbable that he is to be regarded as the author of a *Tafsīr Ibn 'Abbās*, about which Sezgin stated his conviction that it is possible to reconstruct it in 'Alī ibn Abī Ṭalḥa's (d. 120/737) transmission with the help of the traditions found in *Tafsīr al-Ṭabarī*. In agreement with the findings regarding the Mujāhid tradition, 'Alī ibn Abī Ṭalḥa probably may not even be considered as the one who fixed or had fixed in writing *tafsīr* material that belonged to an Ibn 'Abbās tradition.[78] On the other hand, it is not improbable that Ibn 'Abbās's activities are rightly characterized by the designation *turjumān al-Qur'ān*. If the ascriptions are taken to mean that the

[71] Cf. Stauth, p. 105.

[72] Birkeland, pp. 35–42; *QS* 158. Cf. Cook, p. 108 and Juynboll, *passim*, in the index under *raf'*.

[73] Cf. Juynboll, ch. 1.

[74] Cf. al-Zarqānī, ii. 23.

[75] Al-Suyūṭī, *al-Itqān*, iv. 239. See for other such sceptical views on the authenticity of material transmitted from early authorities, Juynboll, pp. 29–30.

[76] *QS*, esp. 216–19.

[77] 'Ibn 'Abbās's *Al-lughāt fī'l-Qur'ān*', *BSOAS* 44 (1981), 15–25 and 'Ibn 'Abbās's *Gharīb al-Qur'ān*', *BSOAS* 46 (1983), 332–3.

[78] Cf. *QS* 158. Wansbrough's qualification that it should be admitted 'that the historical process reflected in *tafsīr* cannot be reconstructed before the beginning of the third/ninth century' should, on the basis of the foregoing, be rejected.

respective traditions were thought to be in the spirit of a type of *tafsīr* of which Ibn 'Abbās was regarded to be the prime exponent, they probably reflect something of a historical fact.[79]

In connection with this, there is a small aspect which tends to be overlooked. In the introduction of *Tafsīr al-Ṭabarī*, Ibn 'Abbās is not called *turjumān al-Qur'ān*;[80] we only find expressed about him the opinion: *ni'ma turjamān al-Qur'ān Ibn 'Abbās*, which means nothing else than: 'What an excellent Qur'ān interpreter Ibn 'Abbās is!'[81] There is no meaning to this phrase other than that Ibn 'Abbās was an excellent representative of the genus of what, in accordance with the *Lisān al-'Arab*, may be defined as *mufassir li-lisān al-Qur'ān*, interpreter of the language of the Qur'ān.[82] The type of exegesis that is found introduced by the *isnād*s that end with Mu'āwiya ibn Ṣāliḥ (d. 158/174) *'an* 'Alī ibn Abī Ṭalḥa *'an* Ibn 'Abbās and by Muḥammad ibn Sa'd's (d. 230/844) family *isnād* that goes back to Ibn 'Abbās is not unlike one of the three major versions of the Ibn Abī Najīḥ/Mujāhid tradition. It may be noted, however, that even when one (or sometimes both) of these Ibn 'Abbās traditions agrees in content with Shibl, Warqā', and/or 'Īsā, which is by no means always the case, there is very often a difference in wording. The basic method of lexical explanation based on paraphrastic equivalence,[83] however, is clearly the same.

What are the implications of all this for a reconstruction of the early history of *tafsīr*? Extrapolating from the analysis of the fixed Ibn Abī Najīḥ/Mujāhid traditions and taking into consideration what the studies mentioned and discussed above have taught us, the following sketch may be drawn by way of a conclusion.

Probably in the time of Ibn 'Abbās, or perhaps even before, people like Ibn 'Abbās and Mujāhid, who were devoted to the

[79] Birkeland, pp. 39–40. In this respect, it seems useful to point out that even if all the ascriptions to Ibn 'Abbās are conscious fabrications, they nevertheless will be fabrications that had to function within the socio-cultural context of the society in question. Ascription of *tafsīr* material to someone who was not remembered as an authority in the field would simply not have been believed. Exaggeration of the role played by such an authority in reality is, of course, a different matter.

[80] As in al-Suyūṭī, *al-Itqān*, iv. 234. Cf. Goldziher, *Richtungen*, 65; *GAS* i. 25; *QS* 158. It may suffice to refer to the *Lisān al-'Arab, s.v. n-'-m.*

[81] Al-Ṭabarī, *Jāmi' al-bayān*, i. 90, *isnād* nos. 104–6; Ibn Kathīr, *Tafsīr* (Beirut, 1970), i. 8, also quotes the tradition in its variant form: *ni'ma al-turjumān li' l-Qur'ān Ibn 'Abbās.*

[82] *Lisān al-'Arab, s.v. t-r-j-m: al-turjumān wa'l-tarjumān al-mufassir li-lisān.*

[83] I have borrowed Wansbrough's concise description (*QS* 146) which eminently fits this type of exegesis.

recitation of Islam's most holy text, became concerned about the right understanding of the recited text. Obscure words and expressions thus were explained in immediate connection with the recitation. This is reflected in traditions as: 'When one of us learned ten verses, he did not go further until he knew their meaning.'[84] Some of these oral glosses found their way into the recitation itself under the guise of variant readings. Thus we find attributed to Mujāhid, for example, the variant readings: *yatashā'amū* instead of *yaṭṭayyarū* in Q. 7/131,[85] *la'arfaḍū* instead of *la'awḍa'ū* in 9/47,[86] and the addition *wa-huwa ab*^*un*^ *lahum* to *al-nabī awlā bi'l-mu'minīn min anfusihim* in 33/6.[87] In the different fixations of the Ibn Abī Najīḥ/Mujāhid tradition we find these variant readings as explanatory glosses.

This method of reading the Qur'ān and having its obscurities, as it were, *stante pede* explained remained as yet rather unsophisticated. Simple synonyms to obscure words were given, apparently hardly any attempts were made to compare scripture with scripture, and certainly no *shawāhid* from poetry were adduced.[88] Embedded in a living tradition, the number of explained words and passages gradually increased in the course of the following generations. Also, material of a different type crept in, such as stories about the life of Muḥammad stemming from the *quṣṣāṣ* and biblical stories from Jewish and/or Christian circles or converts. Only the elements that were considered directly relevant to the recited text, such as factual information and names of places and persons, were added to the store of explanations. Owing to the lack of independent source material, it is not possible to ascertain the precise way in which this store of explanations was guarded and transmitted. It may have been mainly orally, or orally with the help of written notes. It is even quite possible that already, at an early time, lists of explanatory glosses were in circulation. For all three possibilities, arguments from *ḥadīth*, *isnād*-analysis, and literary analysis may be brought forward.[89]

[84] See n. 69, above.

[85] So Shibl, 'Īsā, and Warqā'. See A. Jeffery, *Materials for the History of the Text of the Qur'ān* (Leiden, 1937), 178.

[86] So Warqā'. See Jeffery, p. 279: *awfadū* is probably a printing error for *arfaḍū*.

[87] So Warqā' and 'Īsā. See Jeffery, p. 282.

[88] Both are methods of interpretation belonging to the later stage of textual commentary, see *QS* 142, 202 ff.

[89] In this respect, the discussion about the application of the Parry-Lord theory of oral-formulaic composition to Arabic literature also has some relevance. See M.

However, the evidence is still inconclusive and conflicting and in all probability will remain so. Nevertheless, we may take for granted that as long as this store formed part of a living tradition, there was no special need to ascribe single items of it to single persons. Such a living tradition is the communal patrimony of all those who partake in it.

When, as we now may consider to be certain, people like Shibl, Warqā', and 'Īsā, in the later part of the first half of the second Islamic century, started to record and fix (or have fixed) in writing this store of the living *tafsīr* tradition that they themselves were part of, they had no problem in identifying that tradition. In their case it was *'an* Ibn Abi Najīḥ *'an* Mujāhid.

As had been done before them, they felt obliged to include some relevant material that they had independently acquired and considered to be of an indentifiable and trustworthy origin. This material could be in agreement[90] or in contradiction[91] with the main tradition they represented, or could provide complementary[92] or additional information.[93] Other *tafsīr* scholars of this generation, such as Sufyān al-Thawrī (d. 161/777),[94] Ma'mar ibn Rashīd (d. 153/770; or 154/771),[95] and Ibn Jurayj (d. 149/766 or 150/767),[96] left their own stamp even more clearly on the collections of *tafsīr* material they wrote or had written down in that they were more eclectic. The identification of the sources of the material that this generation of recorders of the then-living *tafsīr* tradition fixed in writing was done, as it were, by labelling the items: *'an* Ibn 'Abbās, or Mujāhid, or 'Ikrima, or al-Zuhrī, etc., thereby identifying traditional trends and not necessarily persons who had transmitted to them the respective material. This is, in my opinion, the reason why many of these proto-*insād*s are defective

Zwettler, *The Oral Tradition of Classical Arabic Poetry: Its Character and Implications* (Columbus, 1978), and the extensive and critical review by G. Schoeler, 'Die Anwendung der oral-poetry-Theorie auf die Arabische Literatur', *Der Islam*, 58 (1981), 205–36 and 'Die Frage der schriftlichen oder mündlichen Überlieferung der Wissenschaften im Frühen Islam', *Der Islam*, 62 (1985), 201–30, with whose well-documented views I largely agree.

90 *Tafsīr Warqā'*, *ad* Q. 31/35, 20/15, etc.

91 *Tafsīr Warqā'*, *ad* Q. 5/95, 55/64, etc.

92 *Tafsīr Warqā'*, *ad* Q. 25/30, 51/7, etc.

93 *Tafsīr Warqā'*, *ad* Q. 24/63, 51/17, etc.

94 *QS* 137–45; Stauth, pp. 119–23, 191–209.

95 Horst, pp. 296 and 300–1; Stauth, pp. 16–17, 123–4, 200–21.

96 Horst, pp. 295, 297; Stauth, pp. 110–14, 189.

according to the later exigencies of sound and proper *isnād* theory. It was in the next generation that their material was transmitted in accordance with the rules that by then had become firmly established: proper *isnād*s were introduced. In this generation again some transmitters added little or nothing, but others like Ādam ibn Abī Iyās supplemented the *tafsīr*s they transmitted from their masters with all kinds of material that on the basis of a sound *isnād* could be regarded as equally or even more authoritative. They had fewer qualms about including even long narratives that had no direct bearing on the meaning of the text of the Qur'ān, as long as these were somehow illuminating and edifying and not flagrantly fantastic. Above all, of course, they had to be validated through a chain of trustworthy transmitters by the great authorities of the past.

Such stories as were found in the works of some authors of the previous generation, like Muqātil ibn Sulaymān (d. 150/767)[97] who had collected these to serve as a background narrative for the often not more than allusive text of the Qur'ān, were in this generation often considered to have no *aṣl*:[98] they had no identifiable source. Probably the later qualification that Muqātil ibn Sulaymān *jama 'a tafsīr al-nās*[99] just meant that this kind of material was thought to stem from the popular store of the *quṣṣāṣ*. To us, in any case, it seems clear that this must have been the origin of this kind of narrative *tafsīr*.[100] Although it originated in circles that were different from those in which paraphrastic tafsīr had developed,[101] elements of this type of *tafsīr* nevertheless found their way more and more into the other type. Opposition from pious people from the end of the first century AH to this type of narrative *tafsīr* may later have been reinterpreted as having been directed against *tafsīr bi'l-ra'y* or *tafsīr* that was not properly *ma'thūr*.

Specialized short commentaries on legal matters, such as those that centred on the question of what parts of the Qur'ān had become abrogated, had also come into being. They may perhaps be traced back to the end of the first century in their nuclear form.

[97] Cf. *QS* 122–36 etc.; A. Rippin, 'Al-Zuhrī, *naskh al-Qur'ān* and the problem of early *tafsīr* texts', *BSOAS* 47 (1984), 23.

[98] Cf. Birkeland, pp. 16–19; al-Suyūṭī, *al-Itqān*, iv. 205.

[99] Cf. Birkeland, pp. 26–7.

[100] Thanks to Wansbrough's research, *QS* 145–8.

[101] Wansbrough admits the possibility of such a parallel development of the haggadic and masoretic type, *QS* 146.

However, if so, they apparently also originated in different circles than those in which a *tafsīr* tradition *à la* Ibn Abī Najīḥ/Mujāhid had developed. The *naskh al-Qur'ān* that is ascribed to al-Zuhrī[102] at least shows an almost total lack of agreement with *Tafsīr Warqā'*.

In the late second or early third century AH, commentaries which specialized in the textual difficulties of the Qur'ān partly drew upon traditional sources, but also introduced more developed notions of grammar, syntax, and style in their analysis of the meaning of the text. If necessary they resorted to ancient poetry and secular rhetorics to prove their point. The names of al-Farrā' (d. 207/822), Abū 'Ubayda (d. 210/825), and later Ibn Qutayba (d. 276/889) come to mind in this regard.[103] From the end of the second century onward, *tafsīr* material of different kinds that could be considered authoritative on the basis of a sound *isnād* was collected more and more into compilatory *tafsīr*s. This process had in fact started when the living tradition had become fixed. It was developed and provided with a sound basis in accordance with the science of *ḥadīth* by men like Ādam ibn Abī Iyās, was continued by men like Muḥammad ibn Ḥumayd al-Rāzī (d. 248/862).[104] and al-Muthannā ibn Ibrāhīm al-Amulī (d. after 240/854),[105] and was crowned by the achievement of Muḥammad ibn Jarīr al-Ṭabarī (d. 311/923).[106]

[102] Ed. Rippin (see n. 97 above), pp. 22–43.
[103] *QS* 206–27.
[104] Cf. Horst, pp. 296, 299, 303–4; Stauth, pp. 130–2.
[105] Cf. Horst, pp. 293, 296, 298–9, 301; Stauth, pp. 125–30.
[106] I am indebted to my colleague Geert Jan van Gelder for his constant willingness to function as a soundboard to incipient ideas and for his questions and suggestions. I thank my wife Vreni Leemhuis-Obrecht, whose critical remarks made me remove at least some obscurities, and Sheila van Gelder-Ottway, who kindly corrected my English in this paper.

2

The Value of the Ḥafṣ and Warsh transmissions for the Textual History of the Qur'ān

ADRIAN BROCKETT

MUSLIMS as well as Orientalists know that some Qur'ān 'readings' are of exegetical, rather than textual, origin.[1] But how can it be known which? Actual copies of the Qur'ān are the obvious place to start from in order to begin to answer that question. This paper illustrates the quality of the differences within and between the two transmissions of the Qur'ān found in print. One of these stems from Kūfa and the other from Medina, and they are more commonly referred to by the names of their respective second-century transmitters, Ḥafṣ (d. 180/796) and Warsh (d. 197/812).[2]

The Ḥafṣ transmission is found in printed Qur'ān copies from everywhere but West and North-West Africa, where the Warsh transmission is employed. The Ḥafṣ transmission is therefore the one found in the vast majority of printed copies of the Qur'ān, and printed copies of the Warsh transmission are rare in comparison.[3]

[1] Al-Suyūṭī cites Abū 'Ubayd as saying (in *Faḍā'il al-Qur'ān*): *al-maqṣad min al-qirā'a al-shādhdha tafsīr al-qirā'a al-mashhūra*; see *al-Itqān fī 'ulūm al-Qur'ān* (Cairo, 1368), 82.

Reference in this paper to the 'Ḥafṣ copy' of the Qur'ān means the 1402 Qatari reprint of the 1342 Cairo 'King Fu'ād text'. It has 827 pages of text with 12 lines to the page, and the frame containing the text measures 18 × 11 cm. The 'Warsh copy' is that published by the Tunis Publishing Company in 1389/1969. It has 648 pages of text, with 16 lines to the page, and a frame containing the text of 9 × 6 cm.

[2] These masters are not considered as the authors of these individual systems, but as authorities for them. As Ibn Khaldūn said, they are merely single names representing whole schools, and in no way are to be considered initiators; see *Ta'rīkh* (Beirut, 1386–7), 782.

[3] Outside West and North-West Africa, the Medinan reading-system has been maintained by the Zaydīya of the Yemen. They refer to it as the reading-system of Nāfi' (see R. B. Serjeant and R. Lewcock, eds., *Ṣan'ā', an Arabian Islamic City* (London, 1983), 316b). Whether or not the Yemeni transmission from Nāfi' was through Qālūn rather than Warsh may become apparent from the findings of the German team at present working on the Geniza of the Great Mosque of Ṣan'ā'. Books on the Qur'ān have been printed in the Yemen, but apparently no actual copies of the Qur'ān. Warsh copies have in fact been printed in Cairo and Saudi

There is no doubt about the fact that copies of the Qur'ān according to other transmissions have existed as well, but none has apparently been printed. For example, the Basrans al-Khalīl (d. *c*.175/791) and Sībawayhi (d. *c*.180/796) had texts that differed in places from both the Ḥafṣ and Warsh transmissions. Also, at least one manuscript according to the Basran reading-system of Abū 'Amr is known to exist.[4] The Qur'ān according to this transmission has in fact been printed at the head and side of the pages of some editions of the commentary of al-Zamakhsharī's (d. 538/1144) *al-Kashshāf* as well, but these multi-volumed works are not considered by Muslims as Qur'ān copies proper.

Qur'ān copies according to other transmissions may well still exist in manuscript, therefore, but they are not readily available for scholarly examination.[5] So it is more practical to document the differences between those transmissions that actually are available in print. On a general level, this provides a step towards a critical apparatus of the Qur'ān,[6] and on a more specific level, it provides the basis for the argument of this paper.

Arabia, and Ḥafṣ copies have been printed in Tunis; see A. Brockett, 'Studies in two transmissions of the Qur'ān', Ph.D. thesis (St Andrews University, 1984), 43, 71.

[4] For a possible reading of Ibn 'Āmir, Hamza, or Ibn Kathīr in manuscript, see N. Abbott, *The Rise of the North Arabic Script* (Chicago, 1939), 63.

[5] Evidence for the text of the Qur'ān from other than textual copies of the Qur'ān is slender, and a couple of examples will illustrate the point. Conflationary misquotations of the Qur'ān are found in some early texts (e.g., the *Risāla* of al-Ḥasan al-Baṣrī, the *Kitāb* of Sībawayhi), but they must be treated with caution as they can be found in some Qur'ān manuscripts themselves.

The Qur'ān citations on the Dome of the Rock are another example. The reading *tamtarūna* (Q. 19/34), as opposed to *yamtarūna* of the Ḥafṣ and Warsh transmissions provides no evidence of a text substantially different from what it is now (cf. P. Crone and M. Cook, *Hagarism: the Making of the Islamic World* (Cambridge, 1977), 18). Differences such as this have no real effect on the meaning; indeed, the extent of the agreement of the inscriptions with the text of the Qur'ān is far more impressive, and strongly suggests that the text must, in fact, have already been fixed. Nor can such inscriptions be considered to be actual copies of the Qur'ān requiring strict adherence to the rules of transmission.

[6] Since Bergsträsser's death, his and Jeffery's plan for a critical edition of the Qur'ān (see G. Bergsträsser, *Plan eines Apparatus Criticus zum Koran* (Munich, 1930), and A. Jeffery, *Materials for the History of the Text of the Qur'ān* (Leiden, 1937), p. vii) has lain dormant. The need and desirability for it, however, is still considered to be there (A. Rippin, 'The Present Status of *tafsīr* Studies', *MW* 72 (1982), 224). A. Welch, who has called for the use of computers for such an exercise ('al-Ḳur'ān', EI^2 v. 409), is now making a new start on a critical edition. See also in this connection D. Brady's review of Loebenstein's *Koranfragmente, JSS* 28 (1983), 376.

1. CONSISTENT DIFFERENCES BETWEEN THE TWO TRANSMISSIONS

In cases where there are no variations within each transmission itself,[7] certain differences between the two transmissions, at least in the copies consulted, occur consistently throughout. None of them has any effect on the meaning. The two major ones concern *hamzat al-qaṭ'* and deflection (*imāla*). As for the former, the Warsh transmission in general has far fewer glottal stops than the Ḥafṣ transmission. There are nevertheless cases of the Warsh copy having a glottal stop where the Ḥafṣ copy has *wāw* or *yā'*.[8] As for deflection, both its forms, that of *alif* towards *yā'* and that of *hamza* towards its vowel, involve the usage of the large dot.[9]

2. THE OTHER DIFFERENCES BETWEEN THE TWO TRANSMISSIONS

The other differences between the transmissions of Ḥafṣ and Warsh, as enshrined in the two copies used for comparison, can be separated into two categories—differences in the vocal forms and differences in the graphic forms.[10]

Such a division is clearly made from a written standpoint, and on its own is unbalanced. It would be a mistake to infer from it, for instance, that because *hamza* was at first mostly outside the graphic form, it was therefore at first also outside the oral form.[11] The

[7] The only variations found in printed Ḥafṣ copies from the Iranian, Indian, Turkish, Egyptian, and North-West African Traditions concern textual division, script, and minor details of orthography and recitation. None has any effect on the meaning. For details, see Brockett, 'Studies', 45–62. Similarly the only variations found between Warsh copies concern orthography or recitation. In general, it was found that the printed Warsh copies and many North-West African manuscripts of the Qur'ān belong to a scrupulously followed tradition. Warsh manuscripts from Spain and the Ḥijāz, on the other hand, are outside this tradition. Again, for details, see Brockett, 'Studies', 77–83.

[8] For an analysis see Brockett, 'Studies', 115–17.

[9] This dot is red in manuscripts but in lithographic reproductions it becomes black. To distinguish it from diacritics belonging to consonants, it is therefore kept large. For an analysis see Brockett, 'Studies', 111–14, 120–1.

[10] The usual term for graphic form is *rasm* and for vocal form is *ḍabṭ*, but *khaṭṭ, kitāb, kitāba,* and *kataba* are also used for the graphic, and *lafẓ* and *nuṭq* for the vocal. For lists, see Brockett, 'Studies', 124–33.

[11] As K. Vollers, for instance, did, eg., *Volkssprache und Schriftsprache im alten Arabien* (Strassburg, 1906), 9, 83 ff. For an attack on Voller's thesis, see T. Nöldeke, *Neue Beiträge zur semitischen Sprachwissenschaft* (Strassburg, 1910), 1–5. The

division is therefore mainly just for ease of classification and reference. However, as a bonus, this division also facilitates consideration of the question whether there was any dislocation between the graphic and vocal transmissions, and, more importantly, between the written and oral traditions. The following two sections attempt to redress the balance in the treatment of the issue by considering the differences from other standpoints as well. Lists of the differences between the two transmissions are long, and might create a first impression of the textual transmission of the Qur'ān being anything but unitary, but the length is deceptive, for the following reasons.

On the graphic side, the correspondences between the two transmissions are overwhelmingly more numerous than differences, often even with oddities like *ayna mā* and *aynamā* being consistently preserved in both transmissions (e.g., Q. 2/148, 3/112 and Q. 4/78, 16/76), and *la'nat Allāhi* spelt both with *tā' ṭawīla* and *tā' marbūṭa* in the same places in both transmissions (Q. 3/61 and 3/87). As well, not one of the graphic differences caused the Muslims any doubts about the faultlessly faithful transmission of the Qur'ān. This aspect will be discussed in the next section.

On the vocal side, correspondences between the two transmissions again far and away outnumber differences between them, even with fine points such as long vowels before *hamzat al-qaṭ'* having a *madda*. Also, not one of the differences substantially affects the meaning beyond its own context. This is discussed in section 4, below. All this points to a remarkably unitary textual transmission in both its graphic and its oral form.[12]

3. MUSLIM ATTITUDES TO THE GRAPHIC DIFFERENCES

One's attitude to graphic differences is indicative of one's attitude to the whole Qur'ān. Many Orientalists who see the Qur'ān as only a written document might think that in the graphic differences can be found significant clues about the early history of the Qur'ān text—if 'Uthmān issued a definitive written text, how can such

orthographic sign for *hamza* was simply a later invention; see 'Abd al-Ṣabbūr Shāhīn, *al-Qirā'āt al-Qur'ānīya fī ḍaw' 'ilm al-lugha al-ḥadith* (Cairo, 1386), 18.

[12] Labīb al-Sa'īd, *The Recited Koran* (Princeton, 1975), 106, makes this point on the oral side, but it applies just as much on the written side too.

graphic differences be explained, they might ask. For Muslims, who see the Qur'ān as an oral as well as a written text, however, these differences are simply readings, certainly important, but no more so than readings involving, for instance, fine differences in assimilation or in vigour of pronouncing the *hamza*. This can adequately be shown by illustrating some Muslim comment on three of the graphic differences occurring in the first five *sūras*.

i. *wawaṣṣā/wa'awṣā (Q. 2/132)*[13]

Whereas Ibn al-Jazarī (d. 833/1429) could spend several pages on the precise pronunciation of the word *bāri'ikum* (Q. 2/54),[14] he notes this graphic difference in a few lines without further comment: 'Nāfi', Abū Ja'far and Ibn 'Āmir read *wa'awṣā*, which was how it was in the texts of the Medinese and the Syrians. The rest of the "ten" [readers] read *wawaṣṣā* which was how it was in their texts.'[15] Likewise, al-Farrā' (d. 207/822) could hardly have shown more succinctly that where the meaning was maintained, the reading was more an oral than a graphic matter: '*wawaṣṣā*: In the texts of the Medinese *wa'awṣā*. Both are correct and commonly heard.'[16] Abū 'Ubayda (d. 210/825) did not consider the reading worth a comment. As a cursory, final remark to his discussion of *wawaṣṣā*, al-Ṭabarī (d. 310/923) mentions that many readers read *wa'awṣā*; since it alters the meaning hardly at all, he does not even mention the fact that there is a graphic difference here.[17] This and the following example are, for al-Dānī (d. 444/1053), two items in a long list,[18] although he adds concerning this particular entry that Abū 'Ubayd (d 224/838) saw *wa'awṣā* in the *imām*, the *muṣḥaf 'Uthmān*.[19] His concluding rationalizations hinge on the fact that the written text has never been separate from the oral one, whether in terms of authorities or actual recitation.[20]

[13] In each instance the word is given, first as it appears in the Ḥafṣ copy, and then, following the oblique, as it appears in the Warsh copy.

[14] Ibn al-Jazarī, *al-Nashr fi'l-qirā'āt al-'ashr* (Cairo, n.d.), ii. 212 ff.

[15] Ibid. 222.

[16] Al-Farrā', *Ma'ānī al-Qur'ān* (Cairo, 1955–72), i. 80; see also *GdQ* iii. 11 n. 6.

[17] Al-Ṭabarī, *Jāmi' al-bayān 'an ta'wīl āy al-Qur'ān*, ed. Shakīr (Cairo, 1958–) iii. 96. For a vigorous rejection of a reading by al-Ṭabarī, because of its effect on the meaning, see below, note 52, and for a general observation on al-Ṭabarī's attitude towards readings, see al-Dhahabī, *al-Tafsīr wa'l-mufassirūn* (Cairo, 1396), i. 214; cf. also *GdQ* iii. 109 n. 3.

[18] Al-Dānī, *al-Muqni' fī rasm maṣāḥif al-amṣār ma'a kitāb al-nuqaṭ*, ed. O. Pretzl (Istanbul, 1932), 109, 116, 118.

[19] Ibid. 109.

[20] Ibid. 123–31, esp. 124.

ii. wasāri'ū/sāri'ū (Q. 3/133)

Ibn al-Jazarī described this difference in exactly the same terms as the previous example.[21] Al-Zamakhsharī also dealt with this difference no differently from many a difference in vocalization.[22] Al-Farrā', in whose exegetical style readings are more prominent than in the work of most other exegetes, did not even think this one worth a mention, nor again did Abū 'Ubayda, or even al-Ṭabarī.

iii. yartadda/yartadid (Q. 5/54)

This difference drew more comment from both Ibn al-Jazarī and al-Zamakhsharī, although still without concern about apparent textual inconsistency. Al-Zamakhsharī states: 'Both *yartadda* and *yartadid* are read. The latter was in the *imām*.'[23] For Ibn al-Jazarī it was more a matter of assimilation than textual divergence:

> Abū Ja'far, Nāfi' and Ibn 'Āmir read *yartadid*, which was how it was in the texts of the Medinese and Syrians. The rest of the 'ten' [readers] read *yartadda*, which was how it was in their texts. All, however, read *yartadid* in [the same phrase in] Q. 2/217 because of the unanimity of the texts and because of the length of *sūrat al-baqara*, which calls for the drawing out [of words] and the extra consonant in this case. Take, for instance, Q. 8/13, where all of the 'ten' are unanimous in not assimilating *waman yushāqiqi'llāha warasūlahu*, and Q. 59/4, where all of them are unanimous in assimilating *waman yushaqqi'llāha*, which could be because of the two contexts' relative affinity for length and brevity.[24]

Whether or not the other occurrence of *waman yushāqiq* (Q. 4/115), which was omitted by Ibn al-Jazarī in *Nashr*, casts doubt on this suggestion of his is not relevant, for what is most noteworthy is that the graphic difference in these instances did not unduly trouble him.

Al-Ṭabarī used the reading for a short grammatical digression, concluding that both forms are chaste and common,[25] but al-Farrā' and Abū 'Ubayda again thought it not worth mentioning.

Sībawayhi also indicated that the reading figured in the discussions on assimilation, when he alluded to it in a chapter on assimilation:

[21] See Ibn al-Jazarī, ii. 242. With the similar cases of *wāw* before a verb being absent in certain readings in Q. 2/116 and 5/53, Ibn al-Jazarī again passes them over with less comment than he gives many a fine difference in vocalization (see pp. 220, 254).

[22] Al-Zamakhsharī, *al-Kashshāf 'an ḥaqā'iq al-tanzīl* (Beirut, n.d.), i. 463.

[23] Ibid. 620.

[24] Ibn al-Jazarī, ii. 255.

[25] Al-Ṭabarī, *Jāmi' al-bayān*, x. 421.

[With geminate verbs] in the jussive, the people of the Ḥijāz keep the consonants separate, and say *urdud* and *lā tardud*. This is the good old classical language. Banū Tamīm, however, amalgamate [and so would say *rudda* and *lā tarudda*].[26]

Here also, al-Dānī cited Abū 'Ubayd as having seen *yartadid* in the *imām*.[27]

On occasion, graphic differences without effect on the meaning can figure more prominently in studies on *qirā'āt*, not however for textual reasons, but for questions of authority. For example, Ibn al-Jazarī discussed the reading *yā'ibādi/yā'ibādī* (Q. 43/68) at greater length than usual,[28] but he made nothing of the graphic difference, arguing simply about authorities. Al-Ṭabarī did not even mention this variant reading.

The definitive limit of permissible graphic variation was, firstly, a consonantal disturbance that was not too major, then unalterability in meaning,[29] and finally reliable authority.[30]

4. THE EXTENT TO WHICH THE DIFFERENCES AFFECT THE SENSE

The simple fact is that none of the differences, whether vocal or graphic, between the transmission of Ḥafṣ and the transmission of Warsh has any great effect on the meaning.[31] Many are differences which do not change the meaning at all, and the rest are differences with an effect on the meaning in the immediate context of the text itself, but without any significant wider influence on Muslim thought. One difference (Q. 2/184) has an effect on the meaning that might conceivably be argued to have wider ramifications; it therefore provides a good illustration of the limit of variation between the two transmissions. The need to detail how each and every difference, apart from this one, has no wider implications may first be satisfied by the following examples.

26 Sībawayhi, *al-Kitāb* (Cairo, 1316), ii. 424.

27 Al-Dānī, *al-Muqni'*, 110, also 116, 118.

28 Ibn al-Jazarī, ii. 176–9; see also al-Dānī, *al-Muqni'*, 36, and al-Dānī, *al-Taysīr fi'l-qirā'āt al-sab'*, ed. O. Pretzl (Istanbul, 1930), 70, 197.

29 Ibn al-Jazarī, i. 13; see also J. Burton, *The Collection of the Qur'ān* (Cambridge, 1977), 149, 206.

30 Al-Dānī, *al-Muqni'*, 121.

31 To disagree with Jones, 'The Qur'ān, II', in *Cambridge History of Arabic Literature* (Cambridge, 1983), i. 244.

(i) The difference *ātaytukum/ātaynākum* (Q. 3/81), for instance, has no effect on the meaning at all. The subject is the same in both, and it is merely a matter of God speaking in the singular or plural of majesty,[32] both of which are often attested.
(ii) The difference between *nunshizuhā* and *nunshiruhā* (Q. 2/259) is one of the root, but it alters the meaning in no way since both roots can mean the same, 'to raise'.[33]
(iii) Similarly, the difference *taqūlūna/yaqūlūna* (Q. 2/140) is merely a matter of direct or indirect address.
(iv) The difference *wattakhidhū/wattakhadhū* (Q. 2/125) is of mood and time, but it also has no effect beyond its own immediate context, being merely a matter of direct address or reported action.
(v) The difference *yakhda'ūna/yukhādi'ūna* (Q. 2/9b) is one related to the stem, but it has no effect beyond its own context, being merely a theological nicety as to pseudo-believers actually deceiving themselves or only trying to.[34]
(vi) The difference *yaqūla/yaqūlu* (Q. 2/214) is a grammatical nicety concerning the government of *ḥattā*.[35]
(vii) Finally, the difference *wakaffalahā/wakafalahā* (Q. 3/37) is a matter of the stem and subject. The second stem reading signifies that God appointed Zakarīyā to look after the wife of 'Imrān, whereas the first stem reading signifies simply that Zakarīyā looked after her.[36] Again, however, this is of no wider import.

It has been said above that no differences between these two transmissions have any great effect on the meaning, so with regard to the one that follows, which might be argued to have an effect beyond its context, it is necessary to set up a criterion as to how to gauge the extent of the effect. A sensible criterion is to judge the extent to which the difference in the readings figures in Islamic

[32] Ibn al-Jazarī, ii. 241.

[33] Lane, *Lexicon*, 2794a, 2795c. Ibn al-Jazarī noted this reading without comment (*Nashr*, ii. 231), as did Abū 'Ubayda, *Majāz al-Qur'ān* (Cairo, 1374, 1381), i. 80. See also al-Ṭūsī, *al-Tibyān fī tafsīr al-Qur'ān* (Najaf, 1375–6): 8, and after him, al-Ṭabarsī, *Majma' al-bayān fī tafsīr al-Qur'ān* (Tehran, 1373–4), i. 12. For other, similar differences, see *GdQ* iii. 140 n. 4. See also Q. 3/120 for a reading with two different roots in the two transmissions, *ḍyr* and *ḍrr*, both meaning the same.

[34] See Ibn al-Jazarī, ii. 207, for comments regarding this reading, showing that he was fully aware that readings could come into being for the purpose of conveying an additional meaning. He suggested that a certain reading did not come about because of the derogatory meaning it would have had towards God.

[35] Sībawayhi, i. 417; al-Ṭabarī, *Jāmi' al-bayān*, iv. 290.

[36] Al-Zamakhsharī, i. 427.

thought outside the context of actual Qur'ān exegesis. While these wider branches of Islamic science were at root also Qur'ān interpretation, the task of exegesis pure and simple was to extract as much information as possible, in whatever branch of science, from each and every Qur'ān utterance. In more specialized works, of grammar or theology for instance, only that Qur'ān material which provided a source for discussion in the particular specialist area was naturally dwelt upon, however. So to look in these specialist works for evidence as to how wide the implications of a given Qur'ān reading might have been is safer than limiting the evidence to the purely exegetical works alone. The latter's demand for comprehensiveness might easily lead to the extent of the effect of a given difference in reading being overestimated.

By means of this criterion, then, a difference that might be thought to have a substantial effect on the meaning turns out to have been an exegete's collector's item, rather than a living legal issue. In Q. 2/184 is read *wa 'alā'lladhīna yuṭīqūnahu fidyat^{un} ṭa'āmu miskīn^{in}* or *fidyatu ṭa'āmi masākīna*. Abū Ja'far, Nāfi', and Ibn 'Āmir read the plural *masākīn*, the rest of the 'ten' (readers) read the singular *miskīn*.[37] At first sight, whether part of the expiation (*fidya*) for not fasting was to feed one pauper or several might be thought to have been just the kind of problem likely to exercise the minds of casuistic legal scholars. In the similar phrase of Q. 5/95 (*fajazā'^{un} mithlu mā qatala . . . aw kaffārat^{un} ṭa'āmu masākīna*), where the atonement is for deliberate killing of game while in *iḥrām*, none of the ten readers is said to have read the singular.[38] Interestingly, Ibn al-Jazarī gave a reason for a plural reading not being read here; in short, it was that in Q. 5/95 the making good of lost life is involved, where the value of a bird, for instance, is clearly less than that of a sheep, rather than the making good of lost days (as in Q. 2/184), where one day is no different from another.

The *fidya*, the expiation for breaking the fast, was divided by the scholars into *qaḍā'* and *kaffāra*. The former involved refasting, that is, making up lost days, and the latter involved a penalty, whether

37 Ibn al-Jazarī, ii. 226.

38 Ibn al-Jazarī, ii. 255. Al-A'raj is reported as having read the singular, since, being a clarification, only one (pauper) needed to be mentioned as standing for the whole category; see al-Zamakhsharī, i. 645. Al-A'raj was a Meccan *mawlā* who died in 130 (*GdQ* iii. 166). He was a teacher of the Basran Qur'ān reader Abū 'Amr, and on the borders of being one of the 'fourteen' Qur'ān readers (*GdQ* iii. 189).

manumission, or (for some) an extra sixty-day fast, or feeding paupers. *Qaḍā'* was only ever one further day for each day missed. The feeding-*kaffāra* was also (for most) on a one-to-one basis.[39] It was taken for granted that the singular reading of Q. 2/184, *miskīn*, meant '[those able must make up by feeding] one pauper [for each day they missed]', and the plural reading, *masākīn*, meant '[the same number of] paupers [as the days they missed]'. Both readings, in other words, meant the same. If, further, the fast was broken in such a way as to require a complete month's penalty, this would obviously require, if it could be replaced by feeding paupers, the feeding of thirty.[40]

In the legal literature the question scarcely figures. In his *Umm*, al-Shāfi'ī (d. 204/820) did not discuss the issue. His only apparent reference to the question is the problem of what expiation should be made for someone who had been remiss in fasting after recovering from an illness, or who had been remiss and then had died before making up for his remission. His answer, that those who had recovered before dying had to have fed on their behalf one pauper an amount of one maund for each day missed,[41] implies a plural understanding. For him, *miskīn* certainly did not mean a total of only one pauper for however many days' fasts had been broken.

A similar plural understanding, without any other even being entertained, is found in Mālikī law, where, however, the feeding-penalty is the quantity of a maund to be shared between sixty paupers.[42] In Zaydī legal works significant discussions are not evident. Ibn al-Murtaḍā (d. 310/922) quotes the Qur'ān verse

[39] 'Ṣawm', *EI*[1] iv. 195: every fast-day was considered an independent ritual act, and so, if broken, had its penalty. For the Mālikī two-to-one penalty, see note 42 below.

[40] This is the gist of al-Ṭabarī's exegesis (*Jāmi' al-bayān*, iii. 439 f.). There is no mention of anyone ever having suggested that only one pauper need be fed for however many days missed.

[41] Al-Shāfi'ī, *Kitāb al-umm* (Cairo, 1381), ii. 104.

[42] Saḥnūn, *al-Mudawwana al-kubrā* (Cairo, 1323), i. 218. Here there seems to be a deliberate rejection of the source of the penalty being the thirty days of the month of the fast. The source is shown rather to be in the supposedly analogous situation of someone going back on the *ẓihār* divorce (i. 219). See also Mālik, *al-Muwaṭṭa'* (Cairo, 1370), i. 296 (*kitāb al-ṣiyām*, *bāb* 9), also p. 307 (*kitab al-ṣiyām*, *bāb* 19), and in al-Shaybānī's recension (Cairo, 1399), p. 123 (*abwāb al-ṣiyām*, 3) where the analogy is explicit. The penalty in the Qur'ān for someone going back on *ẓihār* is precisely manumission, or, if that is not possible, a two-month fast, or, if that is not possible, the feeding of *sixty* paupers (Q. 58/3–4).

with the plural reading and refers to the *ḥadīth* of Abū Hurayra specifying one pauper for each day missed, and does not record any disagreement in the matter.[43]

In *Aḥkām al-Qur'ān*, al-Shāfi'ī's understanding of the verse is given as: 'Those who were able to fast but then became unable, are obliged to make an expiation of feeding one pauper for each day.'[44] The point of the discussion here is the meaning of *yuṭīqūnahu*. For al-Bukhārī also the question concerned *yuṭīqūnahu* alone.[45]

It becomes clear that, for the jurisprudents, the *miskīn/masākīn* difference was insignificant, and that the exegetical tasks were rather to clarify the *alladhīna* and the *hu* in *yuṭīqūnahu*. In that regard, several questions arose. Did this *hu* refer to the fast or the *fidya*? And depending on this, to whom did *alladhīna* refer? Was it those who were unable to fast, or those unable to pay the penalty?

Even in the purely exegetical literature the *miskīn/masākīn* question hardly figured. While citing readings for six other words in this one verse, al-Zamakhsharī, for instance, did not even mention this one.[46] Nor was the plural reading mentioned by al-Farrā' in his explanation of the verse which reads: 'Those able to fast who do not must feed one pauper for every day not fasted.'[47] Al-Ṭabarī, while producing a lengthy discussion about the verse as a whole, simply tagged the *miskīn/masākīn* reading on at the end for the sake of completeness.[48] By the time of the encyclopaedic exegesis of al-Rāzī (d. 606/1209), the question still hardly figured at all. *Yuṭīqūnahu* receives two and a half pages of comment,[49] the plural reading *masākīn*, one line.[50]

It is of relevance, however, to compare al-Ṭabarī's ease of acceptance of this double reading with his sharp rejection of another reading earlier on in the verse. For al-Ṭabarī the *miskīn/masākīn* difference had no wider implication; it had no effect on the rules and regulations of making good a broken fast. He certainly

43 Ibn al-Murtaḍā, *al-Baḥr al-zakhkhār al-jāmi' li-madhāhib 'ulamā' al-amṣār* (Cairo, 1366–8), ii. 257; I am indebted to Prof. W. Madelung for this reference. For the *ḥadīth*, see Ibn Ḥanbal, *Musnad* (Cairo, 1313), ii. 208, 241, 273, 281.

44 Al-Shāfi'ī (ed. al-Bayhaqī), *Aḥkām al-Qur'ān* (Beirut, *c.* 1371), i. 108.

45 Ibn Ḥajar, *Fatḥ al-bārī bi-sharḥ al-Bukhārī* (Cairo, 1378–96), ix. 246 f; al-Bukhārī, *al-Saḥīḥ* (Cairo, 1377–8), vi. 30.

46 Al-Zamakhsharī, i. 355.

47 Al-Farrā', i. 112.

48 Al-Ṭabarī, *Jāmi' al-bayān*, iii. 439–40, out of thirty pages for the verse.

49 Fakhr al-Dīn al-Rāzī, *Mafātīḥ al-ghayb al-mushtahir bi'l-tafsīr al-kabīr* (Tehran, 1390–), v. 78–81.

50 Ibid. v. 81.

indicated a preference for the singular reading, but more for reasons of logic than for any connected with the point at issue. He states: 'It is easy to extrapolate from a single case to many of the same case, but not to deduce from many regarding one.'[51] But he did not reject the plural reading, nor did he make any judgement as to which of the two was earlier. His criterion was not, 'what was original?', but 'what is the clearest reading?'

Earlier on in the verse there was the reading *yuṭawwaqūnahu* for *yuṭīqūnahu*. Al-Ṭabarī's rejection of it provides a vivid illustration of the unassailably unitary nature of the text of the Qur'ān. This reading was support for those scholars who would have *alladhīna* refer to the elderly, who could not fast.

As for the reading *yuṭawwaqūnahu*, it goes against the Qur'ān copies of the Muslims, and no Muslim is allowed to set his own opinion over against what they all have as a hereditary transmission from their Prophet, an indisputable transmission removing all excuses. For what has behind it the authority of the religion is truth and without doubt Divine. And what is confirmed and executed by Divine authority is not to be opposed by opinions, hypotheses or independent theories.[52]

It was not the graphic difference of *wāw* for *yā'* that troubled al-Ṭabarī; he accepted such graphically different readings elsewhere.[53] It was the wider implication that the *meaning* of the reading would have not just on the rules regarding the fast but also on the science of *naskh* that demanded that he reject the reading.[54] Nor did the array of companions and followers as authorities for the reading impress al-Ṭabarī; he cited Ibn 'Abbās, 'Ikrima, Sa'īd ibn Jubayr, 'Ā'isha, 'Aṭā', and Mujāhid for the reading and, for the meaning, he cited 'Alī, Ṭāwūs, and al-Ḍaḥḥāk.[55]

It is not necessary to wander down the ins and outs of the predictably ramified dispute, but suffice it to cite two of al-Ṭabarī's traditions about this reading as tips of exegetical icebergs.

'Ikrima said, *alladhīna yuṭīqūnahu* means those who fast, but *alladhīna yuṭawwaqūnahu* means whose who cannot fast.[56] 'Ikrima read this verse

[51] Al-Ṭabarī, *Jāmi' al-bayān*, iii. 440.
[52] Ibid. iii. 438.
[53] See above, section 3.
[54] See also al-Zamakhsharī, i. 335, and note how in Muslim, *al-Ṣaḥīḥ* (Cairo, 1374), ii. 802, the question of the verse comes under abrogation.
[55] In traditions 2784, 2786, 2790, 2791 of al-Ṭabarī, *Jāmi' al-bayān*.
[56] Ibid. iii. 430. Cf. Lane, *Lexicon*, 1894a, '*ṭawwaqtuhu'l-shay'* means "I made the thing to be [as though it were] his *ṭawq* [or neck-ring]", and thereby is expressed

wa 'alā' lladhīna yuṭawwaqūnahu, and held that it was not abrogated. Old men were required not to fast but to feed one pauper per day.[57]

5. CONCLUSION

Such then is the limit of variation between these two transmissions of the Qur'ān, a limit well within the boundaries of substantial exegetical effect. This means that the readings found in these transmissions are most likely not of exegetical origin, or at least did not arise out of crucial exegetical dispute. They are therefore of the utmost value for the textual history of the Qur'ān. Conversely, a general rule can be drawn that when a reading cited by a scholar is of substantial exegetical (especially legal) effect, then it is most likely not to have been textual in origin, that is, not to have been literally there in the text, written or oral. The value of a comparison of these two transmissions for the textual history of the Qur'ān is thus at least twofold. Firstly, the limits of their variation clearly establish that they are a single text.[58] Secondly, given the undisputed oral preservation of the Qur'ān, it looks far more likely than not that the same limit of variation in text would have applied between all transmissions of the Qur'ān.

The fidelity of oral tradition in the Near East in general is well known,[59] and that of the Arabs in particular.[60] Illiteracy strengthens memory. However, looked at negatively, oral tradition

the imposing [upon one] a thing that is difficult, troublesome, or inconvenient. . . . And [in the Qur'ān] some read, *wa 'alā'lladhīna yuṭawwaqūnahu* meaning, ". . . and upon those who shall have it imposed upon them as a thing that is difficult".'

[57] Al-Ṭabarī, *Jāmi' al-bayān*, iii. 430.

[58] Muir stated this over a century ago: 'The recension of 'Uthmān has been handed down to us unaltered. So carefully, indeed, has it been preserved, that there are no variations of importance,—we might almost say no variations at all,—amongst the innumerable copies of the Qur'ān scattered throughout the vast bounds of the empire of Islam. Contending and embittered factions, taking their rise in the murder of 'Uthmān himself within a quarter of a century from the death of Muhammad have ever since rent the Muslim world. Yet but ONE QUR'ĀN has always been current amongst them. . . . There is probably in the world no other work which has remained twelve centuries with so pure a text.' See W. Muir, *The Life of Mahomet* (London, 1858), i. xiv–xv. This needs to be restated because other, entirely contrasting, views are current. For Muir's 'recension of 'Uthmān', however, now read 'the Qur'ān'.

[59] See, e.g., H. Gunkel, *The Legends of Genesis* (Chicago, 1907), 98 f.

[60] See J. Pedersen, *Israel, its Life and Culture* (London, 1926), 127; H. A. R. Gibb, *Modern Trends in Islam* (Chicago, 1947), 5.

is characterized by variants resulting from words wrongly heard, from words confused with similar sounding words, and from whole episodes being forgotten, misplaced,[61] or reinterpreted.[62] Leaving aside the art of calligraphy, written tradition is characterized by variants resulting from copyists' errors, words read wrongly, revised, or left out by a careless eye, and by random passages getting lost, or being added to on the basis of other sources.[63] Thus, if the Qur'ān had been transmitted only orally for the first century, sizeable variations between texts such as are seen in the *ḥadīth* and pre-Islamic poetry would be found,[64] and if it had been transmitted only in writing, sizeable variations such as in the different transmissions of the original document of the Constitution of Medina would be found.[65] But neither is the case with the Qur'ān. There must have been a parallel written transmission limiting variation in the oral transmission to the graphic form, side by side with a parallel oral transmission preserving the written transmission from corruption.[66] The transmission of the Qur'ān after the death of Muḥammad was essentially static, rather than organic. There was a single text, and nothing significant, not even allegedly abrogated material, could be taken out nor could anything be put in.[67] This applied even to the early caliphs. The efforts of those scholars who attempt to reconstruct any other hypothetical original versions of the (written) text are therefore shown to be disregarding half the essence of Muslim scripture.

The innovation of vocalization did not occur simply because foreigners did not know how to recite correctly; vocalization was

[61] E. Nielsen, *Oral Tradition* (London, 1961), 37.

[62] P. Crone, *Slaves on Horses* (Cambridge, 1980), 7.

[63] Nielsen, p. 36; Crone, *Slaves*, 7 nn. 23–5.

[64] In an organic living tradition, that is a non-written one, a prophet's original message is not regainable. It is inextricable from the additions of the disciples and the disciples' disciples, and so on up until literary fixation. Its historicity cannot therefore be taken at face value; indeed, delving into it can result in its history being turned upside down. Wansbrough's methodology falls into this category. But no Qur'ān reading can be explainable only by oral considerations.

[65] For this text see R. B. Serjeant, 'The *Sunnah Jāmi'ah*, Pacts with Yathrib Jews and the *Taḥrīm* of Yathrib: Analysis and Translation of the Documents Comprised in the so-called "Constitution of Medina" ', *BSOAS* 41 (1978), 1–42 for bibliography and full discussion.

[66] For parallel interplay between written and oral tradition, see Nielsen, pp. 34 ff. See also A. Jeffery, *The Qur'ān as Scripture* (New York, 1952), 17. Cf. the effectively complete absence of acknowledgement of an oral tradition of the Qur'ān in A. Mingana, 'The Transmission of the Koran', *MW* 7 (1917), 223–32, 402–14.

[67] Burton, pp. 239, 162, 188.

not a replacement for oral transmission,[68] nor was it a case of 'stabilisation of the text'.[69] These are literary points of view, Muslim and Orientalist, and at the back of all Muslim discussion of the written form is the question of dating individual parts of the text, behind which is the science of *naskh*. But the Qur'ān was not a literary document. Graphic differences like those illustrated above were not worried about. Indeed, such variations show that the spirit was more important than the letter, and this fact is borne out by *tafsīr*.[70] The problem of foreigners' pronunciation may have been a factor in the spread of vocalization, as also the increasing use of paper over parchment at this time.[71] There is some indication, however, that the move for vocalization came from the wider culture of Iraq,[72] that is, from the Nestorian Christians with their system of dot-vocalization,[73] in which case vocalization would have spread from foreigners, not for them. So an equally feasible factor in its spread would have been straightforward respect for the Qur'ān as the Divine Word, a motivation arising out of the need for beautification rather than for clarification, for reverence rather than reference. There was a continual desire to make the written form of the revelation equal to the perfection of the oral form. The writing became aesthetically more and more reverent.

There can be no denying that some formal characteristics of the Qur'ān point to the oral side and others to the written side, but neither was, as a whole, primary. There is therefore no need to make different categories for vocal and graphic differences between transmissions. Muslims have not. The letter is not a dead skeleton to be refleshed, but is a manifestation of the spirit, alive from the beginning. The transmission of the Qur'ān has always been oral, just as it has always been written.

68 Al-Sa'īd, p. 55.

69 Cf. Goldziher, *Richtungen*, 1; *QS*, 1, *passim*. Diacritical dots seem in fact to have been employed in Arabic writing in pre-Islamic times (see B. Moritz, 'Arabia', *EI*[1], i. 383).

70 Al-Ṭabarī, for instance, frequently accepts, quite willingly, two or more readings as equally valid when the meaning remains unaltered; see, e.g., *ad* Q. 6/96, *Jāmi' al-bayān*, xi. 556; *ad* Q. 56/22, *Jāmi' al-bayān* (Cairo, 1373), xxvii. 176; *ad* Q. 112/4, ibid. xxx. 348.

71 Abbott, *North Arabic Script*, 56.

72 Ibid. 59.

73 Y. H. Safadi, *Islamic Calligraphy* (London, 1968), 13. Also see the vowel diagram in J. B. Segal, *The Diacritic Point and the Accents in Syriac* (London, 1953), 152–3. I would like to thank Dr J. Burton, M. A. Cook, and Dr P. Crone for helpful comments made on earlier drafts of this paper.

3

Quranic Hermeneutics: The Views of al-Ṭabarī and Ibn Kathīr

JANE DAMMEN MCAULIFFE

IT is always intriguing to listen to scholars describe their approaches and explain the methods which guide their work. Occasionally this will take the form of a straightforward exposition of principles. More often, the presentation is allusive, garnered by the student from passing comments, or deduced from an analysis of the finished work. The activity of Quranic exegesis offers no exception to these observations, particularly as represented in the *tafsīr*s of Muḥammad ibn Jarīr al-Ṭabarī and 'Imād al-Dīn Ismā'īl ibn Kathīr. Both of these men have left direct and indirect evidence from which an understanding of their exegetical principles may be gleaned. Both, in other words, have provided their readers with the elements of a hermeneutics.

This last-mentioned term is itself in need of careful explication because of the variety of meanings which the word has been asked to convey, particularly in the last century and a half. The English word 'hermeneutics' is, of course, formed from the Greek infinitive *hermēneuein*. Among the most commonly cited meanings of this verb are 'to explain', 'to translate', and 'to express'.[1] The Swiss theologian and philosopher, Gerhard Ebeling, has noted this three-fold signification and attempted to co-ordinate it under the common rubric of 'interpretation'. Using the Latin deponent, *interpretor*, so as not to beg the question, Ebeling concludes that a situation is 'interpreted (*interpretiert*)' through words, a language-use through explanation and a foreign language through translation.[2] It is this base notion of 'interpretation'—or, more especially, the prerequisites for the same—that came to dominate the range of signification carried by the English cognate, 'hermeneutics'.

[1] Henry George Liddell and Robert Scott, comp., *A Greek-English Lexicon*, rev. edn., ed. Henry Stuart Jones (Oxford, n.d.), i. 690.

[2] G. Ebeling, 'Hermeneutik', *Die Religion in Geschichte und Gegenwart* (Tübingen, 1959), ii. 243.

By the post-Reformation seventeenth century this word had begun to appear in book titles to designate a subcategory of Christian theology. The activity of interpretation was divided into its theoretical and practical aspects. The practice of interpretation was equated with what we would now term 'exegesis', while the term 'hermeneutics' was used to denote the aims and criteria of that practice. In conventional theological usage, then, hermeneutics was the enterprise which identified the principles and methods prerequisite to the interpretation of texts. It is in this classical sense that the term will be applied to the parallel activity within the realm of Quranic scholarship.[3] The question of exegetical methodology will be addressed to two pre-eminent Islamic commentators, al-Ṭabarī and Ibn Kathīr.

Abū Ja'far Muḥammad ibn Jarīr al-Ṭabarī was born in the one-time Sassanian province of Ṭabaristān, a mountainous region which lies behind the southern coast of the Caspian Sea. His birthdate is usually given as 224/838, but occasionally as 225/839. Early evidence of intellectual precocity justified a youth and young manhood spent searching for ever-broader educational horizons.[4] His early forays were only as far south as Rayy (just south of modern Tehran), but eventually he went to Baghdad, using that city as a base for expeditions to such places as Kūfa, Baṣra, Cairo, and parts of Syria.[5] It was, however, to Baghdad, the centre of the 'Abbasid universe, that he always returned and that city saw his reputation grow ever brighter.

By all accounts al-Ṭabarī is acknowledged to be one of the great minds of his era. His biographers are unanimously impressed by the extent and depth of his erudition and the magnitude of his written work. A statement by the eleventh-century historian and jurisconsult al-Khaṭīb al-Baghdādī (d. 463/1071) sums up pages of laudation:

[3] The broader signification of the term (frequently used in the singular form, hermeneutic) is most prominently associated with such twentieth-century thinkers as Wilhelm Dilthey, Hans-Georg Gadamer, and Paul Ricoeur. For a brief historical overview of the theological debate, see James M. Robinson, 'Hermeneutic since Barth', in James M. Robinson and John B. Cobb, Jr., eds., *New Frontiers in Theology*, ii. *The New Hermeneutic* (New York, 1964), 1–77.

[4] Al-Ṭabarī evinced his extraordinary gifts of intellect in that time-honoured Muslim way, youthful memorization of the Qur'ān (in his case by the age of 7); see Yāqūt ibn 'Abdallāh al-Ḥamawī al-Rūmī, *Irshād al-arīb ilā ma'rifat al-adīb*, D. S. Margoliouth, ed. (Cairo, 1925), vi. 429–30.

[5] Muḥammad ibn 'Alī ibn Aḥmad al-Dāwūdī, *Ṭabaqāt al-mufassirīn*, 'Alī Muḥammad 'Umar, ed. (Cairo, 1392/1972), ii. 107–8.

'He had a degree of erudition shared by no one of his era.'[6] Al-Ṭabarī put this vast knowledge at the disposal of his students and those who solicited his legal opinions. Evidently, he sought no high office for himself and refused any he was offered. His professional life was one of persistent scholarship, dedicated teaching, and prolific writing.

Al-Ṭabarī died in his adopted city of Baghdad in 310/923. His written legacy includes two of the fundamental works of Islamic scholarship. The first is a history of the world as he knew it entitled *Ta'rīkh al-rusul wa'l-mulūk*, and the second is his massive commentary on the Qur'ān, *Jāmiʿ al-bayān ʿan ta'wīl āy al-Qur'ān*. This latter work ushers in the classical period of Islamic exegetical activity. Therein is contained the compilation and methodical arrangement of the first two and a half centuries of Muslim exegesis.

Because of the tremendous number of exegetical *ḥadīth*s which it incorporates, this *tafsīr* is usually judged to be a particularly important example of *tafsīr bi'l-ma'thūr*.[7] Yet *Jāmiʿ al-bayān* is far more than simply a collection and compilation of the extant exegetical material. It is a carefully structured work which evinces considerable insight and judgement. That al-Ṭabarī was clearly aware of methodological issues is evident from the very first pages. He has prefaced his work with an introductory section which touches upon a number of hermeneutical considerations.[8] In addition to linguistic and lexical concerns (such as the commonly accepted 'readings' (*qirā'āt*) of the Qur'ān), al-Ṭabarī discusses the problematic status of *tafsīr bi'l-ra'y* (interpretation by personal opinion), the objections of those who oppose all exegetical activity, and the reputations of previous commentators, whether revered or denigrated in the passage of time.

Of particular interest for the subject under consideration is the section which al-Ṭabarī devotes to discussing the various ways by

[6] Al-Dāwūdī, ii. 109; Muḥammad al-Ṣabbagh, *Lamaḥāt fī ʿulūm al-Qur'ān wa-ittijāhāt al-tafsīr* (Beirut, 1974), 185.

[7] Some idea of the magnitude of this compilation is to be found in a perusal of the most recent (and as yet unfinished) edition of the *tafsīr*. The editor has consecutively numbered the *ḥadīth*s which al-Ṭabarī incorporated. This edition has not gone beyond the commentary on Q. 14/25 and yet the enumeration has reached 20,787.

[8] The only extended treatment in Western languages of al-Ṭabarī's introduction to his *tafsīr* is to be found in an article published more than a hundred years ago by O. Loth, 'Tabarī's Korankommentar', *ZDMG* 35 (1881), 588–628.

which an individual may arrive at knowledge of the interpretation (here he uses the term *ta'wīl*) of the Qur'ān.[9] The framework of his remarks is a three-fold division of the Quranic materials. Using Q. 16/44 and 16/64 as warrant, al-Ṭabarī posits the first class of verses as those which can only be interpreted by Muḥammad.[10] The two supporting verses each contain the clause *li-tubayyina* ('so that you may explain') with Muḥammad as the subject of the phrase. This exegete then notes the various kinds of verses which constitute this first class. He summarizes his listing by stating that it comprises those verses which have legal consequences and which may be understood only in the light of the prophet's explanation of them. Consequently, 'the only necessary discussion of them is that whereby the messenger of God explains his interpretation.'[11] According to al-Ṭabarī, this explanation may take two forms. It may involve either a phrase from him (*bi-naṣṣ minhu*) or a convincing demonstration (*bi-dalāla*) 'which he has formulated to show what led him to his interpretation'.[12]

The second class of Quranic material, according to al-Ṭabarī, is that of which only God knows the interpretation. (He offers no explanation for making this the second rather than the first category.) The examples which he cites include texts relating to the future sending of 'Īsā ibn Maryām and the time of the hour of resurrection. To support this position al-Ṭabarī quotes Q. 7/187, marking it as a *muḥkam* verse (a designation which will be explained in a later section of this paper.) This verse, which deals with the problem of those who harassed the prophet for knowledge of the final hour, raises the exegetical question of whether Muḥammad had access to this information. In both his commentary on the verse itself and in the present context, al-Ṭabarī is careful to insist upon God's exclusive possession of such awareness.[13] As for Muḥammad, 'God informed him of its coming only by His portents (*bi-ashrāṭihi*) and of its appointed time only by His signs

[9] Abū Ja'far Muḥammad ibn Jarīr al-Ṭabarī, *Jāmi' al-bayān 'an ta'wīl āy al-Qur'ān*, Maḥmūd Muḥammad Shākir and Aḥmad Muḥammad Shākir, eds. (Cairo, 1374/1954–), i. 73 f.

[10] Ibid. i. 74. [11] Ibid. [12] Ibid.

[13] Ibid. xiii. 298–301. Al-Ṭabarī's commentary on Q. 7/187 concludes with an explanation of the final phrases: *yas'alūnaka ka-annaka ḥafīy^{un} 'anhā qul innamā 'ilmuhā 'inda Allāh wa-lākinna akthara al-nās lā ya'lamūna.* According to al-Ṭabarī that which most people do not know is not, as one might suppose, the time of the final hour; rather, they are ignorant of the fact that God alone possesses this knowledge. Ibid. xiii. 301.

(*bi-adillatihi*).'[14] The prophet had no specific knowledge of the final hour to the point of knowing the precise month and day (*bi-maqādīr al-sinīn wa'l-ayyām*).[15]

Al-Ṭabarī's final classification in this three-fold division is 'that of which everyone who possesses knowledge of the language in which the Qur'ān was sent down knows the interpretation'.[16] The particulars of this linguistic communality are three. They include, first of all, a comprehension of inflectional functioning (*iqāma i'rābihi*). Secondly, there must be recognition of the inherent signification of nouns which are not homonyms (*al-musammayāt bi-asmā'ihā al-lāzima ghayra al-mushtarak fīhā*). The last thing required of the linguistically competent is that they understand the exclusionary nature of descriptive qualifiers (*al-mawṣūfāt bi-ṣifātihā al-khāṣṣa dūna mā siwāhā*).[17] The Quranic example which al-Ṭabarī offers illustrates but one of these three. With a citation of Q. 2/11–12, which contrasts evil-doers with those who do good, he makes the point that no one could be ignorant of the fact that the basic meaning of *ifsād* is connected with something detrimental (*maḍarra*) while *iṣlāḥ* connotes something good.[18] Al-Ṭabarī's point is that these root significations would be understood by any Arabic speaker regardless of whether or not the divinely specified particulars of *ifsād* and *iṣlāḥ* were known.

This analysis of the three categories of Quranic material concludes with the repetition of a *ḥadīth* reported on the authority of both Ibn 'Abbās and the prophet himself. As is not infrequently the case, this supporting documentation does not precisely match al-Ṭabarī's own classification. In both versions of the *ḥadīth*, Muḥammad shares his specialized knowledge with those learned (*'ulamā'*) in religious matters. The final category in this exegete's list is further subdivided by the concepts of language and content respectively, so that ignorance of *ḥalāl* and *ḥarām* is inexcusable in any human being, Arabic-speaker or not. That of which God alone has knowledge is more specifically defined as the *mutashābih*, a term which may now conveniently introduce the second part of this discussion of al-Ṭabarī's hermeneutics.[19]

[14] Ibid. i. 75.

[15] Ibid. [16] Ibid. [17] Ibid.

[18] Ibid. Al-Ṭabarī begs the question with respect to *iṣlāḥ* by repeating the term rather than using a synonym. However, his use of this Quranic citation (Q. 2/11–12) is particularly apt, as it records an instance of meaning deliberately subverted.

[19] Ibid. i. 75–6.

Early in the Qur'ān there occurs a verse which is fundamental to the development of exegetical methodology. Q. 3/7 divides the contents of revelation into two orders, labelling one *muḥkam* and the other *mutashābih*. Al-Ṭabarī's commentary on this verse is among the lengthiest in his *tafsīr*—perhaps a good indication of the importance which he accorded it.

The verse begins with the statement: 'He is the one who sent the book down upon you. In it are *muḥkam* verses—they are the mother of the book (*umm al-kitāb*)—and others are *mutashābih*.' Clearly the principal concerns in the exegesis of this verse section are defining the terms *muḥkam* and *mutashābih* and ascertaining to which Quranic elements they may be applied. Following his customary procedures, al-Ṭabarī approaches this task with a combination of methods. He first presents a preliminary explanation of the statement's significant elements. Accordingly, the *āyāt muḥkamāt* are characterized as 'those which are fortified (*aḥkamna*) by clarity (*bayān*) and detail (*tafṣīl*)'.[20] Al-Ṭabarī then lists six pairs of antonyms under which such verses may be classified: licit and illicit (*ḥalāl wa-ḥarām*), promise and threat (*wa'd wa-wa'īd*), recompense and punishment (*thawāb wa-'iqāb*), command and rebuke (*amr wa-zajr*), informational statement and aphorism/metaphor (*khabar wa-mathal*), and exhortation and admonition (*'iẓa wa-'ibar*).[21] The *āyāt mutashābihāt*, on the other hand, are described as 'similar [al-Ṭabarī uses the term *mutashābihāt* which, of course, begs the question] in vocal utterance, differing in meaning'.[22]

These initial characterizations are then incorporated into a paraphrase of the passage being considered. It is only after this introductory groundwork that al-Ṭabarī reproduces his collection of relevant exegetical *ḥadīth*s, as culled from the *ahl al-ta'wīl*. In systematic fashion he subdivides this aggregation according to the varieties of interpretation therein expressed. The divisions thus formed are five and include within them a total of seventeen *ḥadīth*s. The first group, which contains the largest number of supporting *ḥadīth*s, defines the *muḥkam* verses as abrogating (*nāsikh*) and the *mutashābih* verses as abrogated (*mansūkh*).[23]

[20] Ibid. vi. 170. Discussions of Q. 3/7 may be found in *QS*, and in Daud Rahbar, *God of Justice: A Study in the Ethical Doctrine of the Qur'ān* (Leiden, 1960).

[21] *Jāmi' al-bayān*, vi. 170.

[22] Ibid. vi. 173.

[23] Ibid. vi. 174.

Examples of the former include two passages (Q. 16/151–2 and Q. 17/23–9), which can most aptly be termed short Quranic codes.[24]

Al-Ṭabarī offers as a second range of interpretation those *ḥadīth*s which understand the *muḥkam* verses as the ones 'in which God decisively explains (*aḥkama*) what is permitted and forbidden; the *mutashābihāt* are those which resemble each other in meaning even though their words differ.'[25] The third exegetical position distinguishes these two classes of Quranic material on the basis of their possible plurality of interpretation. On this view, the *muḥkam* verses are those which permit of only one interpretation while the *mutashābih* are amenable to more than one. In the *ḥadīth* from Muḥammad ibn Ja'far ibn al-Zubayr which accompanies this third position, the interpretative plurality of the *mutashābih* verses is explained as a divine test for the worshippers, while the *muḥkam* are accorded such epithets as *ḥujjat al-rabb* (the Lord's [categorical] proof) and *'iṣmat al-'ubbād* (the safeguard for God's servants).[26]

It is the narrative portions of the Qur'ān which are of concern in the fourth exegetical view. The *muḥkam* verses constitute the reports on various peoples and the messengers who were sent to them. By contrast, the *mutashābih* are the repetitions of the same in other parts of the Qur'ān with either similar or different wording.[27] (Al-Ṭabarī leaves unasked the question of which Quranic passage constitutes the base for which the others are the repetitions.) The fifth, and concluding, position reverts to the classification system which al-Ṭabarī has outlined in the introduction to his *tafsīr*. Here the division is made not in terms of differing interpretations or multiple interpretations, but of the very possibility of interpretation at all. While the *muḥkam* verses are accessible to the *'ulamā'*, the *mutaṣhābih* are comprehended by no one—except God Himself. The principal members of this latter class are the so-called 'mysterious letters' with which certain *sūra*s of the Qur'ān begin. Attempts to interpret them are condemned inasmuch as they were evidently the subject, on the part of both Muslims and non-Muslims, of efforts at divination by alphabetic numerology (*ḥisāb al-jummal*).[28]

[24] These two groups of verses list some of the basic principles of Islamic ethics such as revering God as One, respecting parents, protecting children, and safeguarding the wealth of orphans.

[25] Ibid. vi. 176–7.

[26] Ibid. vi. 177.

[27] Ibid. vi. 178.

[28] Ibid. vi. 179–80. For a summary of research on the problems surrounding the

It is this fifth characterization of *muḥkam* and *mutashābih* with which al-Ṭabarī casts his lot. In doing so he restricts the latter to a very small fraction of the total revelation, basing his judgement on the inherent necessity of everything contained in the Qur'ān. According to al-Ṭabarī, there is nothing in the Qur'ān of which people 'have no need nor is there in it that of which they have need but whose interpretation they have no way of understanding'.[29] Given his definition of *mutashābih*, al-Ṭabarī is free to describe as *muḥkam* 'everything which is an exception to it'.[30] He explicitly rejects the notion that the *muḥkam* verses are amenable to but one interpretation. Some, he feels, are explicit and univocal in meaning. For others, 'a free range of many meanings (*taṣarruf fī ma'ān kathīra*)' is conceivable.[31] Al-Ṭabarī then concludes his discussion of this Quranic verse-section by tying it once again to his introductory classification. Among the *muḥkam* verses with plural significations are those for which God alone has provided explanation and those for which the prophet has conveyed the proper sense to his *umma*.[32]

Al-Ṭabarī's exegesis of the rest of Q. 3/7 yields much interesting material, but for the purpose of the present hermeneutical analysis, two items are of particular note. The first is his treatment of the phrase: 'As for those in whose hearts is deviation (*zaygh*), they follow what is *mutashābih* in it, desiring dissension (*al-fitna*), and desiring the interpretation of it (*ta'wīlihi*).' After a lengthy and detailed analysis of the subtleties of this statement, al-Ṭabarī rephrases it. His periphrastic explanation functions as an anti-hermeutic, a statement of how Quranic interpretation should not proceed.[33] The wrongheaded exegete, as characterized by al-Ṭabarī, is one who deliberately seeks out the more obscure Quranic verses and then manipulates their meanings in order to support his own misguided preconceptions. Rather than attempting to understand these verses in the light of those which are clearly *muḥkam*, he ignores the latter, thereby perpetuating his own confusion and that of others.

Unlike some of the previous commentators whom he quotes, al-Ṭabarī is less interested in identifying the individuals or groups

'mysterious letters' and a contribution to the debate see the section of that name (4d) in Alford Welch's article 'al-Ḳur'ān', *EI*² v. 412–4.

[29] *Jāmi' al-bayān*, vi. 180.
[30] Ibid. vi. 181.
[31] Ibid. vi. 181–2.
[32] Ibid. vi. 182.
[33] Ibid. vi. 185.

against whom such charges might be laid than in delineating the type of person who is liable to them.[34] The basic spiritual fault of such a one is the inclination to religious innovation (*bidʿa*). From this follows a preference for the *mutashābih* and the consequent disruption caused by [theological] confusion (*labs*), whether individual or social. The inevitable result is religious wrangling. Those who engage in such quarrels, according to a much-quoted prophetic *ḥadīth*, are the ultimate referents of this divine rebuke.

Contrasted with them is a group which forms the subject of the other important feature of this verse still remaining to be discussed. Following upon the verse's phrase, 'No one knows the interpretation of it but God', is the conjunction 'and' (*wāw*), and the substantive *al-rāsikhūn*. Under the rules of Arabic grammar *al-rāsikhūn*—which is here taken to mean those firmly-rooted (in knowledge)—can function as one of the subjects either of the preceding phrase or of the clause which follows. (This grammatical anomaly alone would, by some accounts, qualify this verse as among the *mutashābih*.) In the first instance, it would mean that *both* God and these *rāsikhūn* share a portion in exegetical knowledge. Al-Ṭabarī, as well as most of the authorities whom he quotes, rejects this interpretation.[35] In so doing he yet again remains faithful to the classificatory system with which he began his *tafsīr*.

This concern with classification would, in fact, seem to be al-Ṭabarī's principal contribution to the development of a Quranic hermeneutical theory. It constitutes for him the necessary first stage in a methodical exegesis. Recognizing to which exegetical category a verse may be assigned determines the subsequent treatment of that verse. In contrast, refusing to recognize the respective *muḥkam* or *mutashābih* character of constituent parts of the Quranic revelation can lead to serious distortion. Whether this is a deliberate or an inadvertent refusal matters little in al-Ṭabarī's view. The resultant interpretative distortion presents a serious difficulty for both the individual and the religious community.

Almost four centuries separate the death of al-Ṭabarī in 310/923 and the birth of Ibn Kathīr in 700/1300 or (701/1301). These were, of course, momentous centuries in the history of Islamic life and

[34] Ibid. vi. 197–8. Among the possible referents mentioned by al-Ṭabarī are the Jews, Christians, Majūs, Saba'ī, or a Ḥurūrī, Qadarī, or Jahmī.

[35] Ibid. vi. 201–4. Most of the *ḥadīth*s mentioned by al-Ṭabarī which support the alternative interpretation are transmitted on the authority of Mujāhid.

thought. The world into which 'Imād al-Dīn Ismā'īl ibn 'Umar ibn Kathīr entered in the first years of the eighth/fourteenth century had seen the maturation of the major forms of Quranic exegesis. The works of such figures as al-Ṭūsī (d. 460/1067), al-Zamakhsharī (d. 538/1144). Fakhr al-Dīn al-Rāzī (d. 606/1209), and Ibn al-'Arabī (d. 638/1240) had left their mark. Inevitably, at least some of this proliferation is reflected—if merely negatively, by a rejection—in the *tafsīr* of Ibn Kathīr. More positively, his *tafsīr* presents us with clear evidence of a conscious application to methodological issues.

Ibn Kathīr was born in the Syrian citadel town of Boṣrā. He spent his early childhood there but, following his father's death, he moved to Damascus at the age of 6 as the ward of his brother.[36] As a Sunnī stronghold, Damascus offered the young Ibn Kathīr a wealth of organized educational opportunity. His teachers ranked among the leading intellectuals of that era and they found in him an eager student of the Islamic sciences, particularly *ḥadīth* and *fiqh*.[37] Later, his own students would praise him as having 'the best memory, of those with whom we studied, for the *matns* of *ḥadīth* and being the most knowledgeable in expounding them, in ranking their transmitters and rating their soundness or faultiness'.[38]

Certainly the most famous of Ibn Kathīr's teachers, and perhaps the one who influenced him most, was the Ḥanbalī theologian and jurisconsult, Taqī al-Dīn Aḥmad ibn Taymīya (d. 728/1328). Ibn Kathīr was only 28 when this great *faqīh* died and it was, therefore, during the periods of intermittent persecution which plagued the last ten years of Ibn Taymīya's life that he knew him. Ibn Kathīr's own career developed quietly in the years following Ibn Taymīya's death, but, over the years, his reputation spread as a scholar of *fiqh*, a teacher of *ḥadīth*, and a prominent *khaṭīb*. According to the exiguous biographical information available, by his sixth decade Ibn Kathīr had become one of the most respected preachers and lecturers in Damascus. He died in 774/1373 and was buried in the cemetery of the Ṣūfīya near his master, Ibn Taymīya.[39]

[36] 'Abd al-Ḥayy ibn al-'Imād, *Shadharāt al-dhahab fī akhbār man dhahab* (Cairo, 1350/1931), vi. 231.

[37] In *fiqh* he studied other Burhān al-Dīn al-Fazārī (d. 729/1329), a leading Shāfi'ī jurisconsult. Under the *ḥāfiẓ* Jamāl al-Dīn al-Mizzī (d. 742/1341) he furthered his acquisition of *ḥadīth*s (he also married his daughter). See al-Dāwūdī, i. 110. Also Henri Laoust, 'Ibn Kathīr, historien', *Arabica* 2 (1955), 43–4.

[38] Al-Dāwūdī, i. 111.

[39] Ibn al-'Imād, vi. 232; al-Dāwūdī, i. 111.

Ibn Kathīr's, *Tafsīr al-Qur'ān al-'aẓīm* is, as might be expected from an author who gained such prominence in the sciences of *ḥadīth*, solidly in the class of *tafsīr bi'l-ma'thūr*. In fact, according to the contemporary scholar 'Abdallāh Maḥmūd Shihāta, it is 'one of the soundest of *tafāsīr bi'l-ma'thūr* if not absolutely the soundest'.[40] Certainly a predominating factor in the formation of the work which merits such an assessment is the attention paid to issues of exegetical methodology.

Ibn Kathīr introduced his work with a clear and careful analysis of correct hermeneutical procedure as he saw it. This section of his introduction begins with the question, 'What is the best of the methods for *tafsīr*?'[41] In his response to this query, Ibn Kathīr outlines a sequence of steps which the Quranic commentator should follow. The first stage and the best procedure is 'to interpret the Qur'ān by the Qur'ān'.[42] Letting the Qur'ān interpret itself presupposes understanding the Qur'ān as a unified body of revelation, one part of which can often clarify another. Ibn Kathīr underscores this by noting that, in the Qur'ān, 'what is said succinctly in one place is treated in detail in another place.'[43] It is only after such intra-scriptural investigation has been exhausted that recourse may be had to the second step of this hermeneutical procedure.

That second step involves examination of the prophetic *sunna*, because the *sunna* is 'a means of laying open the Qur'ān (*shāriḥa lil-Qur'ān*) and a means of elucidating it (*mūḍiḥa lihi*)'.[44] This exegete then offers the Quranic warrant for Muḥammad's exegetical primacy (Q. 16/44 and 16/64), which al-Ṭabarī also cited. He adds to this Q. 4/105, which stresses the prophet's judicial eminence. In line with his Shafi'ite training, Ibn Kathīr underlines the importance of the *sunna*, observing that it, too, was sent down by inspiration (*waḥy*) as the Qur'ān was, although it was not recited [by Gabriel] as was the Qur'ān.[45]

However, when neither the Qur'ān nor the prophetic *sunna* provide adequate resources for the interpretation of a passage, the exegete is encouraged to venture upon the third hermeneutical

[40] 'Abd Allāh Maḥmūd Shiḥāta, *Ta'rīkh al-Qur'ān wa'l-tafsīr* (Cairo, 1392/1972), 176.

[41] 'Imād al-Dīn Abū'l-Fidā' Ismā'īl ibn Kathīr, *Tafsīr al-Qur'ān al-'aẓīm* (Beirut, 1385/1966), i. 7.

[42] Ibid. [43] Ibid. [44] Ibid. [45] Ibid.

step, that of resorting to the sayings of the companions of Muḥammad. These individuals are distinguished, observes Ibn Kathīr, as being 'eye witnesses to the circumstances and situations with which they were particularly involved'. This intimate participation equipped them with the means for 'complete understanding, sound knowledge and righteous action (*al-fahm al-tāmm wa'l-ʿilm al-ṣaḥīḥ wa'l-ʿamal al-ṣāliḥ*)'.[46] Singled out for special mention are the first four caliphs (the *rāshidūn*) and both Ibn Masʿūd and Ibn ʿAbbās.[47]

At this point in his introductory statement on Quranic hermeneutics, Ibn Kathīr interrupts the exegetical sequence he has set forth to discuss two related problems. The first is the use of non-Muslim material in the interpretation of the Qur'ān, specifically that culled from the Jews and Christians. After recording a prophetic *ḥadīth* which sanctions, this, Ibn Kathīr spells out the limitations entailed in such authorization. 'These *al-aḥādīth al-isrā'īlīya*', he maintains, 'are quoted for supplementary attestation (*lil-istishhād*), not for full support (*lā lil-iʿtiḍād*).'[48] From a Muslim perspective they fall into three categories: (i) those things which are known to be true because they are attested to in the Quranic revelation; (ii) those things whose falsehood is certified from the same source; and (iii) that which falls into neither of the other classes.[49] The elements of this third class are, of course, matters of insignificant importance in religious affairs. The implication which Ibn Kathīr conveys is that all such information may permissibly be reported but that there is little point in doing so. Exegetical discord over such matters is of no inherent value and profits no one.[50]

What is particularly interesting, however, is that Ibn Kathīr does not rule the transmission of such discussion out of bounds. This is the second related issue which he addresses. Taking his cue from the divine reference to debate on the number of the 'Companions of the Cave' (Q. 18/22), Ibn Kathīr suggests a similar procedure in analogous cases. The proper course of action is to take into account the various views expressed, ratify the sound, reject the false, and

[46] Ibid. i. 7–8. Noting that Ibn ʿAbbās lived thirty-six years longer than Ibn Masʿūd, Ibn Kathīr exclaims: 'So just think what kind of knowledge he acquired after Ibn Masʿūd!' (ibid. i. 8).

[47] Ibid. [48] Ibid. [49] Ibid.

[50] Ibid. Among the examples Ibn Kathīr records are disputations about the names of the *aṣḥāb al-kahf*, the colour of their dog, the kind of wood from which Moses' staff was formed, and the species of tree from which God spoke to Moses.

then let the matter drop. The last bit of advice is important, 'lest contention and debate lengthen into what is useless and you occupy yourself with it to the exclusion of what is more significant'.[51] Ibn Kathīr concludes this excursus with the admonition not to omit any part of this procedure, especially that of judging the truth or falsity of contending opinions. The responsibility which an exegete assumes for the dissemination of the truth is a serious one.

In returning to the consideration of his sequential, hermeneutical methodology, Ibn Kathīr adds a fourth and final step, that of recourse to the sayings of the followers (*al-tābiʿūn*). Chief of those he mentions is Mujāhid ibn Jabr (d. 104/722), a student of Ibn ʿAbbās. Ibn Kathīr makes clear that this step is not incumbent upon Quranic exegetes but is simply followed by many of them.[52] Furthermore, the sayings of the followers are not an authoritative source when they conflict, that is, 'if they disagree, the statement of some is not authoritative over the statement of others or over those who come after them.'[53]

The final component of this hermeneutical prelude is the author's excoriation of *tafsīr bi'l-ra'y*. What is most roundly condemned under this rubric, judging from the *ḥadīth*s which Ibn Kathīr has presented, is irresponsibly attempting the exegesis of something for which one has no knowledge.[54] On the other hand, he is careful to point out that silence is not the appropriate, or even permissible, response in all cases. There is a correlative obligation to share one's knowledge with those who seek it. To refuse to do so is, indeed, a condemnable act.[55] But Ibn Kathīr recognizes, in concert with al-Ṭabarī, that there are limits to human knowledge. His final comments in this introductory section centre on those various categories of Quranic revelation which al-Ṭabarī discussed in the opening pages of his *tafsīr*. As with this earlier discussion, Ibn Kathīr prominently affirms that the interpretation of some things must be left to God alone.

In the hands of Ibn Kathīr the Quranic statement in Q. 3/7 on *muḥkam* and *mutashābih* verses is less an exercise in hermeneutical classification than an analysis of the causes and effects of misinterpretation, both deliberate and inadvertent. This is apparent

[51] Ibid. i. 9. [52] Ibid. [53] Ibid. i. 10. [54] Ibid. i. 10–12.

[55] Ibid. i. 12. Ibn Kathīr's Quranic support for this injunction is drawn from Q. 3/187 which includes the phrase: 'So explain it [the book] to people and do not hide it.'

even in the summary remarks with which he opens his treatment of this verse. The *muḥkam* verses are characterized as 'plain' (*bayyin*) and 'clear' (*wāḍiḥ*), those whose signification contains 'no ambiguity (*lā iltibās*) for anyone'.[56] Conversely, the *mutashābih* verses are those 'whose signification is obscure in purport (*ishtibāh fī'l-dalāla*) for some or most people'.[57] Given this distinction, the only exegetical option, as Ibn Kathīr clearly states, is to refer the interpretation of the latter, the *mutashābih*, to the former.

As expected, Ibn Kathīr records the numerous *ḥadīth*, many of them also found in al-Ṭabarī, which seek to define these two categories.[58] One of particular interest, quoted on the authority of Sa'īd ibn Jubayr, treats of understanding the designation of the *muḥkam* verses as 'mother of the book' on the basis that 'they are written in all the scriptures (*al-kutub*).' Ibn Kathīr glosses this by adding that 'Muqātil ibn Ḥayyān (d. 150/767) said that this is because there does not exist among people any religion which does not accept them.'[59] His adjudication of these various interpretations is consonant with that of al-Ṭabarī.

Ibn Kathīr's understanding of the subsequent phrases in this verse, however, offers insights not to be garnered from the earlier exegete. The 'deviation' (*zaygh*) of which some are accused is understood precisely in terms of misinterpretation. Not only does it involve following the *mutashābih* without recourse to the *muḥkam* verses, but also, in some cases, perverting the correct signification to make it accord with 'their iniquitous intentions (*maqāṣidihim al-fāsida*)'.[60] The example that Ibn Kathīr offers of such perverse interpretation is the case of those who argue for the divinity of Jesus on the basis of such Quranic expressions as 'word of God' and 'spirit of God', ignoring other parts of the revelation (such as Q. 3/59) which clearly underscore his humanity.[61]

The two instances of the term *ta'wīl* in this verse afford Ibn Kathīr the opportunity to comment more specifically on the consequences of exegetical malfeasance. His paraphrase of the reproach, 'seeking the *ta'wīl* of it (*ibtighā'a ta'wīlihi*)', is couched in

[56] Ibid. ii. 5. [57] Ibid.

[58] Ibid. He includes the one transmitted on the authority of Ibn 'Abbās which identifies the *muḥkam* verses with two sets of 'commandments' found in the Qur'ān, i.e. Q. 6/151–3 and 17/23–39.

[59] Ibn Kathīr, ii. 5. Ascription of these ideas is also made to Muqātil ibn Sulaymān (d. 150/767); see *QS* 149; *GAS* i. 36–7.

[60] Ibn Kathīr, ii. 6. [61] Ibid.

such terms. The verbal noun *ta'wīl* is understood as alteration and/or emendation. The results of such, as attested to by the numerous *ḥadīth*s which Ibn Kathīr reports, are inevitably quarrels and dissension. His test case for exegetically engendered discord is that of the Kharijites 'because', says Ibn Kathīr, 'the beginnings of *bid'a* in Islam occurred with the *fitna* of the Khawārij'.[62] Almost as an afterthought, this exegete includes an unusual prophetic *ḥadīth* which reinforces this depiction of careless and deceptive *ta'wīl*: 'In my *umma* is a people who recite the Qur'ān, tossing it around like a handful of mouldy dates; they interpret it contrary to how it should be interpreted.'[63]

A yet more nuanced consideration of *ta'wīl* appears in Ibn Kathīr's treatment of the relation between the terms Allāh and *al-rāsikhūn*. As was noted in al-Ṭabarī's discussion of the same part of this verse, these terms may either be read as twin subjects or separated, with Allāh standing as subject of the phrase which precedes it and *al-rāsikhūn* acting as such for the phrase which follows it. What distinguishes Ibn Kathīr's analysis of this exegetical problem is the way in which he links these two possibilities to two significations of the word *ta'wīl*. If *ta'wīl* means knowing 'the true natures of things and their essence (*ḥaqā'iq al-umūr wa-kunhuhā*)',[64] then Allāh is the only possible subject of the phrase 'no one knows the interpretation of it but . . .'. However, if *ta'wīl* signifies the exegetical act, if it is a synonym for '*tafsīr* and *bayān* and *ta'bīr*',[65] then Allāh and *al-rāsikhūn* may be understood as twin subjects of the quoted phrase. Ibn Kathīr understands the result of *ta'wīl* in this second sense as a true, if partial, knowledge, one which is of value in itself but which falls far short, of course, of the fullness of divine comprehension.

This exegete then concludes his consideration of the hermeneutical issues raised by this verse with a declaration that echoes the context within which his introductory statement was written, that of the unity of Quranic revelation. Building on the *rāsikhūn*'s proclamation, 'We believe in it; all is from our Lord', he reaffirms the truth and correctness of 'all the *muḥkam* and the *mutashābih*; each one of the two confirms the other and bears witness to it because the whole is from God and nothing from God is in disagreement or opposition.'[66] Those 'firmly-rooted' individuals who can make such an affirmation

[62] Ibid. ii. 8. [63] Ibid. [64] Ibid. ii. 9.
[65] Ibid. ii. 9–10. [66] Ibid. ii. 10.

are then characterized in a prophetic *ḥadīth*. This description might well stand as a summation of the spiritual qualities requisite to the Quranic exegete: 'The one whose right hand does good and whose tongue affirms the truth while his heart is upright, the one whose gluttonous and sexual appetites are restrained, he is one of those "firmly-rooted" in knowledge.'[67]

The evidence of an extended hermeneutical continuum between al-Ṭabarī and Ibn Kathīr is unmistakable. These works are, as previously noted, among the most highly regarded of the *tafsīr bi'l-ma'thūr*. The strong reliance on traditional material is the hallmark of this category of exegetical activity and one in which the *tafsīr*s of al-Ṭabarī and Ibn Kathīr share fully. Similarly they both exhibit a marked concern for matters of organization and arrangement.

Yet, in examining their works for evidence of heremeneutical considerations, rather significant differences may be brought to light. These differences are evident both in the direct treatment of these issues in their respective introductions and in the more allusive discussion which may be gleaned from their treatments of Q. 3/7. One could say that al-Ṭabarī takes a necessary first step in the development of a coherent hermeneutics. He recognizes the diversity of material within the Quranic corpus and imposes upon it a principle of organization. This organizing principle takes the form of systems of classification. In the first instance, that of his introduction, al-Ṭabarī's taxonomy is developed from-the-outside-in. The Quranic verses are theoretically classified in terms of their possible, not to say potential, interpreters. Conversely, the designation in Q. 3/7 of Quranic texts as either *muḥkam* or *mutashābih* works from-the-inside-out. Here it is more a question of the texts themselves than the exegetical capacities of their recipients.

Ibn Kathīr's approach, on the other hand, is far more self-consciously methodological. The very question with which he introduces his hermeneutical inquiry is indicative of this. Even more striking is the fact that he has moved beyond a concern with classification to an emphasis on procedure. He has gone ahead to outline a series of steps by which an adequate exegesis may be conducted. Added to this is his interest in the feasible use of extra-Islamic sources and the methods by which their validity may be

[67] Ibid.

assessed. The precision with which he distinguishes useful from useless exegetical activity is of equal interest. Here again he has isolated, on the basis of a Quranic precedent, the sequential procedure which should be followed.

This preoccupation with exegetical method also marks Ibn Kathīr's analysis of Q. 3/7. Here, however, the negative result of the improper application of such procedure is the predominant concern. To ignore the classifications of *muḥkam* and *mutashābih* or deliberately to pervert their respective interpretations are both presented as instances of hermeneutics gone awry. In similar fashion does this exegete's fluid understanding of the term *ta'wīl* allow for both positive and negative connotations. The range of signification extends from deceitful textual emendation to God's all-encompassing knowledge. Evidently, this very conscious concern with methodology makes Ibn Kathīr equally aware of the dangers of methodological ignorance or deliberate subversion. His own conception of hermeneutics gains a consequent precision and specificity when so carefully delineated against a depiction of the religiously disastrous results of the misuse of such techniques.

4

The Function of *ḥadīth* as Commentary on the Qur'ān, as Seen in the Six Authoritative Collections

R. MARSTON SPEIGHT

I. INTRODUCTION

The *ḥadīth* literature of Islam is concerned with the transmission of reports regarding the example (*sunna*) of Muḥammad. These reports were the object of an intense search during the first two and a half centuries of the Islamic era. They were collected into many written compilations, and gradually six of these became recognized in much of the Sunnī world as the most authoritative ones. The 'six books' (*al-kutub al-sitta*), as they are called, form the basis for this investigation into the role of *ḥadīth* as commentary on the Qur'ān.

Before turning to the collections themselves, it is useful to consider the way in which Muslims view the matter of *ḥadīth* as Qur'ān commentary. The convictions here described were current at the time the literature in question emerged; no attempt will be made to trace the earlier development of these beliefs. Such a task would be arduous in the extreme, due to the scarcity of documentation. The revelation of the Qur'ān through Muḥammad was the most important event, or series of events, in his life. So any attempt to recall and to transmit to the community the example of Muḥammad in word and deed must involve the Qur'ān. This the *ḥadīth* do in various ways. Probably the most common practice is to link the Quranic text with some event in the prophet's life: an encounter, a question from a follower, a difficulty, a triumph, or whatever. By citing the circumstances in which a verse or verses were revealed (*asbāb al-nuzūl*), the *ḥadīth* furnish rudimentary elements for exegesis of the scripture.

Beyond the question of the circumstances of revelation, there is the fact that Muḥammad is considered to be the first exegete of the scripture, that is, after the Qur'ān itself, which is esteemed to be its own best interpreter. The prophet, by his words and his deeds, as recalled and passed on by his companions (*ṣaḥāba*), elucidated many passages of the revealed text. There is a difference of opinion as to how much of it he actually explained to the early community, but this is a theoretical question, since the material that is available today from Muḥammad covers the Qur'ān only in a fragmentary fashion.

The Qur'ān itself announces the role of Muḥammad as the interpreter of the revealed text in Q. 16/44: 'We have revealed to you the message (*dhikr*) so that you might explain to people that which has been revealed to them.' This explanation was more than verbal, for it involved the integral example (*sunna*) of God's messenger. As the science of *ḥadīth* developed and the opinions of scholars emerged regarding the relationship of the *sunna* to the Qur'ān, emphasis was largely placed on the practical nature of scriptural commentary. The *sunna* was seen to be a divine gift to the community enabling it to broaden, deepen, and enrich its practices of worship and its social principles, as announced germinally in the revelations.

Al-Awzā'ī of Damascus (d. 157/774) cited Ḥassān ibn 'Aṭīya (d. *c.*130/748) as saying, 'Revelation came to the messenger of God, and Gabriel provided the *sunna*, which explains (*fassara*) it.'[1] This indispensable function of the *sunna* caused some scholars to make such hyperbolic statements as: 'The Qur'ān needs the *sunna* more than the *sunna* needs the Qur'ān.'[2] A more cautious assessment was that of Ibn Ḥanbal (d. 241/855): 'The *sunna* explains the scripture and clarifies it. . . . The *sunna* abrogates nothing in the Qur'ān. Only the Qur'ān can abrogate what is in the Qur'ān.'[3]

All of the *ḥadīth* containing Muḥammad's clarification of the Qur'ān are told on the authority of his companions. They, like all *ḥadīth*, are furnished with lists of guarantors which ensure their faithful transmission through the generations up to the time of their written compilation. It follows that since the companions actually heard and saw Muḥammad, their recollections should have extraordinary authority. In fact, many times in the *ḥadīth* books, companions give their interpretations of the scripture without claiming that they are quoting the prophet or describing one of his

[1] Abū 'Umar Yūsuf ibn 'Abd al-Barr, *Jāmi' bayān al-'ilm wa-faḍlihi* (Medina, 1388/1968), ii. 234.

[2] Attributed to al-Awzā'ī in ibid. [3] Ibid.

actions. These statements are considered to be the same as if they could be traced to Muḥammad, especially if they have to do with the circumstances in which certain verses were revealed. Other utterances of *ṣaḥāba* on the Qur'ān are also held in great esteem, but, in the view of some, are not in the same category as those coming directly from Muḥammad.[4] So we witness in the *ḥadīth* books not only the explicit *sunna* of the prophet as applied to the Qur'ān, but also the beginning of an effort of reflection and interpretation on the part of the companions. This and the similar effort of the next generation, the successors (*tābi'ūn*), contained a modest expression of individual personal opinion (*ra'y*) in explaining the Qur'ān. There was disagreement among the successors at times, and divergent interpretations of Qur'ān verses have been preserved.[5] It was clear that all of their interpretations could not have come from Muḥammad.[6] They exercised reason and discernment based on, and, to a degree, controlled by the store of religious knowledge called *'ilm*. In early Islam this word had the sense of the practical knowledge of the manner of life recommended by the example of the prophet, that is, the *sunna*. Those believers who acquired *'ilm* were called 'bearers of knowledge', and to be a bearer of *'ilm* meant more than having intellectual knowledge of the way Muslims should live. It meant the practice of a life that demonstrated the *sunna*. M. M. Bravmann has pointed out the way in which *'ilm* and *ra'y* were counterparts in the thought of early Islam.[7]

In the ferment of religious debate, however, there was soon felt the need to limit the use of personal opinion, or independent reason, in interpreting the Qur'ān. Probably this development owed much to the discussions of *ra'y* among early legists,[8] and especially to the emergence of speculative thought in Shī'ī circles and among the theologians who came to be known as the Mu'tazila. The latter have been shown by recent scholarship to have been loyal to the Qur'ān, but to have minimized the use of *ḥadīth* in their

[4] Jalāl al-Dīn al-Suyūṭī, *Tadrīb al-rāwī fī sharḥ taqrīb al-Nawawī* (Medina, 1392/1972), 192–3.

[5] Régis Blachère, *Introduction au Coran* (Paris, 1947), 230.

[6] Muḥammad ibn Aḥmad al-Qurṭubī, *al-Jāmi' li-aḥkām al-Qur'ān* (Cairo, 1361/1942), i. 28. Also see Muḥammad al-Ṭāhir ibn 'Āshūr, *Tafsīr al-taḥrīr wa'l-tanwīr* (Tunis, 1969–73), i. 28.

[7] M. M. Bravmann, *The Spiritual Background of Early Islam: Studies in Ancient Arab Concepts* (Leiden, 1972), 177–88.

[8] Joseph Schacht, *The Origins of Muhammadan Jurisprudence* (Oxford, 1950), 98–132.

arguments.[9] It was only natural that others, advocates of *ḥadīth*, would see their interpretations of the scripture as seriously lacking in *'ilm*, since *ḥadīth* were the principal formal expression of the latter. Thereby comes the force of the key *ḥadīth* text, attributed to Ibn 'Abbās, who said: 'The messenger of God said, "Those who interpret the Qur'ān without knowledge (*'ilm*) will have their place prepared for them in the fire of hell".'[10] From the foregoing, it is only a step to the following: 'Ibn 'Abbās: The messenger of God said, ". . . Those who interpret the Qur'ān by independent reasoning (*ra'y*) will have their place prepared for them in the fire of hell".'[11] And to the text reported by Jundub: 'The messenger of God said, "Those who interpret the Qur'ān by independent reason are wrong even if they arrive at the right meaning".'[12] The people who used *ra'y* were considered wrong because they used a faulty method, ignoring the continuity of interpretation from the time of Muḥammad and thereafter. The last two texts read in the light of the first, and in view of what we know about the complementarity of *'ilm* and *ra'y*, lead us to conclude that the stricture against using *ra'y* was not absolute, but that it constituted a prohibition of any interpretation which lacked the support of *'ilm*.

As the discussions continued and as it was felt by some that partisans of *ra'y* were going far astray in their interpretations, the terminology of polarity emerged, in which *tafsīr bi'l-ra'y*, 'interpretation by the use of reason', was contrasted with *tafsīr bi'l-ma'thūr*, 'interpretation according to what has been handed down, that is, the sayings of the prophet and the venerable companions and successors'. *Bi'l-ma'thūr* covers the same range of meaning as *'ilm*, but it is a less dynamic expression than the latter. Advocates of *tafsīr bi'l-ma'thūr* were convinced that only by the application of *ḥadīth*, the reports received *bi'l-ma'thūr*, could the Qur'ān be properly understood. As the passage of time separated Qur'ān scholars more and more from the era of Muḥammad, and as religious movements ebbed and flowed, all taking inspiration from the Qur'ān, the two types of *tafsīr* here described were often put in contradistinction. Practically, however, it was not possible to separate them in an absolute way.

There was no reason to question, in principle, the validity of

[9] Ibid. 258. See also W. Montgomery Watt, *The Formative Period of Islamic Thought* (Edinburgh, 1973), 309.

[10] Al-Tirmidhī, *al-Jāmi'*, *tafsīr*, 1.

[11] Ibid.

[12] Ibid.

tafsīr based on *ḥadīth*, since Muḥammad's authority was behind it. Ibn Kathīr (d. 774/1373), the great historian and traditionist, wrote that the ancients spoke about the Qur'ān only if they had *'ilm* to support what they said. If they had no such support they kept silent. According to Ibn Kathīr, this should be the practice of all exegetes.[13] Some *ma'thūr* material was discredited, however, due to the widespread practice of inventing (*waḍ'*) *ḥadīth* for various tendentious purposes, and also the adoption of Jewish legends by the community, called *isrā'īlīyāt*, which were transmitted as elements supposedly contributing to an understanding of the Qur'ān.[14]

It was the use of *ra'y* which was most often called into question, however, and an examination of some details of the critique of *ra'y* will help in understanding the exegetical methods of *tafsīr*.

The main objection to the use of *ra'y* was in the case of a scholar who would give an interpretation without regard to the previous conclusions of grammarians and legists, or without the support of *ḥadīth*. It was claimed that such procedure could result only in fanciful or sectarian exegesis. In fact, *hawā* ('fancy, whim') came to be synonymous with *ra'y* in the discourse of some critics of the latter.[15]

Interpreters using *ra'y* were thought to risk going into error because: (i) they ignored the background knowledge of linguistic facts, legal principles, the facts of the abrogation of certain Qur'ān passages, and the accounts of the circumstances of the revelations; (ii) they ignored the context of the verses, or they considered only part of the evidence furnished by the context and overlooked the rest; (iii) they interpreted the Qur'ān to support a particular party or doctrine, in a spirit of narrowness; (iv) they took into account only the lexicographical sense of obscure words, ignoring the light cast upon their meaning by the authorities who lived closer to the time of the revelation; (v) they isolated one meaning of several possible interpretations in order to give it undue emphasis, either knowingly or in ignorance; (vi) they misapplied verses, even when

[13] 'Imād al-Dīn Abū al-Fidā' ibn Kathīr, *Tafsīr al-Qur'ān al-'azīz* (Beirut, 1385/1966), i. 12.

[14] Muḥammad Ḥusayn al-Dhahabī, *al-Tafsīr wa'l-mufassirūn* (Cairo, 1381/1961), i. 157–83.

[15] Al-Qurṭubī, i. 27.

they knew better, simply because they desired Quranic justification for a warning or a teaching which they wished to stress.[16]

From what is known about the history of ideas in Islam during the development of the science of *tafsīr*, it is evident that the polarity between *tafsīr bi'l-ma'thūr* and *tafsīr bi'l-ra'y* was often accentuated by polemics in disciplines other than scriptural exegesis alone, that is, in legal theory, philosophy, theology, and political theory. Practically speaking, even that great monument to *ma'thūr* interpretation which is the commentary of al-Ṭabarī (d. 310/922) contains much that can be labelled as *tafsīr bi'l-ra'y*. That work was accepted by partisans of *ḥadīth* because *ra'y* was exercised in it according to the established principles of *'ilm* and of discernment (*qawānīn 'ilm wa-naẓar*).[17]

2. THE FUNCTION OF *ḤADĪTH* IN EXEGESIS

In order to see how the *ḥadīth* were used in Qur'ān interpretation, examples of the kinds of texts which are found in the collections need to be given. A summary of the ways in which Muslim manuals describe the interpretative function of the *sunna*, of which the *ḥadīth* are a record, will also provide an overview of the function of this material.

i. Asbāb al-nuzūl

The messenger of God was not feeling well, and for two or three nights he did not get up. A woman came to him and said, 'O Muḥammad, I am afraid that your familiar spirit (*shayṭān*) has abandoned you. I have not seen it near you for two or three nights.' Then God revealed. 'By the morning light and by the night when it is calm, your Lord has not left you, nor has He despised you' (Q. 93/1–3).[18]

According to this report, the woman noticed that Muḥammad had apparently lost his inspiration; at least, that is the way she interpreted his lassitude. In her ignorance she attributed his inspiration to a demon. Then, to reassure His messenger, God revealed to him the words which later became *sūra* 93.

At the end of *sūrat al-jumu'a* (Q. 62) is found an exhortation to

[16] Ibn 'Āshūr, i. 24; al-Dhahabī, i. 28; al-Qurṭubī, i. 28, 29.
[17] Al-Qurṭubī, i. 28.
[18] Al-Bukhārī, *al-Ṣaḥīḥ, tafsīr, sūrat al-ḍuḥā* (93).

faithfulness at the communal prayer on Friday. Then, in the last verse, Muḥammad is told to reprimand the frivolous people who, 'when they see a good business transaction or some amusement they hasten away to it, leaving you standing'. Jābir ibn 'Abd Allāh reported the event that led to this verse:

One Friday, while we were gathered around the prophet, a caravan arrived and all of the people hurried over to it, except twelve men. Then God revealed the verse, 'When they see a good business transaction or some amusement, they hasten away to it' (Q. 62/11).[19]

Sūrat al-ḥashr (Q. 59) speaks in verse 9 of those who 'give preference to the poor over themselves, in spite of their own poverty':

Abū Hurayra reported that a guest spent the night at the home of one of the Anṣār. The host had only enough food for himself and for his children. He said to his wife, 'Put the little ones to sleep, and turn out the lamp. Then give to our guest that which we have.' At that time the verse was revealed, 'Those who give preference to the poor. . .'.[20]

Ḥādith of this type are very numerous, and are almost invariably introduced by words, such as, 'then was revealed this verse. . .'. Muslims have noted that all such comments cannot be taken at their face value. The judgement is that sometimes the expression, 'then was revealed this verse . . .', means 'The circumstance just related pertains to this verse . . .'.[21] So many texts which might be classified as *asbāb al-nuzūl* by virtue of their formal characteristics might better be considered as examples of an application to life of the Qur'ān verse in question.

ii. Meanings of Obscure Words

On *sūrat al-baqara* (Q. 2), verse 57, Mujāhid explains, in a note without *isnād*, that the manna which God gave as food to the Hebrew people was a resin (*ṣamgha*) and that *salwā* was a kind of bird. A report that follows, documented by Sa'īd ibn Zayd as coming from Muḥammad, calls attention to the white truffle (*kam'a*) as being similar to manna, and in addition as being a good remedy for eye trouble.[22]

[19] Ibid., *sūrat al-jumu'a* (62).

[20] Muslim, *al-Ṣaḥīḥ*, *ashriba*, 32.

[21] Jalāl al-Dīn al-Suyūṭī, *Asbāb al-nuzūl* (Cairo, 1382/1962), 5, citing Ibn Taymīya.

[22] Al-Bukhārī, *tafsīr*, *sūrat al-baqara* (2).

Sūrat al-kawthar (Q. 108) contains the much disputed word, *kawthar*, in verse 1. The two main interpretations are found reconciled in the following text:

Sa'īd ibn Jubayr reported that Ibn 'Abbās said regarding *kawthar*, 'It is the blessing that God gave Muḥammad.' Abū Bishr said, 'I said to Sa'īd ibn Jubayr, "People think that it is a river in paradise".' Then Sa'īd said, 'The river in paradise is part of the blessing that God gave him.'[23]

iii. The Application of Qur'ān Verses to Life Situations of either the Prophet or his Companions

By relating the Quranic verse to an event, something of the intent of the revealed message is made known:

Ibn Mas'ūd reported that the messenger of God entered Mecca and around the House (of God) were 350 idols. He began to strike them with the rod in his hand and say, 'Truth has come and falsehood has passed away. Truly, falsehood is bound to pass away' (Q. 17/81).[24]

Al-Barā' ibn 'Āzib reported that the messenger of God said, 'When a Muslim is questioned in his grave, he shall testify that there is no god but God and that Muḥammad is the messenger of God. That is what is meant by His word, "God will confirm believers with a steadfast word" (Q. 14/27).'[25]

iv. Reflections by Muḥammad or by his Companions on Verses

Reflections on verses may be historical, eschatological, or they may pertain to the experience of the speaker.

Abū Umāma reported that the messenger of God said, 'No people will go astray after having received guidance, unless they become contentious.' Then the messenger of God recited this verse: 'They only raise an objection to argue; but then, they are contentious people' (Q. 43/58).[26]

v. Explanations of Verses in Response to Queries

'Abd Allāh ibn Mas'ūd reported that when this verse was revealed, '. . . those who believed and did not obscure their faith with iniquity . . .' (Q. 6/82), it troubled the Muslims and they said, 'O Messenger of God, which of us has not wronged himself?' He said, 'That is not it. The verse refers to idolatry (*shirk*). Did you not hear what Luqmān said to his son, "O my

[23] Ibid., *sūrat al-kawthar* (108).
[24] Ibid., *sūrat banī Isrā'īl* (17).
[25] Ibid., *sūrat Ibrāhīm* (14).
[26] Al-Tirmidhī, *al-Jāmi', tafsīr, sūrat al-zukhruf* (43).

son, do not associate any deity with God. Truly, idolatry is a great iniquity" (Q. 31/13)?'[27]

An Egyptian guarantor reported: I questioned Abū'l-Dardā' about this verse. 'They will have the *bushrā* in this life' (Q. 10/64). He said, 'No one has asked me about that verse since I asked the messenger of God about it. And he said to me, "No one has asked me about it since it was revealed except you. It refers to the authentic vision which the Muslim will see or which will be seen in his behalf".'[28]

vi. Details of Ritual Practice and Social Behaviour.

Al-Nu'mān ibn Bashīr reported: 'I heard the prophet say, "Supplication (*du'ā'*) is worship." Then he said, "And your Lord said, 'Supplicate me and I will answer, but if anyone becomes proud in his worship of me, he will go into hell debased' (Q. 40/60)".'[29]

Abū Hurayra reported the prophet as saying: 'Communal prayer is twenty-five times superior to prayer alone. The angels of the night and those of the day assemble at the time of the early morning prayer.' Abū Hurayra added, Recite, if you wish: 'The recitation of the Qur'ān at dawn is always witnessed' (Q. 17/78).[30]

vii. Elements of Qur'ān Science.

The *ḥadīth* cover various other topics, including abrogation of verses, different recitations, discussions among companions on the text, the names and nature of the *sūra*s and the collection of Qur'ān manuscripts.

Salama ibn al-Akwa' reported that when this verse was revealed, '. . . and for those who are able to do so, there is a redemption possible (from fasting), that is, the feeding of a poor person' (Q. 2/184), those who did not want to fast offered the redemption and ate, at least until the following verse was revealed, abrogating the first.[31]

Zayd ibn Thābit reported: When we copied the different manuscripts of the Qur'ān I missed one of the verses from *sūrat al-aḥzāb* that I used to hear the messenger of God recite. The only person with whom I could find it was Khuzayma al-Anṣārī, whose witness the messenger of God judged to be equal to that of two believers. 'Among the believers are those men who have been faithful to that which they promised to God' (Q. 33/23).[32]

27 Ibid., *sūrat al-an'ām* (6).
28 Ibid., *sūrat Yūnus* (10).
29 Ibid., *sūrat al-mu'min* (40).
30 Al-Bukhārī, *tafsīr, sūrat banī Isrā'īl* (17).
31 Muslim, *ṣiyām*, 25, on *sūrat al-baqara* (2).
32 Al-Bukhārī, *tafsīr, sūrat al-aḥzāb* (33).

Ibrāhīm reported: The friends of 'Abd Allāh (Ibn Mas'ūd) came to Abū'l-Dardā', who had been looking for them, until they met. He said to them, 'Who among you recites the Qur'ān the way 'Abd Allāh does?' They replied, 'All of us.' He said, 'And who knows it by heart?' They pointed to 'Alqama. He said to him, 'How did you hear him recite *sūrat al-layl*?' 'Alqama recited, 'By the male and the female.' (Q. 92/3) Abū'l-Dardā' said, 'I testify that I heard the prophet recite it that way, but these people want me to recite, "By the One who created male and female." By God, I will not follow them'.[33]

After citing a number of *ḥadīth* to illustrate how that literature provides interpretation of the Qur'ān, we turn now to the Muslim scholars who have discussed the relationship between the *sunna* and the scripture. In their manuals they suggest a number of general ways in which that relationship is expressed, thus providing a theoretical framework for the subject. The following is a brief summary of their conclusions.

(*a*) The *sunna* details that which is general in the Qur'ān, for example, the five times of prayer, the amounts due for *zakāt*, the beneficiaries of *zakāt*, and the rules for pilgrimage.

(*b*) The *sunna* clarifies what is obscure in the Qur'ān, especially the meanings and applications of words and expressions.

(*c*) The *sunna* contains acts which demonstrate the meanings of the revealed text.

(*d*) The *sunna* gives answers to questions about the rules of worship and behaviour.

(*e*) The *sunna* restricts that which is absolute in the Qur'ān. For example, in Q. 5/38, it is said that the hands of a thief should be cut off as punishment. The *sunna* restricts that penalty to the amputation of the right hand.[34]

Another principle of Muslim understanding is that the *sunna* is both elucidation (*bayān*) of the Qur'ān and supplement.[35] Clearly, the manuals soon leave the field of Qur'ān interpretation in order to pass on to elaboration of the ways in which *sunna* is a source of law.

[33] Ibid., *sūrat al-layl* (92).

[34] See for examples of classifications Al-Dhahabī, i. 55–7; also Shams al-Dīn Ibn Qayyim al-Jawzīya, *I'lām al-muwaqqi'īn 'an rabb al-'ālamīn* (Cairo, 1955), ii. 34 ff.

[35] Muṣṭafā al-Sibā'ī, *al-Sunna wa-makānatuhā fī'l-tashrī' al-Islāmī* (Cairo, 1966), 344.

3. *TAFSĪR* IN THE 'SIX BOOKS'

The *ḥadīth* reveal three main preoccupations of the Islamic community: the person of Muḥammad, piety, and social behaviour. Since the Qur'ān is so vital an element in all three, it is natural that the *ḥadīth* should be a vast repertory of references to the scripture. Whether they have certain sections specifically labelled *tafsīr* or not, all of the 'six books' contain many quotations of Qur'ān verses and comments upon them. These are scattered throughout the compilations.

The most famous of all *ḥadīth* collections is that of Muḥammad ibn Ismā'īl al-Bukhārī (d. 256/870), *al-Jāmi' al-ṣaḥīḥ*. It contains about 2,500 *ḥadīth*, not counting repetitions, numerous Qur'ān quotations, personal remarks by the compiler, and abbreviated reports.

One of the ninety-seven books in the *Ṣaḥīḥ* is entitled *Kitāb al-tafsīr*, and it contains 457 *ḥadīth*, not counting repetitions within the same chapter, having to do with different versions of the same report. All 114 of the *sūra*s are listed, each one as a section, usually composed of several chapters (*abwāb*). Thirty-one *sūras* have no *ḥadīth* pertaining to them, but most of these, as well as the others, have lexical and brief interpretative helps at the beginning of the sections. No *sūra* is completely lacking in comment.

In the introductory comments, and those occasionally interspersed among the *ḥadīth*, al-Bukhārī breaks from his usual habit of supplying an *isnād* for each item of information. He simply writes, 'So-and-so said', and gives that person's interpretations of the meanings of words and expressions from the *sūra* in question, or he gives the information without citing any source. For example:

> On *sūrat al-layl* (Q. 92): Ibn 'Abbās said: '*wa-kadhdhaba bi'l-ḥusnā* (Q. 92/9) is by way of antithesis.' Mujāhid said, '*taraddā* means "to die" and *talaẓẓā* means "to blaze".' 'Ubayd ibn 'Umayr recited this word as *tatalaẓẓā*.
>
> On *sūrat al-ikhlās* (Q. 112): It is said that the word *aḥadu* (q. 112/4) should not take the *tanwīn* as *wāḥid*^{un}.

Some of the companions known as authorities on the Qur'ān, and their successors, are cited as sources of these introductory notes, such as al-Ḥasan al-Baṣrī, Ṭāwus, Ibn 'Abbās, Jābir ibn 'Abd Allāh, 'Umar, 'Ikrima, Mujāhid, Qatāda, and Ibn 'Uyayna. The explanation for this practice of citing material without *isnād* may possibly be seen in the convention of 'preface' (*tarjama*, pl. *tarājim*), which is peculiar to al-Bukhārī among the six books. Throughout the *Ṣaḥīḥ* are found introductory remarks and quotations at the beginning of sections without *isnād*s.

Ibn Ḥajar notes that al-Bukhārī cites information from Ibn 'Abbās at times without *isnād* because the chain of transmission did not satisfy his requirements for authenticity.[36] The Turkish scholar, Fuad Sezgin, has also observed that al-Bukhārī borrowed much of the lexical material in the *Ṣaḥīḥ* from *Majāz al-Qur'ān* by Abū 'Ubayda (d. 210/825).[37]

As for the *ḥadīth* themselves which pertain to particular Qur'ān verses, they are highly selective. Rarely does al-Bukhārī cite more than one text for a verse. The coverage of the Qur'ān is fragmentary. A survey of the primary authorities cited by this compiler shows a total of seventy-six persons, mostly companions. Successors from Mecca, Medina, and Iraq are also cited. Apart from the early individuals who were renowned for their knowledge of the Qur'ān, such as 'Ali, 'Umar, 'Ā'isha, Abū Hurayra, Anas ibn Mālik, Ibn 'Umar, Ibn Mas'ūd, Zayd ibn Thābit, Ubayy ibn Ka'b, and Jābir ibn 'Abd Allāh, plus al-Barā' ibn 'Āzib and Abū Sa'īd al-Khudrī and, from the successors, Mujāhid and Sa'īd ibn Jubayr, nearly all of the other authorities are represented by one or two *ḥadīth* only. So the impression is that one purpose of the *Kitāb al-tafsīr* is to include, with limited material, a wide range of guarantors.

Kitāb al-tafsīr is a sprawling work, similar to the rest of the *Ṣaḥīḥ*. It has many puzzling anomalies, most of them small, but the compiler had a particular pattern of composition in view, which sets this book apart from the rest of the six. Al-Bukhārī is supposed to have compiled *al-Tafsīr al-kabīr*, a large work of Qur'ān interpretation.[38] Extant manuscript evidence of this work has been disputed,[39] but it is possible to see the present *Kitāb al-tafsīr* in the *Ṣaḥīḥ* as either a precursor or an essay of the kind of *tafsīr* work which would combine the technical material of vocabulary and

[36] Shihāb al-Dīn Ibn Ḥajar al-'Asqalānī, *Tahdhīb al-tahdhīb* (Beirut, 1968), viii. 430.

[37] Muhammad Fuad Sezgin, *Buhari'nin Kaynaklari* (Istanbul, 1956), p. xi and Appendix III.

[38] Lajnat iḥyā' kutub al-sunna, *al-Ta'rīf bi-amīr al-mu'minīn fī'l-ḥadīth* (Cairo, 1387/1967), 72.

[39] *GAL* i. 166.

recitations with a record of the evocative and clarifying memories of those who experienced the revelation of the Qur'ān.

Turning to the rest of the *Ṣaḥīḥ* we see that the one *Kitāb al-tafsīr* does not by any means exhaust the interest of this collection for students of Qur'ān interpretation. In the *Kitāb al-faḍā'il* of the Qur'ān is found a conventional setting forth of *ḥadīth* on the language of the revelation, the seven versions (*aḥruf*) of the Qur'ān, the history of the gathering and editing of the revealed text, the persons who were noted for reciting the Qur'ān, and the virtues of reciting certain *sūras*.

The *Kitāb al-tawḥīd* gives an imposing series of chapters on the divine attributes, each one introduced by a Qur'ān text, to which pertain the *ḥadīth* which follow. Elements of eschatology are included here, too, also linked to the Qur'ān. Likewise, the *Kitāb aḥādīth al-anbiyā'* is a vast mosaic of Qur'ān material enriched with stories about twenty-two prophets of God.

By means of his use of *tarājim*, al-Bukhārī highlights the Quranic basis of Islamic worship and behaviour. The chapters of the so-called legal books of the *Ṣaḥīḥ* are introduced by Qur'ān verses giving the revelational basis for belief and practice. So, in a way, the legal *ḥadīth* may be said to be a form of Qur'ān commentary also. None of the 'six books' so explicitly expresses the links between Qur'ān and *sunna* as does the *Ṣaḥīḥ* of al-Bukhārī.

Al-Ṣaḥīḥ by Muslim ibn al-Ḥajjāj (d. 261/875) is second only to the *Ṣaḥīḥ* of al-Bukhārī in renown. It has 3,030 texts, not counting the repetitions. Muslim is noted for his meticulous arrangement of the *ḥadīth* according to subject matter and according to variant readings and multiple chains. The logic of his overall presentation is seen by an opening introduction dealing with the techniques of *ḥadīth* collection and transmission, followed by the first book on doctrine. Afterwards, in books 2 to 37, the conventional rubrics of law occur, dealing with worship and social relations. Books 38 to 41 treat good manners, and the collection closes with thirteen books on eschatology, laudation, pious practices, and other subjects intended for edification. The last book is composed of nineteen reports (thirty-eight including variants) under the heading *tafsīr*. There is no discernible order, however, to these reports. They deal with circumstances of revelation, comments on legal principles, and historical questions. The impression is that this book is composed of miscellaneous items which are grouped under *tafsīr* as a kind of convention. This impression is heightened by the fact that the first twelve *ḥadīth* in the book do not have any chapter (*bāb*) headings, contrary to the practice elsewhere in the collection.

Muslim's *Ṣaḥīḥ* abounds in *ḥadīth* which cite and comment upon the Qur'ān, but, as in other collections, these are scattered throughout the various books. A chapter entitled 'Excellences of the Qur'ān' is found in the 'Book of Prayer for Travellers'. Therein are contained *ḥadīth* telling about the seven versions (*aḥruf*) of the Qur'ān.

Only slightly less important for the question of *tafsīr* than the *Ṣaḥīḥ* of al-Bukhāri is the third of the 'six books', entitled *al-Jāmi'* by Abū 'Īsā Muḥammad ibn 'Īsā al-Tirmidhī (d. 279/892). It is a vast work of forty-six books, and on almost every page are found personal notes by the compiler. These comments regarding the degrees of authenticity of the *ḥadīth*, the different versions of a single report, as well as the various currents of thought and practice in the Islamic world of his time, make the *Jāmi'* unique.

Al-Tirmidhī has included a book of Qur'ān interpretation, *tafsīr al-Qur'ān*, as book 44 in his *Jāmi'*. It contains 393 reports, not counting repetitions from the same primary guarantor. These are attributed to ninety-three authorities, of whom only thirty-eight are the same as those found in al-Bukhārī. So al-Tirmidhī's collection is clearly independent of the *Ṣaḥīḥ*. Its fifty-five authorities, mostly companions, who are not cited in the *tafsīr* of the latter, are represented by one or two *ḥadīth* only. The impression is the same as that gained from al-Bukhārī, that is, that the compiler presents the testimonies of as many personalities as possible within a limited scope of material. In fact, al-Tirmidhī has fewer *ḥadīth* than al-Bukhārī and more primary guarantors. The introductory lexical helps seen in al-Bukhārī are lacking in al-Tirmidhī, and the latter gives reports on only ninety-two of the 114 *sūra*s.

The *Kitāb al-tafsīr* in al-Tirmidhī is, on the whole, arranged in a more orderly way than the corresponding *Tafsīr* of al-Bukhārī. It is preceded by two books on the Qur'ān, the first called *faḍā'il al-Qur'ān*, in which eleven *sūra*s are singled out for mention, and the importance of Qur'ān recitation is set forth. The book (no. 43) immediately preceding the *Tafsīr* is entitled 'Chapters on the recitations'. This section attributes to Muḥammad particular readings of the text in eighteen reports. Then follows a conventional report on the seven versions (*aḥruf*) in which the Qur'ān was revealed, and further reports regarding its ritual recitation. The *Kitāb al-tafsīr* itself opens with texts warning against explaining the Qur'ān according to personal opinion (*ra'y*). It closes with two narrative *ḥadīth* on the primeval history of creation, which refer to the relationship between God and His human creatures.

The three books on the Qur'ān are placed towards the end of the collection, after the legal books, and those on doctrine, eschatology, and good manners. They are followed by a book on devotional practices and a final, very lengthy collection of *ḥadīth* on the life of Muḥammad and his companions. Although the Qur'ān is cited throughout the forty-six books, it is not given as prominent a place as in the *Ṣaḥīḥ* of al-Bukhārī. This is due largely to the important use by the latter of *tarājim* having to do with the Qur'ān.

Three of the six authoritative *ḥadīth* collections are of the *sunan* (plural of *sunna*) type. Their purpose is to present reports containing rules and principles for worship and for social behaviour. Thus, more exclusively than the other collections, *sunan* works are tools for the elaboration of jurisprudence, the fundamental science of Islam. *Ḥadīth* and the Qur'ān are the first two sources for jurisprudence, since they enshrine the revealed law (*sharīʿa*).

The most important of the three *sunan* collections is the *Sunan* of Abū Dā'ūd al-Sijistānī (d. 275/888), containing about 4,800 texts. The overall arrangement of its contents gives an idea of the place of *tafsīr* in the collector's mind. The first thirty-three books deal in conventional fashion with worship and the various societal relationships, beginning with the rules of ritual purity and ending with a short book on rings and the use of gold ornaments. This material constitutes about four-fifths of the collection. It includes a book called *al-Ḥurūf wa'l-qirā'āt*, whose forty *ḥadīth* are mainly devoted to testimonies as to the way in which Muḥammad and various scholars recited portions of the Qur'ān. So the recitation of the scripture is a part of the *aḥkam*, or rules of religion. The exegete of later times, Ibn ʿAṭīya of Andalusia (d. 546/1151), wrote: 'The grammatical inflection (*iʿrāb*) of the Qur'ān is a foundation of the law (*sharīʿa*) for by means of it the meanings of the Qur'ān are established, which are themselves the law.'[40]

The Qur'ān is often in the foreground of the testimonies throughout the legal parts of the *Sunan*. In the *ṣalāt* are found

[40] Abū Muḥammad ʿAbd al-Ḥaqq ibn Ghālib ibn ʿAṭīya, *al-Muḥarrir al-wajīz fī-tafsīr al-kitāb al-ʿazīz* (Rabat, 1395/1975–1400/1980), i. 14.

twenty-seven texts (*abwāb qirā'āt al-Qur'ān wa-taḥzībihi wa-tartīlihi*) containing indications for the ritualistic recitation of the Qur'ān. In the *Kitāb al-witr*, Abū Dā'ūd has a number of *ḥadīth* extolling the excellences of certain *sūra*s of the Qur'ān, presumably in view of their use in the *witr* prayer. Also in this book is the rather curious inclusion of four texts establishing the fact that the Qur'ān was revealed in seven versions, or *aḥruf*. As a result, the fact of the seven *aḥruf* is separated from the section which gives precise readings or recitations (*qirā'āt*).

After the long series of legal books, Abū Dā'ūd has five books whose common trait seems to be subject matter having to do with violence or the disruption of order. There is also an eschatological strain to much of this material. The collection could have been brought logically to a close with these five books. At the end, however, are two books whose places in the order of arrangement are more difficult to ascertain. This is especially true of the next-to-last book, called *Kitāb al-sunna*. A great deal of its material is found elsewhere in the collection. It has texts dealing with the basis for the authority of the *sunna*, biographical details on the first caliphs, texts on doctrines, heresies, and eschatology. Of special interest is a chapter on the Qur'ān, containing five texts, all in a pious vein, recommending respect for the word of God. Another chapter deals with the prohibition of debate and argument about the Qur'ān.

Finally, the *Sunan* of Abū Dā'ūd closes with a long *Kitāb al-adab*, a category which is commonly found in *sunan* collections, but which here is oddly placed. Both of the last two books seem to be of an edificatory nature more than of a legal one.

Another *sunan* collection is that of Ibn Māja al-Qazwīnī (d. 273/887). It contains about 4,000 reports arranged in thirty-seven books. This *Sunan* is designed for ready reference as an instrument for legal science. Matters of theology, principles of *ḥadīth* science, and the laudation texts (called *faḍā'il*) are all relegated to the lengthy introduction.

Tafsīr al-Qur'ān, as such, has no place in Ibn Māja, but the link between *sunna* and Qur'ān is everywhere assumed. Quranic references with their elucidation by the *sunna* are numerous, but they are not highlighted. There is no mention of the seven versions (*aḥruf*), and a group of eleven texts under the heading *thawāb al-Qur'ān* is found in the *Kitāb al-adab*.

Of the three *sunan* collections included in the 'six books', the one by Abū 'Abd al-Raḥmān Aḥmad ibn Shu'ayb al-Nasā'ī (d. 303/915) is the most interesting from the point of view of *tafsīr*. Like Ibn Māja, al-Nasā'ī's concern is exclusively legal, in the broad sense. His collection has no books on laudation, good manners, eschatology, *tafsīr*, or biographical notes. It holds rigorously to the rubrics of worship practices and the rules of the social and economic life. This does not exclude a book on beliefs, for that rubric belongs historically within the purview of jurisprudence. Characteristically, however, al-Nasā'ī names his section on faith *Kitāb al-imān wa-sharā'i'ihi*. The conventional material on the seven *aḥruf*, appropriate recitations for particular times, the history of the beginning of the revelation, and so forth is placed in *Kitāb iftitāḥ al-ṣalāt*. This arrangement agrees with the Islamic understanding that Qur'ān science is an ancillary of the inclusive discipline of jurisprudence (*fiqh*).

Tafsīr ḥadīth figure prominently in many of the fifty-one books of al-Nasā'ī. He often devotes a whole chapter to one Qur'ān text, heading it by the words *Ta'wīl qawl Allāh 'azza wa-jalla*. Al-Nasā'ī also gives a number of different versions and *isnād*s of the *ḥadīth* he cites, quoting them in full. Besides these numerous chapters of *tafsīr* on subjects of *fiqh*, the Qur'ān figures in many other *ḥadīth*, just as it does in all of the collections.

4. CONCLUSION

The 'six books' of authoritative *ḥadīth* encapsulate two centuries or more of Islamic *'ilm*, the word used for knowledge of that which is useful for the worship of God and for life in society. Information about the Qur'ān is an important part of this store of knowledge. In fact, it is impossible to separate Quranic elements from the rest of knowledge, without doing violence to the whole. This is clearly seen in the way the compilers of the *sunan* books integrate their legal material with Quranic data. At the same time, the presence of books entitled *tafsīr al-Qur'ān* in al-Bukhārī, Muslim, and al-Tirmidhī, witness the fact of an independent and parallel development of the science of *tafsīr*. The emergence of a full-blown work of *tafsīr*, such as the *Jāmi' al-bayān* of al-Ṭabarī (d. 310/922), from the same century as that of the great *muḥaddithūn*, is startling evidence of the difference between the concerns of a *mufassir* and a *muḥaddith*.

The *mufassir* was concerned primarily, if not wholly, with the elucidation of the revealed text, for whatever purpose that might serve, and to achieve that end, he was open to several possible sources of information. The *muḥaddith*, on the other hand, was concerned primarily with reporting the *sunna* of Muḥammad, and when the reports he brought involved the Qur'ān text, his effort joined that of the *mufassir*.

The *ḥadīth* material on the Qur'ān is largely reflective and edificatory. But it is also exemplary, didactic, and at times juridical, thus nourishing the adjunct concern of the *ḥadīth* scholars who, along with the lawyers, saw the *sunna* as the key to the application of Quranic principles to the life of Muslim society.

Finally, the *ḥadīth* literature furnishes an instructive view of the kind of information that was and is accessible to the masses of Muslims in their effort to reflect and act upon the Quranic revelation. *Ḥadīth* are short, concrete, vivid, and practical pieces of information. They are also profoundly evocative at times. It is no wonder that they have provided perhaps the primary religious nourishment of the Islamic community. A text recorded in al-Tirmidhī, Muslim, and Ibn Māja reflects in vivid fashion the image of pious believers assembled in a circle of Qur'ān study.

> Abū Hurayra reported that the messenger of God said: '. . . When people sit in a mosque to recite the Book of God and to study it carefully (*yatadārasūnahu*) together, the presence of God (*sakīna*) will descend upon them, mercy will envelop them, and the angels will surround them. . .'.[41]

APPENDIX
THE SIX *ḤADĪTH* COLLECTIONS

Abū Dā'ūd, Sulaymān ibn al-Ash'ath al-Sijistānī, *Sunan abī Dā'ūd*. 4 vols., ed. Muḥammad Muḥyī al-Dīn 'Abd al-Ḥamīd. Cairo: Maṭba'at Muṣṭafā Muḥammad, n.d.

Al-Bukhārī, Muḥammad ibn Ismā'īl, *Ṣaḥīḥ al-Bukhārī*. 9 vols. Cairo: Dār wa-maṭābi' al-sha'b, n.d.

Ibn Māja, Abū 'Abd Allāh, *Sunan*. 2 vols., ed. Muḥammad Fu'ād 'Abd al-Bāqī. Cairo: 'Īsā al-Bābī al-Ḥalabī wa-shurakāhu, 1972.

[41] Al-Tirmidhī, *abwāb al-qirā'āt*, 3.

Al-Mubārakfūrī, Muḥammad ʻAbd al-Raḥmān, *Tuḥfat al-aḥwadhī bi-sharḥ Jāmiʻ al-Tirmidhī*. 10 vols., ed. ʻAbd al-Wahhāb ʻAbd al-Laṭīf and ʻAbd al-Raḥmān Muḥammad ʻUthmān. Al-Madīna al-Munawwara: al-Maktaba al-salafīya, 1963–7.

Muslim ibn al-Ḥajjāj, *Ṣaḥīḥ Muslim*. 5 vols., ed. Muḥammad Fu'ād ʻAbd al-Bāqī. Cairo: al-Ḥalabī, 1955.

Al-Nasā'ī, Abū ʻAbd al-Raḥmān, *Sunan al-Nasā'ī bi-sharḥ al-ḥāfiẓ Jalāl al-Dīn al-Suyūṭī wa-ḥāshiyat al-imām al-Sindī*. 8 vols., ed. Ḥasan Muḥammad al-Masʻūdī. Beirut: Iḥyā' al-turāth alʻArabī, 1348/1930.

5

Legends in *tafsīr* and *ḥadīth* Literature: The Creation of Ādam and Related Stories

M. J. KISTER

STORIES and tales about the prophets and about pious, ascetic, and righteous people of bygone days, the so-called *qiṣaṣ al-anbiyā'*, already circulated widely in the Muslim community of the first century. The origin of these stories, as stated by T. Nagel, must be traced back to pre-Islamic Arabia; they were disseminated in that period by Jews and Christians.[1] The recently published papyrus of Wahb ibn Munabbih (d. 110/728),[2] the papryi edited by the late Nabia Abbott,[3] and the papyri of Khirbet Mird edited by A. Grohmann[4] bear evidence to the fact that in the early period of Islam there were elaborate stories about prophets, sages, and saints which were widely circulated. The *Tafsīr* of Muqātil ibn Sulaymān (d. 150/767)[5] and the *Tafsīr* of 'Abd al-Razzāq (d. 211/827)[6] contain valuable material of the *qiṣaṣ al-anbiyā'*, and reflect the way in which these stories were absorbed and incorporated into the exegetical compilations of the Qur'ān. The important work of Isḥāq ibn Bishr (d. 206/821), *Mubtada' al-dunyā wa-qiṣaṣ al-anbiyā'*, until recently considered lost,[7] has been rediscovered and, I am told, is now being prepared for a critical edition.[8] The importance of this early compilation was pointed out by Nagel in

[1] T. Nagel, 'Ḳiṣaṣ al-anbiyā'', *EI*².

[2] Raif Georges Khoury, *Wahb b. Munabbih, der Heidelberger Papyrus PSR Heid Arab* 23 (Wiesbaden, 1972).

[3] Nabia Abbott, *Studies in Arabic Literary Papyri* i (Historical texts) and ii (Quranic Commentary and Tradition), (Chicago, 1957, 1967).

[4] Adolf Grohmann, *Arabic Papyri from Ḥirbet Mird* (Louvain, 1963).

[5] Muqātil ibn Sulaymān, *Tafsīr al-Qur'ān*, MS Ahmet III, 74, i–ii; also vol. i, ed. 'Abd Allāh Maḥmūd Shaḥāta (Cairo, 1969), including the first six *sūras*.

[6] 'Abd al-Razzāq ibn Hammām, *Tafsīr al-Qur'ān*, MS Cairo, Dār al-kutub *tafsīr* 242.

[7] See Abbott, i. 46: (Document 2, Story of Adam and Eve) '. . . there is a strong possibility that the papyrus with its rather "unique" text could belong to this somewhat discredited and lost work. . . .'

[8] Bodleian Library, MS Huntingdon 388. For using this manuscript I owe thanks to Mrs Ruth Lieber, who is working on an edition of it.

his Inaugural Dissertation, *Die Qiṣaṣ al-anbiyā'*;[9] Nagel devoted five pages to an examination of the personality of Isḥāq ibn Bishr and to a detailed scrutiny of the sources of the *Mubtada'*.[10] The manuscript, which contains the first part of the composition, consists of 218 folios, and ends with the death of Abraham. Nagel's high view of the significance of this rich early source is entirely justified, it would seem.

The Qur'ān contains a great many reports concerning prophets and sages, but these are usually formulated in vague terms and frequently do no more than mention an event or refer to a person who is specified no further. The transmitters of the tales aimed at widening the scope of the stories; they availed themselves of the lore contained in local traditions current in the Arab peninsula in the period of the Jāhilīya, in Christian narratives concerning the life of Jesus, the Apostles, the martyrs, and the monks, in Jewish Biblical legends, and in the utterances of sages and ascetics.[11] This huge mass of material started to infiltrate into the realm of *ḥadīth* and *tafsīr* very early on in the Islamic period, and from the terse reports and utterances, combined with the additional material derived from other sources, a rich tapestry of lively and plastic narrative was woven. As the advent of Islam and the mission of the prophet Muḥammad were, according to the concepts of the Muslim community, part of God's predestination, as they were contained in God's prior knowledge and heralded by the prophets of all ages, the stories of the prophets became an integral part of the books of history, and were duly embedded in the preamble (the *mubtada'*, *bad'*, or *ibtidā'*) with which, as a rule, these compilations began. The Muslim community was eager to learn of the biographies of the prophets of the past because Muḥammad was identified in certain passages of the Qur'ān with their mission and vocation, and especially with the sufferings and persecution which they had undergone. It is evident that these stories had some bearing on current trends within the Muslim community and that they both

[9] Tilman Nagel, *Die Qiṣaṣ al-anbiyā': Ein Beitrag zur Arabischen Literaturgeschichte* (Bonn, 1967).

[10] Nagel, pp. 113–18; see also *GAS* i. 293–4.

[11] Cf. F. Rosenthal, 'The Influence of the Biblical Tradition in Muslim Historiography', in B. Lewis and P. M. Holt, eds., *Historians of the Middle East* (Oxford, 1962), 35–45; and see the exhaustive bibliography on the *qiṣaṣ* literature in Haim Schwarzbaum, *Biblical and extra-Biblical Legends in Islamic Folk Literature* (Walldorf-Hessen, 1982).

reflected and shaped to a certain extent the religious and political ideas of the various factions which made up the community of Islam.

The rich treasure of stories and traditions relating to Ādam, Ḥawwā' (Eve), and their progeny is closely connected to the narrative verses of the Qur'ān which deal with their creation, temptation, vicissitudes, and fate. These stories often present divergent and even contradictory conceptions of these events. The traditions attributed to Muḥammad are frequently accompanied by commentaries, discussions, and analyses provided by theologians, scholars of religious law, and especially by scholars of *ḥadīth*. The scrutiny of some of this material as presented by the *tafsīr* and *ḥadīth* literature may help us gain a better understanding of the ideas and beliefs prevalent in the various divisions of the Muslim community; it may thereby help us reach a better definition of their religious and political attitudes and of the arguments used within their internal struggles.

1. THE CREATION OF ĀDAM AND HIS POSITION IN THE WORLD

A key verse concerning the creation of Ādam is: 'And when thy Lord said to the angels, "I am setting in the earth a viceroy," they said, "What, wilt Thou set therein one who will do corruption there and shed blood, while we proclaim Thy praise and call Thee Holy?" He said, "Assuredly I know that you know not"' (Q. 2/30). This verse is interpreted in several ways. The word *qāla*, 'said', in the phrase, 'Thy Lord said', is not an utterance to which an answer or advice of the angels is expected; God said it in order to inform them, not in order to consult them.[12] As a result, some commentators express the opinion that the question of the angels, 'What, wilt Thou set therein one who will do corruption. . .', does not reflect any objection to God's utterance or a low opinion of the qualities of man. The angels' question is an attempt to solicit knowledge about the purpose of God's deed, 'setting in the earth a viceroy (*khalīfa*)'.[13] Commentators are not unanimous about the identity

[12] Ibn Junghul, *Ta'rīkh*, MS BL Or. 5912, fo. 23v; cf. al-Qurṭubī, *al-Jāmi' li-aḥkām al-Qur'ān* (Cairo, 1387/1967), i. 263; al-Majlisī, *Biḥār al-anwār* (Tehran, 1376–92), xi. 124–6; 'Abd al-'Azīz ibn Yaḥyā al-Kinānī, *Kitāb al-ḥayda* (Damascus, 1384/1964), 167.

[13] Ibn Junghul, fo. 23v; cf. al-Maqdisī, *al-Bad' wa'l-ta'rīkh*, ed. C. Huart (Paris, 1899), ii. 92; see also the explanation in the commentary of al-Ḥasan ibn

of the angels addressed by God. One account gives a different setting in which God's order was uttered—God's command was released to a group of angels who were with Iblīs; other angels residing in the Heavens were not present.[14] According to another opinion, God addressed all the angels.[15] Although the more general opinion of the scholars was that God merely informed the angels about 'setting the viceroy in the earth', some held the view that He consulted them; this interpretation established the moral to be drawn from the story, that is, we too should consult wise and knowledgeable people.[16]

The term *khalīfa* is crucial for the correct understanding of the phrase 'I am setting in the earth a viceroy.' The word denotes a person who replaces another one. Lane records *inter alia*, 'one who has been made, or appointed, to take the place of him who has been before him', 'a substitute', 'successor', 'deputy', 'one who supplies the place of him who has been before'. Almost all commentators take it for granted that *khalīfa* refers to Ādam who was sent as messenger.[17] His prophethood is attested in the Qur'ān and the *sunna* and by *ijmā'*. Some people deny his prophethood, but this denial should be considered *kufr*.[18] Ādam undoubtedly deserved the title *khalīfa*.[19] Some commentators assume that he was the *khalīfa* of the angels who dwelt on earth, others maintain that he

Muḥammad al-Qummī al-Nīsābūrī, *Gharā'ib al-Qur'ān wa-raghā'ib al-furqān* (Cairo, 1381/1962), i. 232, and see the discussion of this subject in Fakhr al-Dīn al-Rāzī, *al-Tafsīr al-kabīr* (Cairo, 1357/1938), ii. 166–70.

[14] See al-Suyūṭī, *al-Durr al-manthūr fi'l-tafsīr bi'l-ma'thūr* (Cairo, 1314), i. 45; also Abū Ḥayyān al-Jayyānī, *al-Baḥr al-muḥīṭ* (Cairo, 1321), i. 140–1; Mītham, *Sharḥ nahj al-balāgha* (Tehran, 1378), i. 173–4; Anon., *Siyar al-anbiyā'*, MS BL Or. 1510, fo. 10r.

[15] Abū Ḥayyān, i. 140; Mītham, i. 173–4.

[16] Abū Ḥayyān, i. 141, al-Nīsābūrī, i. 232; Fakhr al-Dīn al-Rāzī, ii. 166; al-Shawkānī, *Fatḥ al-qadīr al-jāmi' bayna fannayi'l-riwāya wa'l-dirāya min 'ilm al-tafsīr* (Cairo, n.d.), i. 62.

[17] See, e.g., Nūr al-Dīn al-Haythamī, *Majma' al-zawā'id wa-manba' al-fawā'id* (Beirut, 1967), i. 196, 197, viii. 198; al-Suyūṭī, *Jam' al-jawāmi'* (Cairo, 1978), ii. 641; al-Suyūṭī, *al-Durr*, i. 52; Ibn al-Ṣalāḥ, *Muqaddima*, ed. 'Ā'isha 'Abd al-Raḥmān (Cairo, 1976), 650; al-Māwardī, *A'lām al-nubūwa* (Cairo, 1353/1955), 33; al-Qurṭubī, i. 263; Ibn Abī 'Āṣim, *al-Awā'il*, MS Ẓāhirīya, *ḥadīth* 297, fo. 4v; al-Shawkānī, i. 69; al-Daylamī, *Firdaws al-akhbār*, MS Chester Beatty 4139, fo. 15r; Ibn Nāṣir al-Dīn al-Dimashqī, *Jāmi' al-āthār fī-mawlid al-nabī al-mukhtār*, MS Cambridge Or. 913, fo. 141r;al-'Aynī, *'Umdat al-qārī, sharḥ Ṣaḥīḥ al-Bukhārī* (Cairo, 1348), xviii. 83; al-Suyūṭī, *al-Wasā'il ilā ma'rifat al-awā'il* (Cairo, 1400/1980), 17.

[18] 'Alī al-Qārī, *Sharḥ al-fiqh al-akbar li-Abī Ḥanīfa* (Beirut, 1399/1979), 50.

[19] Al-Qurṭubī, i. 263.

was the *khalīfa* of Iblīs in holding sway over the earth. In the opinion of some, the term *khalīfa* should be applied to Ādam and his progeny. This is said to be proved by the words of the angels, 'What, wilt Thou set therein one who will do corruption there and shed blood.' This expression refers to the progeny of Ādam who would do corruption, not to Ādam himself as a person.[20] Some scholars are of the opinion that Ādam was the *khalīfa* of the *jinn*, the sons of al-Jānn.[21] A peculiar tradition says that *fi'l-arḍ* refers to Mecca.[22] According to some, Ādam was entrusted with establishing a rule of truth and justice on earth; others speak of his duties of cultivating the soil, digging canals, and building houses.[23]

The distinctive position of Ādam as a prophet is reflected in the traditions about the books of revelation (*ṣaḥīfa*, *ṣaḥā'if*, or *ṣuḥuf*) which God sent down to him and about the religious injunctions which He ordered him to carry out. Ibn Nāṣir al-Dīn (d. 742/1341) records a report according to which God revealed to Ādam the letters of the alphabet; they were written down on twenty-one pages.[24] Another tradition says that God revealed to him forty books.[25] A tradition quoted from 'Abd al-Raḥmān al-Bisṭāmī (d. 854/1454), *Durrat al-ma'ārif*, says that God granted Ādam the secrets of the letters; this is a piece of information which He did not reveal to the angels. God sent down to him ten books (*ṣaḥā'if*), and so he talked about *'ilm al-ḥurūf*. Ādam wrote three books on the science of letters: *Kitāb al-malakūt*, *Kitāb al-khafāyā*, and *al-Sifr al-mustaqīm*.[26] According to a tradition reported on the authority of Abū Dharr, God sent down to Ādam a book containing the letters of the alphabet. Muḥammad states authoritatively that the letter *lā* *(lām alif)* is one of the twenty-nine letters of the alphabet, and that the number of the letters revealed to Ādam was twenty-nine, including the letter *lā*; he who denies the letter *lā* as one of the letters of the alphabet is guilty of *kufr*; he who does not admit that the number of letters is twenty-nine will not come out from Hell.[27] The first who wrote Arabic, Persian, as well as other scripts was

20 Al-'Aynī, xv. 205.

21 Abū Ḥayyān, i. 140; cf. al-Nīsābūrī, i. 231.

22 Al-Shawkānī, i. 62, 63.

23 Abū Ḥayyān, i. 140.

24 Ibn Nāṣir al-Dīn, fo. 148ᵛ.

25 Pseudo Aṣma'ī, *Qiṣaṣ al-anbiyā'* (included in the *Kitāb al-Shāmil*), MS BL Or. 1493, fo. 8ᵛ.

26 Al-Qundūzī, *Yanābī' al-mawadda* (Kāẓimīya-Qom, 1385/1966), 398.

27 Ibn 'Arāq al-Kinānī, *Tanzīh al-sharī'a al-marfū'a 'an al-akhbār al-shanī'a al-mawḍū'a* (Beirut, 1399/1979), i. 250.

Ādam; he put it down in clay, which he later burnt. Those tablets of burnt clay survived the deluge, were found by the various peoples and applied to writing their languages.[28] Ādam is said to have been the first human being who composed poetry; he composed his verses in Arabic.[29]

Ādam is said to have been the first to have prayed the morning prayer and to have performed two *rak'a*s in this prayer.[30] Al-Mas'ūdī (d. 345/956) records a tradition saying that God revealed to Ādam twenty-one books, Jibrīl taught him the practices of the pilgrimage to Mecca, and God enjoined him to pray, to pay the *zakāt*, to wash from ritual impurity, and to perform the *wuḍū'*.[31] According to another tradition God sent down to Ādam twenty-one books (*ṣaḥīfa*) and enjoined him to perform 50 *rak'a*s. He forbade him to eat pork, carrion, and blood of animals; God also forbade him to lie, to behave treacherously, and to fornicate. God's injunctions were dictated by Jibrīl and written down by Ādam in Syriac. In paradise Ādam spoke Arabic; after his disobedience and expulsion he spoke Syriac.[32] These injunctions and prohibitions seem to have formed the *sharī'at Ādam*, the binding law of Ādam. Muḥammad is said to have acted before his call according to the *sharī'a* of Ādam.[33] Before his death 'Ādam summoned Shīth, ordered him to hide his will (*waṣīya*) from the progeny of Qābīl, and instructed him as to the injunctions and penalty laws enjoined by God.[34] The Shī'ī version of the transfer of the will is slightly more detailed. According to it, God ordered Ādam to hand over to Shīth (= Hibat Allāh) the true name of God (*al-ism al-a'ẓam*) and the Ark of Covenant (*tābūt*) in which the knowledge (*al-'ilm*) and the will (*waṣīya*) had to be deposited. Ādam enjoined Shīth to avoid contact with the progeny of Qābīl.[35]

[28] Muḥammad ibn 'Abd Allāh al-Shiblī, *Maḥāsin al-wasā'il fī ma'rifat al-awā'il*, MS BL Or. 1530, fos. 137ʳ, 138ʳ; cf. al-Qurṭubī, i. 283; al-Suyūṭī, *al-Wasā'il*, 127.

[29] See, e.g, Ibn Hishām, *al-Tījān fī mulūk Ḥimyar* (Hyderabad, 1347), 17–18 (and see ibid. for the denial of this tradition); al-Suyūṭī, *al-Wasā'il*, 122; al-Shiblī, fo. 153ᵛ; Mu'āfā ibn Zakarīyā, *al-Jalīs al-ṣāliḥ al-kāfī wa'l-anīs al-nāṣiḥ al-shāfī*, MS Ahmet III, 2321, fo. 159ᵛ; Ibn Nāṣir al-Dīn, fos. 148ʳ–148ᵛ; al-Mas'ūdī, *Murūj al-dhahab*, ed. C. Pellat (Beirut, 1966), i. 39–40.

[30] Anon., *Siyar al-anbiyā'*, fo. 19ᵛ; 'Abd al-Malik ibn Ḥabīb, *Ta'rīkh*, MS Bodley, Marsh 188, p. 27.

[31] Al-Mas'ūdī, *Akhbār al-zamān* (Cairo, 1357/1938), 51.

[32] Anon., *Siyar al-anbiyā'*, fo. 19ᵛ.

[33] Ibn Ḥajar al-Haytamī, *al-Fatāwā al-ḥadīthīya* (Cairo, 1390/1970), 153.

[34] Anon., *Siyar al-anbiyā'*, fo. 22ʳ.

[35] Al-Mas'ūdī, *Ithbāt al-waṣīya* (Najaf, 1374/1955), 16–17.

2. IBLĪS AND THE *JINN* PRIOR TO ĀDAM

There are many reports about the *jinn* and the angels who ruled on earth before Ādam and who had to be replaced by the rule of Ādam. We have mentioned above the view that the announcement made by God that He was installing a *khalīfa* was directed at the angels who were in the company of Iblīs. Abū Ḥayyān (d. 745/1345) says that God addressed the angels who fought the *jinn* on the side of Iblīs; God intended to lift them to heaven and replace them by Ādam and his progeny. Abū Ḥayyān then gives a short report about the rule of the *jinn* on earth and says that a force of angels was dispatched under the command of Iblīs to fight them.[36]

The reports recorded by Isḥāq ibn Bishr in his *Mubtada'* contain interesting details about the role of Iblīs and give us an idea as to the notions concerning the *jinn* that were current in the early period of Islam. An account given on the authority of Ibn 'Abbās tells the following story about angels and *jinn*. The *jinn* were inhabitants of the earth, the angels were in the heavens. Every heaven had its angels, who performed their special prayers and glorification of God; the higher the heaven, the more powerful was the worship, the glorifications and prayer. According to some they inhabited the earth for 2,000 years, according to others, for only 40 years and 'God knows the truth.'[37]

The other report recorded by Isḥāq ibn Bishr is also given on the authority of Ibn 'Abbās and contains some new details about the classes of the *jinn* and their activities. When God created Sawmā, the father of the *jinn*—it was he who was created from the smokeless fire (*mārij*)—God said to him: '(Say) what is your desire?' Sawmā answered: 'I wish that we should see but remain unseen, that we should disappear in moist ground and that our people of ripe age should be turned young.' These wishes were granted; *jinnī*s see but remain unseen, the dead disappear in moist ground, and a *jinnī* of ripe age never dies before being turned into a young *jinnī*.[38] This report is followed by a short passage which

[36] Abū Ḥayyān, i. 140–1; al-Suyūṭī, *al-Durr*, i. 44–5; al-Kisā'ī, *'Ajā'ib al-malakūt*, MS Hebrew University, AR 8° 63, fo. 39ᵛ.

[37] Isḥāq ibn Bishr, *Mubtada' al-dunyā wa-qiṣaṣ al-anbiyā'*, MS Bodl. Huntingdon 388, fo. 38ᵛ.

[38] Ps. Aṣma'ī, *Qiṣaṣ al-anbiyā'*, fo. 5ᵛ; al-Shiblī, *Ākām al-marjān fī gharā'ib al-akhbār wa aḥkām al-jānn* (Cairo, 1376), 85.

states that when God created Ādam, He asked him about his desire; Ādam said that he desired horses, which were indeed granted to him.[39]

The story about the revolt of the *jinn* on earth and about the expedition of warriors from heaven against them is given in the following passage. God created the *jinn* and ordered them to inhabit and build up the earth. They did so and worshipped God for a very long time. But afterwards they became disobedient towards God and shed blood. Amongst them was an angel called Yūsuf; they killed him. Then God dispatched against them a military force of the angels who dwelt in the lower heaven; this force was of the division of the *ḥinn*. Among them was Iblīs, who stood at the head of a troop of 4,000 warriors.[40] They descended, banned the sons of al-Jānn, and exiled them from the earth to the isles of the sea. Iblīs and the warriors under his command settled on earth. Worship became easy for them[41] and they were inclined to go on dwelling on earth.[42] The report recorded by Abū Ḥayyān has some additional phrases which explain the attitude of the *ḥinn* and of their head, Iblīs. When God announced that He intended to put up a *khalīfa* on earth, He let them know that He had decided to raise the *ḥinn* to heaven, but they did not like the idea, as their worship on earth was of the lightest kind among the angels. This is why they were reluctant to return to heaven.[43] Further, they remembered the case of the prophet (!) Yūsuf who was killed by the *jinn*, and when God told them that He intended to set up a substitute on earth, they asked him: 'Wilt Thou set therein one who will do corruption there?'[44] The report makes it clear that these angels had no knowledge of hidden things. Their question was

[39] Isḥāq ibn Bishr, fo. 38ᵛ; this and the following are recorded in al-Shiblī's *Ākām*, 9–11 where the author quotes the source, Abū Ḥudhayfa Isḥāq ibn Bishr, *al-Mubtada'*.

[40] Isḥāq ibn Bishr, fos. 38ᵛ–39ʳ. The *ḥinn* are defined as the lowest class of the *jinn*; they are nicknamed *kilāb al-jinn*. See al-Shiblī, *Ākām*, 6; al-Fīrūzābādī, *al-Qāmūs al-muḥīṭ* (Cairo, 1371/1952), iv. 218, s.v. *ḥ-n-n*; Ibn al-Athīr, *al-Nihāya fī gharīb al-ḥadīth wa'l-āthār* (Cairo, 1383/1963), i. 453, s.v. *ḥ-n-n*; al-Zamakhsharī, *al-Fā'iq* (Cairo, 1971), i. 325.

[41] In the text of Isḥāq ibn Bishr: *fa-hāna 'alayhim al-'amal*; the intent is elucidated in Abū Ḥayyan, i. 141—*wa-khaffaf 'anhum al-'ibāda*; see also Muqātil ibn Sulaymān, *Tafsīr*, ed. Shaḥāta, i. 29.

[42] Isḥāq ibn Bishr, fos. 38ᵛ–39ʳ.

[43] Abū Ḥayyān, i. 141; also al-Diyārbakrī, *Ta'rīkh al-khamīs* (Cairo, 1283), i. 36.

[44] Isḥāq ibn Bishr, fo. 39ᵛ.

based only on their experience and on what they saw of the corruption of the *jinn*.

An elaborate version of the events and of the position of Iblīs is given in al-Diyārbakrī (d. 990/1582), *Ta'rīkh al-khamīs*; it is told on the authority of Ubayy ibn Ka'b who claimed that he had found it in the Torah. It relates a story of a division of angels called al-Jinn ibn al-Jānn. They were sent down from heaven and God granted them sexual desire. They multiplied in large numbers and for a long period remained righteous and God-worshipping. However, they deteriorated and became corrupt especially when they became addicted to drinking wine; this led them to sodomy, fornication, and murder. A righteous man from among them, called al-Ḥārith or 'Azāzīl, decided to part from the wicked community; he was joined by a thousand honest believers, who settled separately in an isolated place and worshipped God. When the Earth complained of the wrong deeds of the *jinn* community, God ordered 'Azāzīl to send one of his community in order to summon them to abandon disobedience and accept belief. 'Azāzīl sent to them Sahlūt ibn Balāhit; he summoned them to embrace Islam, but they killed him. 'Azāzīl continued to send messengers to them and they went on killing them. The last of the messengers was Yūsuf ibn Yāsif; the *jinn* tortured him and finally killed him by casting him into a copper cauldron filled with boiling oil. Then God sent down against them a troop of angels; they held swords in their hands and fire poured from their mouths. God put them under the command of al-Ḥārith/'Azāzīl and they defeated the wicked *jinn*.[45] It is evident that this account is different from the reports recorded by Isḥāq ibn Bishr; Iblīs (alias al-Ḥārith, alias 'Azāzīl) is one of the *jinn* who, inspired by a deep religious conviction, parts from the sinful community, dedicates himself to the worship of God, and fights at the head of the troops of angels for a victory of righteousness and truth. Nothing is said about the vicissitudes of 'Azāzīl (= al-Ḥārith, Iblīs) after that victory.

A quite different account recorded by al-Diyārbakrī gives interesting details of the career of the pious *jinnī* 'Azāzīl. When the community of the *jinn* deteriorated, he separated himself from them and devoted himself to the fervent worship of God. The angels in heaven admired him so much that they asked God to lift him up to

[45] Al-Diyārbakrī, i. 33.

heaven. God raised him to the lower heaven and he exerted himself in worship there as well. The angels of the second heaven asked God to elevate him, and so he passed all the heavens until God placed him in the highest position, that of the 'Treasurer of the Throne', and entrusted him with its keys. He used to circumambulate the heavens; the angels sought his favours and addressed him as the 'Treasurer of Paradise' and the 'Chief of the Pious (ascetics)'.[46]

Additional traditions concerning the events in the career of Iblīs are no less divergent. Some early traditions reported on the authority of the companions of Muḥammad or of their successors say that Iblīs belonged to the *jinn* who dwelt on earth and who were defeated by the force of the angels dispatched against them. He was young when he was captured and brought to heaven; there, he worshipped God in the company of the angels. When God ordered the angels to bow to Ādam, Iblīs refrained.[47] Other traditions maintain that Iblīs (named al-Ḥārith) belonged to a group of angels created from the fire of *samūm* while other groups were created from light. They were called *al-ḥinn*.[48] Several traditions say that he was one of the dignified angels; God put him at the head of the kingdom of the lower heaven and appointed him as 'Treasurer of Paradise'; the division of angels to which he belonged was called *al-jinn*, because they were the 'Treasurers of Paradise' (*khuzzān al-janna*).[49]

Some accounts stress Iblīs's knowledge, devotion in the worship of God, and his high position. He was the head (*ra'īs*) of the angels in the lower heaven and his *kunya* was Abū Kurdūs; he belonged to the division of angels called *al-jinn*, who were the 'Treasurers of Paradise', and was one of the noble group of angels who were equipped with four wings.[50]

A peculiar tradition says that Iblīs was sent as judge (*qāḍī*) to the *jinn* on earth and that he meted out judgement among them in righteousness for 1,000 years; he was called *Ḥakam* and God approved of this name. However, he grew haughty and insolent and began to cause hatred and dissension to spread among people, and

46 Al-Diyārbakrī, i. 32–3.

47 Al-Ṭabarī, *Ta'rīkh*, ed. M. Abū'l-Faḍl Ibrāhīm (Cairo, 1387/1967), i. 87; id., *Tafsīr*, ed. Shākir (Cairo, n.d.), i. 507, nos. 698–9; Abū Ḥayyān, i. 153.

48 Al-Ṭabarī, *Tafsīr*, i. 502, no. 685.

49 Al-Ṭabarī, *Tafsīr*, i. 503, nos. 688–9; 'Abd al-Malik ibn Ḥabīb, p. 12; Ibn Nāṣir al-Dīn, fo. 136v.

50 Ibn Junghul, fo. 24r; cf. al-Suyūṭī, *al-Durr*, i. 50.

for 2,000 years they shed blood in internal wars. Then God sent a fire and burnt the people. Having seen what had happened, Iblīs went up to heaven and became a fervent and devout worshipper at the side of the angels.[51] Some scholars denied his provenance from the angels and based their argument on Q. 18/50, *kāna min al-jinn*. Al-Ṭabarī (d. 310/923) provides a harmonizing solution in his *Tafsīr*. It is possible that God created one part of His angels from light and another part from fire; Iblīs could possibly belong to that group of angels who were created from fire and he may have also been created from the fire of *samūm*. The fact that Iblīs had offspring can be explained by the hypothesis that God installed in him sexual desire, an impulse which was denied to other angels. The fact that he was from the *jinn* does not mean that he was not an angel, as the angels also belong to the category of the *jinn*, because they are invisible to the sight of human beings.[52] Al-Ṭabarī's opinion can be traced back to Ibn Qutayba (d. 276/889)[53] and is echoed in al-Shiblī (d. 769/1367), *Ākām al-marjān*.[54]

Indeed, the pivot of lengthy discussions was the question whether Iblīs belonged to the angels or to the *jinn*.[55] According to some scholars Iblīs was an angel; he was metamorphosed (*musikha*) by the order of God, and having been banned from the community of angels, he joined the *jinn*.[56]

Descriptions of Iblīs's odd and perverse ways of copulation and parturition and several lists of his sons are actually given in the literature.[57] One of his descendants, Hāma ibn al-Hīm, is said to

[51] Al-Ṭabarī, *Ta'rīkh*, i. 88.

[52] Al-Ṭabarī, *Tafsīr*, i. 508; Ibn Ḥajar al-Haytamī, pp. 61, 125; Fakhr al-Dīn al-Rāzī, ii. 213–15, 218 and xxi. 3, 124, 136–7; al-'Aynī, xv. 167–8; Mītham, i. 174.

[53] Ibn Qutayba, *Tafsīr gharīb al-Qur'ān*, ed. Aḥmad Ṣaqr (Cairo, 1378/1958), 21; this assumption is strongly refuted in Ibn Ḥazm, *al-Iḥkām fī uṣūl al-aḥkām* (Cairo, 1398/1978), 511–16.

[54] Al-Shiblī, *Ākām*, 7.

[55] See, e.g., al-Nasafī, *Tafsīr* (Cairo, n.d.), i. 42, iii. 67; al-Shawkānī, i. 66, 191, iii. 130; Mītham, i. 174; 'Abd al-Jabbār, *Tanzīh al-Qur'ān 'an al-maṭa'in* (Beirut, n.d.), 22; al-Ṭabarī, *Tafsīr*, i. 502–8; al-Qurṭubī, x. 25; Fakhr al-Dīn al-Rāzī, xxi. 136; Ibn Abī'l-Ḥadīd, *Sharḥ nahj al-balagha* (Cairo, 1964), i. 110; al-Suyūṭī, *al-Durr*, iv. 227; Anon., *Siyar al-anbiyā'*, fo. 4^v; al-Ṭabarsī, *Majma' al-bayān fī tafsīr al-Qur'ān* (Beirut, 1380/1961), i. 180–3; al-Rāzī, *Masā'il al-Rāzī wa-ajwibatuhā min gharā'ib āy al-tanzīl* (Cairo, 1381/1961), 202–3.

[56] See, e.g, al-Rāzī, *Masā'il*, 202–3; al-Suyūṭī, *al-Durr*, iv. 227; Ibn Abī'l-Ḥadīd, vi. 435–6.

[57] See, e.g., Isḥāq ibn Bishr, fos. 52^v–53^v; al-Kisā'ī, fo. 42^v (also fo. 39^r); al-Majlisī, lxiii. 306–7 and xi. 237; al-Daylamī, *Firdaws al-akhbār*, MS Chester Beatty 3037, to. 74^r; Muḥammad ibn Ḥabīb, *al-Muḥabbar*, ed. Ilse Lichtenstädter (Hyderabad, 1361/1942), 395; al-Shiblī, *Ākām*, 176–7; al-Suyūṭī, *al-Durr*, iv. 226.

have visited Muḥammad; the prophet taught him some chapters of the Qur'ān and welcomed his conversion to Islam.[58]

Everybody is, in fact, accompanied by a satan and even Muḥammad had his satan; God however helped the prophet, and as a result, his satan embraced Islam.[59] Muḥammad pointed out the difference between his satan and the satan of Ādam: 'My satan was an unbeliever but God helped me against him and He converted to Islam; my wives were a help for me. Ādam's satan was an infidel and Ādam's wife was an aid in his sin.'[60]

Scholars devoted long discussions to the question of where the angels got their knowledge that man would cause corruption on earth. Some assumed that God disclosed it to them, others conjectured that they might have seen it on the heavenly tablet (*al-lawḥ al-maḥfūẓ*); some commentators surmised that they learnt it by analogy from the corruption and decline which had previously befallen the realm of the *jinn* on earth.[61] A different explanation of the sources of information available to the angels is supplied in an account traced back to Mujāhid. Iblīs was given the rule of the lower heaven of this world and of the heaven of the earth. It was written in the highest firmament in the presence of God that from

[58] See, e.g., Isḥāq ibn Bishr, MS Ẓāhirīya 359 (*majmū'a*), fos. 126^{v}–127^{r}; 'Umar ibn Muḥammad al-Mawṣilī, *al-Wasīla* (Hyderabad, 1397/1977), iv^{2}. 81–3; al-Majlisī, lxiii, 303, 99–101; Ibn 'Arabī, *Muḥāḍarat al-abrār wa-musāmarat al-akhyār* (Beirut, 1388/1968), i. 98–9; al-Shawkānī, *al-Fawā'id al-majmū'a* (Beirut, 1392), 498, no. 1377; Ibn al-Jawzī, *al-Mawḍū'āt* (Medina, 1386/1966), i. 207–8; al-Suyūṭī, *al-La'ālī al-maṣnū'a fī'l-aḥādīth al-mawḍū'a* (Cairo, n.d.), i. 174–8; al-Fākihī, *Ta'rīkh Makka*, MS Leiden Or. 463, fos. 371^{v}–372^{r}; and see Muḥammad ibn Ḥibbān al-Bustī, *Kitāb al-majrūḥīn* (Cairo, 1976), i. 136–7 (on the authority of Isḥāq ibn Bishr); Ibn 'Arāq, i. 238–9, no. 23 (on the authority of Isḥāq ibn Bishr); al-Damīrī, *Ḥayāt al-ḥayawān* (Cairo, 1383/1963), i. 208; Ibn Ḥajar al-Haytamī, 70, 234; al-'Uqaylī, *Kitāb al-ḍu'afā'*, MS Ẓāhirīya, *ḥadīth* 362, fo. 19^{r} (on the authority of Isḥāq ibn Bishr); al-Muttaqī al-Hindī, *Kanz al-'ummāl* (Hyderabad, 1377/1958), vi. 82–4, no. 650.

[59] See, e.g., Aḥmad ibn Ḥanbal, *Musnad* (Beirut, 1398/1978), iii. 309; al-Dārimī, *Sunan* (n.p., n.d.), ii. 320; Ibn Dayba', *Taysīr al-wuṣūl ilā jāmi' al-uṣūl* (Cairo, 1390/1970), iii. 285, no. 4; al-Ṣāghānī, *Mabāriq al-azhār fī sharḥ mashāriq al-anwār* (Ankara, 1328), i. 309; al-Sukkarī, *Juz'*, MS Ẓāhirīya, *majmū'a* 18, fo. 237^{r}; Ibn Ḥajar al-Haytamī, p. 72; Ibn al-Jawzī, *Talbīs Iblīs* (Beirut, 1368), 34; al-Ṭaḥāwī, *Mushkil al-āthār* (Hyderabad, 1333), i. 30–1; al-Dhahabī, *Mīzān al-i'tidāl* (Cairo, 1382/1963), iv. 59–60, no. 8293; 'Abd al-Razzāq, *Tafsīr*, fos. 37^{r}–37^{v}.

[60] See, e.g., al-Munāwī, *Fayḍ al-qadīr: sharḥ al-Jāmi' al-ṣaghīr* (Beirut, 1391/1972), iv. 440, no. 5885; al-Suyūṭī, *al-Durr*, i. 54; al-Daylamī, MS Chester Beatty 3037, fo. 109^{v}.

[61] See, e.g., Abū Ḥayyān, i. 142; al-Nīsābūrī, i. 232–4; al-Qurṭubī, i. 274–7; al-Ṭabarī, *Tafsīr*, i. 454–72; Ibn Junghul, fo. 23^{v}.

early on it was in God's knowledge that He would set up a *khalīfa* on earth and that there would be bloody events and calamities. Iblīs saw the document and read it (while the angels did not know it); when God mentioned Ādam to the angels, Iblīs informed them that Allāh would bring about a creation which would shed blood and that He could order the angels to bow to this *khalīfa*. Thus when God said: *innī jā'il^un fī'l-arḍi khalīfat^an*, the angels remembered what Iblīs had said to them and they questioned: *a-taj'alu fīhā man yufsidu fīhā*.[62]

A short report quoted in other sources affords us a glimpse of the way by which secret information was passed from certain rather suspect sources. The angels, according to this report, got the information from Hārūt and Mārūt, who in their turn got it from an angel who was superior to them and whose name was al-Sijill.[63] A more detailed version is recorded in Ibn Kathīr's (d. 774/1373) *Tafsīr*. Hārūt and Mārūt were the helpers of the angel al-Sijill. Al-Sijill had the privilege of looking at the *umm al-kitāb* three times a day. Once he cast a glance at a tablet that was forbidden to him, and learnt from it of God's plan to create Ādam and of the events that would follow. He disclosed this information to his two helpers. When God announced that He was going to establish a *khalīfa* on earth, it was Hārūt and Mārūt who asked: *a-taj'al* . . . Ibn Kathīr marks the tradition as one of the *isrā'īlīyāt* stories.[64]

The question of the angels, *a-taj'al*, 'Wilt thou set therein . . .', was asked according to another report in quite different circumstances. When, having committed his sin, Ādam was expelled from paradise and sent down to earth, the angels asked God the fateful question: *a-taj'al*. God bade them to choose two angels who would be sent down to earth and whose deeds would subsequently be watched and tested. They chose Hārūt and Mārūt who descended to earth and whose way of life was one of corruption and depravity. For their sins they must undergo pain and suffering until the present day. The profligate Zuhara (Venus) was hung up in the sky as a star and remains there until now.[65]

[62] Isḥāq ibn Bishr, fos. 39ʳ–39ᵛ.

[63] Ibn Junghul, fo. 23ᵛ; Ibn Kathīr, *al-Bidāya wa'l-nihāya* (Beirut and Riyad, 1966), i. 71.

[64] Ibn Kathīr, *Tafsīr* (Beirut, 1385/1966), i. 123–4.

[65] Nūr al-Dīn al-Haythamī, vi. 313; Ibn Kathīr, *Tafsīr*, i. 241–3; al-Suyūṭī, *al-Durr*, i. 46; Anon., *Qiṣaṣ al-anbiyā'*, MS Leiden Or. 14027, fo. 11ʳ; and cf. the different reports in al-Ṭabarī, *Tafsīr*, ii. 419–35; also Yaḥyā ibn Sallām, *Tafsīr* (*Mukhtaṣar* by Ibn Zamanīn), MS Qarawīyīn 40/34, p. 15; al-Tha'labī, *Tafsīr*, MS

3. ĀDAM AS *KHALĪFA*

The word *khalīfa* became the pivot of a heated discussion in connection with the need to establish an authoritative ruler over the Muslim community. Al-Qurṭubī (d. 671/1273) scrutinizes the orthodox Sunnī views, while he also records the Shī'ī views. It was here, in the crucial problem of the exclusive right of the Shī'a to get the Caliphate, that the miraculous elements of the *qiṣaṣ al-anbiyā'* became part and parcel of the Shī'ī arguments. The Sunnī view was necessarily based on the notion that the exclusive right of Quraysh to be granted the Caliphate was legitimate on the basis that it had been affirmed in the meeting of the Saqīfat Banī Sā'ida; the precedent thus arose from the authority of the Caliphate being ceded to another person (as happened in the case of Abū Bakr who transferred the Caliphate to 'Umar before his death) or it being authorized by an electoral body entrusted with the appointment of the Caliph (as in the case of 'Uthmān).[66] In his account of the Sunnī arguments, al-Qurṭubī records the rejection of the Shī'ī interpretation of the widely circulating traditions: *man kuntu mawlāhu fa-'alīy*[un] *mawlāhu* and *anta minnī bi-manzilati Hārūn min Mūsā illā annahu lā nabīya ba'dī*. The Sunnī argument emphasizes the differences in the position of Hārūn as opposed to 'Alī: Hārūn shared the prophethood with Mūsā, while 'Alī did not share the prophethood with Muḥammad. Hārūn was the brother of Moses, while 'Alī was not Muḥammad's brother. Muḥammad's intention was not that 'Alī would be his *khalīfa*; this is indicated by the fact that Hārūn died before the death of Mūsā and was not his *khalīfa*; the *khalīfa* of Mūsā was Yūsha' (Joshua). If Muḥammad had the intention to intimate that 'Alī would be his successor, he would have said: *anta minnī bi-manzilati Yūsha' min Mūsā*. As to the tradition in *man kuntu mawlāhu*, al-Qurṭubī quotes the opinion of scholars to the effect that the tradition was not considered to be sound; philological

Berlin, Sprenger 409, pp. 148–52 (according to some reports Hārūt and Mārūt were sent down in the period of Idrīs; according to another report three angels were sent down); Ibn Ḥajar al-Haytamī, pp. 61–2; Fakhr al-Dīn al-Rāzī, *Tafsīr*, ii. 167–8, 170; Ibn Abī'l-Ḥadīd, vi. 436; al-Shawkānī, *Fatḥ al-qadīr*, i. 122–3; al-Suyūṭī, *al-La'ālī*, i. 158; Nāṣir al-Dīn al-Albānī, *Silsilat al-aḥādīth al-ḍa'īfa wa'l-mawḍū'a* (Beirut, 1384), 204–7; Ḥamza al-Iṣfahānī, *al-Durrat al-fākhira fī'l-amthāl al-sā'ira* (Cairo, 1972), ii. 555.

[66] See, e.g., al-Qurṭubī, i. 264–5; Ibn Kathir, *Tafsīr*, i. 124.

analysis and comparison with other traditions in which the word *mawlā* appeared proved that the Shīʿī interpretation was misleading. An additional argument was the recording of the circumstances in which Muḥammad uttered the tradition; when ʿAlī quarrelled with Usāma ibn Zayd, Usāma said to ʿAlī: 'I am not your *mawlā*, I am the *mawlā* of the Prophet.' Then Muḥammad is said to have uttered: *man kuntu mawlāhu fa-ʿAlīy^{un} mawlāhu*. This tradition is also said to have been uttered on another occasion; when ʿĀ'isha was suspected of having had an affair with a Muslim warrior as reported in the *ḥadīth al-ifk*, ʿAlī advised Muḥammad to find another woman as wife: 'There are many women', said ʿAlī. ʿĀ'isha was offended by his words; hypocrites in Medina calumniated ʿAlī and tried to get rid of him. Then Muḥammad uttered the saying: *man kuntu mawlāhu*, thus refuting the calumnies of the hypocrites. Yet another tradition is found. Muḥammad used to appoint a deputy when he left Medina for an expedition. When he appointed ʿAlī and left for the expedition of Tabūk, the hypocrites claimed that he left him at Medina because he hated him. Another rumour which was bruited about in Medina by wicked people said that he left ʿAlī merely in charge of his family. The saying of the hypocrites were denied when Muḥammad said about ʿAlī: *kadhabū, bal khallaftuka kamā khallafa Mūsā Hārūna*.[67]

The Shīʿa's conception of the caliphate on earth was defined with great precision: there existed only four *khulafā'* on earth, of whom ʿAlī was the fourth. That is why ʿAlī could say, 'He who does not say that I am the fourth of the four Caliphs, on him falls God's curse.' The four Caliphs were Ādam, Dāwūd, Hārūn, and ʿAlī.[68] This statement was also uttered by al-Khiḍr and was confirmed by Muḥammad. A story says that the prophet walked one day with ʿAlī in Medina. They met a Bedouin with a long beard who addressed ʿAlī: 'O, Amīr of the Faithful, Peace be upon you, the fourth Caliph!' The man disappeared and Muḥammad explained to ʿAlī that it was al-Khiḍr and told him that the first Caliph was his ancestor Ādam, the second was Hārūn (the successor of Mūsā), the third was Dāwūd, and that he was the fourth. 'O ʿAlī', said the prophet, 'You are indeed my successor (*khalīfatī*) after my death

[67] Al-Qurṭubī, i. 265–8; see also al-Bukhārī, *al-Ta'rīkh al-kabīr* (Hyderabad, 1380), vi. 241, no. 2277.

[68] Al-Katakānī, *Kitāb al-burhān fī tafsīr al-Qur'ān* (Tehran, 1375), i. 75.

and you will pay my debts.'[69] In his thorough and fundamental work on the concept of *nūr Muḥammad*,[70] Uri Rubin gave a lucid exposition of the Shīʿī concept of the prerogatives for authority and about the legacy of Muḥammad.

Ādam was surnamed Abū Muḥammad.[71] He is the only person distinguished by this *kunya* in paradise in order to display the honour of the prophet Muḥammad.[72] Muḥammad was invested with prophethood before the creation of Ādam.[73] In the first month of the pregnancy of Āmina, his mother, she saw in her dream a tall man who gave her the good tidings that she would give birth to the Lord of the Messengers; the tall man was Ādam.[74] When Muḥammad was born he disappeared for a short time; he was brought to the presence of Ādam, who kissed him on his forehead and told him that he would be the lord of Ādam's progeny and that those who adhered to his faith and uttered his *shahāda* would gather on the day of resurrection under the banner of Muḥammad.[75]

God created the world for the sake of Muḥammad; Ādam saw on the throne of God the *shahāda*, 'There is no god except God, Muḥammad is the messenger of God', and when Ādam begged God to forgive him his sin, he invoked the merit of Muḥammad to his aid.[76] On Ādam's forehead was a blaze of light which was to be transferred through the generations down to Muḥammad; it was the light of Muḥammad.[77]

[69] Niʿmat Allāh al-Mūsawī al-Jazā'irī, *al-Anwār al-nuʿmānīya*, (Tabriz-Teheran, 1380), i. 267.

[70] Uri Rubin, 'Pre-existence and Light: Aspects of the Concept of Nūr Muhammad', *Israel Oriental Studies*, 5 (1975), 62–119.

[71] Rubin, p. 71; Ibn ʿAsākir, *Ta'rīkh* (Beirut, 1399/1979), ii. 345; al-Qurṭubī, i. 279; al-Suyūṭī, *al-Durr*, i. 62; al-Thaʿlabī, p. 84; al-ʿAynī, xv. 204.

[72] Al-Suyūṭī, *al-Durr*, i. 62; al-ʿAynī, xv. 204.

[73] Al-Bukhārī, *al-Ta'rīkh*, vi. 68–9, no. 1736; Ibn Taymīya, *al-Rasā'il al-kubrā* (Beirut, 1392/1972), ii. 357 (see the evaluation of this *ḥadīth* by Ibn Taymīya); Nāṣir al-Dīn al-Albānī, pp. 316–17, nos. 302–3; al-Munāwī, v. 53, no. 6424; al-Ṣāliḥī, *al-Sīra al-sha'mīya* (Cairo, 1392/1972), i. 96–107.

[74] Al-Ṣaffūrī, *Nuzhat al-majālis wa-muntakhab al-nafā'is* (Beirut, n.d.), 354.

[75] Al-Ṣaffūrī, p. 355.

[76] Rubin, p. 106; Ibn Abī'l-Dunyā, *al-Ishrāf fī manāzil al-ashrāf*, MS Chester Beatty 4427, fos. 5r, 5v; Muḥammad al-Madanī, *al-Itḥāfāt al-sanīya fī'l-aḥādīth al-qudsīya* (Hyderabad, 1358), 140, no. 679; Ibn 'Asākir, ii. 344 (2 versions); ʿAlī ibn Burhān al-Dīn al-Ḥalabī, *Insān al-ʿuyūn fī sīrat al-amīn al-ma'mūn* (= *al-Sīra al-ḥalabīya*) (Cairo, 1382/1962), i. 241; al-Samarqandi, *Tafsīr*, MS Chester Beatty 3668, i. 15r; al-Thaʿlabī, p. 87; Isḥāq ibn Bishr, fos. 54r, 55r; Nāṣir al-Dīn al-Albānī, no. 403; cf. al-Zurqānī, *Sharḥ al-mawāhib al-ladunīya* (Cairo, 1327), v. 242–3.

[77] Rubin, pp. 91–6.

Shīʿī traditions give an extended version of the inscription on the throne; the *shahāda* included an addition mentioning ʿAlī.[78] An almost identical inscription was on the gate of paradise.[79] A tradition traced back to Ibn ʿAbbās says that when God created Ādam, He put him up in His presence and then Ādam sneezed; God inspired in him the formula of praise and gratitude to God and said, 'Ādam, you praised Me, therefore I swear by My power and splendour that were it not for two servants whom I intend to create at the end of time (*fī ākhir al-zamān*) I would not have created you.' Ādam inquired about their names and God showed him two lines of light on His throne; the first line read, 'There is no god save God, Muḥammad is the prophet of mercy, ʿAlī is the key of Paradise', and the second line read, 'I bind myself by oath that I shall have mercy upon him who would be faithful to both of them (*man wālāhumā*) and I shall punish (*uʿadhdhibu*) him who would be hostile towards them.'[80] The Shīʿī traditions record extended inscription formulas which incorporate Muḥammad and other members of ʿAlī's family: ʿAlī, Fāṭima, al-Ḥasan, and al-Ḥusayn. God explained to Ādam that these are 'better than Ādam and all of God's creatures'; had it not been for them God would not have created paradise, the earth, hell, and the sky.[81]

Another report on an expanded Shīʿī inscription is linked with the term *yawm ʿarafa* and with the stipulations associated with the forgiveness of sins. When Ādam was in paradise, he one day looked at the throne and saw lines of light containing the names of Muḥammad and the members of the *ahl al-bayt*; this took place on the eighth day (of his stay in paradise). On the next day God acquainted him with their rank and position and stated that had it not been for them He would not have created Ādam or anyone else. This day was called *yawm ʿarafa*. Later, after God had refused to accept Ādam's repentance, Jibrīl visited him and encouraged him to ask God's forgiveness 'by the merit' (*bi-ḥaqq*) of Muḥammad, ʿAlī, Fāṭima, al-Ḥasan, al-Ḥusayn, and the Imāms whose names were written on the throne. This was in fact the content of the phrase of Q. 2/37: *fa-talaqqā Ādamu min rabbihi kalimātⁱⁿ fa-tāba ʿalayhi*. Then God revealed to Ādam: 'O Ādam, had you not invoked me with these names I would not have accepted your repentance; I

[78] Al-Madanī, p. 144, no. 695; cf. Rubin, p. 107.
[79] Al-Madanī, p. 150, no. 730.
[80] Niʿmat Allāh al-Mūsawī, i. 228–9. [81] Ibid. i. 243.

swear that there will be no sinner who invoked Me with these names but that I shall forgive his sins.'[82]

As a counterpart to the Shī'ī conception that there were inscriptions in heaven legitimizing the claims of the Shī'ī Imāms and emphasizing the usurpatory character of the rule of the first Caliphs and their Umayyad successors, there were the Sunnī orthodox traditions which upheld the legitimacy of the first three 'Guided Caliphs'. Many traditions record predictions of Muḥammad concerning the virtuous character of the rule of the first three Caliphs and of the merits of the first Umayyad rulers. To this category belongs the tradition quoted by Rubin according to which Muḥammad saw on the night of the *mi'rāj* in each heaven an inscription: 'Muḥammad is the prophet of God and Abū Bakr is his successor.'[83] On the throne is written: *lā ilāh illā Allāh Muḥammad rasūl Allāh Abū Bakr wa-'Umar wa-'Uthmān, yuqtalu shahīd*^{an}.[84] A tradition reported on the authority of Ibn 'Abbās says that on every tree and on every leaf there is an inscription: *lā ilāh illā Allāh, Muḥammad rasūl Allāh, Abū Bakr al-ṣiddīq 'Umar al-fārūq 'Uthmān dhū'l-nūrayn.*[85] Here only the three guided caliphs are mentioned; 'Alī is ignored. Another tradition recorded on the authority of Quṭba ibn Mālik is similar in content; when Muḥammad laid the foundations of the mosque at Qubā', three of his companions were with him: Abū Bakr, 'Umar, and 'Uthmān. Quṭba passed by and asked him: 'O Messenger of God, you laid the foundation of the mosque and with you is only this (tiny) group of three persons?' Muḥammad answered: 'These are the people entitled to successorship (*wulāt al-khilāfa*) after my death.'[86] 'Umar himself gained the highest praises from Muḥammad who said that, had he not been sent as a prophet, 'Umar would have been sent.[87]

[82] Ibid. i. 247.

[83] Rubin, p. 107 n. 21: the tradition is indeed recorded in Ḥasan 'Arafa, *Juz'*, MS Chester Beatty 4433, fo. 125^{r}; Anon., *Manāqib al-ṣaḥāba*, MS BL Or 8273, fo. 22^{v}.

[84] Rubin, p. 107 n. 22; Anon., *Manāqib al-ṣaḥāba*, fo. 22^{v}; cf. Anon., *A Collection of* ḥadīth, MS, Hebrew University, Yahuda Ar. 1050, fo. 8^{r}.

[85] Anon., *Manāqib al-ṣaḥāba*, fo. 22^{v}; al-Nāzilī, *Mafza' al-khalā'iq, manba' al-ḥaqā'iq* (Cairo, 1293), 37 (from al-Ṭabarānī).

[86] Al-Suyūṭī, *Jam' al-jawāmi'* (Cairo, 1978), ii. 590; Ibrāhīm ibn Muḥammad al-Ḥusaynī al-Ḥanafī, *al-Bayān wa'l-ta'rīf fī asbāb wurūd al-ḥadīth al-sharīf* (Beirut, 1400/1980), ii. 136, no. 749; Ibn Ḥibbān al-Bustī, i. 277.

[87] Al-Basawī, *al-Ma'rifa wa'l-ta'rīkh* (Baghdad, 1401/1981), ii. 500; Anon., *Manāqib al-ṣaḥāba*, fo. 6^{v}; al-Suyūṭī, *al-Ḥāwī li'l-fatāwī* (Cairo, 1378/1959), i. 572; Ibn 'Adī, *al-Kāmil fī ḍu'afā' al-rijāl*, MS Ahmet III, 2943/1, fo. 349^{v}; al-Muḥibb al-

Several of ‘Umar’s precepts proved to be congruent with the will of God and some Quranic verses confirmed his suggestion.[88] The few traditions quoted give us some insight into the ongoing and uninterrupted competition between the Shī‘a and their opponents as to the position of ‘Alī and his descendants, the Imāms, and the rights of Shī‘ī aspirants to the Caliphate. Shī‘ī missionaries tried to explicate to their adherents the deliberate forgeries circulated by the Umayyad officials.[89] They themselves circulated stories and reports about the Caliphs which contained defamations not less abusive than those which their opponents told of the Shī‘ī leaders.[90]

Having made these remarks on the use of the word *khalīfa* it should be noted that there is a variant reading of this word: *khalīqa*.[91] This reading, not widely current, could have changed the content of the discussion or even made it entirely superfluous.

4. ĀDAM'S CREATION IN THE WORLD

The stories about the creation of Ādam are abundant and often divergent or contradictory; only a few aspects of these stories can be treated here. Well known are the stories about Iblīs who, when he heard that God was about to command an angel to bring a handful of dust for the creation of Ādam, went down in order to persuade the earth to refuse to hand over material.[92] The earth indeed tried to refuse and asked for God's protection when the angels came to take the dust. Two of the angels could not stand against the beseeching of the earth and returned to God without the required dust. The third angel disregarded the beseeching of the earth and preferred to carry out God's command to return carrying

Ṭabarī, *al-Riyāḍ al-naḍira fī manāqib al-‘ashara* (Cairo, n.d.), i. 199; Ibn ‘Abd al-Ḥakam, *Futūḥ Miṣr*, ed. Charles Torrey (Leiden, 1920), 288.

[88] See e.g., Anon., *Manāqib al-ṣaḥāba*, fo. 3ʳ; al-‘Aynī, ii. 284–5 and iv. 143–4; Maḥmūd Ḥasan Rabī‘, *Risāla shahī al-samar bi-muwāfaqāt ‘Umar* (Cairo, 1373/1954), 122–8; see additional bibliography in ‘Maḳām Ibrāhīm’, *EI*², vi.

[89] See e.g., Sulaym ibn Qays al-Kūfī, *Kitāb al-saqīfa* (Najaf, n.d.), 138–9.

[90] See, e.g., al-Katakānī, i. 498–500 (Abū Bakr and ‘Umar depicted as eating and drinking wine in Ramaḍān, and denouncing their allegiance to Muḥammad and to Islam).

[91] See Abū Ḥayyān, i. 140; al-Qurṭubī i. 263; al-Tha‘labī, p. 409; Fakhr al-Dīn al-Rāzī, *Tafsīr*, ii. 166.

[92] See, e.g., al-Kisā’ī, *The Tales of the Prophets*, trans. and annotated by W. M. Thackston, Jr. (Boston, 1978), 22; al-Kisā’ī, *‘Ajā’ib al-malakūt*, fo. 47ʳ; Anon., *Qiṣaṣ al-anbiyā’*, MS Leiden OR. 14027, fo. 5ᵛ.

the dust; this angel became the Angel of Death.[93] The versions of the story telling of the dust brought to the presence of God usually say that it was gathered from different places on the earth and that is the reason why mankind consists of different colours.[94] Other reports say that the dust for the shaping of Ādam's body was collected from the 'six earths'; the major part of it was taken from the Sixth Earth, which is called *adāma*, the word from which the name of Ādam is derived. The dust was not gathered from the Seventh Earth because that is where hell is found.[95] Another tradition, attributed to Wahb, gives a detailed list of the parts of Ādam's body, mentioning their provenance from the various earths; but in this tradition his shank and his feet were from the dust of the Seventh Earth.[96] Another type of tradition lists the members of Ādam's body and gives the various regions of the world from which they were taken; his head was from the dust of the Ka'ba, his breast from the dust of al-Daḥnā, his back and his belly from the dust of India, his hands from the dust of the East, and his legs from the dust of the West.[97] Different data are provided by al-Daylamī (d. 509/1115) in a tradition on the authority of Abū Hurayra; Ādam's head and forehead were from the dust of the Ka'ba, his body from Jerusalem, his thighs from Yaman, his shanks from the dust of the Ḥijāz, his right hand from the East, his left hand from the West, his skin from the dust of al-Ṭā'if, his heart from Mawṣil, his spleen and his lungs from the region of al-Jazīra.[98] Another list of the parts of the body of Ādam and their qualities according to their provenance is given by al-Suyūṭī (d. 911/1505) in his *al-Kalām 'alā khalq Ādam wa-dhikr wafātihi*

[93] Isḥāq ibn Bishr, fos. 40v–41r; al-Samarqandī, i. 13r; cf. Anon., *Siyar al-anbiyā'*, fo. 11v; al-Khāzin, *Tafsīr* (Cairo, 1381), i. 39; al-Saqsīnī, *Zahrat al-riyāḍ wa-nuzhat al-qulūb al-mirāḍ*, MS Hebrew University, Yahuda Ar. 571, p. 8; Ibn Ṭāwūs, *Sa'd al-su'ūd* (Najaf, 1369/1950), 33; al-Mas'ūdī', *Murūj*, ed. C. Pellat (Beirut, 1964), i. 33.

[94] See, e.g., al-Qurṭubī, i. 280; al-Shabrakhītī, *Sharḥ 'alā'l-arba'īna ḥadīth (!) al-Nawawīya* (Beirut, n.d.), 288; cf. al-Samarqandī, i. 13r; al-Bayhaqī, *al-Asmā' wa'l-ṣifāt* (Cairo, 1358), 362–3; Ibn Khuzayma, *Kitāb al-tawḥīd* (Cairo, 1387/1968), 63–4; al-Tha'labī, p. 84; al-Khāzin, i. 40; al-Saqsīnī, p. 8; 'Abd al-Razzāq, fo. 2v; Anon., *Siyar al-anbiyā'*, fos. 11r–11v; Ibn Fūrak, *Mushkil al-ḥadīth* (Hyderabad, 1362), 25–6; al-Nuwayrī, *Nihāyat al-arab* (Cairo, 1357/1938), xiii. 11.

[95] Isḥāq ibn Bishr, fo. 41r; cf. al-'Aynī, xv. 204 (called Ādam because he was created from *adīm al-arḍ*, or because the dust of the earth is called in Hebrew *ādām*; the second *ā* in the word is shortened into *a* in the name *ādam*; see also al-Tha'labī, p. 84.

[96] Al-Shabrakhītī, p. 289. [97] Ibid. [98] Al-Daylamī, fo. 77v.

'alayhi al-ṣalāt wa'l-salām. The tradition is transmitted on the authority of Ibn 'Abbās. God created the head of Ādam from the dust of Jerusalem, his face from the dust of paradise, his teeth from the Kawthar (said to be a river in paradise), his right hand from the Ka'ba, his left hand from Persia, his feet from India, his bones from the mountain (perhaps meaning Jabal, the mountainous province in Persia), his pudenda from Babylon, his back from Iraq, his heart from paradise, his tongue from al-Ṭā'if, and his eyes from the Ḥawḍ, the pond with a delicious beverage from which the believers will be given permission to drink on the day of resurrection. As his head is from Jerusalem, it became the place of reason and sagacity; as his face is from paradise, it became the place of beauty and comeliness; as his teeth are from the Kawthar, they became a spot of sweetness; as his right hand is from the Ka'ba, it became the place of assistance; as his back is from Iraq, it became the place of strength; as his pudenda are from Babylon, it became a place of lust; as his bones are from al-Jabal, they became the place of rigidity; as his heart is from paradise, it became the place of belief; as his tongue is from al-Ṭā'if, it became the place of the *shahāda*.[99] It is obvious that we have stories closely akin to the type of *faḍā'il al-buldān* or *faḍā'il al-amākin*; places have distinctive features, which affect the people living in these places. There are traditions saying that Ādam was created from the dust of Mecca.[100] Others claim that he was created from the dust of al-Jābiya.[101] Sa'īd ibn Jubayr said that God created Ādam from the dust of Dajnā.[102] Al-Ḥasan (probably al-Baṣrī) reported that his breast (*ju'ju'*) was from Ḥimā Ḍarīya.[103] Some reports say that God created Ādam from the dust of al-Daḥnā;[104] in the *wādī* of al-Daḥnā (between Mecca and al-Ṭā'if) God is said to have performed the act of the covenant with the progeny of Ādam, which was in his loins.[105] Ādam alighted in

99 Al-Suyūṭī, *Ithnā 'ashara rasā'il* (!) (Lahore, n.d.), 25–7; al-Saqsīnī, pp. 8–9.

100 Isḥāq ibn Bishr, fo. 42r.

101 Al-Daylamī, fo. 77v; Ibn al-Jawzī, *al-Mawḍū'āt*, i. 190; al-Muttaqī al-Hindī, vi. 64, nos. 548–9; Nāṣir al-Dīn al-Albānī, pp. 357–8, no. 354; al-Munāwī, *Fayḍ al-qadīr*, iii. 445, no. 3927; Ibn 'Arāq, i. 232, no. 11; al-Suyūṭī, *Jam' al-jawāmi'*, i. 520, 167.

102 Al-Qurṭubī, vi. 388; cf. al-Ṭabarī, *Ta'rīkh*, i. 121; Ādam alighted in Daḥnā in India; and see Isḥāq ibn Bishr, fo. 64v; Daḥnān in India.

103 Al-Qurṭubī, vi. 388; Ibn 'Asākir, *Ta'rīkh Dimashq* (*tahdhīb*) (Beirut, 1399/1979), ii. 343; al-Bakrī, *Mu'jam mā ista'jam* (Cairo, 1368/1949), 859.

104 Yāqūt, *Mu'jam al-buldān*, s.v. al-Daḥnā; al-Suyūṭī, *al-Durr*, i. 48; Ibn 'Asākir, ii. 343; Ibn Junghul, fo. 25r.

105 Isḥāq ibn Bishr, fo. 67v.

the *wādī* of al-Daḥnā when he was expelled from paradise.[106] On a mountain outside Nabulus, Ādam prostrated himself to God.[107] He is said to have dwelt in a village in the vicinity of Bayt Lihya in the region of Damascus.[108] There are several other places connected with the life of Ādam; some of them serve as places of pilgrimage, though not necessarily favoured by orthodox scholars.

Ādam was created on Friday, the best day of the week; he was introduced to paradise on that day and was expelled from paradise on that day. His repentance was accepted on Friday and he died on Friday.[109] As the angels bowed to Ādam on Friday, this day became a feast day for the believers.[110]

5. ĀDAM'S CREATION BY GOD

One aspect of the story of the creation of Ādam became the pivot of a heated discussion between the anthropomorphistic scholars and their opponents.[111] The important verse which speaks of God's creation of Ādam with His own hands, Q. 38/75, 'Said He: Iblīs, what prevented thee to bow thyself before that I created with My own hands', is in fact the bone of contention between the two opposing theological schools. The question is whether the expression 'My own hands' should be understood as referring literally to God's hands, or metaphorically. Tradition enlarged the scope of the role of God's hands in the process of creation. God is said to have made three things with His own hands: the creation of Ādam, the writing of the Torah, and the planting of the trees of paradise. Some

106 Ibn Kathīr, *al-Bidāya*, i. 80.

107 Yāqūt, s.v. Nabulus. According to a Samaritan tradition, Ādam was created from the dust of the mountain of Gerizim at Nabulus (see Z. Ben-Ḥayyim, 'A fragment from Memar Marqa, an unknown version', in *Studies in the Literature of the Talmud, the Language of the Songs and the Exegesis of the Bible* (Tel-Aviv, 1983), 126 and 131 (in Hebrew).

108 Ibn 'Asākir, ii. 341.

109 Nūr al-Dīn al-Haythamī, ii. 167; Yaḥyā ibn Ma'īn, *al-Ta'rīkh wa'l-'ilal*, MS Ẓāhirīya, *majmū'* 112, fos. 8v, 9v; Anon., *Siyar al-anbiyā'*, fos. 11r, 12r, 15v; 'Abd al-Malik ibn Ḥabīb, p. 16; 'Abd al-Razzāq, fo. 2r; Anon., *Qiṣaṣ al-anbiyā'*, MS Leiden Or. 14027, fo. 14v; al-Bukhārī, *al-Ta'rīkh*, iv. 44, 220, 1911.

110 Anon., *Qiṣaṣ al-anbiyā'*, fo. 7r.

111 See Ibn Khuzayma's censure of the Jahmīya and Rāfiḍī views: *Kitāb al-tawḥīd*, 41; and see A. J. Wensinck, *The Muslim Creed* (London, 1965), 66–70, 73–4.

traditions add a fourth object: the Pen.[112] Al-Ash'arī (d. 324/935) records the tree of Ṭūbā as the fourth thing.[113]

It is evident that the anthropomorphists interpreted the 'hands' literally; others rendered this expression as 'power', 'ability', 'favour', or 'grace'. Some argued that the expression 'hands' serves for emphasis with the aim of stressing that Ādam was God's own creation.[114] Abū Ḥayyān records two readings: *bi-yadayya* ('with My two hands') and *bi-yadī* ('with My hand'), and explains the word as ability and strength.[115] Al-Shawkānī (d. 1250/1832) records the various meanings attributed to the word *yad* and the two readings mentioned above. The meaning 'ability' or 'strength' is rejected because the dual cannot denote strength and ability; it denotes two attributes of God.[116] Further, al-Shawkānī records another opinion that the two hands are used metaphorically emphasizing God's deed; the expression 'with My two hands' thus denotes: 'I, myself, created him.' In another formulation quoted by al-Shawkānī, the aim of the expression is, as in the former explication, to stress that God created Ādam without mediation (*wāsiṭa*) and attributed the creation to Himself, in this way bestowing special honour on Ādam, although He is the Creator of all things.[117] More explicit about the mediators is al-Nawawī (d. after 1888): 'Before him whom I created with My own hands' means 'whom I created by My power and will' without the mediation of a father and mother.[118] Explanations of the kind mentioned above are given in other commentaries as well.[119] Al-Ash'arī, however, criticizes severely the widely current interpretations; basing himself on the sound usage of the Arabic language, al-Ash'arī states that 'God's two hands' mentioned in the verse cannot denote 'favour' or 'grace'. God's two hands cannot denote, as some commentators maintain, strength; their recourse to the meanings of

[112] 'Abd al-Razzāq, fos. 91^r–91^v; al-Ṭabarī, *Tafsīr* (Bulaq, 1329), xviii. 2 (from 'Abd al-Razzāq), xxiii. 119; al-Suyūṭī, *Jam' al-jawāmi'*, i. 168, 510; id., *al-Durr*, iii. 121, v. 321; al-Bayhaqī, *al-Asmā' wa'l-ṣifāt* (Cairo, 1358), 318; al-Muttaqī al-Hindī, vi. 65, nos. 556–9.

[113] Al-Ash'arī, *al-Ibāna 'an uṣūl al-diyāna* (Cairo, n.d.), 36.

[114] See, e.g., al-Nīsābūrī, xxiii. 107.

[115] Abū Ḥayyān, vii. 410; and see Ibn Bābūyah (al-Shaykh al-Ṣadūq), *al-Tawḥīd* (Najaf, 1386/1966), 104.

[116] Al-Shawkānī, *Fatḥ al-qadīr*, iv. 445.

[117] Ibid. iv. 445.

[118] Al-Nawawī, *Marāḥ labīd* (Cairo, 1305), ii. 233.

[119] Al-Wāḥidī, *al-Wajīz fī tafsīr al-Qur'ān al-'azīz* (on margin of al-Nawawī's *Marāḥ*), ii. 233; al-Nasafī, iv. 47; al-Qurṭubī, xv. 228; al-Katakānī, iv. 64.

ayd as found in Q. 51/47, *wa'l-sāma' banaynāhā bi-ayd^{in}*, has nothing to do with 'the two hands', because the plural of *yad* as 'favour' or 'grace' is *ayād^{in}*. If the meaning of the hand in the verse were 'power' (*qudra*), Adam would not have obtained any distinction over Iblīs because Iblīs was also created by God's power as He did everything else. 'God's hands' are however not the same as the hands of a human being.[120] Ibn Khuzayma (d. 311/923), too, uses the same arguments in rejecting the meanings 'favour' and 'strength.' He who explains the two hands of God as meaning 'strength' (*quwwa*) adducing *ayd* as proof, should be sent to the *kuttāb* to be taught proper Arabic.[121] Al-Bayhaqī (d. 458/1066) reiterates the arguments which refute the interpretation of God's hands as either God's body extremities (*jāriḥa*), as favour, or as power; the word must be understood as denoting two attributes to God connected with the creation of Ādam.[122] Fakhr al-Dīn al-Rāzī (d. 606/1209) scrutinizes the various explanations of the word *yad* in the verse; having rejected them all, he chooses to explain it as a metaphor which denotes the keenness and care with which the work was carried out.[123]

Another tradition concerning the creation of Ādam became the subject of keen debate; it concerned the utterance of Muḥammad according to which God created Ādam in his image (*inna Allāh 'azza wa-jalla khalaqa Ādam 'alā ṣūratihi*).[124] This is usually coupled with a further tradition which says that Ādam was 60 cubits in height when created, that God sent him to greet the angels and that his greeting became the current greeting of the Muslim community. Everybody entering paradise will be 60 cubits high; people have been gradually losing their height.[125] Ibn Qutayba scrutinizes the interpretations of the scholars concerning this

120 Al-Ash'arī, pp. 36–9.

121 Ibn Khuzayma, *Kitāḥ al-tawḥid*, 85–7.

122 Al-Bayhaqī, *al-Asmā'*, 319; also Ibn Fūrak, *Mushkil al-ḥadīth* (Hyderabad, 1362), 169–73.

123 Fakhr al-Dīn al-Rāzī, *Tafsīr*, xxvi. 229–32, and see the commentary of the tradition about God's creation of Eden and His planting of the trees with His own hand: al-Munāwī, iii. 444, no. 3926.

124 Ibn Qutayba, *Kitāb ta'wīl mukhtalif al-ḥadīth* (Cairo, 1326), 275; Ibn Abī'l-Ḥadīd, iii. 227.

125 Ibn Khuzayma, p. 41; Muḥammad Ḥabīb Allāh al-Shinqīṭī, *Zād al-Muslim fīmā ittafaqa 'alayhi al-Bukhārī wa-Muslim* (Beirut, 1387/1967), i. 180–1, no. 427; al-Munāwī, iii. 445, no. 3928; al-Bayhaqī, *al-Asmā'*, 289–91; al-Suyūṭī, *Jam' al-jawāmi'*, i. 510.

utterance. Some of them assume that the suffix *hi* in *ṣūratihi* goes back to Ādam; but this interpretation is rejected by Ibn Qutayba, as it is obvious that God created Ādam in his shape and the beasts in their shape. According to some scholars, this indicates that God created Ādam following an image that was with Him; this interpretation is also rejected, as God did not create any of His creatures according to a model.[126] The interpretation of this tradition is further complicated if one takes into account another saying of Muḥammad in which he forbade disforming the face of an adversary because God created it in his shape (that is, in the shape of the adversary's face). This is again rejected by Ibn Qutayba, as it is obvious that Ādam's face was similar to that of his posterity.

A further complication arises from a peculiar utterance which states explicitly that God created Ādam in the image of *al-Raḥmān*. It is undeniable that *al-Raḥmān* is identical with Allāh; the Arabic of the sentence is clumsy and the utterance simply indicates that God created Ādam in the image of God.[127] Ibn Qutayba concludes that the tradition of God's creation of Ādam indicates that Ādam was created in paradise having the same shape that he retained when removed to earth. But Ibn Qutayba himself is uncertain as to whether this was the intention of Muḥammad's statement. He quotes the verse from the Torah, where it is said that 'God created Ādam in His shape', and points out that it fits in with the interpretation of the *ḥadīth*, according to which the suffix *hi* refers to God.[128] According to a more moderate interpretation, God's creation of Ādam in His shape alludes to some of God's attributes, like knowledge and power.[129]

As we have seen, traditions say that Ādam was 60 cubits high at the time when he was created.[130] According to other reports, Ādam's head reached up to heaven and his legs touched the earth when he was first sent down from paradise and alighted in India;

[126] Cf. Ibn Ṭāwūs, p. 33.

[127] Ibn Qutayba, *Kitāb ta'wīl*, 278; and see the thorough scrutiny of the traditions in Ibn Fūrak, pp. 6–14.

[128] See, e.g., Genesis 1: 26–7.

[129] Ibn Ḥajar al-Haytamī, pp. 290, 292; and see the comments in al-Munāwī, iii. 445–7.

[130] Al-Majlisī, xi. 115; al-'Iṣāmī, i. 78, 80; Ibn Nāṣir al-Dīn, fo. 140^r; al-Ṣāliḥī, i. 165–6; al-Qurṭubī, i. 320, vi. 388; al-'Aynī, xv. 208–9; Anon., *Siyar al-anbiyā'*, fos. 12^v–13^r; al-Khāzin, i. 39; al-Shabrakhītī, p. 289.

the angels were afraid of him, and his stature was reduced to 60 cubits. Ādam was thereby cut off from the voices of the angels and their praises of God and became sad; God gave him solace by causing the House in Mecca to descend on earth and by ordering Ādam to set out to Mecca to perform the *ṭawāf*.[131] Divergent stories say that he was so tall that the clouds rubbed his head and he became bald; his baldness was inherited by his posterity. His height was then reduced to 60 cubits.[132] Some sources are critical of these fabulous stories; many believers reject the story that Ādam's height was reduced to 60 cubits, as this is unnatural; baldness, say the physicians, stems from humidity in the brain.[133] Ādam is said to have been the most beautiful of creatures; he was beardless (*amrad*) and his descendents got a beard only later on.[134] According to a divergent tradition, Ādam prostrated himself when he received the good tidings that God accepted his repentance, and asked God for more beauty. God granted him a black beard; this will remain the adornment of men until the day of resurrection.[135]

Ibn Kathīr, in fact, records on the authority of Ka'b al-Aḥbār that Ādam is the only man in paradise with a long black beard which reaches down to his navel.[136] It is evident that we have here two contradictory views about the beauty of man: a young beardless ephebe and a man with a full black beard.

6. THE LANGUAGE OF ĀDAM

Wa-'allama ādama'l-asmā'a kullahā, 'and He taught Ādam the names, all of them' (Q. 2/31), is interpreted in several different ways

[131] Al-Azraqī, p. 12; cf. Ibn Nāṣir al-Dīn, fo. 140^v; cf. 'Abd al-Razzāq, *al-Muṣannaf* (Beirut, 1970–2), v. 91, no. 9090, and v. 93, no. 9096.

[132] Al-Qurṭubī, vi. 388, i. 319; cf. al-Majlisī, xi. 127 (his head reaching the sky, his feet treading on the Safā; reduced to 70 cubits); al-'Iṣāmī, i. 77 (70 cubits); al-'Aynī, xv. 209; al-Tha'labī, p. 168; al-Suyūṭī, *al-Wasā'il*, 142.

[133] Al-Maqdisī, *al-Bad'*, ii. 99.

[134] Ibid., ii. 100.

[135] Al-Majlisī, lxxvi. 110; also al-'Iṣāmī, i. 571; and see the description of the hairless Ādam in Anon., *Qiṣaṣ al-anbiyā'*, MS Leiden Or. 14027, fo. 15^r.

[136] Ibn Kathīr, *al-Bidāya*, i. 97; Ibn Junghul, i. 28^v; al-Suyūṭī, *al-Durr*, i. 62 (Ādam had no beard when alive; men's beards originated only after Ādam, but in paradise he is the only person with a beard, a black one reaching down to his navel). Another tradition says that the only person with a long black beard in paradise is Moses; see al-Suyūṭī, *al-Durr*, i. 62; al-Dhahabī, *Mīzān al-i'tidāl*, ii. 286, no. 3763; al-Daylamī, *Firdaws al-akhbār*, MS Chester Beatty 4139, fo. 112^r; 'Alī al-Qārī, *al-Asrār al-marfū'a fī'l-akhbār al-mawḍū'a* (Beirut, 1391/1971), 124, no. 83.

in the commentaries on the Qur'ān. God taught him, according to the commentators, one of the following things: the names of all the creatures, the names of events which happened in the past or which will happen in the future, all the languages (so that he could speak with each of his sons in a special language), the names of all the stars, the names of the angels, the names of his progeny, or the names of the various species of His creatures; or He taught him everything, including even the grammar of Sībawayh.[137]

Some traditions say that the secret language which God taught Ādam was Syriac.[138] An early report states that God taught Ādam the names in Syriac in order to hide from the angels the knowledge thus acquired.[139] Al-Suyūṭī records a tradition saying that Ādam spoke Arabic in paradise; when he committed the sin, he began to speak Aramaic, but after God accepted his repentance he reverted to Arabic.[140] The early 'Abd al-Malik ibn Ḥabīb (d. 239/854) has a more detailed account of the language of Ādam; Ādam is included in the list of prophets whose language was Arabic. He descended from paradise speaking Arabic because Arabic was the language of God, of the angels and the people of paradise. This is supported by the words spoken by Muḥammad to Salmān al-Fārisī: 'You should love the Arabs because of three things: your Qur'ān and your prophet are Arab and your language in paradise will be Arabic.' 'Abd al-Malik ibn Ḥabīb explains the position of Arabic in comparison with Aramaic: Ādam and his progeny spoke Arabic; in a later period Arabic degenerated (*ḥurrifa*) into Syriac, which is akin to Arabic.[141]

Shī'ī tradition explains that God taught Ādam the names of the prophets, the names of Muḥammad, 'Alī, Fāṭima, al-Ḥasan, al-Ḥusayn, the names of the prominent men of their family, the names of the righteous men of the Shī'a, and the names of the rebellious men of their opponents.[142] 'Then He presented them unto the

[137] Abū Ḥayyān, i. 145–6; cf. al-Ṭabarsī, i. 168–9; al-Majlisī, xi. 146. Knowledge of language (*'ilm al-lugha*) follows in importance the perception of the unity of God; God showed the angels the superiority of Ādam by his knowledge of language (see al-Samarqandī, i. 13^{v}).

[138] Al-Ṣāliḥī, i. 364.

[139] Yaḥyā ibn Sallām, p. 7.

[140] Al-Suyūṭī, *al-Durr*, i. 58; and see a similar report in al-Mas'ūdī, *Akhbār al-zamān*, 49.

[141] 'Abd al-Malik ibn Ḥabīb, p. 19; see also René Dagorn, *La Geste d'Ismaël* (Paris, 1981), 289–90.

[142] Al-Majlisī, xi. 117.

angels' (Q. 2/31) is consequently explained as meaning that God presented unto the angels the spectres of the prophets and the Imāms as lights within shadows.[143] The angels committed themselves to faith and obedience, and undertook to recognize the excellence of 'Alī and of the Shī'ī Imāms.

The Shī'ī idea of the superiority of 'Alī and the Imāms provides the reason why God ordered that the angels prostrate themselves in front of Ādam. Because the angels became convinced that the Shī'i Imāms surpass them in rank and position, they prostrated when they were ordered to do so.

A clear exposition of the Shī'ī idea is given in a story in which Muḥammad is made to reply to the hypocrites who asked him whether 'Alī was superior to the angels. He explained that the angels gained honour only through their love of himself and 'Alī and through the acceptance of their *wilāya*. Adherents of 'Alī who cleansed their hearts from deceit, hatred, and the impurity of sins are purer and better than the angels. As the angels believed that they surpass the creatures on earth, God created Ādam, taught him all the names, ordered him to test their knowledge through questions and to show them that they were inferior. Then He ordered them to prostrate themselves to Ādam. Muḥammad stresses that the Shī'a are constant in their struggle against oppressive rulers, that they suffer and grieve as a result of the persecution of their enemies, and that they subdue their lust and desire; the angels do not need to cope with such difficulties and do not suffer pain as do the Shī'ī adherents. The angels perceived that Ādam possessed the light of these noble creatures and they therefore prostrated themselves to Ādam.[144] Muḥammad repeated the same idea in another tradition in which he emphasized the superiority of the Shī'a over the angels: God put us into the loins of Ādam and ordered the angels to prostrate themselves to him as a mark of honour and glorification for us; their prostration was thus an act of worship for God and one of rendering homage and obedience to Ādam, because we were in his loins. How can we not be considered superior to the angels when they prostrated

143 Ibid. xi. 117.

144 Ibid. xi. 137–8; cf. the story of the conversation of the angels with God, in which they boasted of their fast. God replied: 'You fast because you do not desire food, but these human beings are better than you, because they need food; nevertheless they fast.' Thus the human beings are superior to the angels; see al-Zandawaysitī, *Rawḍat al-'ulamā' wa-nuzhat al-fuḍalā'*, MS BL Add. 7258, fo. 267^{v}.

themselves to Ādam?[145] In a third tradition, the prophet mentions again the prostration of the angels as an argument for the superiority of himself, 'Alī, Fāṭima, al-Ḥasan, and al-Ḥusayn over the angels. 'I, 'Alī, Fāṭima, al-Ḥasan and al-Ḥusayn were in the pavilion of the Throne. We glorified God and the angels glorified Him by our glorification; this was two thousand years before the creation of Ādam. When God created Ādam he ordered the angels to prostrate themselves to him, but He did not order us to do so.' The expression *'ālūna* (contained in the rebuke addressed at Iblīs: *istakbarta am kunta min al-'ālīn* in Q. 38/75) refers to the five who were in the pavilion of the Throne.[146] A tradition which fits in with the Shī'ī story states that the place where the angels prostrated themselves to Ādam was al-Kūfa (which was a Shī'ī stronghold).[147]

The Sunnī explanations of the command given to the angels to prostrate themselves to Ādam are concise and touch upon the problem whether one is permitted to prostrate oneself in front of a human being. Some scholars argue that the prostration was only done in the direction of Ādam; others claim that the prostration was no more than an act of bowing (*inḥinā'*) towards Ādam, or that *li-ādam* means 'with Ādam' (that is, Ādam serving as *imām*), or that the prostration was in front of God and the bowing was to Ādam as a mark of respect for Him. Finally, some commentators claimed that it was a real prostration to Ādam, but that this was not yet forbidden at that time.[148]

7. THE CREATION OF EVE AND HER CHILDREN

The creation of Ḥawwā' and the time when this took place formed the subject of another discussion. The verse in the Qur'ān, *wa-qulnā yā ādamu skun anta wa-zawjuka'l-jannata* (Q. 2/35), does

[145] Al-Majlisī, xi. 140, 150–1.

[146] Ibid., xi. 142. According to a Shī'ī tradition, the cherubs behind the throne are people of the Shī'a, of the First Creation—ibid., xiii. 224.

[147] Al-'Ayyāshī, *Tafsīr* (Qom, 1371), i. 34, no. 18; al-Katakānī, i. 79; al-Majlisī, xi. 149; al-Burāqi, *Ta'rīkh al-Kūfa* (Najaf, 1379/1960), 59 (more precisely, the outskirts of al-Kūfa, *ẓahr al-Kūfa*, by which probably Najaf is meant).

[148] See, e.g., al-Ṭabarī, *Tafsīr*, i. 512; al-Jaṣṣāṣ, *Aḥkām al-Qur'ān* (Qusṭanṭīnīya, 1338), i. 32; al-Tha'labī, p. 84; see Isḥāq ibn Bishr, fo. 43ʳ; Anon., *Siyar al-anbiyā'*, fo. 13ᵛ; see further al-Khāzin, i. 41; al-Nasafī, i. 40, iii. 67; al-Shawkānī, *Fatḥ al-qadīr*, i. 66, iii. 130; Ibn Abī'l-Ḥadīd, i. 100; 'Abd al-Jabbār, p. 22; Ibn Nāṣir al-Dīn, fo. 137ᵛ; Abū Ḥayyān, i. 152–3; al-Nīsābūrī, i. 260–1.

not indicate when and how Ḥawwā' was created. The best-known traditions transmit the story that Ḥawwā' was created from the rib of Ādam during his sleep.[149] A widely current tradition of Muḥammad states that 'the woman was created from a crooked rib; if you are eager to set her aright you will break her; so treat her with gentleness and you will live with her.'[150] Al-Māwardī (d. 450/1058) records that story of her creation from a rib, and adds several anecdotes concerning the meeting of the couple and their marriage; as in other sources, al-Māwardī quotes two alternative opinions, that Ḥawwā' was created either before Ādam entered paradise, or after that event. A short passage in his report, an individual view expressed by one scholar, deserves particular attention: Abū Baḥr says that God created her from the material from which He created Ādam.[151] Shī'ī compilations recorded this version, tracing it back to the utterances of the Shī'ī Imāms. The Imām al-Bāqir said: 'God created Ḥawwā' from the remainder of the clay from which He created Ādam.'[152] A more detailed report is attributed to Wahb (ibn Munabbih?): God created Ḥawwā' from the remainder of the clay of Ādam, forming her in Ādam's shape. God put sleep on Ādam and showed it (!) to him; it was the first dream on earth. When Ādam awoke, Ḥawwā' was sitting at his head. He asked who she was and God replied that she was the person whom he had seen in his dream.[153] A Shī'ī Imām, Abū Ja'far, remarks angrily on the opinion that Ḥawwā' was created from Ādam's rib, 'They lie! Was God powerless to create her from material other than Ādam's rib?' He quoted on the authority of one of his ancestors the following utterance of Muḥammad: God took a handful of clay, mixed it with His right hand (both of His hands were right hands) and created Ādam from it; from a remainder of

[149] See, e.g., al-Suyūṭī, *al-Durr*, i. 52; Ibn 'Asākir, ii. 349; al-Samarqandī, i. 14[r]; al-'Aynī, xv. 212; al-Ṣaffūrī, p. 288; al-Saqsīnī p. 10; al-Shawkānī, *Fatḥ al-qadīr*, i. 70; al-Ṭabarsī, i. 187; Ibn Nāṣir al-Dīn, fo. 141[r].

[150] Ibn Qutayba, *'Uyūn al-akhbār* (Cairo, 1349/1930), iv. 77; al-Shaykh al-Mufīd, *al-Ikhtiṣāṣ*, (Najaf, 1390/1971), 334; al-Munāwī, ii. 388, nos. 2111–2; al-Sulamī, *Ādāb al-suḥba* (Jerusalem, 1954), 82 n. 245 (and see the refs. of the editor); 'Abd al-Malik ibn Ḥabīb, p. 8; al-Qurṭubī, i. 301–2; al-Majlisī, xi. 222; Ibn Kathīr, *al-Bidāya*, i. 74; al-Bayhaqī, *Shu'ab al-īmān*, MS Reisu'l-kuttāb Muṣṭafā Ef. Sulaymānīya 219, fo. 133[v]; al-Tha'labī, p. 85.

[151] Al-Māwardī, *A'lām al-nubūwa*, 32; also Ibn Nāṣir al-Dīn, fo. 140[v] (quoting al-Māwardī).

[152] Al-Majlisī, xi. 99.

[153] Ibid. xi. 115 no. 42.

the clay He created Ḥawwā'[154] The reason for the anger of the Shī'ī Imāms is indicated by a tradition recorded by Ibn Bābawayh al-Qummī (d. 381/991). People say that Ḥawwā' was created from the left rib of Ādam, remarks one of the followers of the Imām. The Imām, Abū 'Abd Allāh, says in rage: 'Did God lack the power to create a wife for Ādam from something other than his rib? This is a slander which makes it possible to say that Ādam had sexual intercourse with himself as Ḥawwā' was [created] from his rib. What is the matter with these people? May God judge between us and them.' Even some of the beasts are in the habit of killing themselves when they notice that they have had intercourse with one of their sisters, the Imām observes. Further, the Imām gives a short report on the independent creation of Ḥawwā'.[155] A harmonizing version is recorded by Ni'mat Allāh al-Mūsawī (d. 1130/1718): Ḥawwā' was created from the clay prepared for Ādam; every part of the body of Ādam was made separately in order to put the parts together during creation. In this way, Ḥawwā' was created from the clay of Ādam's rib.[156] But it was not only Ḥawwā' who was created from the remainder of Ādam's clay; some other useful creatures originated from this left-over. God created from this remainder the palm tree, and Muḥammad bade the believers honour this tree, which is the aunt of the believers.[157] Prophets and Imāms used to put green branches of palm trees in the graves during the burial; there is indeed an utterance of Muḥammad recommending this custom; but it was later branded by the opponents of the Shī'a as a Shī'ī *bid'a*.[158] From this remainder God also created, according to a tradition recorded by Ibn 'Asākir (d. 600/1203), the pomegranate and the vine.[159] Some Muslim

[154] Ibid. xl. 116.

[155] Ibn Bābawayh al-Qummī, *'Ilal al-sharā'i'* (Najaf, 1385/1966), 17–18; also al-Majlisī, xi. 222; Ni'mat Allāh al-Mūsawī, i. 240.

[156] Ni'mat Allāh al-Mūsawī, i. 241–2.

[157] See, e.g., al-Suyūṭī, *Jam' al-jawāmi'*, i. 140; al-Munāwī, ii. 94, no. 1432; Ibn al-Jawzī, *al-Mawḍū'āt*, i. 183–4; Ni'mat Allāh al-Mūsawī, i. 232; Ibn 'Asākir, ii. 343; al-Jāḥiẓ, *Kitāb al-ḥayawān* (Cairo, 1385/1965), i. 212; al-Suyūṭī, *al-La'ālī*, i. 155; Nāṣir al-Dīn al-Albānī, pp. 282–3, nos. 261, 263; Anon., *Siyar al-anbiyā'*, fo. 12^{v}. A peculiar story records a convincing proof that the palm tree was created from the remainder of Adam's clay and is different from any other tree. Like a human being the palm tree dies when its top is cut off; see al-Samarqandī, *Majma' al-ḥikam*, MS Bratislava, fo. 87^{v}.

[158] Ni'mat Allāh al-Mūsawī, i. 232.

[159] Ibn 'Asākir, ii. 343; al-Suyūṭī, *al-La'ālī*, i. 156; Nāṣir al-Dīn al-Albānī, no. 262; al-Munāwī, iii. 450, no. 3937; al-Suyūṭī, *Jam' al-jawāmi'*, i. 511.

scholars report that pigeons[160] and locusts were also created from it.[161]

The same criteria used for criticizing the traditions about Ḥawwā' were applied to the traditions about the children of Ādam and Ḥawwā' as well. According to the current tradition, Ḥawwā' gave birth to a great number of sets of twins. The sons of Ādam were permitted to marry their sisters on condition that they would not marry their own twins.

There was an eminent descendant of 'Alī, 'Alī ibn al-Ḥusayn, who justified these marriages and adopted the story of the creation of Ḥawwā' from Ādam's rib. When he was asked about that, his attention being drawn to the fact that this was a Majūsī practice, he replied that the deeds of Ādam and his children had been carried out before the prohibition of these deeds was issued. Their actions were in harmony with their law (*sharī'a*).[162] The tradition that the sons of Ādam married their sisters, says a Shī'ī Imām, only strengthens the arguments of the Majūs. The Shī'i story about the progeny of Ādam is as follows. Ḥawwā' gave birth to seventy sets of twins; after Qābīl murdered his brother Hābīl, Ādam was overcome by grief and abstained from intercourse with Ḥawwā' for 500 years. Then he had intercourse with her and she bore two children: Shīth and Yāfith, who did not have twin siblings. When they became mature for marriage, God sent down two *ḥūrī* girls: Baraka for Shīth, Munzala for Yāfith. The progeny of Shīth and Yāfith are the prophets and messengers of mankind.[163] This account contains no information about the marriages of the other sons of Ādam.

In another version it is again the Imām Abū 'Abd Allāh who is asked about the marriages of the sons of Ādam with their sisters and who flatly denies the account, arguing that Ādam's belief was identical with that of Muḥammad; had Ādam done it, the prophet would have followed his example. Further, the Imām gives a short résumé of the marriages of Ādam's children. Ādam's monstrous daughter, 'Anāq, was killed by ravaging beasts. The son Qābīl (born after 'Anāq) grew up and married a *jinnī* girl, Jihāna, sent for

[160] See Ni'mat Allāh al-Mūsawī, i. 232.

[161] Al-Damīrī, *Ḥayāt al-ḥayawān*, i. 188; al-Kisā'ī, trans. W. M. Thackston, Jr., p. 58; al-Suyūṭī, *al-Durr*, iii. 110.

[162] Al-Majlisī, xi. 226.

[163] Ibid. xi. 224; Ibn Bābawayh, pp. 19–20 (with the variants: Nazla and Munzala); al-'Iṣāmī, i. 67–8.

him by God. Later Hābīl was born, and when he grew up God sent down a *ḥūrī* girl called Turk (!); Hābīl married her. After a time, God bade Ādam transmit to Hābīl the greatest name of God, the legacy of prophethood, and the lists of names which God taught him. Ādam carried out God's order. However, Qābīl envied Hābīl; a test of a sacrifice proved that Hābīl had the right to the prophetic legacy. Qābīl disregarded the test of fire (which consumed the sacrificial ram of Hābīl) and killed his brother, guided in his plan by Iblīs. Qābīl was advised by Iblīs to build a temple for the worship of fire on the spot where the fire consumed the sacrifice of Hābīl; he was the first worshipper of fire. Ādam came to the place where Qābīl killed Hābīl and wept for forty days, cursing the earth which accepted the blood of his son; this place is the *qibla* of the congregational mosque of al-Baṣra. On the day when Hābīl was killed, his wife, the *ḥūrī* Turk, bore a child; Ādam named it Hābīl; the child was thus Hābīl ibn Hābīl. Afterwards God granted Ādam a child; Ādam named him Shīth or Hibat Allāh. Shīth grew up and married a *ḥūrī* girl named Nā'ima sent for him by God; she bore him a girl and Ādam named her Ḥūrīya; when she grew up she married Hābīl ibn Hābīl. All the creatures are in fact the progeny of Shīth. Before his death Ādam conveyed the prophetic legacy to Shīth, bidding him hide it from Qābīl and enjoin his descendants to transmit it to Nūḥ.[164]

The material discussed in this paper, all the traditions, utterances, stories, and tales, as well as the assumptions and arguments of the Muslim scholars, add up to no more than a drop in the sea when compared to the totality of the lore transmitted about Ādam in the Islamic sources. The few examples brought together in this paper may serve as an illustration of the manner in which Muslim scholars coped with the body of material handed down to them, showing how they adapted it for answering the pressing questions of their period.

[164] Al-Majlisī, xi. 226–9; about the worship of fire of Qābīl see al-'Iṣāmī, i. 86.

PART II

GENRES OF *TAFSĪR*

6

The Exegetical Genre *nāsikh al-Qur'ān wa mansūkhuhu*

DAVID S. POWERS

ALTHOUGH the doctrine of abrogation (*naskh*) has recently attracted the attention of several scholars interested in the collection of the Qur'ān[1] and the formation of Islamic law,[2] it nevertheless remains the case that the *naskh* phenomenon, in and of itself, is still poorly understood. But if, as Muslim scholars maintain, an understanding of *naskh* is essential to a proper understanding of the Qur'ān, it behoves us to try and appreciate the complexity and sophistication of this phenomenon, as understood by the Muslim scholars themselves. A first step in this direction has already been undertaken by A. Rippin, who has edited an early *naskh* text ascribed to Ibn Shihāb al-Zuhrī (d. 124/742).[3] In an effort to advance our understanding of the *naskh* phenomenon still further, I propose here to survey the historical development of the *naskh* literature, to summarize the classical understanding of the *naskh* phenomenon, to clarify some of the details and dynamics of the way in which abrogation works, and to identify several special or unique verses that are singled out by the authorities on abrogation.

[1] In *The Collection of the Qur'ān* (Cambridge, 1977), John Burton argues that the explanations found in the Islamic sources as to how the Qur'ān came to assume its present shape were introduced, at a relatively late date, by jurists seeking support for their theories about abrogation. The final text of the Qur'ān, according to Burton, was produced by Muḥammad himself. John Wansbrough comes to a very different conclusion in his *QS* 191–202, where he argues that the final text of the Qur'ān emerged from what were originally independent traditions that were brought together a century or more after the death of Muḥammad. Remarkably, Wansbrough, like Burton, finds support for his theory in the doctrine of abrogation.

[2] See David S. Powers, 'On the Abrogation of the Bequest Verses', *Arabica* 29 (1982), 246–95, where it was argued that the doctrine of abrogation was first applied to the bequest verses (Q. 2/180 and 2/240) a generation or more after Muḥammad's death.

[3] A. Rippin, 'Al-Zuhrī, *naskh al-Qur'ān* and the Problem of Early *tafsīr* Texts', BSOAS 47 (1984), 22–43. Surveys of *naskh* have been attempted by Ahmad Hasan, 'The Theory of *naskh*', *IS* 4 (1965), 181–200; Qamaruddin Khan, 'Incidence of Abrogation (*naskh*) in the Qur'ān', *Iqbal*, 15 i (1966), 8–46.

1. THE DEVELOPMENT OF THE LITERARY GENRE

The commentators and legists find Quranic sanction for the doctrine of abrogation in four verses. The term *naskh* itself occurs twice in the Qur'ān, each time with a different connotation. Q. 2/106 is generally understood as signifying, 'Whatever verse (*āya*) we replace (*nansakh*) or cause to be forgotten, We bring a better or the like to it.'[4] In Q. 22/52, on the other hand, the term *naskh* is taken in the sense of 'to cancel, annul, or suppress': 'We never sent any messenger or prophet before thee, but that Satan cast into his fancy, when he was fancying; but God annuls (*yansakh*) what Satan casts.' Islamic tradition teaches that this verse was revealed to Muḥammad after he had recited two short verses in which he appeared to have recognized the Arabian goddesses al-Lāt, al-'Uzza, and al-Manāt, mentioned in Q. 53/19: 'These are the exalted ones, whose intercession is to be hoped for.' Q. 22/52 came to inform Muḥammad that these two verses had been inserted into the revelation by Satan.[5] Further Quranic support for the doctrine of abrogation was found in Q. 16/101, which mentions *tabdīl* ('replacement'), not *naskh*: 'And when We exchange (*baddalnā*) a verse (*āya*) in place of another'. Finally, several companions, followers, and successors of Muḥammad are reported to have taken the terms *muḥkamāt* and *mutashābihāt* in Q. 3/7 ('It is He who sent down upon thee the book, wherein are *muḥkamāt* verses that are the Essence of the Book, and other *mutashābihāt*') as referring to the abrogating and abrogated verses, respectively.[6]

[4] Recently, however, Burton has suggested that the term *āya* here refers to an individual ritual or legal obligation, and that the verb '*yansakh*' means 'modification'. Q. 2/106 would accordingly refer to the modification of an earlier, Jewish ritual or legal regulation by a later, Islamic one. As support for this assertion, Burton notes that Q. 2/106 occurs immediately before a series of modifications introduced by Muḥammad (*sic*) in both the ritual and legal spheres: *qibla*, pilgrimage rites, dietary laws, talio, bequests, and fasting. See Burton, *Collection*, 235–7. See also his 'The Exegesis of Q. 2:106 and the Islamic Theories of *naskh*: *mā nansakh min āya aw nansahā na'ti bi khairin minhā aw mithlihā*', *BSOAS* 48 (1985), 452–69, and 'The Interpretation of Q. 87, 6–7 and the theories of *nasḫ*', *Der Islam*, 62 (1985), 5–19.

[5] A. Welch, 'al-Ḳur'ān,' *EI*² v. 404; Burton, *Collection*, 62, 235.

[6] Al-Ṭabarī, *Jāmi' al-bayān 'an ta'wīl āy al-Qur'ān*, ed. Shākir (Cairo, 1954–68), iii. 172–3, where this opinion is attributed to Ibn 'Abbās, Ibn Mas'ūd, Qatāda, al-Rabī', and al-Ḍaḥḥāk. This identification may have been prompted by the fact that in the *naskh* literature a verse that is not abrogated is classified as being *muḥkama*, i.e., in force or effective.

But even if the Qur'ān does sanction the doctrine of *naskh* in the sense of the replacement of one legal ruling by another, it nevertheless remains the case that the overwhelming majority of pairs of abrogated and abrogating verses are not identified as either 'abrogated' or 'abrogating'.[7] Hence, it becomes essential to determine the relative chronology of the two verses because, if one mistakes the abrogating verse for the abrogated, Muslims would be adhering to a legal ruling that has been suppressed and, at the same time, they would be neglecting a ruling that has been commanded. It is for this reason that the literary genre *al-nāsikh wa'l-mansūkh* developed hand-in-hand with the *asbāb al-nuzūl* on the one hand, and *uṣūl al-fiqh* on the other.[8]

Although companions of Muḥammad are reported to have discussed *naskh*, and even to have disagreed over the abrogation of a particular verse, references to the generation of the companions in the *naskh* literature are relatively infrequent.[9] It is, rather, during the generation of the successors (*tābiʿūn*) that the *naskh* phenomenon seems to have come into its own. In the classical texts on abrogation we frequently encounter references to disagreements among *tābiʿīs* over the status of a particular verse. For example, although the majority of scholars consider Q. 2/62 to have been abrogated by Q. 3/85, Mujāhid ibn Jabr (d. 104/722) and al-Ḍaḥḥāk ibn Muzāḥim (d. 105/723) considered the verse to be *muḥkama*. Other *tābiʿīs* mentioned frequently in the sources include: Nakhaʿī (d. 94/712), Muslim ibn Yasār (d. 101/719), Shaʿbī (d. 104/722), Ṭāwūs (d. 106/724), al-Ḥasan al-Baṣrī (d. 110/728), 'Aṭā' ibn Abī Rabāḥ (d. 114/732), Muḥammad al-Bāqir (d. 114/732), Qatāda (d. 118/736), and Muqātil ibn Sulaymān (d. 150/767). It is perhaps not surprising then that in both literary and

[7] The one explicit reference to the replacement of one legal ruling with another is the change of the *qibla* (Q. 2/143–4); but even here, the Qur'ān only refers indirectly to 'the *qibla* to which you formerly prayed'.

[8] On the *naskh–asbāb* connection, see A. Rippin, 'The Quranic *asbāb al-nuzūl* Material: An Analysis of its Use and Development in Exegesis', Ph.D. Thesis (McGill University, 1981); on the *naskh–uṣūl* connection see W. Hallaq, 'Was the Gate of *ijtihād* closed?', *IJMES* 16 (1984), 6, where al-Ghazālī is cited as mentioning familiarity with the *naskh* phenomenon as one of the prerequisites for exercising *ijtihād*.

[9] But see Ibn Salāma, *al-Nāsikh wa'l-mansūkh* (Cairo, 1315/1899), 142–3, where 'Alī and Ibn 'Abbās disagree over the abrogation of Q. 4/94; 'Alī maintained that the verse was abrogated by Q. 4/115 and 4/48, while Ibn 'Abbās held that it remained *muḥkama*.

manuscript sources we find evidence for the emergence of the
nāsikh al-Qur'ān literary genre during the course of the second/
eighth century.[10] The earliest treatises on the subject of abrogation
are attributed to Qatāda, al-Zuhrī, al-Ḥārith ibn 'Abd al-Raḥmān
(d. 130/747), 'Aṭā' al-Khurasānī (d. 135/757), Muqātil, and 'Abd
al-Raḥmān ibn Zayd (d. 183/798). Although the reliability of these
ascriptions may, in certain cases, be questioned it is not my
intention here to enter into a discussion of this issue.[11] Rather, I
propose to survey the *nāsikh al-Qur'ān* literature as manifested in
several standard, well-established texts: al-Naḥḥās (d. 338/949),
Kitāb al-nāsikh wa'l-mansūkh fī'l-Qur'ān al-karīm;[12] Hibat Allāh
ibn Salāma (d. 410/1020), *al-Nāsikh wa'l-mansūkh*;[13] and Ibn al-
'Aṭā'iqī (d. c. 790/1308), *al-Nāsikh wa'l-mansūkh*.[14] Reference will
also be made to al-Zuhrī's *Naskh al-Qur'ān*, and Ibn Khuzayma al-
Fārisī (death date unknown), *Kitāb al-mujāz fī'l-nāsikh wa'l-
mansūkh*, where appropriate.

The treatises on abrogation, even the earliest ones, were probably
intended to serve as handbooks for commentators and legal
scholars. Due to the great complexity of the *naskh* phenomenon, as
well as the importance of abrogation for determining the law,
specialists in both the Qur'ān and Islamic law needed short
reference works that provided a convenient overview of the entire
phenomenon. Ibn Salāma, for example, indicates that he wrote his
treatise, *Nāsikh al-Qur'ān*, after observing that the commentators
'were unable to master the science of abrogation, or to memorize it,
and frequently mixed one part of it with another'.[15] Similarly, al-
Fārisī indicates that he wrote his treatise on abrogation 'in order to
facilitate memorization of the text by those who wish to do so'.[16]

The treatises on abrogation are generally composed of two

[10] For lists of books on *naskh* see esp. Muṣṭafā Zayd, *al-Naskh fī'l-Qur'ān al-
karīm* (Cairo, 1963), 290–395. Sezgin, *GAS*, and Ḥajjī Khalīfa, *Kashf al-ẓunūn*, also
contain many entries for works on this topic.
[11] As has been done by Rippin, on the basis of an analysis of a manuscript
attributed to al-Zuhrī. See his '*al-Zuhrī*', 43.
[12] Cairo, 1323/1905.
[13] On the margin of al-Wāḥidī, *Asbāb al-nuzūl* (Cairo, 1315/1899). A new
edition of Ibn Salāma alone has recently become available, ed. Zuhayr al-Shāwīsh
and Muḥammad Kan'ān (2nd printing, Beirut, 1986).
[14] Najaf, 1389/1969.
[15] Ibn Salāma, p. 8.
[16] Ibn Khuzayma al-Fārisī, *Kitāb al-mujāz fī'l-nāsikh wa'l-mansūkh*, published
with al-Naḥḥās, *Kitāb al-nāsikh wa'l-mansūkh* (Cairo, 1905), 260.

sections: a short introduction in which the author explains the doctrine of abrogation in theoretical terms, and the treatise itself, in which the abrogated and abrogating verses of the Qur'ān are enumerated. A typical introduction includes the following six chapters: (i) exciting interest in the study of the abrogated and abrogating verses; (ii) disagreement among scholars regarding that which the Qur'ān and the *sunna* may abrogate; the meaning of *naskh*, and its derivation; (iii) the various modes of *naskh*; (iv) the difference between *naskh* and *badā'*; (v) mention of some relevant *ḥadīth*; (vi) the *sūra*s in which both abrogating and abrogated verses are mentioned.[17]

One notices among the classical authors a predilection for classification. Ibn Salāma, Ibn al-'Atā'iqī, and al-Fārisī classify the 114 *sūra*s of the Qur'ān according to whether or not they contain abrogating and/or abrogated verses. Ibn Salāma identifies forty-three *sūra*s that contain neither abrogating nor abrogated verses, six that contain abrogating verses only, one that contains abrogated verses only, and twenty-five that contain both abrogated and abrogating verses.[18] Such lists may have facilitated memorization of the text.

The body of the text itself is almost always divided into chapters or sections that follow the standard *sūra* order of the Qur'ān, from *sūrat al-fātiḥa* to *sūrat al-nās*. The author will indicate the name of the *sūra*, whether it was revealed in Mecca or Medina, or in both cities, and the number of abrogated verses that it contains.[19] He will then take up the abrogated verses serially, following the order in which they appear in the Qur'ān; for example, in *sūra* 2, al-Naḥḥās mentions the first abrogated verse, Q. 2/144, the second abrogated verse, Q. 2/165, and so on.[20]

When discussing a particular abrogated verse, an author will

[17] Al-Naḥḥās, pp. 4–12.

[18] Ibn Salāma, pp. 9–10.

[19] Occasionally, there may be a discrepancy between the number of abrogated verses the author says are in a given *sūra*, and the number of abrogated verses he actually cites. See, e.g., Ibn Salāma, pp. 207–11, where the author indicates that *sūrat al-naḥl* contains four abrogated verses, but then proceeds to enumerate five verses that were abrogated.

[20] Once again, there are occasional discrepancies, as, e.g., when Ibn al-'Atā'iqī (p. 62) refers to Q. 24/4 as the first abrogated verse in the *sūra*, and Q. 24/3 as the second. Such discrepancies are, in all likelihood, due to scribal error. Two works appear to contradict this ordering of their presentation: Abū 'Ubayd (d. 224/838) and 'Abd al-Qāhir al-Baghdādī (d. 429/1037); see *QS* 198–9 for details and significance.

generally quote either the entire verse or, more often, those words in it which are considered to have been abrogated; then he will quote the abrogating verse. If the abrogation of a particular verse was the subject of controversy, this will be mentioned in passing, and if the author himself has doubts about the abrogation of a particular verse, he may say, at the end of his discussion, *wa fīhi naẓar*, roughly, 'this is open to question.'

With the exception of al-Naḥḥās, the *naskh* specialists generally do not provide an extensive treatment of the arguments for or against the abrogation of a particular verse; rather, disagreements among earlier generations are mentioned, but only in summary form. Thus these texts are not of much use to the scholar who wants to trace the historical development of the status of a particular verse, for which one must refer to other sources such as the *ḥadīth* collections, Qur'ān commentaries, and legal texts.[21]

The number of verses that are considered to have been abrogated increased dramatically between the eighth and eleventh centuries (al-Zuhrī mentions 42 abrogated verses, al-Naḥḥās, 138, and Ibn Salāma, 238), at which point an upper limit seems to have been reached (Ibn al-'Atā'iqī identifies 231 abrogated verses, and al-Fārisī, 248). The rapid increase in the number of abrogated verses can be explained, I think, by two major factors. First, the doctrine of abrogation may have been invoked, subsequent to the death of Muḥammad, in order to reconcile discrepancies that had developed between the Qur'ān and the *fiqh*, as I have argued, for example, with respect to the abrogation of Q. 2/180 and 2/240.[22] I would caution, however, that examples of this phenomenon must be demonstrated on a case-by-case basis, and should not be taken for granted. Second, and more important, was the expansion of the semantic range of the term *naskh* to include phenomena that did not originally fall within its scope. Al-Faḍalī, the modern editor of Ibn al-'Atā'iqī, makes an important distinction between *naskh uṣūlī* and *naskh tafsīrī*. The jurisprudents (*uṣūlī*s), he explains, use the term *naskh* in the sense of 'replacing one legal ruling with another due to the termination of the effective period of the earlier ruling'.[23] The commentators, on the other hand, extend the parameters of the term *naskh* to include, in addition to the above: 'specification, exception, abandoning a legal rule because circumstances have

[21] See, e.g., Powers, 'Abrogation'.
[22] Ibid. [23] Ibn al-'Atā'iqī', p. 7.

changed, and mutual cancellation'.[24] As an example of 'abandoning adherence to a legal rule because circumstances have changed', al-Faḍalī cites the sword-verse (*āyat al-sayf*) which, as we shall see below, may have accounted for over 100 additional instances of abrogation. Similarly, the inclusion of the idea of 'exception' within the scope of abrogation may account for an additional fifteen cases of abrogation. Thus, by redefining the term *naskh*, the commentators brought within the scope of abrogation a large number of verses which, according to the jurists, do not constitute instances of abrogation.[25]

There also appears to have been a reaction, among certain scholars, to the wholesale application of the *naskh* doctrine to verses of the Qur'ān. Sensitive, perhaps, to theological considerations, e.g. the possible confusion of *naskh* and *badā'* (see below), some scholars endeavoured to reduce the number of abrogated verses by harmonizing the apparent contradiction between pairs of abrogated and abrogating verses: al-Suyūṭī (d. 911/1505) recognized only twenty instances of true abrogation, and Shāh Walī Allāh (d. 1762) reduced that number to five.[26] Ibn al-'Atā'iqī, on the other hand, while citing 231 instances of abrogation, appendixes the phrase *wa fīhi naẓar*, indicating doubt or uncertainty, to his discussion of twenty-six verses.[27]

2. THE CLASSICAL UNDERSTANDING OF THE *NASKH* PHENOMENON

Familiarity with the science of abrogation was considered to be essential for a proper understanding of the Qur'ān. Ibn Salāma states that the starting-point of any proper investigation of the Qur'ān is the 'science of the abrogating and abrogated verses', as related on the authority of the ancient *imāms*; indeed, anyone who engages in the scientific study of the Qur'ān without having

[24] Ibid.

[25] Ibid.

[26] These figures are mentioned in Ernest Hahn, 'Sir Sayyid Ahmad Khān's *The Controversy over Abrogation (in the Qur'ān)*: An Annotated Translation', *MW* 64 (1974), 124.

[27] Q. 2/173, 2/180, 2/190, 2/192, 2/221, 2/228, 3/86–8, 4/93, 5/109, 5/111, 6/15, 8/1, 8/33, 9/1–2, 9/97, 11/15, 20/115, 21/98–100, 24/3, 38/88, 76/29. See Appendix A for a full listing of abrogated verses in Ibn Salāma.

mastered the doctrine of abrogation is 'deficient' (*nāqiṣ*).[28] Textual support for this requirement is generally found in an anecdote told about the fourth caliph, 'Alī ibn Abī Ṭālib, who expelled a preacher from the mosque in Kūfa because he talked about the Qur'ān without being familiar with the science of abrogation. One version of this anecdote runs as follows:

> It has been related about the Commander of the Faithful, 'Alī ibn Abī Ṭālib . . . that one day he entered the Friday mosque in Kūfa, where he saw a man known as 'Abd al-Raḥmān ibn Dābb, a follower of the Abū Mūsā al-Ash'arī. The people had gathered around him in order to ask questions, but he was mixing commands with prohibitions, and permissions with restrictions. 'Alī asked him, 'Can you distinguish between the abrogating and abrogated verses?' He replied, 'No.' Then 'Alī said, 'You destroy yourself and you destroy others. Of whom are you the father?' He said, 'I am the father of Yaḥyā.' 'Alī said, 'You are only talking in order to increase your reputation!'[29] And he grabbed his ear and twisted it. Then he said, 'Do not tell stories in our mosque ever again.'[30]

Various definitions are given for the meaning of the term *naskh*. According to al-Naḥḥās, the term may be used in two different ways. Sometimes *naskh* means 'to remove or eliminate', as in the sentence 'The sun eliminated (*nasakhat*) the shade', that is, the sun removed the shade and took its place. This is the sense in which the word *naskh* is used in Q. 22/52, 'God eliminates (*yansakh*) what Satan casts.' More commonly, however, especially in the treatises on abrogation, the word *naskh* is used in the sense of 'to move from one place to another', as in the sentence, 'I copied (*nasakhtu*) the book', that is, transferred the words from one place to another.[31] Referring to the second of these two usages, Ibn Salāma defines *naskh* as 'to raise/remove (*raf*') something', for the abrogating verse removes the legal content (*ḥukm*) of the abrogated verse.[32]

Al-Faḍalī gives three definitions of the word *naskh*: (i) 'Removal/elimination' (*izāla*), as in the sentence, 'The sun removed (*nasakhat*) the shade.' Used in this sense, the *naskh* of one verse by another refers to the removal/elimination of the earlier verse's legal force (*ḥukm*); (ii) 'change' (*taghayyur*), as in the sentence, 'The wind

[28] Ibn Salāma, pp. 4–5.
[29] Literally, 'You are the father of "acknowledge me"', *anta abū i'rafūnī*.
[30] Ibn Salāma, pp. 5–6; cf. Rippin, 'al-Zuhrī', 28; al-Naḥḥās, p. 5; Ibn al-'Atā'iqī, p. 22.
[31] Al-Naḥḥās, p. 7.
[32] Ibn Salāma, pp. 9–10; cf. Ibn al-'Atā'iqī, p. 22.

changed (*nasakhat*) the traces of the house'; (iii) 'cancellation', as in the sentence, *nasakhahu*, i.e., 'he cancelled it (*abṭalahu*) and something took its place.' It is in this sense that al-Faḍalī cites al-Layth (d. 175/791) and al-Farrā' (d. 207/822), each of whom defined *naskh* as the abandonment/removal/cancellation of the legal force of an earlier verse by a later one.[33]

These definitions are related, of course, to the three different modes of abrogation recognized by the authorities; of these three, the first two are quite rare, while the third describes the great majority of instances of abrogation dealt with in the treatises on abrogation. (i) Abrogation of both wording and ruling (*naskh al-ḥukm wa'l-tilāwa*). Anas ibn Mālik (d. *c.*92/710), for example, related that during the lifetime of Muḥammad, the believers used to recite a *sūra* equal in length to *sūra* 9 ('Repentance'), but that he could only remember one verse from this *sūra*, namely, 'If the son of Adam had two valleys made of silver. . .'.[34] Similarly, Ibn Mas'ūd (d. *c.*33/653) mentions a verse that he had both committed to memory and written in the *muṣḥaf*; later, however, he could not remember the verse, and the page on which it had been written in the *muṣḥaf* was blank. Muḥammad, upon being informed of the disappearance of the verse, said, 'It was removed' (*rufi'at*).[35] The most famous example of this mode of abrogation is the so-called Satanic verses (see above). (ii) Abrogation of the wording but not of the ruling (*naskh al-tilāwa dūna'l-ḥukm*). The most famous example of this mode of abrogation is the 'stoning verse', which, according to 'Umar, read as follows: 'The adult male and the adult female, when they fornicate, stone them outright, as an exemplary punishment from God. God is mighty, wise.'[36] (iii) Abrogation of the ruling, but not of the wording (*naskh al-ḥukm dūna'l-tilāwa*). This is the mode of abrogation which occurs most frequently in the Qur'ān; according to Ibn al-'Atā'iqī, this type of abrogation can be found in sixty-three *sūra*s.

There was considerable disagreement over the scope and parameters of abrogation, especially with regard to (*a*) the relationship between Qur'ān and *sunna*, and (*b*) which verses of the Qur'ān, if any, are susceptible to abrogation. With regard to the

[33] Ibn al-'Atā'iqī, p. 7.
[34] Ibn al-'Atā'iqī, p. 23; cf. Ibn Salāma, pp. 10 ff.
[35] Ibn al-'Atā'iqī, p. 23; cf. Ibn Salāma, pp. 10 ff.
[36] See Burton, *Collection*, index, s.v. 'stoning penalty'.

first issue, al-Naḥḥās lists five different opinions: according to the Kufans, the Qur'ān may abrogate both the Qur'ān and the *sunna*; al-Shāfi'ī agreed that the Qur'ān abrogates the Qur'ān, but argued that the *sunna* does not abrogate the Qur'ān; according to one unidentified group, the *sunna* abrogates both the Qur'ān and the *sunna*; another unidentified group maintained that the *sunna* abrogates the *sunna*, but is not abrogated by the Qur'ān; finally, a certain Muḥammad ibn Shujjā' is reported to have said that, in light of the clear contradictions between the above four positions, no one of them is preferable to the other.[37]

There is also considerable disagreement over the scope of abrogation within the Qur'ān itself. At one extreme, there were apparently certain people who argued that 'the Qur'ān does not contain either an abrogating or an abrogated verse';[38] these people, according to Ibn Salāma, 'have deviated from the truth and, by virtue of their lying, have turned away from God'.[39] At the other extreme were those scholars who maintained that any narrative, positive command, or prohibition in the Qur'ān may be abrogated.[40] While there was general agreement on the susceptibility of commands and prohibitions to abrogation, the status of narratives was debated; some denied that narratives may be abrogated, while others made an exception for narratives that contained a legal ruling (*ḥukm*) or had the sense of a command.[41] Al-Naḥḥās formulates the opinion of the leading scholars of his time in the following terms: 'Abrogation only takes place with regard to acts of devotion (*muta'abbadāt*), because it is within God's power to make His creation worship Him in whatever manner He chooses, and until whatever point in time He desires, but subsequently to have them worship Him in a different manner. Abrogation, therefore, may take place with respect to commands and prohibitions, and whatever has the sense of a command or a prohibition [viz., a narrative].'[42]

Naskh in the sense of intra-scriptural abrogation was, of course, rejected by the Jews on the grounds that the idea of abrogation of divine law implies the recognition of *badā'* ('mutability of the

37 Al-Naḥḥās, pp. 5–6.
38 Ibn Salāma, p. 26; cf. al-Naḥḥās, pp. 2–3.
39 Ibn Salāma, p. 26.
40 Al-Naḥḥās, pp. 2–3.
41 Ibid. 3; Ibn Salāma, p. 22.
42 Al-Naḥḥās, p. 3; al-Naḥḥās also mentions that some people claim that the *imām*—perhaps the Shī'ī *imām*—may abrogate whatever verse he wishes.

divine will').[43] Muslims were sensitive to this implication (it may lay behind the contention of some Muslims that there are no abrogated or abrogating verses in the Qur'ān), and they sought to counter it by drawing a distinction between *naskh* and *badā'*. Al-Naḥḥās includes a discussion of the difference between these two terms in his treatise on abrogation, something which, to the best of his knowledge, had never before been mentioned in a *naskh* treatise.[44] *Naskh*, according to al-Naḥḥās, refers to something that had previously been permitted, but has now become forbidden, or vice versa, due to God's desire to improve the situation of His worshippers. Abrogation, then, does not involve any change in the divine will, but rather, God's recognition of the fact that the situation of His worshippers would change over time. God knew, at the outset, what these changes would be, and He knew it would eventually become necessary to abrogate the original command or prohibition. As examples of this, al-Naḥḥās cites the change in the direction of prayer, from Jerusalem to Mecca, the abrogation of Q. 50/12 ('O believers, when you conspire with the Messenger, before your conspiring advance a freewill offering'), and God's granting Muslims permission to work on the Sabbath, after having earlier prohibited Jews from working on that day.[45]

Badā', on the other hand, refers to the abandonment of something that had been firmly resolved upon as, for example, when one says, 'Go to so-and-so', but later you say, 'Don't go to him'; or when you say, 'Plant such-and-such in this year', but then you say, 'Don't do that.' This, according to al-Naḥḥās, is *badā'*; *naskh*, on the other hand, refers to the abrogation of some command or prohibition that God had meant to apply only during the lifetime of a certain prophet, or during a certain period of time, knowing from the outset that this *ḥukm* would remain in force until such time as circumstances changed, and a new *ḥukm* would be required.[46]

3. THE DYNAMICS OF ABROGATION

To speak of abrogated and abrogating 'verses' of the Qur'ān frequently distorts the actual dynamics of the abrogation pheno-

43 'Badā'', *EI*² i. 850–1.
44 Al-Naḥḥās, p. 4.
45 Ibid. 9–10.
46 Ibid. 10.

menon, for, in a great many instances, only part of a verse, and sometimes only one word, is either abrogated or abrogates. Q. 2/183–4, for example, stipulate some of the requirements associated with the fast during the month of Ramaḍān:

For days numbered; and if any of you be sick or if he be on a journey, then a number of other days; and for those who are unable to fast, a redemption by feeding a poor man. Yet better it is for him who volunteers good, and that you should fast is better for you, if you but know.

This verse presents the believer with the option of either fasting or, if he is unable to complete the fast, breaking the fast and feeding a poor man. But the next verse in the Qur'ān, Q. 2/185, restates the rules for fasting without mentioning the option of feeding a poor man: 'The month of Ramaḍān, wherein the Qur'ān was sent down to be a guidance to the people, and as clear signs of the Guidance and the Salvation; so let those of you, who are present at the month, fast it.' Ibn al-'Atā'iqī explains that the words, 'so let those of you, who are present at the month, fast it', in Q. 2/185 abrogate the second half of Q. 2/184, but the first half of that verse ('for days numbered; and if any of you be sick or if he be on a journey, then a number of other days') remains in force.[47] Similarly, in Q. 2/228, which stipulates the waiting-period for divorced women, only the words 'in such time their mates have better right to restore them' are abrogated by Q. 2/229 ('Divorce is twice; then honourable retention or setting free kindly'); whatever precedes or follows the abrogated phrase remains in force.[48]

A single verse may deal with two discrete subjects, each of which is abrogated by a different verse. Q. 2/219, for example, first treats the subject of wine, and then charity:

They will question thee concerning wine, and arrow-shuffling. Say: 'In both is heinous sin, and uses for men, but the sin in them is more heinous than the usefulness.' They will question thee concerning what they should expend. Say: 'The abundance.' So God makes clear His signs to you; haply you will reflect.

According to Ibn Salāma, the first half of the verse, dealing with wine, is abrogated by Q. 4/43 ('Draw not near to prayer when you are drunken'), while the second half of the verse, dealing with

[47] Ibn al-'Atā'iqī, pp. 32–3.

[48] Ibn Salāma, pp. 87–92; Ibn al-'Atā'iqī, pp. 35–6. Another example: the words 'or hide it' in Q. 2/284 are abrogated by the opening phrase of Q. 2/286.

charity, is abrogated by Q. 9/103 ('Take of their wealth a free-will offering').[49]

The progressive banning of the drinking of wine has made the phenomenon of sequential abrogation of verses widely known. After first praising wine as one of the signs of His grace to mankind (Q. 16/67), God refers to this substance as a mixed blessing in Q. 2/219; in Q. 4/43, He orders the believers not to come to prayer 'when you are drunken until you know what you are saying'; finally, God prohibited wine entirely in Q. 5/90, 'O believers, wine and arrow-shuffling, idols and divining arrows are an abomination, some of Satan's work; so avoid it; haply so you will prosper.'[50]

Another less well-known example of sequential abrogation deals with a theological subject. When God revealed Q. 3/102 ('O believers, fear God as He should be feared'), the Muslims asked Muḥammad to explain to them what was meant by the words 'as He should be feared'. Muḥammad responded that God should be obeyed, remembered, and thanked, not disobeyed, forgotten, and blasphemed. But the Muslims, who considered this verse to be a hardship, said to Muḥammad, 'O Messenger of God, we cannot bear it.' He replied, 'Do not say, as the Jews have said, "We hear and disobey;" rather, say, "We hear and obey".' Subsequently, God revealed Q. 22/78 ('and struggle for God as is His due'). This only made matters worse, for the verse was understood as meaning, 'Act as He acts', and was considered to impose an even greater burden than Q. 3/102. Finally, God relieved the Muslims of this burden by revealing Q. 64/14 ('So fear God as far as you are able'), which abrogated Q. 3/102 and 22/78.[51]

One factor which may have contributed to the gradual increase in the number of verses that were considered to have been abrogated (see above) was the inclusion of the idea of 'exception' within the scope of abrogation. For example, there are several verses in the Qur'ān which describe the punishment of the hypocrites, the ungodly, etc., and then, in the next verse, exempt from this punishment those who repent and make amends. Q. 4/145 states: 'Surely the hypocrites will be in the lowest reach of the Fire;

[49] Ibn Salāma, pp. 72 ff; according to Ibn al-'Atā'iqī (pp. 34–5), who treats Q. 2/219a and 2/219b as separate instances of abrogation, Q. 2/219a was abrogated by 5/90.

[50] See 'Khamr', *EI*²; Rippin, 'al-Zuhrī', 40.

[51] Ibn Salāma, pp. 106–8; see also Ibn al-'Atā'iqī, pp. 38–9.

thou wilt not find for them any helper.' But an exception is made in Q. 4/146: 'Save such as repent, and make amends, and hold fast to God.'[52] Most of the classical and post-classical authors consider this to be an instance of abrogation.

In many cases, the exceptive, abrogating clause occurs in the same verse as the abrogated phrase. Q. 2/233 opens with the statement, 'Mothers shall suckle their children two years completely, for such as desire to fulfil suckling.' Later in the same verse, however, we find, 'But if the couple desire by mutual consent and consultation to wean'. The commentators consider this to be a case of abrogation. Similarly, in Q. 4/22 we read, 'And do not marry women that your fathers married, unless it be a thing of the past.' The phrase 'unless it be a thing of the past' is considered to have abrogated what precedes it.[53] By my count, exceptive particles account for at least sixteen instances of abrogation.

4. SPECIAL VERSES

The *naskh* specialists single out a small number of abrogated or abrogating verses for certain distinctive qualities which they manifest, e.g. the verse which abrogates the greatest number of other verses, the verse which remained in force for the longest time before being abrogated, the only verse that abrogates itself, and the only two verses that deviate from a rule regarding the order in which pairs of abrogated and abrogating verses appear in the Qur'ān.

The distinction of abrogating the greatest number of verses in the Qur'ān belongs to Q. 9/5, known in Arabic as *āyat al-sayf* ('the sword verse'), which abrogated no less than 124 other verses.[54] This verse, which commands the believers to 'slay the idolators wherever you find them, and take them, and confine them, and lie in wait for them at every place of ambush', abrogates every other verse in the Qur'ān which commands or implies anything less than a total offensive against the non-believers.[55] The abrogated verses

[52] Other examples of this phenomenon: Q. 3/88–9, 19/59–60, 24/4–5, 25/69–70, 26/224–7, 103/2–3.

[53] Ibn al-'Atā'iqī, pp. 41–2; other examples: Q. 2/191, 2/196, 2/229, 4/19, 4/23, 5/108, 9/5.

[54] Ibn Salāma, p. 184; Ibn al-'Atā'iqī, p. 53.

[55] See Appendix B for a list of the verses abrogated by Q. 9/5.

occur in fifty-three *sūras*, some of which precede Q. 9/5, while the majority follow it.[56] For example, the words 'aggress not' in Q. 2/190 ('And fight in the way of God with those who fight with you but aggress not: God loves not the aggressors') were abrogated by Q. 9/5; similarly, the phrase 'then, if they fight you, slay them' in Q. 2/191 was abrogated by Q. 9/5, due to the defensive tendency it articulates; and the same holds for the words 'fighting in it [viz., the holy month] is a heinous thing' in Q. 2/217.

Also considered to have been abrogated by Q. 9/5 are all those verses in which God commands Muḥammad to say that he is merely a warner (Q. 15/89, 19/39, 22/49, 35/24a), or in which the Divinity tells His prophet to be patient (Q. 40/55a, 50/39a, 68/48a), to be forgiving (Q. 45/14a), or to turn away from those who reject God (Q. 53/29a). In all of these verses, a distinction is made between *ma'nā* and *lafẓ*; since these verses are not phrased in the form of a command, it is only the *ma'nā*, or sense, of the verse that is abrogated, not the actual phrasing.

Remarkably, the sword verse, which abrogated no fewer than 124 other verses, is itself considered to have been abrogated by the conditional clause with which it concludes: 'But if they repent, and perform the prayer, and pay the alms, then let them go their way; God is All-forgiving, All-compassionate.' Small wonder, then, that Ibn al-'Aṭā'iqī refers to the sword-verse as one of the marvels (*'ajā'ib*) of the Qur'ān![57]

Similar to *āyat al-sayf* is *āyat al-zakāt* which specifies who is to receive charity, and abrogates every other verse dealing with this subject: by my count, however, only three verses are so affected: Q. 2/215, 7/199a, and 9/34.

The distinction of remaining in force for the longest amount of time before being abrogated is conferred upon the words 'and I know not what shall be done with me or with you' in Q. 46/9: 'Say: "I am not an innovation among the Messengers, and I know not what shall be done with me or with you. I only follow what is revealed to me; I am only a clear warner." ' This verse was revealed in Mecca in the year AD 612. For the next ten years, the polytheists in Mecca used to insult Muḥammad by saying, 'How is it possible for us to follow a man who does not know what shall be done with himself or his followers?' And for the first six years after the *hijra*,

[56] On the significance of this, see the discussion of *tartīb*, below.
[57] Ibn al-'Aṭā'iqī, p. 53.

the hypocrites of Medina insulted Muḥammad in a similar manner.[58] Then, in the year AD 628, several verses were revealed which clarified the phrase 'what shall be done with me': 'Surely, We have given thee a manifest victory . . . God is All-knowing, All-wise' (Q. 48/1–4). But Muḥammad's followers, although pleased, were not entirely relieved, because Q. 48/1–4 did not clarify their fate. Then, we are told, God revealed Q. 33/47: 'Give good tidings to the believers that there awaits them with God great bounty.' Still later, Q. 48/5 was revealed, informing the believers that they would be admitted into paradise. Finally, when the Medinese hypocrites and Meccan polytheists objected that God had still not clarified the phrase 'what shall be done with you', God revealed Q. 48/6, which refers to the punishment of the male and female hypocrites, and the male and female polytheists.[59] These verses, collectively, abrogated Q. 46/9b, which had been revealed sixteen years earlier; no other abrogated verse remained in force for as much time as this one.

The *naskh* specialists also considered it unusual that a single verse should contain both an abrogated command and its abrogator. According to Ibn Salāma's father, Abū 'Abd Allāh al-Qāsim ibn Salāma, there is only one verse in the Qur'ān 'which combines both the abrogating and the abrogated' (*jama'a'l-nāsikh wa'l-mansūkh*), namely, Q. 5/105; 'O believers, look after your own souls. He who is astray cannot hurt you, if you are rightly guided.' Al-Qāsim ibn Salāma apparently maintained that the phrase 'He who is astray cannot hurt you' was abrogated by the phrase 'if you are rightly guided', and that this was the only occurrence of such a phenomenon in the entire Qur'ān. Now, we have already considered a series of verses which, according to Ibn Salāma and Ibn al-'Atā'iqī, are abrogated by an exceptive clause that occurs in the abrogated verse; we have also considered the sword verse, Q. 9/5a, which, according to the same two authors, was abrogated by the qualifying phrase in Q. 9/5b. Clearly, al-Qāsim ibn Salāma either did not consider the latter examples to constitute instances of abrogation, or considered Q. 5/105 to be qualitively different from them (although the nature of this distinction eludes me). In either case, it should be noted that Hibat Allāh ibn Salāma, the son, is reported to have said, 'It is not as he [viz., al-Qāsim], and others, said',[60] which could either mean that Q. 5/105 does not combine the abrogating

58 Ibn Salāma, pp. 279–80.
59 Ibid. 282.
60 Ibid. 152–4.

and abrogated, or that it is not the only verse in the Qur'ān that does so.

To Q. 7/198 belongs the distinction of being one of the few verses in the Qur'ān in which a phrase that is *muḥkama* (effective) is sandwiched between two phrases that are abrogated: 'Take the abundance, and bid to what is honourable, and turn away from the ignorant.' The phrase 'Take the abundance' is abrogated by Q. 9/102 ('Take of their wealth a freewill offering, to purify them and to cleanse them thereby'); the middle section of the verse, 'And bid to what is honourable', is effective, while the last phrase, 'and turn away from the ignorant', is abrogated by *āyat al-sayf*. Ibn Salāma remarks that this phenomenon makes Q. 7/198 one of the most remarkable of the abrogated verses (*a'jab al-mansūkh*).[61]

Finally, two pairs of abrogated and abrogating verses are singled out as wonders (*'ajā'ib*) because they fail to conform to a pattern that is supposed to have governed the arrangement of pairs of abrogated and abrogating verses in the Qur'ān. This phenomenon deserves close attention, inasmuch as it may shed some light on aspects of the collection of the Qur'ān.

Q. 2/240 reads as follows: 'And those of you who die leaving wives, let them make testament for their wives, provision for one year without expulsion.' According to the legal scholars, the injunction to leave a bequest for one's wife was abrogated by Q. 4/12, which awards a surviving spouse a specific fractional share of the estate, whereas the time period that is stipulated here—one year—was abrogated by Q. 2/234, which reduces this period to four months and ten nights: 'And those of you who die, leaving wives, they shall wait by themselves for four months and ten nights.' What is important to note here is that part of Q. 2/240 is considered to have been abrogated by a verse that is recited/written earlier in the same chapter.

Similarly, Q. 33/52, which places restrictions on the women Muḥammad may marry ('Therefore women are not lawful to thee') is held to have been abrogated by a verse which precedes it in the same chapter, Q. 33/50 ('O Prophet, We have made lawful for thee thy wives whom thou hast given their wages').

Now, according to Ibn Salāma, these are the only two instances in the Qur'ān 'in which the abrogating verse occurs before the

[61] Ibn Salāma, p. 170; see also Ibn al-'Atā'iqī, pp. 52–3 and p. 69, where he notes that the beginning and end of Q. 40/77 were abrogated by *āyat al-sayf*.

abrogated verse', something which he considered unusual, indeed wondrous (*min a'ājīb al-mansūkh*).[62] This statement suggests a rule or principle according to which pairs of abrogated and abrogating verses should be arranged in the Qur'ān: the abrogated verse, which, by definition, must have been revealed prior to the abrogating verse, must also be written/recited before the abrogating verse. Indeed, it is not difficult to find numerous examples of pairs of abrogated and abrogating verses which adhere to this pattern, whether in the same *sūra* (e.g., Q. 2/115 is abrogated by 2/144, and 2/184 is abrogated by 2/185) or across *sūra*s (e.g., Q. 2/180 is abrogated by Q. 4/11–12, and 4/33 is abrogated by 8/75, etc.). But at the same time, there are over 100 exceptions to the rule; eighty-two of the 124 verses abrogated by Q. 9/5, the sword verse, occur later in the Qur'ān than 9/5 itself;[63] and there are at least twenty other exceptions to the rule in cases that do not involve *āyat al-sayf*.[64] What sense, then, are we to make of Ibn Salāma's statement that the abrogation of Q. 2/240 and 33/52 constitutes an exception to a rule that the abrogating verse must follow the verse it abrogates?

Al-Zuhrī's *Naskh al-Qur'ān*, an early treatise, may shed some light on this question.[65] Unlike most of the classical treatises, in which upwards of 250 instances of abrogation are cited, al-Zuhrī's treatise, by my count, refers to only forty-two instances of abrogation. Furthermore, in all but three cases, the abrogated verse does, in fact, precede the abrogating verse. The three pairs of verses that deviate from this rule are Q. 17/24 (abrogated) and 9/113 (abrogating), 17/110 (abrogated) and 7/205 (abrogating), and 15/94–5 (abrogated) and 9/5 (abrogating).[66] Thus, at the time al-Zuhurī's text was compiled, the great majority of the recognized instances of abrogation conformed to Ibn Salāma's pattern.

Ibn Salāma was apparently not the only legal scholar who believed that the abrogated verse must precede the abrogating verse. After mentioning the abrogation of Q. 2/286 by 2/185 (a

[62] Ibn Salāma, pp. 95, 258–9; see also Ibn al-'Atā'iqī, pp. 36–7, 66–7.
[63] See Appendix B.
[64] e.g., in Ibn Salāma: Q. 2/158b (abrogated)–2/130 (abrogating), 2/240–2/234, 2/286–2/185, 4/9–2/182, 4/10–4/5, 4/24–4/12, 4/93–4/48, 5/107–4/14, 6/68–4/139, 6/121–5/5, 9/99–9/97, 13/6–4/48, 16/67–5/90, 29/46–9/29, 42/20–17/18, etc.
[65] See Rippin, 'al-Zuhrī'.
[66] Al-Zuhrī indicates that Q. 2/240 is abrogated by 4/11–12, without mentioning 2/234, and he does not cite 33/52.

deviation from the pattern), he indicates that some scholars 'maintain that God abrogated Q. 2/286 with a verse that comes after it'.[67] Similarly, al-Shāfi'ī's contention that Q. 4/24 was abrogated by 23/5–7, and not by 4/12, as others argued, may have been motivated, in part, by a concern with proper arrangement (*tartīb*) of verses.[68] A statement attributed to 'Alī ibn Abī Ṭālib to the effect that Q. 4/93 was abrogated 'by two verses, one before it and one after it', may have been prompted by similar considerations.[69] Finally, it is reported that when Ibn al-Zubayr asked 'Uthmān ibn 'Affān why he wrote Q. 2/240 in the Qur'ān, when it had been abrogated by 2/234, the latter replied, 'Leave it alone, my nephew. I do not move any part of it from its place.'[70] The reference to 'moving a verse from its place' may be an allusion to the question of *tartīb*.

Despite the fact that the pattern had been violated over a hundred times, later authors continued to make reference to it. Fakhr al-Dīn al-Rāzī (d. 607/1210) cites the phenomenon of *tartīb* as one of the grounds for his contention that Q. 2/240 was not abrogated by 2/234.

> The abrogating verse should be revealed after the abrogated one. If it was revealed subsequently, then it is preferable that it should also be read subsequently, because this arrangement is better. As for the abrogating verse being read before the abrogated one, even if this were permissible in general, still, it is considered to be a poor arrangement, and the word of God must be free from such defects, to the extent possible. Since Q. 2/240 is recited after 2/234, it is preferable that it not be considered to have been abrogated by it.[71]

Thus, in the midst of the seeming 'disorderliness' of the Qur'ān there emerges a conscious, deliberate, and rational pattern according to which a small body of verses are supposed to have been arranged. This phenomenon, which has not previously been recognized, must somehow be reconciled with the various theories that have been advanced to explain the collection of the Qur'ān. Of course, this new datum can easily be integrated into either of the

[67] Ibn Salāma, p. 101.
[68] Ibn al-'Atā'iqī, p. 42.
[69] Ibn Salāma, pp. 142–3.
[70] Al-Bukhārī, *al-Ṣaḥīḥ*, (Leiden, 1862–98), iii. 209–10; Powers, 'Abrogation', 266; Rippin, 'al-Zuhrī', 73.
[71] Al-Rāzī, *al-Tafsīr al-kabīr* (Cairo, 1934–62), vi. 170; see also Powers, 'Abrogation', 289.

two major positions regarding the date at which the Qur'ān was fixed in its present shape. At least two scenarios are possible. (i) The Qur'ān, according to the traditional Muslim account, was revealed to Muḥammad seriatim over a period of twenty-two years. The chronological order in which individual verses had been revealed would have been known to his companions, if only in a rudimentary fashion, and at least some of these companions would have been able to distinguish between pairs of abrogated and abrogating verses. At the time of the collection of the Qur'ān, during the caliphate of 'Uthmān, approximately forty instances of abrogation had been identified, and the persons responsible for fixing the order of the text imposed a distinct pattern of arrangement upon pairs of abrogated and abrogating verses. Subsequently, the scope of the term *naskh* was extended to include many verses that had originally been considered *muḥkama*; but, since the text of the Qur'ān had been fixed by AD 656, it was frequently impossible to adhere to the desired pattern. Nevertheless, certain scholars continued to refer to the pattern, even though it no longer accurately described the phenomenon of abrogation. (ii) It may be objected, however, that the Muslim community could not possibly have worked out the implications of *naskh* as early as, say, AD 656. Thus, if one accepts the traditional Muslim account of the collection of the Qur'ān, then the pattern that has been identified is merely a coincidence. But the pattern can be integrated with the theory of sceptics, such as Wansbrough, who argue that the Qur'ān was not fixed in its final shape for at least a century after Muḥammad's death. During the course of the first century AH, *naskh* could have emerged as an important hermeneutical device designed, first and foremost, to reconcile discrepancies that had arisen between the Qur'ān and the *fiqh*. Over the course of the century, a small corpus of forty abrogated and abrogating verses were identified, fitted into a chronological grid according to which the former was revealed prior to the latter, and, finally arranged in the Qur'ān in such a way that, in any given pair of abrogated and abrogating verses, the sequence in which the two members of the pair appear reflects the chronological order in which they were supposedly revealed. Then, during the course of the second and third centuries AH, the scope of the term *naskh* was extended so that it was no longer possible to adhere to the pattern. God knows best!

APPENDIX A
ABROGATED VERSES ACCORDING TO IBN SALĀMA

Sūra 2: 3, 62, 83, 109, 115b, 139, 158b, 159, (5/3*), 178a, 180, 183, 184, 190b, 191, 192, 196a, 215, 217, 219a, 219b, 221, 228a, 229b, 233a, 240, 256a, 256a, 282, 284b, 286.
Sūra 3: 20b, 28b, 86–8, 97b, 102, 111, 145b, 186.
Sūra 4: 7, 8, 9, 10, 15, 17, 22a, 23, 24, 29, 33, 42, 63, 64b, 71, 80b, 81, 83, 90, 91, 92b, 93, 145.
Sūra 5: 2b, 13, 33, 45, 102a, 105a, 106b, 107, 108a.
Sūra 6: 15, 66b, 68, 70, 91b, 104b, 106, 107, 108, 112, 121, 135, 137, 158.
Sūra 7: 183a, 199a, 199c.
Sūra 8: 1, 33, 61a, 65, 72b, 73.
Sūra 9: 1, 5a, 7, 34, 35, 39, 41, 80, 98.
Sūra 10: 15b, 20, 41, 46, 99, 102, 108b.
Sūra 11: 12b, 15, 121–2.
Sūra 13: 6, 40.
Sūra 14: 34b.
Sūra 15: 3, 85, 88, 89, 94b.
Sūra 16: 67, 82, 106b, 125.
Sūra 17: 23b, 24, 54, 110.
Sūra 18: 29.
Sūra 19: 39, 59b, 71, 75, 84a.
Sūra 20: 114b, 130, 136.
Sūra 21: 98–100.
Sūra 22: 52, 68, 78.
Sūra 23: 54, 96.
Sūra 24: 3, 4, 6, 27, 31, 54b, 58.
Sūra 25: 68–9.
Sūra 26: 224–6.
Sūra 27: 92.
Sūra 28: 55.
Sūra 29: 46, 50.
Sūra 30: 60.
Sūra 32: 30.
Sūra 33: 48, 52.
Sūra 34: 25.
Sūra 35: 23.
Sūra 36: 76.
Sūra 37: 174–5, 178–9.
Sūra 38: 70, 88.
Sūra 39: 3b, 13, 15, 39, 40, 41b, 46.
Sūra 40: 12b, 55b.
Sūra 41: 34.
Sūra 42: 5b, 6b, 15b, 20, 23, 39–40, 48.
Sūra 43: 83, 89.
Sūra 44: 59.
Sūra 45: 13.
Sūra 46: 9, 35.
Sūra 47: 4, 37.
Sūra 50: 29, 45.
Sūra 51: 19, 54.
Sūra 52: 31, 48.
Sūra 53: 29, 39.
Sūra 54: 6.
Sūra 58: 12.
Sūra 60: 8, 9.
Sūra 70: 5, 42.
Sūra 73: 1, 5, 10, 19.
Sūra 74: 11.
Sūra 75: 16.
Sūra 76: 8, 24.
Sūra 80: 11.
Sūra 81: 28.
Sūra 86: 17.
Sūra 88: 22.
Sūra 95: 8.
Sūra 103: 2.
Sūra 109: 6.

APPENDIX B

VERSES ABROGATED BY *ĀYAT AL-SAYF* ACCORDING TO IBN SALĀMA

Sūra 2: 83, 139, 190, 191, 192, 217, 256.
Sūra 3: 20b, 28b.
Sūra 4: 63, 80b, 81, 83, 90, 91.
Sūra 5: 2b, 102.
Sūra 6: 66b, 91b, 104b, 106, 107, 108, 112b, 135, 137b, 158b.
Sūra 7: 183a, 199c.
Sūra 8: 73.
Sūra 9: 5a, 7.
Sūra 10: 20, 41, 46, 99, 102, 108b, 109b.
Sūra 11: 12b, 121–2.
Sūra 13: 40.
Sūra 15: 3, 85, 88, 89, 94b.
Sūra 16: 82, 106b, 125.
Sūra 17: 54.
Sūra 19: 39, 75, 84a.
Sūra 20: 130, 136.
Sūra 22: 68.
Sūra 23: 54, 96.
Sūra 24: 54b.
Sūra 27: 92.
Sūra 28: 55.
Sūra 29: 50.
Sūra 30: 60.
Sūra 32: 30.
Sūra 33: 48.
Sūra 34: 25.
Sūra 35: 23.
Sūra 36: 76.
Sūra 37: 174–5, 178–9.
Sūra 38: 70, 88.
Sūra 39: 3b, 15, 39–40, 41b, 46.
Sūra 40: 12b.
Sūra 41: 34.
Sūra 42: 6b, 15b, 48.
Sūra 43: 14.
Sūra 46: 35.
Sūra 47: 4.
Sūra 50: 29, 45.
Sūra 53: 29, 39.
Sūra 54: 6.
Sūra 60: 8–9.
Sūra 68: 44, 48.
Sūra 70: 42.
Sūra 73: 10.
Sūra 74: 11.
Sūra 76: 8, 24.
Sūra 86: 17.
Sūra 93: 22.
Sūra 95: 8.
Sūra 109: 6.

7

The Rhetorical Interpretation of the Qur'ān: *i'jāz* and Related Topics

ISSA J. BOULLATA

I

THE powerful effect of the Qur'ān on the minds of those who first heard it recited in the lifetime of Muḥammad is reflected in the text of the Holy Book itself. Muḥammad's contemporaries were certainly not rhetoricians or literary critics. But they had sufficient innate abilities to recognize the verbal power of the Qur'ān[1] and thus to react to it positively or negatively. Those who opposed its message accused Muḥammad of things that were meant to dismiss the Qur'ān as an authentic divine revelation and negate Muḥammad's claim to prophethood. Noting the Qur'ān's spell and its enchanting influence on new converts,[2] they charged that its enthralling words recited by Muḥammad were mere magic and that they were only the speech of ordinary human beings (Q. 74/24–5). Associating the rhythmic wording of the Quranic message and its recurring periods of rhyme and assonance with the style of pagan Arab poets and even more with that of soothsayers, they accused Muḥammad of being a poet (*shā'ir*) and a soothsayer (*kāhin*). Muḥammad's detractors were aiming not only at defaming the Quranic style but also at degrading the source, and hence the authenticity, of his message claimed to be from God. A poet was believed to have an inspiring demon (*shayṭān*), and a soothsayer was thought to have contact with mysterious, non-human forces often represented by various idols (*aṣnām*). Furthermore, Muḥammad was accused of being a *majnūn*, someone possessed by *jinn*, a madman, hence not a

[1] See, e.g., the account given in Ibn Hishām, *al-Sīra al-nabawīya*, ed. Muṣṭafā al-Saqqā, Ibrāhīm al-Abyārī, and 'Abd al-Ḥafīẓ Shalabī, 2nd edn. (Cairo, 1955), 270–1, of al-Walīd ibn al-Mughīra's view of the verbal power of the Qur'ān and his advice to Muḥammad's opponents.

[2] See, e.g., ibid. 342–6 for an account of how 'Umar ibn al-Khaṭṭāb, a staunch opponent of Muḥammad, had a change of heart on reading a Quranic passage that his sister Fāṭima was trying to conceal from him.

true prophet worthy of being listened to, believed, and followed at the cost of abandoning the tribal gods of tradition (Q. 36/36). Worse still, his unheard-of Quranic self-styled revelation was said to be mere fabrication (Q. 38/7) in which he was being helped by other people (Q. 25/4). It was said to be made of the stuff of dreams and falsehood (Q. 21/5). Even later on, when Muḥammad's message was beginning to take root and hold its ground, the Quranic text, particularly its didactic narrative parts, were considered by opponents to be mere tales, legends, or fables of the ancients capable of being imitated (Q. 8/31 and 25/5).

In the face of this barrage of accusations, the Qur'ān retorted with continual strong denials and by affirming the divine source of Muḥammad's revelation, and even by challenging the opponents in various ways. The Qur'ān declared that Muḥammad was no soothsayer, or madman, or poet (Q. 52/29–31). His recitation was that of a noble messenger, a revelation from God (Q. 69/40–3). It was not poetry, but rather a clear reminder and warning which was to be recited (Q. 36/69–70). At any rate, poets were followed by wrongdoers and went astray except for believing ones, as the Qur'ān asserted (Q. 26/224–7).

One of the effective ways in which the Qur'ān retorted was to challenge its opponents and Muḥammad's by repeatedly asking them to produce anything like it. When they claimed he invented it, they were challenged by the Qur'ān to produce a discourse like it (Q. 52/33–4). And when they claimed he fabricated it, they were challenged to bring forth ten similar fabricated *sūra*s and seek the help of anybody but God for that purpose (Q. 11/13). On another occasion, the Quranic challenge was even reduced to the production of one *sūra* only (Q. 10/38). But in a defiant and authoritative affirmation, the Qur'ān said conclusively that if humans and *jinn* were to combine their efforts, they would not produce a similar Qur'ān even if they helped one another (Q. 17/88). And in a later passage, it further asserted that sceptical opponents would definitely never be able to produce even a single *sūra* similar to any of its *sūra*s (Q. 2/23–4).

II

The fact that the Quranic challenge (*taḥaddī*) has never been taken up successfully, either in Muḥammad's lifetime or later on,[3] gave Muslim thinkers cause to consider this as a divine authentication of the Qur'ān and proof of the veracity of his prophethood. This argument was put forward by several Arab writers among the early Muslim philologists, but most forcefully by the Mu'tazilī al-Jāḥiẓ (d. 255/869), particularly in his *Ḥujaj al-nubūwa* where he said that the pagan Arabs who were masters of verbal eloquence were unable to rise to the Quranic challenge, in spite of strong motivation on account of their tribal pride and their opposition to Islam, and in spite of the fact that meeting the challenge would have been easier for them than engaging the Muslims in battle as they did, only to lose eventually.[4]

By the early part of the third/ninth century, this Quranic phenomenon of rendering humans incapable of imitating the Holy Book or any part of it in content and form came to be referred to as *i'jāz* (incapacitation). Developing into a technical term by the end of that century, it referred from then on to the miraculous inimitability of the Qur'ān.

Under the influence of early Muslim thinkers like al-Jāḥiẓ and others who emphasized the eloquence of the Qur'ān, the word *i'jāz* later became increasingly associated with the Qur'ān's rhetorically unsurpassable and sublime style. Some thinkers, however, believed that the idea of *i'jāz* should not be too narrowly identified with the unique stylistic supremacy of the Qur'ān. Early in the discussion, the Mu'tazilī al-Naẓẓām (d. 232/846) introduced the concept of the *ṣarfa* (turning away). He maintained that the *i'jāz* of the Qur'ān

[3] There were a few attempts recorded in the Islamic tradition. What remains of their texts, understandably suppressed by orthodoxy, are snippets of ludicrous parodies that have a hollow ring to them and that do no credit to their authors. See, e.g., al-Ṭabarī, *Annales* (Leiden, 1879–1901), i. 1933–4; and al-Bāqillānī, *I'jāz al-Qur'ān*, ed. Aḥmad Ṣaqr (Cairo, [1954]), 238–40. For an account of other intended or attempted imitations of the Qur'ān, see Ignaz Goldziher, *Muslim Studies*, ed. S. M. Stern (London, 1971), ii. 363–5. See also Rudi Paret, 'The Qur'ān, I', in A. F. L. Beeston, T. M. Johnstone, R. B. Serjeant, and G. R. Smith, eds., *Arabic Literature to the End of the Umayyad Period* (Cambridge, 1983), 212–13. Paret says the Quranic challenge 'was not meant seriously but as a rhetorical device', ibid. 215. For an analysis of recently published fragments imitating the Quranic style and attributed to Ibn al-Muqaffa', see Josef van Ess, 'Some fragments of the *Mu'āraḍat al-Qur'ān* attributed to Ibn al-Muqaffa'', in Wadād al-Qāḍī, ed., *Studia Arabica et Islamica: Festschrift for Iḥsān 'Abbās on his Sixtieth Birthday* (Beirut, 1981), 151–63.

[4] Al-Jāḥiz, 'Ḥujaj al-Nubūwa', in Ḥasan al-Sandūbī, ed., *Rasā'il al-Jāḥiẓ* (Cairo, 1933), 143–4. For a similar argument exalting the Quranic eloquence, see also 'Alī ibn Rabban al-Ṭabarī (d. *c.*250/864), *Kitāb al-dīn wa'l-dawla* (Cairo, 1923), 44–5.

consisted in God's preventing the Arabs from imitating it by turning them away from that potentiality and taking away their competence and knowledge. This notion was accepted only by a few, like Hishām al-Fuwaṭī (d. *c.*218/833), 'Abbād ibn Sulaymān (3rd/9th century), and al-Rummānī (d. 386/996). But the general Muslim consensus rejected the concept of *ṣarfa* and continued to hold to the stylistic supremacy of the Qur'ān as an inseparable component of the idea of *i'jāz*, constituting with other components the *mu'jiza*, the confirmatory miracle of Muḥammad's prophethood, specially heightened in view of his illiteracy. Other components of *i'jāz* were argued to be the contents of the Qur'ān, including its information about the distant past, its prophecies of coming mundane events and future eschatological happenings, its statements about God, the world of spirits, and the universe, and its proclamations about man and society—all of which were deemed beyond the knowledge of any human being, let alone an unlettered one like Muḥammad.

The literature on the idea of *i'jāz* continued to grow from the third/ninth century onwards. There was general acceptance of the *i'jāz* as a miracle proving Muḥammad's prophethood. But what constituted this miracle was a subject that continued to engage Muslim thinkers as works on it multiplied. In 1933, Abdul Aleem surveyed the major extant works that developed it into a Muslim doctrine.[5] In the 1950s, Na'īm al-Ḥimṣī offered a more detailed survey of the literature on the development of the theological doctrine and its creedal and aesthetic ramifications.[6] More recently, in 1964, 'Abd al-Karīm al-Khaṭīb devoted the whole first volume of his two-volume book, *I'jāz al-Qur'ān*, to an analysis of previous works on the topic as an introduction to his own view expounded in the second volume.[7]

In view of the extensive literature on this subject and the helpful surveys of it just mentioned, we will confine ourselves in the limited

[5] Abdul Aleem, "Ijazu'l-Qur'ān [*sic*]', *IC* 7 (1933), 64–82 and 215–33.

[6] Na'īm al-Ḥimṣī, *Ta'rīkh fikrat i'jāz al-Qur'ān* (Damascus, 1955), originally a series of articles under the same title in *Majallat al-majma' al-'ilmī al-'Arabī*, 27 (1952), 240–63; 418–33; 571–86; 28 (1953), 61–78; 242–56; 29 (1954), 104–14; 239–51; 417–24; 573–9; 30 (1955), 106–13; 299–311.

[7] 'Abd al-Karīm al-Khaṭīb, *I'jāz al-Qur'ān* (Cairo [1964]), i, *al-I'jāz fī dirāsāt al-aqdamīn* and ii, *al-I'jāz fī mafhūm jadīd*. Reprinted as: *I'jāz al-Qur'ān: al-i'jāz fī dirāsāt al-sābiqīn. Dirāsa kāshifa li-khaṣa'iṣ al-balāgha al-'Arabīya wa ma'ayīrihā*, i. (Beirut, 1975); and *I'jāz al-Qur'ān fī dirāsa kāshifa li-khaṣā'iṣ al-balāgha al-'Arabīya wa ma'āyīrihā: al-i'jāz fī mafhūm jadīd*, ii (Beirut, 1975).

space of this article to a brief account of only some of the most important contributions to the development of the idea of *i'jāz* beyond what has been said above.[8]

III

One such contribution is al-Rummānī's *al-Nukat fī i'jāz al-Qur'ān.*[9] It is one of the earliest systematic works having the word *i'jāz* in their title. Its main thrust is the rhetorical uniqueness of the Qur'ān, though it also discusses related topics. According to its Mu'tazilī author, there are seven components to the idea of *i'jāz*, and they are: (i) the abandonment of imitating the Qur'ān despite abundant motives, (ii) the Qur'ān's challenge to everyone, (iii) the *ṣarfa*, or God's turning of humans away from imitation, (iv) the Qur'ān's *balāgha*, that is, its rhetoric, its aesthetic effectiveness, (v) the Qur'ān's truthful information concerning future events, (vi) the Qur'ān's breach of custom, that is, in literary genres, and (vii) analogy of the Qur'ān to all other inimitable miracles.

Of these components, al-Rummānī writes at length only about *balāgha* which he defines as 'the conveying of meaning in the best of verbal forms'. The elements of *balāgha* are ten according to him, namely, (i) concision, (ii) simile, (iii) metaphor, (iv) harmony, (v) periodic rhyme and assonance,[10] (vi) paronomasia, (vii) variation, (viii) implication, (ix) hyperbole, and (x) beautiful rendition. He explains each in detail and gives many examples from the Qur'ān affirming that the Qur'ān is the highest kind of *balāgha*, the lower kinds alone being within human powers.

Al-Khaṭṭābī (d. 388/998), a Sunnī contemporary, rejected the concept of *ṣarfa* in his *Bayān i'jāz al-Qur'ān*,[11] since the Qur'ān categorically says (Q. 17/88) that humans and *jinn* will never

[8] For a short account of the development of the idea of *i'jāz*, see Gustave E. von Grunebaum, 'I'djāz', *EI*², iii. 1018–20, and the introduction to his *A Tenth-century Document of Arab Literary Theory and Criticism* (Chicago, 1950). See also my article, 'I'jāz', in *Encyclopedia of Religion* (New York, 1987) v. 87–8.

[9] Published in *Thalāth rasā'il fī i'jāz al-Qur'ān*, ed. Muḥammad Khalaf Allāh and Muḥammad Zaghlūl Salām (Cairo, n.d.), 67–104.

[10] *Fawāṣil*, a term which von Grunebaum renders as 'rhythmization' in his *A Tenth-century document*, 118.

[11] Published in *Thalāth Rasā'il*, 17–65. For a French translation and study, see Claude-France Audebert, *Al-Ḫaṭṭābī et l'inimitabilité du Coran: Traduction et introduction au Bayān i'ǧāz al-Qur'ān* (Damascus, 1982).

produce the like of the Qur'ān, whereas the *ṣarfa* implies they could if only God had not deterred them. He equally rejects the idea of Quranic prophecy of future events as a component of *i'jāz*, because not every verse of the Qur'ān tells of the future and because the Quranic challenge (Q. 2/23) is to produce one *sūra* of it without specification of content matter. He accepts the rhetorical uniqueness of the Qur'ān as a component of its *i'jāz*, but he says he wants to be specific in this regard and not like his predecessors.

Al-Khaṭṭābī argues that all speech is made up of three elements: (i) words conveying meaning, (ii) ideas subsisting in words, and (iii) structure organizing both. He maintains that humans cannot imitate the Qur'ān because their knowledge does not encompass all the words of Arabic, all the ideas in them, and all the varieties of structure. Furthermore, they cannot imitate the Qur'ān because it has the most eloquent wording, conveying the best ideas, presented in the most beautiful structure. Al-Khaṭṭābī stresses the fact that rhetorical effectiveness results not only from the choice of words but also from the order in which words are put. A change of wording or of order alters the meaning otherwise intended or impairs the beauty otherwise obtained.

Al-Khaṭṭābī gives detailed analysis of Quranic verses as examples of his approach and shows excellent literary taste and subtlety. He ends his treatise by pointing to the powerful psychological effect of the Qur'ān as an aspect of its *i'jāz* resulting, not from its imagery as al-Rummānī believed, but from the totality of its rhetorical uniqueness.

Al-Bāqillānī (d. 403/1013), an Ash'arī theologian who authored one of the earliest comprehensive books on the subject entitled *I'jāz al-Qur'ān*,[12] accepts the rhetorical uniqueness of the Qur'ān and the excellence of its style, but he does not think that *i'jāz* consists in this alone. He considers the Qur'ān's information about future events as the first component of its miraculous character. The second is that, despite Muḥammad's illiteracy and ignorance of the

[12] The best edition is that of al-Sayyid Aḥmad Ṣaqr (Cairo, [1954]). On al-Bāqillānī, see J. Bouman, *Le Conflit autour du Coran et la solution d'al-Bāqillānī* (Amsterdam, 1959), with bibliography. See also Angelika Neuwirth, 'Ṭarīqat al-Bāqillānī fi iẓhār i'jāz al-Qur'ān', in Wadād al-Qāḍī, ed., *Studia Arabica et Islamica*, 281–96 (Arabic section), in which she studies al-Bāqillānī's method of deducing Quranic *i'jāz* from his empirical, stylistic analysis of *naẓm* and its rhythm of *kalimāt* (structural rhetorical units) within Quranic verses and she disagrees with G. von Grunebaum's contention that al-Bāqillānī did not put *i'jāz* on an empirical basis.

contents of the books of the ancients, the Qur'ān gives accounts of great happenings from the creation of Adam onwards to Muḥammad's prophethood. As for its style, he says: 'it is original structure, wonderful composition, reaching the ultimate in rhetoric to the extent that creatures' inability to achieve it is recognized'. He adds that its unprecedented excellence, despite the length of the Qur'ān and its variety of subjects, remains of one sublime quality, unlike the writings of the best authors, which are invariably uneven. To prove the uncustomary character of the Quranic style, al-Bāqillānī quotes several eloquent orations and epistles of Muḥammad, his companions, and others for contrast with the Qur'ān by the reader. He also offers a detailed literary critique of Imru'l-Qays's *mu'allaqa* and of al-Buḥturī's *lāmīya*, both acclaimed masterpieces of poetic achievement, and he points out what he considers to be weaknesses and defects in them. Furthermore, al-Bāqillānī makes a detailed study of the Arabic figures of speech occurring in the Qur'ān and used by the poets. Basing his argument on these acts of comparison, he concludes that the Qur'ān is superior to all literary products in Arabic. His vigorous support of the rhetorical uniqueness of the Qur'ān, however, is accompanied by reservation because *i'jāz*, in his view, does not depend on rhetoric, though it is enhanced by it.[13] For much rhetoric can be learnt, and it is what cannot be learnt of it that indicates *i'jāz*.[14] The Qur'ān's rhetoric is of the inimitable sublime kind that runs evenly through all the Holy Book. Human rhetoric, on the other hand, can be neither sublime nor even, in any literary product.

In contrast, the Mu'tazilī theologian 'Abd al-Jabbār (d. 415/1025) insists on the stylistic excellence of the Qur'ān as an intrinsic constituent of its *i'jāz*, and he emphasizes that it is its *faṣāḥa* (eloquence) that has rendered the Arabs unable to imitate it. In volume xvi of his extensive *al-Mughnī fī abwāb al-tawḥīd wa'l-'adl*, he explains that *faṣāḥa* results from the excellence of both wording and meaning, but not necessarily in any particular literary genre.[15] He says that there are degrees of *faṣāḥa* depending on the choice of words and the manner they are arranged in a text with a view to proper syntax and rhetorical effect.[16] 'Abd al-Jabbār does not ignore the importance of meaning but he emphasizes that it is

[13] Al-Bāqillānī, *I'jāz al-Qur'ān*, 169–70.
[14] Ibid. 417.
[15] See 'Abd al-Jabbār al-Asadābādī, *al-Mughnī fī abwāb tawḥīd wa'l-'adl*, xvi, *I'jāz al-Qur'ān* (Cairo, 1960), 197.
[16] Ibid. 199.

faṣāḥa that gives meaning its excellence, and that the Qur'ān's *faṣāḥa* is of the highest rank.

The choice and arrangement of words, referred to as *naẓm*, were discussed in earlier works entitled *Naẓm al-Qur'ān*, such as those of al-Jāḥiẓ, now lost, al-Sijistānī (d. 316/928), al-Balkhī (d. 322/933), and Ibn al-Ikhshīd (d. 326/937). Other authors discussed aspects of *naẓm* in books of other titles such as al-Khaṭṭābī, al-Bāqillānī, and 'Abd al-Jabbār. But it was 'Abd al-Qāhir al-Jurjānī (d. 470/1078), an Ash'arī theologian, who elaborated and systematized the theory of *naẓm* in his *Dalā'il al-i'jāz* and related it to all figures of speech in his *Asrār al-balāgha*.[17] He argued that single words as such have no specific distinction over one another and that ideas as such do not exist without words, hence they cannot be judged separately. It is *naẓm* that creates distinctive style by the choice and arrangement of words to bring out meaning. Words arranged differently convey different meanings. Thus the best style is one which has the best construction possible for the meaning intended, and that is achieved by choosing the most expressive words for the purpose and placing them in the most likely arrangement. According to al-Jurjānī, the Qur'ān uses the best *naẓm* which, when the Arabs heard it, they realized they were unable to match.[18] Because degrees of stylistic excellence are subtle, only taste and sensibility based on long aesthetic experience and literary knowledge can help one achieve discernment.[19]

Al-Jurjānī may be considered to be the earliest author to analyse *naẓm* at length and expound a theory of meaning in Arabic stylistics.[20] Following him, others offered better organization of materials such as Fakhr al-Dīn al-Rāzī (d. 606/1209) and al-Sakkākī (d. 626/1229), but many among them may be rightly charged with submerging the study of Arabic rhetoric in complicated, dry rules.[21]

However, as far as the rhetorical interpretation of the Qur'ān

[17] *Dalā'il al-i'jāz*, ed. Muḥammad 'Abduh and Muḥammad al-Shanqīṭī, annotated and published by Rashīd Riḍā (Cairo, 1321/1902). *Asrār al-balāgha*, ed. Hellmut Ritter (Istanbul, 1954). There are other editions of both books.

[18] *Dalā'il al-i'jāz*, 42. See further, al-Jurjānī, *al-Risāla al-shāfiya* in *Thalāth rasā'il*, 105–44.

[19] *Dalā'il al-i'jāz*, 192 and 343–51.

[20] See the study on him by Kamal Abu Deeb, *Al-Jurjānī's Theory of Poetic Imagery* (Warminster, 1979). See further the bibliography in ibid. 324–33.

[21] See Shawqī Ḍayf, *al-Balāgha: taṭawwur wa ta'rīkh* (Cairo, 1965).

goes, there is no book on Qur'ān exegesis that has better used the growing science of rhetoric in understanding the sacred text and shedding light on its *i'jāz* and its inimitable beauty and expressiveness than *al-Kashshāf* of al-Zamakhsharī (d. 538/1144).[22] In spite of the Mu'tazilite doctrines that permeate this work, Muslims hold it in high esteem, not least because of its immense contributions to rhetorical exegesis. Whereas al-Jurjānī used examples from Arabic poetry more than from the Quranic text to build up his theory of *naẓm* and expound his analysis of figures of speech, al-Zamakhsharī's book is a verse-by-verse running commentary on the Qur'ān, occasionally using quotations from Arabic poetry as additional proof-texts, but consistently taking advantage of every sentence or phrase treated seriatim to analyse the stylistic elements in it that lead to its aesthetic effectiveness, and repeatedly showing the matchless excellence of the Quranic text and its meaning. He often makes cross-references to other verses of the Qur'ān in his commentary to reinforce his analysis. Putting to practical purposes al-Jurjānī's theories of construction and meaning, al-Zamakhsharī goes even beyond him in elaborating details of rhetorical analysis and in uncovering further rhetorical elements that escaped his predecessor.[23]

Later medieval writers hardly added anything new on *i'jāz* and its analysis.[24] A major development in a related field was the fact that the science of rhetoric (*balāgha*) was eventually divided into three branches: *'ilm al-ma'ānī*, *'ilm al-bayān*, and *'ilm al-badī'*,[25] the study of which, however, was increasingly encumbered with sterile complications and barren discussions almost totally divorced from

[22] Al-Zamakhsharī, *al-Kashshāf 'an ḥaqā'il ghawāmiḍ al-tanzīl* (Beirut, 1947) in 4 vols. There are other editions (without the word *ghawāmiḍ* in the title). For studies on al-Zamakhsharī and his *al-Kashshāf*, see Muṣṭafā al-Ṣāwī al-Juwaynī, *Manhaj al-Zamakhsharī fī tafsīr al-Qur'ān wa bayān i'jāzihi* (Cairo, 1959); Aḥmad al-Ḥūfī, *al-Zamakhsharī* (Cairo, 1966); and Darwīsh al-Jundi, *al-Naẓm fī kashshāf al-Zamakhsharī* (Cairo, 1969). For further information, see Dionisius A. Agius, 'Some Bio-bibliographical Notes on Abū'l-Qāsim Maḥmūd b. 'Umar al-Zamakhsharī', in *Al-'Arabiyya (Journal of the American Association of Teachers of Arabic)*, 15, nos. 1–2 (1982), 108–30.

[23] See esp. Ḍayf, *al-Balāgha*, 219–70.

[24] Al-Zarkashī (d. 794/1392), *al-Burhān fī 'ulūm al-Qur'ān* (Cairo, 1972), and al-Suyūṭī (d. 911/1505), *al-Itqān fī 'ulūm al-Qur'ān* (Cairo, 1951), summarize the efforts of predecessors in Quranic studies and compile encyclopaedic information including sections on *i'jāz*.

[25] For short accounts, see *EI*[2] i. 857–8 (*badī'*), 981–3 (*balāgha*), and 1114–16 (*bayān*), v. 898–902 (*al-ma'ānī wa'l-bayān*).

literary texts and aesthetic pursuits. They contributed to no new creative interpretations of the Qur'ān for several centuries.

IV

In the twentieth century, Muḥammad 'Abduh (d. 1905) returned to a common sense of rational simplicity and directness, and he discussed *i'jāz* briefly in his *Risālat al-tawḥīd*,[26] omitting detailed analysis of the syntactical and rhetorical elements of the Quranic style and concentrating on the inimitable miracle as proof of Muḥammad's prophecy, unmatched by Arabs and others. Muṣṭafā Ṣādiq al-Rāfi'ī (d. 1937), on the other hand, devoted a whole volume to *I'jāz al-Qur'ān wa'l-balāgha al-nabawīya*,[27] in which he asserts that *i'jāz* consists in two things, namely, the insufficiency of human capability to attempt the miracle and the persistence of this inability throughout the ages.[28] He repeats the argument for the unmatchable style (*uslūb*) of the Qur'ān which the Arabs recognized they could not imitate because of its overpowering eloquence and psychological effects.[29] He then gives a detailed analysis of *naẓm* by studying its three linguistic elements: (i) the letters and their sounds, (ii) the words and their sounds, and (iii) the sentences and their words.[30] He concludes that the Quranic *naẓm* is the highest type of composition because of its superhuman perfection.

Although much modern Qur'ān exegesis 'is still largely traditional',[31] there are a few attempts at introducing a new approach to the issue of *i'jāz*. I am not thinking here of the so-called 'scientific' interpretation of the Qur'ān in which modern scientific principles and discoveries are read into the Quranic text and all modern science is deduced from it, hence the claim that the Qur'ān forestalls modern science[32] and the attendant claim that herein lies its *i'jāz*. Nor am I thinking of Rashad Khalifa's computerized

[26] Muḥammad 'Abduh, *Risālat al-tawḥīd*, ed. M. Rashīd Riḍā, 16th edn. (Cairo, 1373), 144–51. But see his longer discussion in *Tafsīr al-Qur'ān al-ḥakīm*, 4th edn. (Cairo, 1373), i. 190–229 at Q. 2/23–4.

[27] Muṣṭafā Ṣādiq al-Rāfi'ī, *I'jāz al-Qur'ān wa'l-balāgha al-nabawīya*, 6th edn. (Cairo, 1956).

[28] Ibid. 156. [29] Ibid. 213–40. [30] Ibid. 241–82.

[31] J. J. G. Jansen, *The Interpretation of the Koran in Modern Egypt* (Leiden, 1974), 17.

[32] Ibid. 35–54. See also J. M. S. Baljon, *Modern Muslim Koran Interpretation (1880–1960)* (Leiden, 1961), 88–98.

research of the Qur'ān that led him to believe the *i'jāz* lies in a consistent mathematical code system based on the number 19 which, he argues, is the proof of the miracle of the Holy Book unveiled by him in printouts that he diligently produces as a visual presentation of a long-hidden secret.[33] All these efforts are forced in one way or another.

I am, rather, thinking of attempts that have come to consider the principles of Arabic rhetoric developed in the past as insufficient to probe the aesthetic character of the Arabic text of the Qur'ān because, at best, they do not go beyond analysis and assessment of the single sentence. In his book, *al-Naẓm al-fannī fi'l-Qur'ān*,[34] 'Abd al-Muta'āl al-Ṣa'īdī tries to look at the Qur'ān as a whole. Basing himself on the Islamic tradition regarding the chronological order of the *sūras* of the Qur'ān, and on certain notions of *'ilm irtibāṭ al-āyāt* (the science of the relationship of verses), especially the ideas of Burhān al-Dīn al-Biqā'ī (d. 885/1480) in *Naẓm al-durar fī tanāsub al-āy wa'l-suwar*,[35] al-Ṣa'īdī tries to show that each *sūra* is a well-knit unit constructed around a main theme with an introduction, a logical enlargement of the subject, and an ending. Furthermore, he tries to show the connections that bind one *sūra* to the one following it in the received Quranic text. His approach, however, is strictly thematic and topical, and his aim is to show the unity of the Quranic message and its harmonious continuity in its literary or textual presentation. He is not interested in studying the aesthetic aspects of this unity and harmonious continuity. His ultimate aim, as he explains in the epilogue,[36] is to prepare the way for the appearance of *al-muṣḥaf al-mubawwab*, a Qur'ān in which the margins are not used to indicate its quantitative division and sub-division into *ajzā'* (parts), *aḥzāb* (portions), and *arbā'* (quarters), but rather to indicate the sections into which each *sūra* is divided with regard to the elements of the theme developed in it, and to show the harmony of its interrelated ideas and the order of its total structure.[37]

[33] Rashad Khalifa, *Quran: Visual Presentation of the Miracle* (Tucson, 1982). See also his annotated translation of the Qur'ān, *Quran: The Final Scripture (Authorized English Version)* (Tucson, 1981).

[34] 'Abd al-Muta'āl al-Ṣa'īdī, *al-Naẓm al-fannī fi'l-Qur'ān* (Cairo, n.d.).

[35] For manuscripts of this book, see *GAL* ii. 142 and *SI* 178.

[36] Al-Ṣa'īdī, *al-Naẓm al-fannī*, 375–8.

[37] I have not seen the *muṣḥaf mubawwab* referred to by Jansen, *Interpretation*, 14, n. 46, which, he says, appeared in 1969 compiled by Muḥammad Bāqir

In contrast, Sayyid Quṭb (d. 1966) did give his attention to a study of the aesthetic aspects of the Quranic style in an article published in 1939.[38] He developed his approach more fully in 1944, concentrating on the stylistic unity of the Qur'ān in a book entitled *al-Taṣwīr al-fannī fī'l-Qur'ān*.[39] He also applied it in greater detail to Quranic scenes of resurrection in his book *Mashāhid al-qiyāma fī'l-Qur'ān*.[40] All along he felt the need for a new approach to study the *i'jāz* and find the general principles of the artistic beauty in the Qur'ān and the pervading characteristics which distinguished that beauty from all other expressions of verbal beauty in Arabic literature.[41] In his view, al-Zamakhsharī succeeded only occasionally in perceiving it, while al-Jurjānī did arrive at the greatest success possible for a scholar of his age and could have achieved a breakthrough but was bogged down with the issue of 'meaning and wording'.[42]

Quṭb recognizes that scholars mention three elements in the contents of the Qur'ān that are commonly believed to constitute its *i'jāz*, namely (i) its meticulous legislation that is good for all times and places, (ii) its information about the unknown that comes true in future years, and (iii) its sciences on the creation of the universe and man.[43] But he holds that this is true of the Qur'ān as a whole, and does not explain why the Arabs were impressed by it even when only a few *sūra*s of it had been revealed before any of the above contents. His explanation is that the Qur'ān, right from the beginning of revelation, had an uncanny verbal power to influence hearts and minds because of its way of expression.

According to Quṭb, the preferred way of expression in Quranic

al-Muwaḥḥid al-Abṭaḥī with reference to his *al-Madkhal ilā al-tafsīr al-mawḍū'ī* (Najaf, 1969), 8. The book of al-Sayyid Muḥammad Bāqir al-Ṣadr, *Muqaddimāt fī'l-tafsīr al-mawḍū'ī li'l-Qur'ān* (Beirut and Kuwait, 1980), is a series of lectures on the Qur'ān using what he terms a topical (*mawḍū'ī*) exegetical method as opposed to the traditional one he terms disjunctive (*tajzī'ī*), and comes out with a unitary Quranic world-view on history, man, society, and nature.

[38] See Sayyid Quṭb, 'al-Taṣwīr al-fannī fī'l-Qur'ān al-karīm', *al-Muqtaṭaf*, 94, no. 2 (Feb. 1939), 206–22 and no. 3 (Mar. 1939), 313–18.

[39] Sayyid Quṭb, *al-Taṣwīr al-fannī fī'l-Qur'ān*, 3rd printing (Cairo, n.d. [1951?]).

[40] Sayyid Quṭb, *Mashāhid al-qiyāma fī'l-Qur'ān* (Cairo, n.d.).

[41] Sayyid Quṭb, *al-Taṣwīr*, 32.

[42] Ibid. 26–31. See also Sayyid Quṭb, *al-Naqd al-adabī: uṣūluhu wa manāhijuhu* (Cairo, 1960), 129–32 for a brief discussion of al-Jurjānī to whom the book is dedicated as the first Arab literary critic to have established criticism on a scientific and theoretical basis without sacrificing its artistic and spiritual nature (ibid. 3).

[43] Quṭb, *al-Taṣwīr*, 17.

style is artistic *taṣwīr* (portrayal, representation). Apart from legal material which forms only a small part of the Qur'ān, over three-quarters of the Holy Book exhibits one uniform and established way, one pervasive and consistent characteristic, that may have variations but is, in the final analysis, informed by one great rule—the rule of *taṣwīr*.[44]

Quṭb argues that the Qur'ān speaks in palpable images to express abstract ideas and psychological states, to depict events and scenes perceived by the senses, and to portray human types and human nature. The Quranic style imparts vividness, immediacy, and dynamism to its images so that abstract ideas take on shape or movement; psychological states become perceptible tableaux or spectacles; events and scenes, and stories turn into actual and dramatic appearances; human types are fleshed out as present and living beings; and human nature becomes embodied and visible. *Taṣwīr* in the Qur'ān is not a stylistic embellishment: it is an established method, a comprehensive characteristic, using variations in colour, movement, tone, and sound, and employing harmonious patterns and artistic sequences to offer an effective image to the eyes, the ears, the senses, as well as the imagination, the heart, and the mind.[45] Meaning and wording do not exist separately, and it is because of the way the Qur'ān fuses them together in its style based on *taṣwīr* that it achieves its distinction and powerful effect.[46]

Throughout his two books *al-Taṣwīr al-fannī* and *Mashāhid al-qiyāma*, Quṭb quotes the Qur'ān and analyses at length the texts chosen to support his view. He leaves no doubt at the end of his analysis that he has brought a fresh insight to the issue of *i'jāz*.

Another modern scholar of note in this respect is 'Abd al-Karīm al-Khaṭīb, who published a two-volume work entitled *I'jāz al-Qur'ān* in 1964.[47] In the second volume of this work, al-Khaṭīb presents the idea of *i'jāz* in what he calls 'a new understanding', which is his own. According to him, there are four aspects to the Qur'ān's *i'jāz*, all of which contribute to its miraculous character and its incapacitating, powerful effect.

The first of these is the fact that the Qur'ān deals with absolute truth (*al-ṣidq al-muṭlaq*). It treats of all universal, religious, and mundane realities and presents them to humankind for what they are.

[44] Ibid. 32–4 and 206.
[45] Ibid. 35 and 196–204.
[46] Ibid. 194–5.
[47] See n. 7, above.

The second is the authoritative tone of the Qur'ān because of its exalted provenance (*'ulūw al-jiha*). The Qur'ān speaks in the manner of one who possesses and controls everything, supervises and determines everything, without being obstructed or deterred in any way.

The third is the Qur'ān's excellence of rendition (*ḥusn al-adā'*), which al-Khaṭīb equates with the *naẓm*, that is, the composition and style of the Qur'ān whereby superb ideas are presented in the most beautiful and perfect form. This, he says, is the aspect of *i'jāz* that most scholars have dealt with at length because of its manifest uniqueness.

The fourth aspect is the Qur'ān's spirituality (*rūḥānīya*), for the Qur'ān conveys God's *amr* (command, decree, judgement, will), and it is a spirit proceeding from His Spirit that has put on speech and been clothed in words.[48]

These ideas have obvious a priori theological premisses, a fact which highlights many other discussions on *i'jāz*. One modern scholar of note, however, wanted to base her interpretation on philological principles only: she is 'Ā'isha 'Abd al-Raḥmān, widely known by her pseudonym Bint al-Shāṭi'.[49] As far as I know, she is the first Muslim woman ever to write Qur'ān exegesis—a two-volume work, *al-Tafsīr al-bayānī li'l-Qur'ān al-karīm*, published in Cairo in 1962 and 1969, and reprinted. She has other books on Quranic studies,[50] all of which are admittedly said to follow the method she acquired from her professor at Fu'ād I University in Cairo (later her husband), Shaykh Amīn al-Khūlī (d. 1966).[51] His method is expounded in his book, *Manāhij tajdīd fi'l-naḥw wa'l-balāgha wa'l-tafsīr wa'l-adab*.[52] He himself never wrote an exegesis

48 'Abd al-Karīm al-Khaṭīb, *I'jāz al-Qur'ān . . .*, 2nd edn. (Beirut, 1975), ii. 193–250.

49 See I. J. Boullata, 'Modern Qur'ān Exegesis: A Study of Bint al-Shāṭi''s Method', *MW* 64 (1979), 103–13. See also Jansen, *Interpretation*, 68–76. For biographical information on her, see C. Kooij, 'Bint al-Shāṭi': A Suitable Case for Biography?', in Ibrahim A. El-Sheikh, C. Aart van de Koppel, and Rudolph Peters, eds., *The Challenge of the Middle East: Middle Eastern Studies at the University of Amsterdam* (Amsterdam, 1982), 67–72.

50 See a partial list of seven books in Boullata, 'Modern Qur'ān Exegesis', 104, n. 1, to which may be added, among others, *Min asrār al-'Arabīya fi'l-bayān al-Qur'ānī* (Beirut, 1972) and *al-Qur'ān wa qaḍāyā al-insān* (Beirut, 1972).

51 On Amīn al-Khūlī, see Jansen, *Interpretation*, 65–8 and *passim*.

52 Cairo, 1961; see esp. pp. 307–17. For a summary of his method, see Boullata, 'Modern Qur'ān Exegesis', 104–5.

apart from a number of essays treating selected Quranic topics,[53] but he strongly advocated a topical approach to the study and exegesis of the Qur'ān, and argued for a philological interpretation based on the chronological sequence of the text and the semantics of its own usage of Arabic.[54]

In her book *al-I'jāz al-bayānī li'l-Qur'ān wa Masā'il Ibn al-Azraq* published in Cairo in 1971, 'Ā'isha 'Abd al-Raḥmān disagrees with those who ascribe the *i'jāz* of the Qur'ān to anything but its unique style, although she recognizes that *i'jāz* defies all attempts at definition. She humbly ventures certain philological observations and arrives at conclusions, not all of which are without theological overtones. She agrees with al-Khaṭṭābī and al-Jurjānī regarding Quranic *naẓm* and that a word cannot be differently placed in a sentence without impairment of meaning or loss of beauty.[55] But she goes beyond them both in perception and argument. According to her, not even one letter or one particle in the Qur'ān is otiose or elliptic. Even the mysterious letters which were variously explained in over twenty unlikely ways by predecessors are for her meaningful openings of certain *sūra*s, their function being (1) to draw attention to the fact that the Qur'ān is made up of language consisting of similar letters joined together and composed miraculously into matchless revelation leading to *i'jāz*, and (2) to introduce material that refers to the Qur'ān, the Book or the revelation, and mentions its opponents, its challenge to them, and its support by God despite opposition.[56] Prepositions that have been considered by grammarians and exegetes as otiose (*zā'id*) are not only used for emphasis, as is known, but are used so in certain constructions exclusively and not in others, as her painstaking survey shows.[57] The ideas of grammarians and exegetes that certain particles are to be considered elliptical (*maḥdhūf*) is shown to be incorrect,[58] as for example at Q. 2/184 where *alladhīna yuṭīqūnahu* ('those who endure it') is believed by some to mean *alladhīna lā yuṭīqūnahu* ('those who do not

[53] Such as: *Min hadyi'l-Qur'ān: al-qāda . . . al-rusul* (Cairo, 1959); *Min hadyi'l-Qur'ān: fī Ramaḍān* (Cairo, 1961); and *Min hadyi'l-Qur'ān: fī amwālihim* (Cairo, 1963).

[54] Amīn al-Khūlī, *Manāhij Tajdīd*, 304–7.

[55] 'Ā'isha 'Abd al-Raḥmān, *al-I'jāz al-bayānī* (Cairo, 1971), 126.

[56] Ibid. 166–7. This view agrees with that of certain past exegetes like al-Ṭabarī, al-Zamakhsharī, ibn Kathīr, and al-Rāzī, though 'Ā'isha 'Abd al-Raḥmān develops it further with fresh conclusions. See ibid. 139–43.

[57] Ibid. 168–77.

[58] Ibid. 178–86.

endure it'), 'it' being the fast of Ramaḍān. 'Ā'isha 'Abd al-Raḥmān argues that the phrase is affirmative and that the negative *lā* is not necessary, otherwise the Qur'ān would have used it. Her interpretation is that the Qur'ān refers to those who, on fasting, endure so much hardship that their sufferance is exhausted, such as the terminally ill or frail old persons. They should make sacrifice by feeding a needy person rather than performing the fast, just as the rest of the verse says.[59]

Furthermore, 'Ā'isha 'Abd al-Raḥmān has shown by pinpointed evidence that the Qur'ān chooses its wording very meticulously and that no vocable can be replaced by what some linguistics usually call a synonym,[60] even when it is derived from the same root.[61] For example, *ānasa* in Quranic usage consistently means seeing something pleasant and comforting, whereas *abṣara* means seeing in general.[62] Similarly, *zawj* always means spouse in the context of procreation, whereas *imra'a* means wife in the context of barrenness or widowhood.[63] Likewise, *ins* refers invariably to humans in full visibility and geniality as contrasted with *jinn*, whereas *insān* always refers to man as a responsible being, capable of bearing God's trust and being tested by good and evil.[64]

'Ā'isha 'Abd al-Raḥmān studies inductively other aspects of Quranic usage and offers fresh ideas and new interpretation, uncovering certain consistencies never observed before, such as those regarding the use of the passive voice in Quranic scenes of the day of resurrection which, in her view, emphasize the passivity of the universe and the spontaneity of all creation in obeying the overwhelming events of the day.[65] These and other observations of hers transcend traditional Arabic syntax and rhetoric as she attempts to capture the reality that lies behind Quranic expression. Her conclusion is that the Qur'ān, being neither prose nor verse, is a literary genre of its own that is of the highest eloquence and of matchless stylistic perfection.

[59] Ibid. 184.
[60] Ibid. 198–214. See also Boullata, 'Modern Qur'ān Exegesis', 109–10.
[61] 'Ā'isha 'Abd al-Raḥmān, *al-I'jāz al-bayānī*, 215–20.
[62] Ibid. 200–1.
[63] Ibid. 212–13.
[64] Ibid. 216–18.
[65] Ibid. 222–5. See also Boullata, 'Modern Qur'ān Exegesis', 110.

V

In modern Western scholarship, the focus of attention in Quranic studies has not been aesthetic and rhetorical, the field having been dominated to a large degree by critical concerns.[66] When Western scholars dealt with the idea of *i'jāz*, they merely placed it in the historical perspective of a growing Islamic theology[67] or in the dialectical experience of a developing Muslim community.[68] Those among them who treated Quranic style were motivated by a desire to analyse and dissect the text for purposes of establishing its chronological sequence of revelation, such as Theodor Nöldeke and Régis Blachère,[69] or for purposes of shedding light on its redaction, such as Richard Bell and John Wansbrough.[70] These Quranic studies are, of course, legitimate and apply the methods and principles of textual and historical criticism developed in the study of other sacred books and literatures, though their conclusions must often remain speculative. But other studies seem to have ulterior motives transparently covered by thin scholarship.

In contrast, Gustave E. von Grunebaum dealt with *i'jāz* in particular, and rightly placed it in the context of the development of Arab literary theory and criticism[71] as well as of Islamic thought in general.[72] But he seems to have had little sympathy with what it really meant to Muslim religiosity and piety.

[66] For a survey of Western scholarship on the Qur'ān, see *Bell's Introduction to the Qur'ān*, rev. and enlarged by W. Montgomery Watt (Edinburgh, 1970), 173–86. See also Charles J. Adams, 'Islamic Religious Tradition', in Leonard Binder, ed., *The Study of the Middle East* (New York, 1976), esp. 61–6; Charles J. Adams, 'Islam', in C. J. Adams, ed., *A Reader's Guide to the Great Religions*, 2nd edn. (New York, 1977), esp. 421–8; and A. T. Welch, 'al-Ḳur'ān', *EI*[2] v. 400–29.

[67] See, e.g., A. S. Tritton, *Muslim Theology* (London, 1947) and J. Bouman, *Le Conflit autour du Coran.*

[68] See *QS*, esp. 77–83 and 231–2, where it is argued that the dogma of *i'jāz* developed more as an assertion of the canonical status of the Qur'ān in the Muslim community than as proof of Muḥammad's prophethood. See also his *The Sectarian Milieu: Contents and Composition of Islamic Salvation History* (Oxford, 1978).

[69] *GdQ*. See also Régis Blachère, *Le Coran: Traduction selon un essai de reclassement des sourates*, 3 vols. (Paris, 1947–51).

[70] Richard Bell, *Introduction to the Qur'ān* (Edinburgh, 1953) and id., *The Qur'ān Translated, with a Critical Re-arrangement of the Surahs*, 2 vols. (Edinburgh, 1937–9). See also id., 'The style of the Qur'ān', *Transactions of the Glasgow University Oriental Society*, ii (1942–4), 9–15, and *QS*, chs. 1 and 2.

[71] Von Grunebaum, *A Tenth-century Document.*

[72] Ibid. See also id., 'I'djāz', *EI*[2] iii. 1018–20.

One of the few Western scholars to recognize this meaning and to appreciate the aesthetic and rhetorical features of the Qur'ān was Arthur J. Arberry, who made a most erudite and sensitive study of the message as well as the intricate and richly varied rhythms of the Qur'ān[73] which, according to him, constitute its 'undeniable claim to rank amongst the greatest literary masterpieces of mankind'.[74]

Introducing his own translation of the Qur'ān, Arberry says, 'This very characteristic feature—"that inimitable symphony," as the believing Pickthall described his Holy Book, "the very sounds of which move men to tears and ecstasy"—has been almost totally ignored by previous translators.'[75] He devised 'rhythmic patterns and sequence-groupings' in his English translation to correspond with the Arabic patterns and sequences that, he deemed, varied according to subject-matter. His translation is one of the best English renditions and, indeed, note its title *The Koran Interpreted*, one of the finest rhetorical interpretations. Though he admits it is a 'poor echo . . . of the glorious original',[76] he says, 'Each Sura will now be seen to be a unity within itself, and the Koran will be recognized as a simple revelation, self-consistent to the highest degree.'[77]

In conjunction with current interest in structural (and structuralist) studies of literature, including Arabic literature,[78] Quranic studies are taking advantage of this approach which may throw light on the nature of *iʿjāz*. In this regard, mention must be made of the study of Angelika Neuwirth, *Studien zur Komposition der mekkanischen Suren*,[79] which, though limited to the Meccan *sūra*s, offers an interesting insight. The author says the Qur'ān has yet to be treated in its own essence as a liturgical discourse and a recitation text. She accepts the *sūra*s as units, and proceeds to

[73] Arthur J. Arberry, *The Holy Koran: An Introduction with Selections* (London, 1953), see 'Introduction', esp. 18–19.

[74] Arthur J. Arberry, *The Koran Interpreted*, 2 vols. (London, 1955), also in 1 vol. (Oxford, 1964). See ibid., introduction, x.

[75] Ibid. x. [76] Ibid. xiii. [77] Ibid. xi.

[78] See, e.g., Mary Catherine Bateson, *Structural Continuity in Poetry: A Linguistic Study in Five Preislamic Arabic Odes* (Paris and The Hague, 1970); Renate Jacobi, *Studien zur Poetik der altarabischen Qasīde* (Wiesbaden, 1971); Andras Hamori, *On the Art of Medieval Arabic Literature* (Princeton, 1974); Raymond P. Scheindlin, *Form and Structure in the Poetry of al-Muʿtamid ibn ʿAbbād* (Leiden, 1974); and Michael Zwettler, *The Oral Tradition of Classical Arabic Poetry: Its Character and Implications* (Columbus, Ohio, 1978).

[79] Berlin and New York, 1981.

analyse the intricate patterns of rhythm, rhyme, and assonance within each as well as the structure of the verses and their sequence-groupings that contribute to the form of the specific unique genre that a *sūra* is.

Pierre Crapon de Caprona's work, *Le Coran: aux sources de la parole oraculaire: Structures rhythmiques des sourates mecquoises*[80] also studies the Meccan *sūra*s in a similar fashion, but attempts to go further in his systemic investigation of the rhythmic continuity within the *sūra*s and looks for what he calls 'metrical affinities'. He finds mono-patterned *sūra*s, double-patterned *sūra*s, and multi-patterned *sūra*s, though he also claims there are 'textual deteriorations' where the text does not fit his theory.

Both these studies of Quranic rhythms and structures in the *sūra*s and the whole Qur'ān need refinement, if only because of a large degree of arbitrariness they exhibit, and the fact that their grasp of accentuation in the original Arabic text remains to be improved. But they point to the need for a new trend in Western scholarship that studies the Qur'ān for itself and as a literary text, a scripture having its own proper referential system, and independently of any other consideration.

Yet the Quranic 'inimitable symphony' is not only rhythm and rhyme. Other aspects of it must also be addressed in a similar fresh way for a fuller understanding.[81] As Charles J. Adams has said, 'The study of the Qur'ān for its own sake as the basic document of the Islamic community must now be fostered and encouraged, and study of this kind stands in the first rank of importance for the deepened understanding of Islam as a religion.'[82] Only after such studies are undertaken can the idea of *i'jāz*, among other things, be better apprehended and its function in the Islamic faith be more fully appreciated.

[80] Paris, 1981.

[81] See, e.g., Fazlur Rahman, *Major Themes of the Qur'ān* (Minneapolis, 1980); Kenneth Cragg, *The mind of the Qur'ān* (London, 1973); Toshihiko Izutsu, *Ethico-religious Concepts in the Qur'ān* (Montreal, 1966); and Daud Rahbar, *God of Justice* (Leiden, 1960). Mention should also be made of Mohammed Arkoun's efforts in Quranic studies, particularly his book *Lectures du Coran* (Paris, 1982) where he calls for new methodologies and attitudes that go beyond philology, transcending the historical criticism of Orientalists and the traditionalism of Muslim scholars, and insisting that the language of the Qur'ān is religious language to be treated differently from other uses of language, with the help of modern semiotic and structural approaches and in the light of anthropological and socio-cultural disciplines. See esp. in ibid., 'Comment lire le Coran?', 1–26 and 'Peut-on parler de merveilleux dans le Coran?', 87–108.

[82] Charles J. Adams, 'Islamic Religious Tradition', 65.

8

Lexicographical Texts and the Qur'ān

ANDREW RIPPIN

I. LEXICOGRAPHY AND LEXICOLOGY

Lexicography has been classically understood to be the art of dictionary-making. In modern times, this art has become a more fully conscious science (according to some people, at least) under the influence of linguistic theory; in fact, it would now be argued that underlying every dictionary can be said to be some sense of a theory of language. European dictionaries of the nineteenth century, for example, often reflect the emphasis of unusual detail and explanation tied to history, and generally encompass the whole language and provide a normative slant while emphasizing the part played by the written language. All this reflects an understanding of language which is normative in its written form and is supposed to be unchanging in its character; such dictionaries are, in sum, the result of Romantic linguistics with its historical emphasis. The Oxford masterpiece, *A New English Dictionary on Historical Principles*, is, of course, a prime example of the type.

Recent scholarly activity has manifested itself both in the emergence of the study of dictionaries—in itself a historical study—and in the creation of other forms of dictionaries—dictionaries of usage (a linguistic description of language), conceptual dictionaries (synchronic rather than historical or universal), and notional dictionaries (as opposed to alphabetical). As a result, comprehensive works are being supplemented today by inventories of vocabulary used by 'a particular author or field or technique in relation to a precise historical or geographical situation or event'.[1]

Just how the notion of a dictionary is to be defined is somewhat problematic. Some would want to define it stringently such that it is equal to a former sense of 'lexicon', so that the word 'dictionary' becomes reserved for a total inventory of language, however that

[1] Bernard Quedama, 'Lexicology and Lexicography', *Current Trends in Linguistics*, 9 (1972), 436–7.

concept be defined and limited; opposed to dictionaries, therefore, would be things such as 'concordances', 'glossaries', 'vocabularies', and 'word books'.[2] Others[3] see the idea of a dictionary as more inclusive, being defined more simply as a work dealing with lexical meaning. It is in this sense that the word will be used in this paper.

Lexicology has only recently been distinguished as a field of study separate from lexicography. It is the field which attempts to look at the morphological structure and the semantic function of lexical units and to analyse the use of vocabulary.[4] It is, therefore, the science underlying lexicography. One of the crucial questions faced by lexicology revolves around the definition of the lexical unit; some consensus has been reached such that the term is to be identified with 'a complete linguistic sign for which the "consubstantiality" of the name (*significant*) and the sense (*signifié*) will not be questioned, even if determination appears delicate'.[5]

2. APPROACHES TO QURANIC VOCABULARY

In analysing the vocabulary of the Qur'ān, the Arabs of the classical period developed several approaches. The literary genres resulting from this activity have already been outlined in masterful form by John Wansbrough in his *Quranic Studies: Sources and Methods of Scriptural Interpretation*.[6] The aim of this paper, therefore, is fairly modest; what I hope to do here is to clarify and expand the treatment of Wansbrough, adding a little to the scope of his

[2] Allen Walker Read, 'Approaches to Lexicography and Semantics', *Current Trends in Linguistics*, 10 (1973), 166.

[3] Ladislav Zgusta, *Manual of Lexicography* (The Hague and Paris, 1971); also Yakov Malkiel, 'A Typological Classification of Dictionaries on the Basis of Distinctive Features', in Fred W. Householder and Sol Saporta, eds., *Problems in Lexicography: Report of the Conference on Lexicography held at Indiana University, November 11–12, 1960* (Bloomington, 1960), 23.

[4] For a good introductory treatment see Sydney M. Lam, 'Lexicology and Semantics', in Archibald A. Hill, *Linguistics Today* (New York, 1969), 40–9.

[5] Quedama, p. 401.

[6] See pp. 202–27; see also his *The Sectarian Milieu: Content and Composition of Islamic Salvation History* (Oxford, 1978), ch 1. The recent publication of Sezgin's *GAS* viii: *Lexikographie bis ca. 430 H.* (Leiden, 1982) has added immensely to the material available on this topic. Basic works on Arabic lexicography include F. Rundgren, 'La lexicographie Arabe', in P. Fronzaroli, ed., *Studies on Semitic Lexicography* (Firenze, 1973); S. Wild, *Das Kitāb al-'Ain und die Arabische Lexikographie* (Wiesbaden, 1965); J. A. Haywood, *Arabic Lexicography* (Leiden, 1965).

observations, and, most importantly, indicating possibilities for further areas of exploration and attention.

Three kinds of texts are to be examined. The *gharīb* works are the most prominent. These texts are the closest to the modern sense of lexicography; they are dictionaries of 'difficult words'. Note that there is implicit in that statement a comparative sense; included in these dictionaries are words which later authors found difficult to understand in terms of the language usage of their day. Of course, this lexicographical insight of the notion of what difficulty is all about is modified by observations which hold just as true for medieval Arabic works as they do for modern English dictionaries; such dictionaries are constrained by a number of factors including convenience and especially convention, as well as, in modern times, commercial viability. As a result of these factors, certain words simply entered the stock of 'difficult words' and were passed down through the generations as such. Dictionaries of this type work on the level of synonymity, whether that be expressed by a single lexeme or by a phrase. Vocabulary studies such as these go back to the earliest studies of language in many cultures; direct parallels are to be seen in the Greek works from the fifth to the first centuries BC cataloguing 'difficult words' in Homer.[7]

Employing a typology of dictionaries such as that proposed by Yakov Malkiel[8] could provide a number of useful criteria for classifying these *gharīb* works. Malkiel provides a three-fold categorization with ten subdivisions:

i. Range

(*a*) Density of entries in relation to total lexical stock. In theory, there would be no problem of a changing lexicon for the *gharīb* works, since they are based upon a fixed corpus of scriptural text, so the density will only vary according to the author's perception of the task; all will be severely limited compared to the entire stock of Arabic lexemes, but will vary in the proportion of the vocabulary of the Qur'ān treated. The only other variable factor here may be the treatment of variant readings to the text of scripture.

(*b*) Number of languages involved. While no bilingual dictionaries

[7] R. L. Collison, *A History of Foreign-language Dictionaries* (London, 1982), ch. 1.

[8] Malkiel, pp. 3–24. See also Ali M. al-Kasimi, *Linguistics and Bilingual Dictionaries* (Leiden, 1977), ch. 1.

as such have been uncovered in this research, the role of the interlinear translation, because of its very special character, may need to be considered here. The recent review article concerned with Janos Eckmann's *Middle Turkic Glosses of the Rylands Interlinear Koran Translation*[9] by A. J. E. Bodrogligeti brings up this aspect very clearly: 'In dealing with the primary source one must remember that "The Rylands interlinear Koran translation" is not what Turcologists have up to now taken it for: it is not the Qur'ān in three—Arabic, Persian and Turkic—languages. It is the Qur'ān in Arabic with Persian and Turkic interlinear glosses. The glosses translate words or phrases mostly in isolation, irrespective of their grammatical, and often even semantic context.'[10]

(*c*) Extent of concentration on purely lexical data. Here one will have to consider infiltration of commentary (the encyclopedic approach) and excessive verbiage in definition. Itemization of proper names would also be a factor.

ii. Perspective

(*a*) The fundamental dimension, that is, synchronic versus diachronic. Such an issue is of little concern, for the medieval Arab lexicographers seem to have had few qualms over having a mixed historical perspective in their works; dictionaries of the Qur'ān are ahistorical but not synchronic, if by that is meant the absence of archaism. Note, too, that such Quranic dictionaries are not etymological (or diachronic) for the most part, although a text such as *Al-lughāt fī'l-Qur'ān* ascribed to Ibn 'Abbās (d. 68/687)[11] may well be argued to be of some relevance to this category with its identification of tribal dialects, a clear and thorough-going backwards-looking perspective.

(*b*) Arrangement of entries. Possibilities here are conventional (that is, alphabetic, popularly seen as a defining character of a dictionary), semantic, or arbitrary. *Gharīb* works display variation as to whether they are arranged according to the words as actually employed in the Qur'ān or according to the root of the word. They

[9] Budapest, 1976.

[10] A. J. E. Bodrogligeti, 'Ghosts, Copulating Friends and Pedestrian Locusts in Some Reviews of Eckmann's "Middle Turkic glosses" ', *JAOS* 104 (1984), 455.

[11] Printed in numerous versions, e.g., as Ibn Ḥasnūn, *al-Lughāt fī'l-Qur'ān* (Beirut, 1972). On this text see A. Rippin, 'Ibn 'Abbās's *Al-lughāt fī-Qur'ān*', *BSOAS* 44 (1981), 15–25, and id., 'Ibn 'Abbās's *Gharīb al-Qur'ān*', *BSOAS* 46 (1983), 332–3.

also vary in following alphabetical order or the order of occurrence in the text of scripture.

(*c*) The tone of the work. Possibilities here range from detached through preceptive, normative, didactic, to facetious. The normative (that is, a Muslim theological perspective) is universal in the *gharīb* works.[12]

iii. Presentation

(*a*) Definition. The glosses provided in most *gharīb* works are generally very specific as compared to being fully comprehensive for the language or for the text as a whole.

(*b*) Verbal documentation. Two elements enter here. Is the full passage of the text cited in order to provide the context, or are shorter segments or simple bare references given? Is there any indication of frequency of usage? Secondly, what other type of material is adduced to provide a context: literary or oral (living) examples; historical or contemporary material?

(*c*) Graphic illustration. Of this I am not aware of any applicability to Quranic vocabulary texts.

(*d*) Special features. This would include the use of abbreviations, linking words (especially prominent in some texts), indications of pronunciation (perhaps crucial when considering variants), and designation of the social plane of the lexeme (perhaps a phenomenon parallel to the citation of dialects in the aforementioned *lughāt* text).

In the second category of texts to be examined are the works known as *al-wujūh wa'l-naẓā'ir*, which would seem to fall under the modern classification of semantic lexicology. The works deal with homonyms (two words which are spelt in the same manner but which are perceived—either by native speakers and/or etymology[13]—to have different roots because of the inability to determine any connection between two senses of the word) and polysemy (where words have different senses of meaning and can

[12] For the normative character of Arab lexicography, see the work of Lothar Kopf, especially 'Religious Influences on Medieval Arabic Philology', *SI* 5 (1956), 33–59, and 'The Treatment of Foreign Words in Medieval Arabic Lexicology', *Scripta Hierosolymitana*, 9 (1961), 191–205; both articles are reprinted in his *Studies in Arabic and Hebrew Lexicography* ed. M. H. Goshen-Gottstein (Jerusalem, 1976), 19–45 and 247–61 respectively.

[13] See Zugusta, pp. 74 and 77.

be classified according to those different senses). Whether this is taken at a root level or on the level of the form of the word is one matter which needs to be noted. Since these texts deal with the written text of the Qur'ān, as studied by scholars (a significant clarification in light of Wansbrough's understandings of the function of these texts[14]), the question of homophones (words which are spelt differently but sound the same) does not generally arise. Homographs (where words are written in the same way but are pronounced differently) are a phenomenon that exists (most especially as revealed in discussion over variant readings—this may, one should note, provide some material related to homophones also), but that does not appear to enter into the consideration of the *wujūh* texts—another factor impinging on Wansbrough's understanding of the function of these works. In general, one may say that the *wujūh* texts analyse the semantic diversity on the level of context and not by syntax or any other such means. It should be noted that polysemy was studied by the ancient Greeks as a part of their investigations into language; they appear to have desired to develop principles in order to distinguish nuances of senses of words.[15] The Arab use of this mode of vocabulary classification, therefore, has a long heritage prior to the development of Quranic exegesis.

Finally, the phenomenon of the texts known as *mushtabihāt* does not seem to fall easily under any modern scholarly category. Perhaps the best one can do is call the mode of analysis 'phraseological lexicology'.[16] On the other hand, these texts do follow an ancient tradition, like the *gharīb* and the *wujūh* texts, in this case one of 'enumeration of scriptural examples', and therefore it could be argued, on these grounds, that the category lies outside lexicology altogether and that, as such, it performs a totally different function, such as that of homelitic indexation.

[14] See *QS* 202–27.

[15] See Gene B. Gragg, 'Redundancy and Polysemy: Reflections on a Point of Departure for Lexicology', in Donka Farkas, Wesley M. Jacobsen, Karol W. Todrys, eds., *Papers from the Parasession on the Lexicon, Chicago Linguistic Society, April 14–15, 1978* (Chicago, 1978), 174–83.

[16] Cf. Wansbrough's characterization, *Sectarian Milieu*, 61: 'phraseological commocation'.

3. BEGINNINGS OF QURANIC LEXICOGRAPHICAL INTEREST

There are two areas of related lexicographical interest which, while standing somewhat outside the genres of literature being treated in this paper, may well provide the background material from which the lexicographical tradition developed. The first type of material which must be considered, though it is not necessarily historically first, is formed from lexicographical intrusions into the text of the Qur'ān. These consist of simple glosses to the text, and were first isolated by Goldziher and subsequently analysed by Bergsträsser.[17] This material is evidenced in variant readings, and, in fact, lexicographical synonymity is one of the traditional ways of disposing of any supposed significance to the existence of variants within the Quranic textual tradition.[18] Just how the interaction between this kind of material and the lexicographical tradition might have worked is difficult to assert, primarily because of the lack of hard historical data for the ordering of the emergence of the variants; the influence could have worked either way.

Even more significant, perhaps, is the existence of early works of *tafsīr*; examples of commentaries on the Qur'ān which are essentially 'Arabic translations' of the scripture are worthy of note. Most significant in this regard would be the work known as *Tanwīr al-miqbās min tafsīr Ibn 'Abbās*, the work ascribed variously to al-Kalbī (d. 146/763),[19] Ibn 'Abbās,[20] and al-Fīrūzābādī (d. 817/1415),[21] but which has its most likely origins in the third or fourth Muslim centuries.[22] The approach is continued in a work such as *Tafsīr al-Jalālayn* of Jalāl al-Dīn al-Maḥallī (d. 864/1459) and Jalāl al-Dīn al-Suyūṭī (d. 911/1505).[23] Perhaps early lexicographical works should be seen as extracts of such texts, putting into some more readily accessible form the crucial and most

[17] Goldziher, *Richtungen*, 3–32; *GdQ* iii. 57–115, as assessments of extra-canonical readings especially; *QS* 203–4.

[18] See, e.g., Ahmad von Denffer, *'Ulūm al-Qur'ān. An Introduction to the Sciences of the Qur'ān* (Leicester, 1983), 115–16.

[19] *GAS* i. 34–5; *QS* 130–7, 140–6.

[20] *GAS* i. 27.

[21] *GAL* S ii. 235.

[22] See A. Rippin, 'Al-Zuhrī, *naskh al-Qur'ān* and the Problem of Early *tafsīr* Texts', *BSOAS* 47 (1984), 23–4.

[23] In many prints, e.g., Beirut, 1978, with a marginal print of al-Suyūṭī, *Lubāb al-nuqūl fī asbāb al-nuzūl*.

'difficult' pieces of information. The style of commentary found in *Tanwīr al-miqbās*, because it is devoid of most textual and grammatical analysis,[24] many well have lent itself to such lexicographical extraction. Still, the lack of historical evidence makes it hard to argue the matter one way or the other.

4. *GHARĪB* WORKS

'Difficulty', as manifested in the variety of Arabic writings which go under this title, is conceived in a variety of ways: foreign words, dialect words, bedouin words, or lexical oddities (in the tradition of *hapax legomenon*). While some works devoted to Quranic vocabulary tend to isolate one aspect of this 'difficult' tradition, others tend to be more all-inclusive. A few examples will prove illustrative.

The work of Ibn Qutayba (d. 276/889), *Tafsīr gharīb al-Qur'ān*,[25] is a straightforward work presenting the lexical difficulties of the Qur'ān in *sūra* order and providing glosses to each entry generally connected simply by *ay*, with a moderate amount of poetry and proverbial material adduced to support the suggestions. The book is preceded by a treatment of the names of God (a total of 26)[26] and by a list of meanings of words which occur frequently in the Qur'ān and are, for the most part, prominent theological terms.[27] Forty such words are presented in this way.

Al-Sijistānī's (d. 330/942) *Nuzhat al-qulūb fī gharīb al-Qur'ān*[28] is perhaps the most famous book of its type; there are few other books of *tafsīr* listed in Sezgin[29] which have such a large number of manuscript copies still in existence. Al-Sijistānī created a dictionary composed on an alphabetic principle of the first letter of the word as it appears in the text of the Qur'ān,[30] further subdivided according to whether the first vowel of the word is a *fatḥa*, *kasra*, or

24 See *QS* 130–37, 140–6.

25 Ed. A. Ṣaqr (Beirut, 1978).

26 pp. 6–20.

27 pp. 21–37.

28 Available in many editions, here Beirut, 1983 ('third printing'). A. Jeffery, *Foreign Vocabulary of the Qur'ān* (Baroda, 1938), 8 n. 3, makes reference to al-Sijistānī's view on the language of the Qur'ān, but I have not been able to find Jeffery's reference in the edition of al-Sijistānī available to me. On al-Sijistānī's work, see Josef Feilchenfeld, *Ein einleitender Beitrag zum ġarîb al-ḳur'ân nebst einer Probe aus dem Lexikon des Seġestâni* (Wien, 1892).

29 *GAS* i. 43–4.

30 See J. A. Haywood, pp. 96–7, for the historical significance of this.

ḍamma.[31] Within that basic order, the text would appear to follow the sequence of the words as they occur in the Qur'ān. For the most part, the author provides simple glosses bridged by *ay*; intra-Quranic proofs are used frequently, applying the principle of definition by context. Occasionally poetry is adduced and, more frequently, comparisons are made to profane speech (introduced by *yuqālu*, 'one says'). On occasion, also, explanatory exegetical remarks are added, including items such as occasion of revelation reports. On some occasions, the author seems to be led into conceptually related passages.[32] On other occasions, he will cite the number of meaning-aspects (*wajh*) for a given word.[33]

Al-Rāghib al-Iṣfahānī's (d. 502/1108) *al-Mufradāt fī gharīb al-Qur'ān*[34] is a far more complete work and is virtually a complete inventory of Quranic vocabulary rather than a simple dictionary of 'difficult' words. Checking the entries under the letter *thā'*, for example, shows that all words beginning with that letter are included, with the apparent omission of the root *thā'-rā'-yā'*.[35] The author has pursued a rigorous application of alphabetic ordering according to roots, as compared to al-Sijistānī's alphabetic treatment on the word level.[36]

There are a large number of other works in this genre,[37] but these three books are typical ones, dealing with 'difficult' vocabulary on an intuitive, ill-defined level. This is well illustrated by the tremendous variation in the number of words treated in the various texts; there are, as one would indeed expect, no criteria for determining what is a 'difficult' word. At the same time, it is in these kinds of texts that the conventional nature of the enterprise will be most clearly revealed, in that certain words are always considered a part of the stock of *gharīb* lexemes.

There are, however, other works to be included within the consideration of this genre, composed of texts which use different criteria or different lexicological principles than the general type of books in order to isolate words for attention or to provide a

31 See al-Sijistānī, p. 2, for his explanation of this.

32 See, e.g., ibid. 126–7.

33 See, e.g., ibid. 111 on *al-ṣāmid*.

34 Cairo, n.d.

35 See ibid. 76–82.

36 Cf. the treatment by al-Sijistānī of words beginning with *thā'*: pp. 64–7.

37 See, e.g., *GAS* i. 557 (Zayd ibn 'Alī); *GAS* viii. 24, 173, 225 (the famous work of Abū 'Ubayd al-Harawī), 230; see also al-Zarkashī, *al-Burhān fī 'ulūm al-Qur'ān*, ed. Muḥammad Abū'l-Faḍl Ibrāhīm (Cairo, 1957), i. 291–6, for a brief review of the genre.

unifying approach to the topic of 'difficult words'. Foreign words are listed by al-Suyūṭī, for example, in his famous *al-Mutawakkilī*.[38] Elsewhere I have given extensive attention to a text dealing with dialect words attributed to Ibn 'Abbās;[39] this classification is then followed in texts found in al-Suyūṭī and al-Zarkashī (d. 794/1391)[40] (foreign words also find their place in the text). The *Masā'il Nāfi' ibn al-Azraq*[41] is a listing of words whose meanings are known best by the Bedouin, as is proven by the citation of poetry in every instance; while the words treated in such a text may not substantially differ from the collective *gharīb* tradition, the external criterion by which words found their entry into the text is at least specified (be it fictious historically, and spurious in terms of poetical *shawāhid*). There do not appear to be any texts which isolate *hapax legomenon* as such, however.[42]

5. *WUJŪH*

Muqātil ibn Sulaymān (d. 150/767) is universally designated as the first author in this genre. His work goes under a variety of names, *Kitāb al-wujūh wa'l-naẓā'ir* and *al-Ashbāh wa'l-naẓā'ir* being two popular titles.[43] The work contains 186 words presented in some sort of conceptual order, although that is certainly unclear. The initial words treated, *hudā*, *kufr*, and *shirk*, indicate the theological import which the author considered of utmost importance in his treatment of the subject. The analysis provides the number of meanings or aspects (*wujūh*) of each word and a gloss for each meaning, and then provides the parallel passages or analogues (*naẓā'ir*) in which the word is used in that sense. By no means are all

[38] Cairo, 1926, ed. and trans. W. Bell; see also al-Suyūṭī, *al-Itqān fī 'ulūm al-Qur'ān* (2 vol. Ḥalabī edn., Cairo, 1951), i. 135–41, and cf. his *al-Muhadhdhab fīmā waqa'a fī'l-Qur'ān min al-mu'arrab*, published in *al-Mawrid*, i (1971), 101–24.

[39] See n. 11, above.

[40] Al-Zarkashī, i. 282–90; al-Suyūṭī, *al-Itqān*, i. 133–5.

[41] See Rippin, 'Lughāt', 15–16.

[42] Cf., however, Sa'adyā Gaon, *Tafsīr al-sab'īna lafẓat al-farīda*. The very existence of this text raises questions as to whether or not something similar is not to be found somewhere for the Qur'ān. For general considerations, see F. E. Greenspahn, *Hapax Legomena in Biblical Hebrew* (Chico, 1984).

[43] See *QS* 208. The work is published (Cairo, 1975). See also P. Nwyia, *Exégèse coranique et langage mystique* (Beirut, 1970), 25–61, and N. Abbott, *Studies in Arabic Literary Papyri, ii: Qur'anic Commentary and Tradition* (Chicago, 1967), 92–106.

the verses provided in the analysis (that is, the concordance function of the text is incomplete), and the analysis of the number of *wujūh* would seem to be primarily dictated by the context of employment rather than clearly distinguishable meanings. The words treated are, for the most part, religiously significant terms, but a few particles are also included for analysis. Wansbrough's conclusion concerning the text is that its function was to elucidate scriptural imagery, and is therefore exegetical,[44] rather than to provide a neutral index of vocabulary.[45]

Ibn Qutayba's *Ta'wīl mushkil al-Qur'ān*[46] is a text of a different character both from his own contribution to the *gharīb* genre and from many other works in the *wujūh* category. Lexicography is never a straightforward art; the problem of the metaphorical versus literal usage of words, for example, depends upon the reader's perspective and, in the case of the Qur'ān, is very much dependent upon theological presuppositions. Ibn Qutayba appears to recognize the importance of such factors and he acts to get them straightened out first in *Mushkil*, before entering into semantic classifications.[47] The author appears to go through the Qur'ān according to *sūra*s selected in a random order, isolating figures of speech for attention. In this respect, the book is a rhetorical analysis of the Qur'ān along the lines of that of Abū 'Ubayda (d. 210/825), *Majāz al-Qur'ān*,[48] a book which, it could be argued, is of the *gharīb* type.[49] But part of Ibn Qutayba's book is also of the *wujūh* type. He has a chapter which covers both technical and theological words which covers single words with multiple meanings,[50] and also a chapter on words which substitute one for another in certain places, for example, *fī makān 'alā*.[51]

[44] *QS* 211.

[45] A similar approach in the inverse is found in Muqātil *apud* al-Malaṭī, *al-Tanbīḥ wa'l-radd 'alā ahl al-aḥwā' wa'l-bida'* (Istanbul, 1949), 72–80; see *QS* 210–11.

[46] Ed. A. Ṣaqr (2nd printing, Cairo, 1973). On the work see Gérard Lecomte, *Ibn Qutayba (mort en 276/889): L'Homme, son oeuvre, ses idées* (Damscus, 1965), 295–9.

[47] See W. Heinrich, 'On the Genesis of the *ḥaqīqa–majāz* dichotomy', *SI* 59 (1984), 130–2.

[48] Cairo, 1954–62.

[49] See Wansbrough's analysis, '*Majāz al-Qur'ān*: Periphrastic Exegesis', *BSOAS* 33 (1970), 247–66; E. Almagor, 'The Early Meaning of *majāz* and the Nature of Abu 'Ubayda's Exegesis', in *Studia Orientalia Memoriae D. H. Baneth* (Jerusalem, 1979), 307–26; W. Heinrichs, n. 47, above. Note that al-Zarkashī, *al-Burhān*, i. 291, lists this work as one of the *gharīb* genre.

[50] *Mushkil*, 439–563.

[51] Ibid. 565–78.

The work by al-Damaghānī (d. 478/1085), *Iṣlāḥ al-wujūh wa'l-naẓā'ir fī'l-Qur'ān al-karīm*,[52] is very similar to that of Muqātil's, although slightly more expansive. The author states in his introduction that he has examined the work of Muqātil and 'others' but has found them to be lacking because of the omission of too many words. Al-Damaghānī then provides an alphabetic listing of the words, enumerating the different meanings of a given word which are provided by glosses introduced by *ay* after a given verse is cited in support. He then gives the *naẓā'ir* for each meaning, those verses being introduced by *kaqawlihi* or *mithlahā*. The actual analysis provided is frequently the same as that in Muqātil (see, for example, the word *sabab*[53]), but the material has been expanded. Under the letter *alif*, al-Damaghānī provides thirty-eight entries while Muqātil scatters entries for only twenty of these lexemes throughout his book. Both texts treat particles (and here are parallel to Ibn Qutayba, *Ta'wīl mushkil al-Qur'ān*), as well as substantives.

Ibn al-Jawzī's (d. 597/1200) work on *wujūh* is available in two printed versions, *Nuzhat al-a'yun al-nawāẓir fī 'ilm al-wujūh wa'l-naẓā'ir*[54] and *Muntakhab qurrat al-'uyūn al-nawāẓir fī'l-wujūh wa'l-naẓā'ir*.[55] The latter of these is an abbreviated version, prepared according to the author for ready reference, while the former is an expansive treatment ordered alphabetically and numbered according to the number of *wujūh*. The work does not provide any evidence of a reworking of the genre, but rather is a restatement of earlier works. Ibn al-Jawzī's exegetical statements are perhaps the prime contribution. Even then, many of the analyses are preceeded by the statement that: 'Many of the exegetes say that [this word] appears in the Qur'ān with [a certain number] of *wajh*', once again reflecting this conservative and conventional nature of the lexicographical enterprise.

There are a number of other books available on the subject of *wujūh*, for the topic itself seems to have become one of theological importance; al-Zarkashī is explicit in stating that the notion of

[52] See *GAL* i. 373; Beirut, 1970.

[53] See A. Rippin, 'The Exegetical Genre *asbāb al-nuzūl*: A Bibliographical and Terminological Survey', *BSOAS* 48 (1985), 12–14.

[54] Ed. Sayyida Mihr al-Nisā' (Hyderabad, 1974). On the text in general see A. J. Arberry, 'Synonyms and Homonyms in the Qur'ān', *IQ* 13 (1939), 135–9, and Ḥātim Ṣāliḥ al-Ḍāmin, review in *al-Mawrid*, 15 (1986), 169–80.

[55] Ed. Fu'ād 'Abd al-Munajjim (Alexandria, *c.*1979).

wujūh is a part of the miraculous character of the Qur'ān,[56] and looking at a work such as al-Rummānī's (d. 386/996) *al-Nukat fī i'jāz al-Qur'ān*[57] indicates the way this was conceived. While al-Rummānī does not use the *wujūh/naẓā'ir* terminology, his category of *tajānus*[58] is conceived as a very similar phenomenon, although it is not elaborated in any systematic way as found in the *wujūh* texts. Al-Rummānī argues that a part of the aesthetic effectiveness of the Qur'ān is to be found in this notion which he defines as being of two kinds: totally resemblant, where the words are identical but have different meanings, and resemblant as such, where only the same root is employed with the words having different meanings. Notable in al-Rummānī's treatment of the topic is the impact of theology and the *sharī'a* on the analysis. For example, in his treatment of the case of a totally resemblant word-employment in Q. 2/194: *fa-man i'tadā 'alaykum, fa-i'tadā 'alayhi*, 'Whoever commits aggression against you, commit aggression against him', al-Rummānī glosses the phrase as 'that is, repay that person with that which is deserved in a just way, except that God used for the sense of "that which is deserved" the word "commit aggression" in order to confirm the notion of equality in quantity'. For al-Rummānī, there is a difference between the use of the verb *i'tadā* in the first and second cases, the first being used as 'outright aggression', the second being used as 'appropriate force'.[59]

Al-Zarkashī and al-Suyūṭī, as has previously been pointed out by Abdus Sattar,[60] seem to have a slightly different sense of *wujūh* and *naẓā'ir* than some of the earlier writers. *Wujūh* and *naẓā'ir* are seen by these two writers to be different topics, homonyms and synonyms respectively, rather than interrelated subjects. That is, the term *naẓā'ir*, for al-Zarkashī and al-Suyūṭī,[61] is reserved for the study of words with only one *wajh*, while *wujūh* treats those who

[56] Al-Zarkashī, i. 102; also see al-Suyūṭī, *al-Itqān*, i. 141.

[57] Published in *Thalāth rasā'il fī i'jāz al-Qur'ān*, ed. M. Zaghlūl Salām and M. Khalaf Allāh (Cairo, 1956), 75–113.

[58] Al-Rummānī, pp. 99–100.

[59] Ibid. 99.

[60] Muhammad Abdus Sattar, '*Wujūh al-Qur'ān*: A Branch of *tafsīr* Literature', *IS* 17 (1978), 138–40; this article also contains references to other works in the *wujūh* genre, as does *GAS* viii. Especially noteworthy is the text by al-Mubarrad, *Mā ittafaqa lafẓuhu wa-ikhtalafa ma'nāhu* (Cairo, 1931), see *GAS* viii. 98; I have not been able to locate a copy of this book. See also Yaḥyā ibn Sallām, *al-Taṣārif: al-tafsīr al-Qur'ān mimmā ishtabahat asmā'hu wa taṣarrafat ma'ānihi* (Tunis, 1979), especially the editor's introduction.

[61] Al-Zarkashī, i. 102; al-Suyūṭī, *al-Itqān*, i. 141–2.

have many. Note that al-Zarkashī's presentation of *wujūh* is fairly limited; he gives the outline of *hudā* in seventeen *wujūh* and then goes on to quote a few examples of multiple aspects of words on the authority of Ibn Fāris.[62]

Finally, it should be noted that none of the texts examined seems to distinguish either explicitly or implicitly between homonymity and polysemy. That topic probably deserves a fuller and broader-based study.

Wansbrough has argued that lexicographical/phraseological analyses or 'semantic collation'—as found in texts entitled *wujūh*—were constructed for the purpose of asserting the conceptual unity of the Qur'ān in the same way in which the hermeneutic of analogy and the separation into *muḥkam* ('clear verses') and *mutashābih* ('ambiguous verses') functions.[63] Indeed, it is hard to see what other purpose these texts could serve; they certainly have no particular functional attributes, not being designed for easy reference or the like. They may reflect simply an impulse to collect, but underneath that lies a view of the text of the Qur'ān, as indeed Wansbrough has argued. Whether such motivation was actually conscious on the part of the compilers of these texts I would tend to doubt; it is more a case of an underlying assumption being given conceptualization.

6. *MUSHTABIHĀT*

'Alī ibn Ḥamza al-Kisā'ī is famed as a Qur'ān reciter and transmitter of a *qirā'a* of the Qur'ān (one of the 'seven'). He is said to have died somewhere between 179/795 and 192/807. A work known under two titles is ascribed to him: *Kitāb al-mutashābih fī'l-Qur'ān* (manuscript Paris 665/4) and *Kitāb al-mushtabihāt* (manuscript Beyazit 436).[64] As compared to later books with this same title (or at least, that of the Paris manuscript) which deal with the obscurities of the Qur'ān (that is, as a result of Q. 3/7) and often see this term as equivalent to metaphorical expressions, al-Kisā'ī takes the word in the more literal sense of the 'resemblances' in the

[62] Al-Zarkashī, i. 103–4 on *hudā* (from Muqātil); i. 105–11 provides a rather random list of lexemes from Ibn Fāris, *al-Afrād* (see *GAS* viii. 214).

[63] *QS* 215.

[64] See *QS* 212 n. 8; the Beyazit MS is given the title *Kitāb al-mutashābihāt* at the end.

Qur'ān.[65] The text is ordered by the number of occurrences of a given phrase—once, twice, three to ten times, fifteen times, and twenty times—and within each of those a *sūra* order is followed for citing examples. For the most part, verse order is followed within the *sūra* listings, but this is not consistent. When dealing with examples of what are considered unique phraseologies in the Qur'ān, the text selects a certain phrase of Quranic diction and contrasts it to the rest of the Qur'ān either by displaying how that text states something elsewhere or by stating that there is nothing in the Qur'ān like the phrase in question. When the phraseology is not unique (that is, the phrase occurs between two and twenty times), the text cites the examples of identical scriptural statements where they are found in the text.

The text raises two issues. First, on what basis are phrases selected for comparison—lexical, grammatical, theological, word order, inflectional, and/or orthographical? Second, what is the ultimate purpose of the text?

To question one it seems that the text works on all levels, but with the least amount of emphasis on the semantic value of the phrase. For example, a comparison is made between Q. 2/21: 'O people, serve your Lord', and the rest of the Qur'ān where it is stated: 'Fear your Lord.' The point is not that these two sentences mean the same thing but use different words (that is, are working on the semantic–synonym level), but rather it is that the construction is supposedly unique (although Wansbrough points out that the basis on which this uniqueness is asserted is still unclear).[66]

Although there do not appear to be any books which treat the text of the Qur'ān in quite the same way, a similar listing of material is found in al-Zarkashī.[67] Especially significant here is the treatment of the unique instances, where an attempt is made to classify the instances according to their differences (for example, particles present/absent). Al-Zarkashī has thereby attempted to add some sort of system to al-Kisā'ī's beginning exploration of the genre.[68]

[65] See *QS* 212 ff.—Wansbrough terms this 'distributional analysis of Quranic diction'; see also *GAL* S i. 178.

[66] *QS* 213–14.

[67] Al-Zarkashī, i. 112–54, covering unique expressions and then expressions which occur the following number of times: 2 (i. 133), 3 (i. 137), 4 (i. 140), 5 (i. 144), 6 (i. 145), 7 (i. 146), 8 (i. 147), 9 (i. 147), 10 (i. 148), 11 (i. 149), 15 (i. 151), 18 (i. 151), 20 (i. 152), 23 (i. 153).

[68] Al-Zarkashī, i. 112–32; al-Suyūṭī, *al-Itqān*, ii. 114–16, and refs. given there to other works.

Wansbrough has suggested that, one, this mode of analysis is a short step on from the *wujūh* texts—that is, it is a move from semantic distribution to phraseological distribution—and that, two, there is some connection between this approach and later ones under the same title, which differ because of the impact of rhetorical exegesis and the doctrine of *i'jāz*.[69] It could also be suggested, especially in the light of the way al-Zarkashī formulates the 'unique instances', that there is a connection between Abū 'Ubayda's 'periphrastic exegesis' and the *mushtabihāt*.

Sidney Towner's book *Rabbinic 'Enumeration of scriptural examples'*[70] may be of some help in determining the ultimate purpose of these listings of Quranic phrases. Towner states that 'listing' is an ancient phenomenon which was used 'for systematizing observations about nature, geography and man and as pedagogical and mnemonic tools for conveying information to students and posterity'.[71] This kind of listing trend can easily be identified in a book such as the *Sīra* of Ibn Isḥāq (d. 151/768).[72] However, there is, for Towner, a difference between enumeration of proverbial examples, as just defined, and the enumeration of scriptural examples which, while the latter may have evolved from the former, seems to have an exegetical function, at least within the context of Rabbinic literature. Within the Quranic context, this function may be termed a 'hermeneutical tool', acting just as do other terminological devices (*nāsikh/mansūkh*, *muḥkam/mutashābih*, *tafsīr/ta'wīl*) to demonstrate the unity of the scriptural text, be that on a conceptual, phraseological, or semantic level.

7. CONCLUSIONS

With interest increasing in lexicography and lexicology in general, attention to Arabic, and specifically Quranic, data will undoubtedly prove popular and rewarding in the coming years. One area which will repay a full and broad investigation is the historical development of profane and religious lexicography in relationship to the use of poetry as resource material for definitional analyses. The connection of this to the emergence of the arguments concerning

69 *QS* 215.

70 Leiden, 1973.

71 Towner, p. 4.

72 See *Sectarian Milieu*, ch. 1.

the inimitability of the Qur'ān as compared to the human compositions found in poetry will prove crucial.

The citation of the figure of Ibn 'Abbās in the context of much of this lexicographical material must be viewed in terms of the overall picture of the establishment of a fixed religious system called 'Islam';[73] lexicography provides one element, small yet important, in the overall context, most especially the notions related to the status of the Arabic language, but also as connected to the establishment of the Qur'ān as an authoritative source within the emergent Muslim community.

[73] See C. Gilliot, 'Portrait "mythique" d'Ibn 'Abbās', *Arabica*, 31 (1984), 127–84.

PART III

SECTARIAN DIMENSIONS OF INTERPRETATION

9

The Speaking Qur'ān and the Silent Qur'ān: A Study of the Principles and Development of Imāmī Shī'ī *tafsīr*

MAHMOUD AYOUB

SHĪ'Ī piety has occupied an important place in the devotional life of Muslim society. For Muslims, the Qur'ān is a guide through this life and into the next. Thus, the science of understanding the Qur'ān (*tafsīr*) may be regarded as the child of piety, of fear of God's punishment for ignorance and hence disobedience, and of hope in God's mercy and reward for understanding and hence obedience. For the Shī'ī community, the Qur'ān is all that and more. *Tafsīr* is also the child of frustration and disappointment, of hope and exultation. It is the child of the ethos of martyrdom and eschatology. Through *tafsīr*, the link between the faithful and their spiritual guides, the Imāms, is established. *Tafsīr* is the humanization of the divine word and the divinization of the human spirit.

Shī'ī *tafsīr* in its entirety is too vast a subject for any comprehensive treatment, let alone a comparative presentation. Because scholarship has focused on Sunnī Islam, much needs to be done to familiarize the Western student of religion with Shī'ī thought and piety. It is this latter task which this brief study takes as its aim. Turning to a vast corpus of Shī'ī literature that is largely unknown or unread in the West, we shall first present the Shī'ī concept of the Imām in relation to revelation. Then we shall very briefly sketch the history of Shī'ī *tafsīr*, pointing out only its broad lines of development. Then we shall be able to present its main principles. Finally, in order not to keep our discussion purely theoretical, we shall follow the development of *tafsīr* on one crucial verse: verse 67 of *sūra* 5.

1. THE IMĀMS AND THE QUR'ĀN

As the revealed Word of God for Muslims, the Qur'ān has, like all other sacred scriptures, a human dimension without which it cannot be fully understood or appreciated. This dimension is first exemplified in Muḥammad, the recipient of the divine Word and its transmitter and first interpreter for humanity. The second and equally important aspect of this dimension is the Qur'ān's life in the community and its own life through its power and by its authority. Through their unquestioning acceptance of the Qur'ān, successive generations of Muslims have provided strong attestations to its authenticity for them. Through their interiorization of the eternal Word of God, 'free from the limitations of sounds and letters', they have given it power and vitality through the sciences of *tilāwa* or *qirā'a* (recitation or reading), *kitāba* or *naskh* (writing or copying), and *tafsīr* (interpretation or exegesis).

Divine–human communication by means of the Qur'ān is expressed in the two terms for divine revelation: *tanzīl*, literally 'sending down', and *tafsīr*, the human unveiling of its meaning. The process of *tafsīr* continues to grow with the life of the community, guiding it through life's vicissitudes and consoling it in times of despair and tragedy. Yet it may be said that as God transcends creation while remaining the immanent Lord of its history, so also His Word transcends human history while participating in it. The Qur'ān participates in human history in that it is a book of guidance which must be understood and pondered if it is to serve as the moral and spiritual guide for human conduct.[1] It transcends human history, however, in that its real meaning is known only to God.[2] Transcendence is not simply an expression of power and majesty, but also the safeguarding of the absolute against any confusion with the relative. Hence Muslims, and especially Shī'ī Muslims, have insisted that God revealed to Muḥammad both the Qur'ān and its exegesis.[3] The sacred text of the Qur'ān, or what is contained 'between the two covers', is what Muḥammad taught the generality of the faithful. Its exegesis, however, he reserved for the Imāms, the elect of his household (*ahl al-bayt*). The Imāms have a

[1] See Q. 2/1–5, 47/24. [2] See Q. 3/7.

[3] Shaykh al-Ṭā'ifa Abū Ja'far al-Ṭūsī, *Tafsīr al-tibyān*, ed. Aḥmad Ḥabīb Quṣayr al-'Āmilī (Najaf, n.d.), i. 4, author's introduction.

unique relation to the Qur'ān; this gives Shī'ī *tafsīr* its unique character. Islam holds a prophetic view of history. Prophets are seen as humanity's guides to God and as its human models. Adam, who was placed on the earth as God's vicegerent (*khalīfa*),[4] was also the first prophet. This divine vicegerency, however, is not the inheritance of the elect only. This is because Adam and his progeny are seen not only as prophets, but also as imperfect creatures prone to corruption and the shedding of blood on earth. Thus, prophets are distinguished from the rest of humankind by the important quality of protection (*'iṣma*) from error and imperfection. Prophets therefore share in some way with the Qur'ān the divine quality of transcendence.

The Qur'ān stands midway between God and humanity, mediated by Muḥammad, who, for Muslims, is humanity's chief exemplar. Prophets, in turn, stand between the divine Word and humanity, mediated by the Imāms, who are its exemplars. Thus it may be further said that in a special sense, prophets are the vicegerents of God on earth and the Imāms are the vicegerents of the prophets, as well as their successors. Through their humanity, human beings share in a general way the privilege of God's vicegerency, a privilege dependent upon piety and faith.[5] Prophets and Imāms, on the other hand, are distinguished by the inheritance of divine knowledge. Thus the prophet Muḥammad and his descendants, the Imāms, alone know the full meaning of the Qur'ān, since it was to them that it was primarily addressed, and through them to the rest of humankind. In a long dialogue between Ja'far al-Ṣādiq, the sixth Imām of the Shī'ī community, and Abū Ḥanīfa, the founder of one of the four Sunnī schools of jurisprudence, the Imām declared: 'God gave this knowledge [that is, knowledge of the Qur'ān] only to the true People of the Book to whom it was sent down. . . . It belongs to the elect of the descendants of our prophet. . .'[6]

The Qur'ān possesses a special status with God. It was with God, preserved in the well-guarded tablet (*al-lawḥ al-maḥfūẓ*), and its power here on earth is said to be beyond the capacity of the hard mountains to bear.[7] It is for humanity a source of healing and blessing in this life, and of solace and bliss in the life to come.

[4] See Q. 2/30–7.

[5] See Q. 24/55.

[6] Quoted in al-Sayyid Abū'l-Qāsim al-Mūsawī al-Khū'ī, *al-Bayān fī tafsīr al-Qur'ān* (Beirut, 1394/1974), 267.

[7] See Q. 85/22, 59/21.

The Imāms share these qualities with the Qur'ān and have indeed been identified with it. They were with it before creation, formed from God's light. It was for their sake that all things were brought into being. Thus, in the course of a long apologetic introduction, the editor of *Tafsīr al-Qummī* asserts that '[the Imāms] are the purpose of the creation, and the purpose of their creation is the purpose of the Truth [that is, God]'. He argues further that since God created all creatures in order that they may worship Him, it follows that worship cannot be truly achieved without faith in God as He is. Faith cannot be attained except through knowledge. Such knowledge, moreover, can only be communicated by an apostle who speaks on God's behalf and by an Imām who relates the apostle's teachings and interprets his message. The author thus concludes that it is incumbent upon God to appoint the Imām and to guide people to Him. 'It is not therefore farfetched [to assert] that the Qur'ān was sent down concerning them and for them.'[8]

In a long and well-known tradition related by both Shī'ī and Sunnī traditionists (with many variants), the Qur'ān is presented as the 'greater weight' (*al-thaqal al-akbar*) and the Imāms as the 'lesser weight' (*al-thaqal al-aṣghar*). In a version related on the authority of Umm Salama (one of Muḥammad's wives), we are told that during his last illness, the prophet said in the presence of many of his companions: 'I am soon about to be received. . . . I am telling you before I am taken up that I shall leave with you as representatives after me the book of my Lord, and my progeny, the people of my household.'[9] In another version quoted by al-'Ayyāshī in proof of the authority (*walāya*) of 'Alī, it is related that Muḥammad went on to say regarding *ahl al-bayt* that 'the All-Gracious, All-Knowing told me that they [the two weights] shall not be separated until they meet me [on the day of resurrection]. . . . Do not precede them, for you would go astray, and do not fall behind them, for you would perish. Do not teach them, for they are of greater knowledge than you.'[10]

The Qur'ān states that Muḥammad will complain to God on the day of resurrection, saying, 'O Lord, my people have made this

[8] Abū'l-Ḥasan 'Alī ibn Ibrāhīm al-Qummī, *Tafsīr al-Qummī*, ed. al-Sayyid al-Mūsawī al-Jazā'irī (Najaf, 1386), i. 18–19.

[9] Mullā Muḥammad Bāqir al-Majlisī, *Biḥār al-anwār* (Tehran, 1387), xcii. 79.

[10] Abū'l-Naṣr Muḥammad ibn Mas'ūd ibn 'Ayyāsh al-Sulamī al-Samarqandī, *Tafsīr al-'Ayyāshī*, ed. Hāshim al-Rasūlī al-Maḥallātī (Qom, n.d.), i. 4.

Qur'ān abandoned' (Q. 25/30). On the basis of this verse, Shīʿī piety has endowed the Qur'ān with a quasi-human personality. The Qur'ān itself will therefore contend before God with the people, interceding for some and condemning others. Since the two weights are linked in Shīʿī tradition, both will be questioned on the day of judgement as to the people's love for Muḥammad's family and their abiding by the teachings of the Qur'ān; thereby shall they be judged, and rewarded or punished.[11]

It is a well-known principle in the history of religions that traditions relate a previous history which serves as a prelude to a central event around which human history is said to revolve. Thus biblical history and even human wisdom were seen by the early Church Fathers as *preparatio evangelica*. Likewise in Muḥammad, as Seal of the Prophets, and in the Imāms, as his vicegerents, Shīʿī Muslims have seen the *raison d'être* of all creation. Acceptance of their authority is an essential aspect of faith. The sixth Imām declared that 'God made our authority (*walāya*) the pole (*quṭb*) of the Qur'ān and the pole of all scriptures. Around it the clear (*muḥkam*) verses of the Qur'ān revolve; through it scriptures were elucidated and through it faith becomes manifest.'[12]

Prophethood (*nubūwa*) and vicegerency (*waṣīya*) may be seen as concentric circles within which history moves. Every prophet from Adam to Muḥammad had twelve successive vicegerents who inherited his knowledge and carried on his mission. The vicegerents are one with their respective prophets—that is, as extensions of their prophetic existence. The Imāms did not possess revelation (*waḥy*); that was their main distinction from the prophet. They were none the less *muḥaddathūn*, that is, people spoken to by angels. Because Muḥammad was the last prophet and the Qur'ān was the final revelation, the prophetic circle continues only through the *imāma*, which shall continue until the day of resurrection. 'Alī, the first Imām, is said to have challenged his audience, saying, 'Ask me about the book of God! For by God, there is no verse of the book of God sent down by day or night, on a journey or while present [that is, while at home], about which the Apostle of God did not teach me its recitation and exegesis.' Ibn al-Kawwā, a controversial disciple of the Imām, asked, 'What about verses which were sent down while you were not with him?' The Imām

[11] See nn. 9 and 10, above.

[12] Al-ʿAyyāshī, i. 5.

answered, 'Whatever was sent down of the Qur'ān to the Apostle of God in my absence, the Prophet recited it to me when I had returned, saying, "O 'Alī, God sent down after you left such-and-such, and such-and-such is its exegesis." Thus he taught me its exegesis and the reason for its revelation.'[13] It is also related that Ibn 'Abbās, Ibn Mas'ūd, and other companions of Muḥammad learned *tafsīr* from 'Alī, who acquired all his knowledge of the Qur'ān from the prophet, who in turn was taught by God.[14] 'Alī and the Imāms after him knew not only the exegesis of the Qur'ān but that of all previous relevations. Again, 'Alī is said to have declared, 'were the cushion [that is, seat of learning in an assembly] to be doubled for me, I would judge among the people of the Torah in accordance with what God had revealed in it until it returns to God bearing witness that I did judge in accordance with what God revealed in it.' He is said to have asserted the same concerning the Gospel and its people and the Qur'ān and its people.[15]

The Shī'ī community considers the Imāms as associates of the Qur'ān. Therefore, the twelfth Imām, who is believed to be in the world yet concealed from the view of its inhabitants, is daily addressed in the *ziyāra* (pilgrimage liturgy) following the prayers: 'Peace be upon you, O Master of the Age! Peace be upon you, O Friend (*walī*) of the Merciful! Peace be upon you, O Associated (*sharīk*) of the Qur'ān.' It is further believed that the Qur'ān, which 'Alī wrote down from the dictation of Muḥammad, with its true exegesis (*ta'wīl*) was passed down from one Imām to the next and is now with the hidden Imām, who will disclose it and judge by it when he returns as the expected *mahdī*. On the basis of this assertion (as will be seen later), extremist Shī'ī *'ulamā'*, such as al-Kāshānī (the author of the *Tafsīr al-ṣāfī*) and al-Majlisī, have claimed that the Qur'ān we now have has been altered. It is related that the fifth Imām, Muḥammad al-Bāqir, said: 'Had it not been that [some] things were added to the book of God and others deleted, our right would not have been obscured from anyone with discernment. When our *qā'im* [the one raised up by God, that is, the twelfth Imām] shall appear and speak, the Qur'ān will confirm his words.'[16]

Inasmuch as the Imāms possess the true and limitless meaning of the Qur'ān, they keep alive the sacred Book as a moral and spiritual

[13] Al-Majlisī, xcii. 78–9.
[14] Ibid. 105
[15] Al-'Ayyāshī, i. 15.
[16] Ibid. 13.

guide. They are the 'speaking' (*nāṭiq*) Qur'ān, while the Qur'ān after the death of Muḥammad remains the 'silent' (*ṣāmit*) Qur'ān.[17] This identification of the written and recited word of God with the Imāms was poignantly expressed in a fascinating tradition attributed to 'Alī: 'God, exalted be He, is One, unique in His unity.. He uttered a word which became a light. From that light He created Muḥammad and created me and my progeny. Then God uttered another word which became a spirit. God made it to dwell in that light and made the light to dwell in our bodies. Thus, we are the spirit of God and His words. . . .'[18]

The Qur'ān was not only revealed to Muḥammad as the book of guidance meant for humanity, but was also addressed especially to him and his family, and revealed concerning them. Because the generality of Muslims read the Qur'ān without its true exegesis, which Gabriel brought to Muḥammad with the revelation, they commit the great error of alteration (*taḥrīf*) of the eternal Word of God. The sixth Imām, Ja'far al-Ṣādiq, said: 'Had the Qur'ān been read as it was sent down, you would have found us named in it.'[19] In a tradition related on the authority of other Imāms, and even Muḥammad, we are told that 'the Qur'ān was sent down in four quarters . . . one quarter concerning us and another concerning our enemies. Another quarter contains obligations (*farā'iḍ*) and precepts (*aḥkām*) and another what is lawful (*ḥalāl*) and what is prohibited (*ḥarām*). To us belong the favours (*karā'im*) of the Qur'ān.'[20] We shall return to the problem of *taḥrīf* when we discuss the basic principles of Shī'ī *tafsīr*. Before doing that, however, we must consider briefly the development of Shī'ī *tafsīr*.

2. THE DEVELOPMENT OF SHĪ'Ī *TAFSĪR*

Sunnī commentators in the early period of *tafsīr* relied primarily on prophetic traditions and those of the companions and their

[17] This idea is more clearly expressed in Ismā'īlī literature. It is implied however in many of the traditions from the Imāms that deal with their relationship to the Qur'ān. See, e.g., Abū Ja'far ibn Muḥammad ibn Ya'qūb al-Kulīnī al-Rāzī, *al-Uṣūl min al-kāfī*, ed. 'Alī Akbar al-Ghifārī (Tehran, 1388), i. 169, 192, 213.

[18] Al-Majlisī, liii. 46.

[19] Al-'Ayyāshī, i. 13.

[20] Furāt ibn Ibrāhīm ibn Furāt al-Kūfī, *Tafsīr Furāt al-Kūfī*, ed. Muḥammad 'Alī al-Ghurawī Urdūbādī (Najaf, n.d.), 1. For this and other versions see also al-'Ayyāshī, i. 9.

successors. This approach to the Qur'ān is known as *tafsīr bi'l-ma'thūr* (interpretation by means of prophetic tradition). Even though *tafsīr* in accordance with one's opinion (*ra'y*) or personal reasoning (*ijtihād*) was categorically rejected from the beginning,[21] later generations were obliged to resort to *ijtihād* in the face of the many contradictory and spurious traditions put in the mouth of Muḥammad, his companions, and their successors. Shī'ī commentators, on the other hand, relying on the Quranic proof texts, accepted Muḥammad's authority, and in accordance with the tradition of the 'two weights', already cited, then accepted that of his descendants as second to his authority.[22]

The first generation of Shī'ī commentators were disciples of the Imāms. Men like Zurāra ibn A'yun, Muḥammad ibn Muslim, and others close to the disciples of the fifth and sixth Imāms were among the first authorities in the Shī'ī community on *tafsīr* and other religious sciences. Even though *tafsīr* works have been attributed to some of these early traditionists,[23] nothing has come down to us. Their traditions have, however, been preserved in the works of the second generation of commentators. Most important among these are Furāt ibn Ibrāhīm ibn Furāt al-Kūfī, Abū'l-Naṣr Muḥammad ibn Mas'ūd al-'Ayyāshī al-Samarqandī, Abū'l-Ḥasan 'Alī ibn Ibrāhīm al-Qummī, and Muḥammad ibn Ibrāhīm al-Nu'mānī. Furāt lived during the Imamate of the ninth Imām, Muḥammad al-Jawād, and may have lived until the first years of the tenth century. He was one of the foremost authorities on Shī'ī tradition and one of the teachers of the famous traditionist, al-Qummī.[24] Al-'Ayyāshī, his contemporary, was a Sunnī scholar who accepted the Ja'farī rite (*madhhab*) and became an outstanding scholar in many of the religious sciences. Only the first volume of his work has come down to us, and even then in an abbreviated form.[25] Al-Qummī related *ḥadīth* traditions from his father, who

[21] Abū Ja'far Muḥammad ibn Jarīr al-Ṭabarī, *Jāmi' al-bayān 'an ta'wīl āy al-Qur'ān*, ed. Maḥmūd Muḥammad Shākir and Aḥmad Muḥammad Shākir (Cairo, 1954), i. 77–9.

[22] See Sayyid Muḥammad Ḥusayn Ṭabāṭabā'ī, *al-Qur'ān fī'l-Islām*, trans. Sayyid Muḥammad al-Ḥusaynī (Beirut, 1393/1973), 59–60.

[23] Āghā Buzurg Ṭihrānī, *al-Dharī'a ilā taṣānīf al-Shī'a* (Tehran, 1355/1936), iv. 231 ff.

[24] Furāt, *Tafsīr Furāt al-Kūfī*, from p. 2 of the introduction, and Ṭabāṭabā'ī, *al-Qur'ān*, 60.

[25] Al-'Ayyāshī, i. from the *jīm* and *dāl* letter pages of editor's introduction, and Ṭabāṭabā'ī, p. 60.

learned from many of the disciples of the Imāms. Al-Qummī died *c.*307/919–20.[26] Al-Nu'mānī (d. 360/971) was a student of al-Kulīnī (the author of *al-Kāfī*, one of the four canonical collections of the Shī'ī *ḥadīth*). He left an important *tafsīr* related on the authority of Ja'far al-Ṣādiq, which is as yet unpublished. His important treatise on *tafsīr*, reproduced in al-Majlisī's encyclopaedic work *Biḥār al-anwār*, provides a very important source of early Shī'ī *tafsīr*.[27]

These commentators simply compiled the traditions of the first generation without any comments of their own. As the period of the living Imāms extended over only approximately three centuries, the first and second generations of Shī'ī commentators cannot be precisely distinguished, as they clearly overlapped. They represent, in our view, the formative or pre-classical period of Shī'ī *tafsīr*. The third generation of Shī'ī commentators extended over a very long period, well into the sixteenth century AD. They include al-Sharīf al-Raḍī (d. 405/1015) and his famous brother, al-Sayyid al-Murtaḍā (d. 436/1044), and Abū Ja'far al-Ṭūsī (d. 460/1067), who was known as Shaykh al-Ṭā'ifa (pre-eminent jurist of the Shī'ī rite), and who was a student of al-Murtaḍā, whose views on the Qur'ān he represented. Al-Ṭūsī's commentary, *al-Tibyān fī tafsīr al-Qur'ān*, represents an important approach in Shī'ī *tafsīr*. His disciple Abū 'Alī al-Faḍl ibn al-Ḥasan ibn al-Faḍl al-Ṭabarsī (d. 548/1153), along with the predecessors just mentioned, represents what may be considered as the classical period of Shī'ī *tafsīr*. These commentators not only took a broad approach to *tafsīr*, drawing on Shī'ī as well as Sunnī tradition, but also took a view of the Qur'ān which rejected many of the earlier (as well as later) Shī'ī popular claims regarding the inauthenticity of the 'Uthmanic recension of the Qur'ān in favour of a Shī'ī recension.

Later commentators belonging to this group were Mullā Ṣadrā al-Shīrāzī (d. 1050/1640), Hāshim al-Baḥrānī (d. 1107/1695), 'Alī al-Ḥuwayzī (d. 1112/1700), and Mullā Muḥsin Fayḍ al-Kāshānī (d. 1191/1777), whose *Tafsīr al-ṣāfī* will be used in this essay as a representative of this school. These commentators lived during the period of the rise and consolidation of Shī'ī power in Iran. In contrast to the approach of what we have called the classical period, they took a polemical approach to earlier and especially

[26] See al-Qummī, pp. 8 f.

[27] See al-Majlisī, xciii. 1–97. The treatise purports to relate traditions from 'Alī on different topics of Quranic exegesis.

Sunnī *tafsīr*. They took literally the traditions of the first and second generations, and used them as ammunition against their opponents. The author of *al-Ṣāfī*, for instance, goes so far as to suggest that the first transmitters of the tradition from the Imāms were restrained by *taqīya* (concealment of one's principles in the face of persecution), which meant that much of the tradition may consequently have been lost. This, of course, left great scope for new ideas in *tafsīr* in the name of recovering the tradition. Thus we see that from the point of view of new emphases and elaborations of the tradition Shī'ī *tafsīr* has continued to evolve with the changing social and political times.[28]

The final stage of the development of Shī'ī *tafsīr* is the contemporary one. Generally speaking, modern works such as *al-Mīzān fī tafsīr al-Qur'ān* of Muḥammad Ḥusayn Ṭabāṭabā'ī and *al-Bayān fī tafsīr al-Qur'ān* of al-Sayyid Abū'l-Qāsim al-Khū'ī try to speak from within the long theological and philosophical tradition to the men and women of today. In some important respects, these commentators resemble in their approach those of the classical period. Thus al-Khū'ī, for example, felt obliged in his work to counter not only traditional Sunnī ideas of the Qur'ān, but some Shī'ī notions as well.[29] (Unfortunately, only one volume of this interesting work has come out, and the author has told me that he does not intend to continue.)

3. PRINCIPLES OF SHĪ'Ī *TAFSĪR*

Muslims have insisted that the Qur'ān must be understood if it is to be followed. They have insisted, further, that 'no one knows its exegesis, save God' (Q. 3/7). Shī'ī Muslims have unanimously agreed, however, that 'those who are firmly rooted in knowledge' (Q. 3/7) possess a measure of this divine knowledge unavailable to the rest of humanity. These are the Imāms, the true vicegerents of the prophet and heirs to the knowledge of all prophets from Adam to Muḥammad.[30] Indeed, in a sense it is through the Imāms that the

[28] See Mullā Muḥsin Fayḍ al-Kāshānī, *al-Ṣāfī fī tafsīr kalām Allāh al-wāfī* (n.p., 1286), 2–3. This continues to be borne out by new *tafsīr* works coming out of Iran and out of other Shī'ī centres that have been touched by the Islamic revolution in that country.

[29] See al-Khū'ī, from p. 200, and *passim*.

[30] See al-Kulīnī, i. 223–6, 238–42. See also n. 62, below.

revelation continues. The Imāms are not prophets, that is, recipients of *waḥy* (direct revelation); yet as people spoken to (*muḥaddathūn*) by angels, they are recipients of a special non-Quranic kind of revelation.[31] Their mission is not a legislative one, which is the special prerogative of an apostle (*rasūl*) sent by God with a new sacred law (*sharīʿa*). Rather, the Imāms receive the true and full meaning of the prophetic revelations, which includes the correct exegesis of legal precepts, knowledge of the concealed (*ghayb*), and elucidation of the Qur'ān's references to past history and prophecies of future events. Thus the sixth Imām is said to have declared: 'We are the people of a household among whom God continues to send one who knows His book from its beginning to its end. We possess such knowledge of God's sanctions and prohibitions as would oblige us to keep its secret, not telling anyone about it.'[32]

It follows from all this that the Qur'ān has many levels or dimensions of meaning. The most important principle of Shīʿī *tafsīr* therefore is that 'the Qur'ān has an outer dimension (*ẓahr*) and an inner dimension (*baṭn*); its inner dimension has yet another dimension, up to seven inner dimensions.'[33] Thus, in accordance with this principle, the Qur'ān must have many references beyond the apparent meaning. After asserting the exoteric and esoteric dimensions of the Qur'ān, Jaʿfar al-Ṣādiq concludes that 'the beginning of a verse may be sent down concerning one thing, its middle concerning another, and its end concerning yet another thing. [The Qur'ān] is constituted by speech which is closely connected and executed in various ways.'[34] The fifth Imām explained the esoteric and exoteric dimensions of the Qur'ān more simply but significantly as follows: 'The exoteric reference of the Qur'ān is to those concerning whom it was sent down; its inner reference is to those who acted like them.'[35]

The second unique principle of Shīʿī *tafsīr* is that of *jarī* (continued pertinence of applicability) and *inṭibāq* (analogic application). *Jarī* means that the Qur'ān must always have a reference that should take place as an event in history. Here again

[31] See ibid. i. 176–7 and 238–42. See also Mahmoud Ayoub, *Redemptive Suffering in Islam* (The Hague, 1978), 57–65.

[32] Al-ʿAyyāshī, i. 16.

[33] Ṭabāṭabāʾī, *al-Qur'ān*, 28; see also al-ʿAyyāshī, i. 11 ff. and al-Ṭūsī, i. 9, where a moderate view of *ẓāhir* and *bāṭin* is advocated.

[34] Al-ʿAyyāshī, i. 11.

[35] Ibid.

the apparent reference of a verse, or its literal sense, is its *ẓahr*, or outer dimension, while its continued application or relevance is its *baṭn*, inner dimension. In a tradition related on the authority of Khaythama (an important disciple of the fifth and sixth Imāms), the fifth Imām said:

> The Qur'ān was sent down in thirds: one third concerning us and those we love, another concerning our enemies and the enemies of those who were before us [that is, earlier prophets and their vicegerents] and one third is *sunna* [life example of bygone generations] and *mathal* [parable]. Were a verse to be revealed concerning a people and were it to die with their death, nothing would remain of the Qur'ān. Rather, the beginning of the Qur'ān continues to apply just like its end, so long as the heavens and the earth remain. Furthermore, to every people there is a revealed portion which they recite and in accordance with which they live in happiness or misery.[36]

The *baṭn* and *ẓahr* of the Qur'ān have also been identified with the principles of *ta'wīl* and *tanzīl*, respectively. *Tanzīl* refers to the sacred text, that is, its having been sent down. *Ta'wīl*, on the other hand, has two important senses. The first is that *ta'wīl* is synonymous with *tafsīr*, that is, the elucidation of the text by bringing its meaning to its original or first (*awwal*) level. The second sense of *ta'wīl* is that basic level of meaning which only God knows. Both senses are acceptable; the first because the Qur'ān must be understood, pondered, and followed. As for the second sense, the Qur'ān itself asserts that it has a level of meaning hidden with God and preserved from human contact.[37] Yet the Qur'ān makes an exception of 'those who are purified'.[38] This indicates, according to the Shī'ī view, that 'there are those who perceive the truths of the Qur'ān and its *ta'wīl*'.[39] Such favoured people possess this knowledge only through direct instruction by God. Ṭabāṭabā'ī explains that 'those who are purified are they who touch the Quranic reality and are empowered to delve into the depths of the sciences of the Qur'ān'.[40]

Two other principles follow from those of *ẓāhir* and *bāṭin*, namely *nāsikh* and *mansūkh* (abrogating and the abrogated verses), and *muḥkam* (unambiguous verses containing legal precepts or statements allowing of only one apparent meaning) and *mutashābih*

[36] Al-'Ayyāshī, i. 10. See also Ṭabāṭabā'ī, *al-Qur'ān*, 51–2.
[37] See Q. 43/1–4. [38] See Q. 56/79.
[39] Ṭabāṭabā'ī, *al-Qur'ān*, 48.
[40] Ibid. 49; see also the important corroborating text in Q. 33/33.

(verses allowing of more than one meaning; literally, verses which may accept similar, and hence confusing, significations). Since these two principles are basic to the science of *tafsīr* in general, we shall indicate only their Shīʿī aspects.

According to a tradition from the fifth Imām, abrogating verses are those which continue unchanged in application or relevance, and abrogated verses are those which have already been fulfilled. *Muḥkam* verses are those which must be followed, while the *mutashābih* are those verses which resemble one another in meaning. It must, however, be observed that there are three verses in the Qur'ān relating to this problem. According to one (Q. 11/1), the Qur'ān is all *muḥkam*. According to another (Q. 39/23), the Qur'ān is all *mutashābih*. According to the third verse (Q. 3/7) there are in the Qur'ān both *muḥkam* and *mutashābih* verses. It may therefore be argued that the Qur'ān, for God, the prophet, and his descendants the Imāms, is all *muḥkam* because it is all known. For the *ʿulamā'* the Qur'ān contains both, in accordance with their own knowledge. For those who have no knowledge, the Qur'ān is all *mutashābih*. Thus the sixth Imām said: '*Muḥkam* is that which must be followed and *mutashābih* is that which is obscured to the one ignorant of its meaning.'[41] It is, however, necessary for people to try and understand the *mutashābih* of the Qur'ān by means of its *muḥkam*. The eighth Imām, ʿAlī al-Riḍā, offered the following counsel: 'Whoever returns the *mutashābih* of the Qur'ān to its *muḥkam* is guided to the straight path.'[42]

These principles and their Shīʿī interpretations raise in different ways the question of *taḥrīf* (alteration). We cannot enter into this thorny problem in any detail; let it suffice to observe that *taḥrīf* has been more of an accusation or point of contention than a principle. Abū Jaʿfar al-Ṭūsī, for instance, writing at a time of relative stability, categorically rejected not only the principle of *taḥrīf*, but also any suggestion that the Qur'ān in use is not the true and authentic Qur'ān which Muḥammad left. He even rejected the time-honoured tradition of the seven modes or dialects (*aḥruf*) according to which the Qur'ān was supposedly sent down to Muḥammad. Rather, al-Ṭūsī argued, the Qur'ān was sent down from the One in one mode.[43]

41 Ibid. 39.

42 Ibid. 39.

43 Al-Ṭūsī, i. 7. This tradition is attributed to the sixth Imām. The general issue has been much discussed in scholarly circles; see *GdQ* ii. 93–112; Goldziher,

Al-Kāshānī, on the other hand, writing at a time of Shīʿī struggle for consolidation in eighteenth-century Iran, came close to rejecting the Qur'ān now in use, alleging all kinds of intentional distortions by the enemies of the prophet's family who were then in power. Al-Kāshānī alludes to the assertion that those who collected the Qur'ān after Muḥammad altered and distorted its meaning by omitting all direct references to the Imāms.[44] After giving a long list of alterations, supported by traditions from the Imāms, the author concludes that:

> the Qur'ān which is in our hands is not the entire Qur'ān sent down by God to Muḥammad. Rather, there is in it that which contradicts that which God had sent down. There is, moreover, in it that which was altered and changed. There were many things deleted from it, such as the name of ʿAlī in many places and the phrase *āl Muḥammad* (the family of Muḥammad), as well as the names of the 'hypocrites', where they occur. . . . The Qur'ān, furthermore, was not arranged in accordance with the pleasure of God and his apostle.[45]

Al-Kāshānī had to contend, however, with the weight of the tradition from the Imāms and such men of great learning and high status in the community as Ibn Bābawayh, al-Murtaḍā, al-Ṭūsī, al-Ṭabarsī, and many others, who had asserted the absolute authenticity of the Qur'ān. Therefore, after raising some of the objections to his own arguments in favour of *taḥrīf*, he concludes (but only by way of respect to the tradition) that the Qur'ān as it now stands is the word of God which, if interpreted correctly, contains all that the community now needs in the way of legal sanctions and prohibitions, as well as the necessary proofs of the Imāms' high office as its guardians and sole authorities on its exegesis. The Qur'ān which is in our hands must, the author argues, be followed during the occultation (*ghayba*) of the twelfth Imām. It must, however, be assumed that the true Qur'ān in all respects is with him.[46]

Al-Khūʾī, writing in our own day, offers the most sustained argument against any kind of alteration or change in the Qur'ān

Richtungen, 263–309; J. Eliash, 'The Shīʿite Qur'ān', *Arabica* 16 (1969), 15–24; E. Kohlberg, 'Some Notes on the Imāmite Attitude to the Qur'ān', in S. M. Stern, A. Hourani, V. Brown, eds., *Islamic Philosophy and the Classical Tradition* (Oxford, 1972), 209–24.

[44] See al-Kāshānī, p. 12, for some interesting interpretations in support of this claim.

[45] Ibid. 13.

[46] See ibid. 15.

from the start. He therefore argues against both Sunnī and Shīʿī traditional ideas. He rejects the notion of different readings of the Qur'ān as being simply the independent efforts (*ijtihād*) of the reciters. He also rejects all the traditions concerning the collection of the Qur'ān by the caliphs as a fantasy contradicting the book itself, *sunna*, consensus, and reasoning. To be sure, he writes, ʿUthmān had the Qur'ān collected in his time, but this does not mean that he collected the *āya*s and *sūra*s in one book. Rather, he unified (*jamaʿa*) the community of Muslims on the recitation of one official (*imām*) text.[47] He argues that Shīʿī authors cannot evince the ʿUthmanic collection of the Qur'ān as proof of *taḥrīf*.

Al-Khū'ī argues patiently against every tradition attributed to the Imāms that asserts *taḥrīf* of the Qur'ān. It cannot be possible for the Muslims, he contends, to follow or hold on to the two weights if the greater of the two (the book of God) is untrustworthy. Such traditions, then, must either be falsely attributed to the Imāms on the authority of single transmitters, or they refer to *taḥrīf* of *ta'wīl*, not *tanzīl*. This is because, al-Khū'ī argues, there is no linguistic reason to restrict *tanzīl* to the text. Rather, in many places of the Qur'ān (Q. 12/6, 101, 18/78, and 18/82, for example), *ta'wīl* is said to be part of the *waḥy* (direct revelation). Thus he argues against those who hold that ʿAlī's *muṣḥaf* is the true one, and that the one which is in our hands is false. As for the additional materials not found in the Qur'ān now in use but contained in this recension of ʿAlī, he argues that 'any additions in ʿAlī's recension (even if such a claim is true) are not part of the Qur'ān, that is, the Qur'ān which the Apostle enjoined be transmitted to the community'.[48]

Al-Khū'ī regards *naskh* (abrogation) and especially *naskh al-tilāwa* (suppression of a recited verse) to be a kind of *taḥrīf*, and therefore unacceptable. *Naskh* is, to be sure, possible, but only the prophet or one of the Imāms can determine what has been abrogated and when. Al-Khū'ī discusses all the alleged abrogated verses, whether they be purely textual or legal precepts, and shows that they actually stand unchanged. It may be of interest to observe that he particularly rejects the stoning verse as having at any time been part of the Qur'ān.[49] Had the verse really been part of the Qur'ān, the community would have accepted it on the testimony of ʿUmar, which was not the case; therefore the verse must be rejected.

[47] Al-Khū'ī, pp. 257–8. [48] Ibid. 225–6.
[49] See ibid. 277–87 and esp. 285.

The practice of stoning, however, may be based solely on *sunna*.

The preceding discussion should suffice to demonstrate that Shīʿī *tafsīr* has been a dynamic and ongoing activity in the life of the community. Perhaps its most unique feature is its insistence upon the continued validity and relevance of the sacred text to human life at all times. This is achieved through the Holy Family's human mediation between the divine and the rest of humanity. The Imāms continue to be regarded as the speaking Qur'ān, addressing humanity through the hope and inspiration which the living Imām (albeit in occultation) continues to give to the community. Our discussion, however, has so far been theoretical and expository. We shall therefore conclude this study with a sample of Shīʿī *tafsīr*. The verse we have chosen is both historically important and controversial.

4. AN EXAMPLE OF SHĪʿĪ *TAFSĪR*

The fifth *sūra* of the Qur'ān (*sūrat al-mā'ida*) was the last major *sūra* to be revealed. It marks the end of Muḥammad's career and signals the actual foundation of a new community, which was to be religiously, socially, and economically independent. Verse 67 of this *sūra* reads as follows: 'O Apostle, convey that which was sent down to you from your Lord; for if you do not, you will not have conveyed his message. God will protect you from the people; surely God guides not the rejecters of faith.'

Ṭabāṭabā'ī observes that this verse falls between two verses dealing with the 'people of the book'. It does not belong in theme, subject, or sequence to the verses surrounding it. It indicates a kind of danger which faces Muḥammad if he does not convey the message of his Lord, as we see in the phrase, 'God will protect you from the people.' The danger here indicated at the time of the revelation of the verse could not have been from the Jews, Christians, or even the associators of Mecca. Thus the verse must have been revealed singly and meant to deal with a particular situation.[50]

The verse no doubt puzzled commentators, for some suggested that it was revealed at the beginning of Muḥammad's mission. Apparently there was at that time no threat of the sort indicated by

[50] Sayyid Muḥammad Ḥusayn Ṭabāṭabā'ī, *al-Mīzān fī tafsīr al-Qur'ān*, vi. 42–3.

the words 'For if you do not, you will not have conveyed His message.' Furthermore, the language of the verse—its command and threat—are markedly different from those of the first three *sūra*s dealing with Muḥammad's mission: Q. 73, 74, and 96. In these early *sūra*s, the prophet was commanded to rise up and warn, that is, to guide his compatriots to faith in God and to inform them of its consequences for their lives. In this verse, it is a specific message or precept which is intended.

That this verse was seen by early Sunnī commentators and traditionists as referring to ʿAlī is fairly certain. It is related that Ibn Masʿūd said, 'We used to recite at the time of the Apostle of God, "O Apostle, convey that which was revealed to you from your Lord, that ʿAlī is the master (*mawlā*) of the people of faith".'[51]

Shīʿī commentators have rested the argument of ʿAlī's authority on Muḥammad's *ḥadīth*, which asserted that, 'He whose master I am, ʿAlī is also his master.' This *ḥadīth* is also related on the authority of many of the prophet's companions, including Saʿd ibn Abī Waqqāṣ, Abū Saʿīd al-Khudrī, and ʿUmar ibn al-Khaṭṭāb; it was also related by Ibn Ḥanbal. We are further told on the authority of Abū Hurayra that when Muḥammad was transported to heaven, he said, 'I heard a voice from beneath the Throne, saying, "ʿAlī is the sign of guidance (*āyat al-hudā*) and the beloved of those who have faith in me. Convey this to ʿAlī!" ' When Muḥammad descended from heaven, he forgot. Thus God sent down to him, 'O Apostle, convey that which was sent down to you from your Lord.'[52]

For commentators of the classical tradition such as al-Ṭūsī and al-Ṭabarsī, the verse was surely revealed concerning ʿAlī, but other interpretations were not ruled out. Al-Ṭabarsī reviews the different traditions, namely that the verse was revealed in Mecca to reassure the prophet against the people of Quraysh, that it was because of *taqīya* (as related on the authority of ʿĀ'isha), or, according to some traditions, that Muḥammad, during the early days of his mission, walked around with a bodyguard. When God revealed the verse, 'God shall protect you from the people', Muḥammad dismissed his bodyguard.[53] The bodyguard tradition has also been related by

[51] Ibid. vi. 58–9.
[52] Ibid. vi. 59.
[53] Abū ʿAlī al-Faḍl al-Ḥasan al-Ṭabarsī, *Majmaʿ al-bayān fī tafsīr al-Qur'ān* (Beirut, 1380/1961). On al-Ṭabarsī, see Musa O. A. Abdul, *The Qur'ān: Shaykh Tabarsi's Commentary* (Lahore, 1977).

Furāt ibn Ibrāhīm al-Kūfī, one of the earliest Shī'ī commentators, on the authority of Muḥammad al-Quraẓī. Furāt also relates on the authority of Zayd ibn Arqam, a well-known companion of the prophet, the famous saying, 'He whose master I am, 'Alī is also his master.' He relates on the authority of the fifth Imām that God revealed the command to the prophet to convey this injunction. Muḥammad, however, was afraid that the people would not accept it, so God sent down the verse. Thus on the way back from his last pilgrimage, the prophet took 'Alī's hand at Ghadīr Khumm (a spring between Mecca and Medina), where he made this famous declaration.[54]

Al-'Ayyāshī relates the story or 'occasion' behind the revelation of this verse in a series of *ḥadīth*s. God had commanded Muḥammad to designate 'Alī as his successor, but Muḥammad feared that the Muslims would not accept 'Alī and would instead accuse him of favouring his cousin. God therefore sent down the verse, and Muḥammad declared 'Alī's authority (*walāya*) over the people at Ghadīr Khumm. In another tradition, al-'Ayyāshī relates that Gabriel came to Muḥammad with the verse during the farewell pilgrimage. The prophet waited three days until the pilgrimage caravan reached Ghadīr Khumm, where he called for congregational prayers, after which he addressed the people, saying, 'Who is dearer to you than your own selves?' They all answered, 'God and His Apostle.' After repeating the same question and receiving the same answer three times, he made the statement: 'He whose master I am, 'Alī is also his master.'[55]

In al-'Ayyāshī we witness a growth of a tradition in which the authority of 'Alī was to be declared or taught to the people along with the fundamentals of Islam, such as prayers, almsgiving (*zakāt*), fasting, and pilgrimage. According to a tradition related on the authority of the fifth Imām, God sent the command to Muḥammad with Gabriel to guide the community to their rites of worship and finally to the authority of 'Alī. The prophet protested, saying, 'My Lord, my community are men close to Jāhilīya.' Thus God sent down the verse, and Muḥammad carried out God's command at Ghadīr Khumm. In another tradition, also related on the authority of the fifth Imām, we are told that when the verse was sent down, Muḥammad gathered the Muslims together and announced to

[54] Furāt, pp. 36–41.
[55] See al-'Ayyāshī, i. 331–2.

them that his end was near. He delivered all the commands of God, and for the last one, he said, 'O people of Islam! Let him who is present tell the one who is absent. I entrust them who believed me and accepted faith in me with the authority (*walāya*) of 'Alī. His authority is my authority and my authority is the authority of my Lord.'[56]

Al-Qummī relates the verse to the farewell pilgrimage and adds dramatic elements to the story suggesting another stage in the growth of the tradition. He quotes a long and highly embellished version of Muḥammad's farewell pilgrimage sermon. Several times during the sermon the prophet was reported to have fallen silent, then turning his face to the right to have said: 'Yes, if God wills, 'Alī ibn Abī Ṭālib.' He was addressing the angel Gabriel, who was urging him to declare 'Alī's imamate over the community to the assembled crowd of pilgrims.[57] After the pilgrimage, God revealed to Muḥammad the verses, 'When victory from God and conquest have come and you see people enter into the religion of God in troops, proclaim the praise of your Lord and beg forgiveness of Him, for he is truly relenting' (Q. 110). Then, Muḥammad again gathered the people to announce his approaching end and to relate to them the famous tradition of the two weights, which we have already discussed. Four men vowed never to allow the imamate to continue in the family of Muḥammad. They bound themselves by a written covenant in the Ka'ba. Unfortunately the men are not identified.

Al-Qummī then relates the incident of Ghadīr Khumm and 'Alī's designation in the presence of all Muslims who repeatedly affirmed their allegiance, each time Muḥammad repeating, 'O God, bear witness!' Then lifting 'Alī's hand for all to see, he declared, 'He whose master I am, 'Alī is also his master. O God, be a friend to him who befriends him and enemy to the one who is his enemy. O God, grant support to him who supports him. Forsake whomever forsakes him and love whomever loves him.' Then lifting his eyes to heaven Muḥammad continued, 'O God, bear witness over them, and I shall bear witness.' 'Umar asked, 'O Apostle of God, is this from God and from his Apostle?' Muḥammad answered, 'It is from God and His Apostle. 'Alī is the commander of the people of faith, Imām of the godfearing and leader of the people of nobility who

[56] Ibid. i. 333–4.
[57] Al-Qummī, i. 172.

shall come on the Day of Resurrection bearing the marks of their piety. God shall make him sit at the bridge [extending over Hell and leading to Paradise, which all humankind shall traverse] on the Day of Resurrection where he shall send his friends (*awliyā'*) to Paradise and his enemies to the Fire.'[58]

Many of Muḥammad's companions complained, and fourteen of them conspired to kill him. These were among the people who apostatized after his death. They gathered in an ambush at a place between Mecca and Medina. As Muḥammad approached the spot by night, however, Gabriel advised him of their plot. Muḥammad called each one out by name, and so they all ran away in fright. They later denied under oath having plotted against him.[59]

Al-Kāshānī provides the most developed form of the tradition. In his presentation, theology, hagiography, piety, and polemics meet. He clearly relates the event at Ghadīr Khumm to Q. 3/5 which declares God's favour to the community, protects their faith, and accepts Islam as their religion. Al-Kāshānī first presents a phrase-by-phrase commentary on the verse: 'O Apostle, convey that which was sent to you from your Lord' (that is, concerning 'Alī); 'for if you do not, you would not have conveyed his message' (that is if you neglect what was sent down to you concerning the authority of 'Alī and conceal it, you would be deserving of punishment as though you did not convey anything of the messages of your Lord); 'God will protect you from the people' (that is, from their ability to touch you with any evil). The men who accompanied Muḥammad on his farewell pilgrimage and learned from him the fundamentals of religion were 70,000, the same number as those who were with Moses in the wilderness. The people of Moses revoked their covenant with God by worshipping the calf; the people of Muḥammad did likewise because they later revoked their covenant with God concerning the authority of 'Alī. Shī'ī piety holds the notion that prophetic history continuously repeats itself, hence the analogy between Moses and his people and Muḥammad and his people. Al-Kāshānī then quotes a long colloquy between God and Muḥammad on *walāya*.[60] For the rest, we shall let the text speak for itself. After the pilgrimage, Gabriel again came to Muḥammad and said:

[58] Ibid. i. 173–4.
[59] See ibid. i. 174–5.
[60] Al-Kāshānī, p. 132.

God sends you salutations of peace and says to you that your end is near. . . . Transfer the knowledge you possess, the sciences which you inherited from prophets who were before you, the ark[61] and all the signs of former prophets which are in your possession to your vicegerents and successor, My incontrovertible proof (*ḥujja bāligha*) over My creation, 'Alī ibn Abī Ṭālib. Raise him up to the people as a beacon and renew his covenant and allegiance. Remind them of the allegiance which I took from them and of My covenant with which I bound them to the *walāya* of My friend, their master and the master of all men and women of faith, 'Alī ibn Abī Ṭālib. I did not receive the soul of any prophet before I perfected My religion and completed My favour through the acceptance of the *walāya* of My friends and enmity towards My enemies. For this is the perfection of the profession of My Oneness and My religion and the completion of My favour to My creation. It is through following My Friend and obedience to Me. I have never left My earth without a *qā'im* [the awaited Mahdī], who is My proof over My creation. 'Today I have perfected your religion for you' (Q. 5/3) through the *walāya* of My *walī* . . . 'Alī, My servant and the vicegerent of My Prophet. . . . Obedience to him is obedience to My Prophet. Whoever obeys ['Alī] obeys Me and whoever disobeys him disobeys Me. I made him a sign between Me and My creatures. Whoever recognizes him is a person of faith (*mu'min*) and whoever denies him is a rejecter of faith (*kāfir*). Whoever associates rivals with allegiance to him is an associator (*mushrik*). Whoever comes to Me accepting his *walāya* shall enter Paradise, and whoever comes to Me with enmity towards him shall enter the Fire.[62]

5. CONCLUSIONS

We have suggested in this essay that Shī'ī *tafsīr* has been a continuous and open-ended process and that it has been formed and nurtured by concrete circumstances in the social, political, and religious life of the community. A new and important chapter is now in the making through the Islamic revolution in Iran. This may be seen in a number of new *tafsīr* works which have since come out bearing the stamp of the revolution and its ideology. The emphasis in these works is not on hagiography and eschatology but rather on the socio-political and economic realities of the twentieth century.

[61] Shī'ī tradition asserts that Muḥammad inherited the Ark of the Covenant from Moses, which he bequeathed to the Imāms along with his own armour and sword, as signs of their authority. See al-Kulīnī, i. 233, and also 232–8.

[62] Al-Kāshānī, pp. 132–3.

The Islamic revolution of Iran, however, is still firmly rooted in Shī'ī piety, eschatology, and messianic hope. Hence, in a very real sense for Shi'ites, the final and real conclusion of Shī'ī *tafsīr*, as indeed, of Shī'ī history altogether, lies not in the writing of commentaries, but rather in the appearance of the hidden Imām, for whose return they pray daily.

10

Ismāʿīlī *ta'wīl* of the Qur'ān

ISMAIL K. POONAWALA

ISMĀʿĪLĪS make a fundamental distinction between aspects of religion, the *ẓāhir* (exterior) and the *bāṭin* (interior). The former aspect consists of exterior aspects, such as knowing the apparent meaning of the Qur'ān and performing the obligatory acts as laid down in the *sharīʿa*, the religious law. The latter aspect is comprised of knowing the hidden, inner, true meaning of the Qur'ān and the *sharīʿa*. They further maintain that it is the *nāṭiq* (lawgiver-prophet)[1] who receives revelation (*tanzīl*) and promulgates the *sharīʿa*, while it is his associate and deputy, the *waṣī* (plenipotentiary),[2] who expounds the *bāṭin* through the science of *ta'wīl*.[3] The *ẓāhir*, therefore, varies from prophet to prophet in accordance with each epoch, whereas the *bāṭin* remains unchanged and is universally valid. Despite this twofold division of religion into exoteric and esoteric aspects, Ismāʿīlīs stress that both are not only complementary to each other, but that they are also intertwined with each other like body and soul. One without the other, therefore, cannot exist.[4]

[1] A term used for the lawgiver–prophet. According to the Ismāʿīlī doctrine there are seven *nuṭaqā'*: Adam, Nūḥ, Ibrāhīm, Mūsā, ʿĪsā, Muḥammad, and the Qā'im. See Zāhid ʿAlī, *Hamāre Ismāʿīlī madhhab kī ḥaqīqat aur uskā niẓām* (Hyderabad, 1954), 129; Abū Yaʿqūb al-Sijistānī, *Kitāb al-iftikhār* (a critical edition has been prepared by Ismail K. Poonawala and will be published soon), ch. 6.

[2] The *waṣī* is also called *al-asās* (foundation). According to the Ismāʿīlī doctrine, every *naṭīq* appoints his *waṣī*, or *asās*, who succeeds him and is, in turn, succeeded by the *imām*. See Al-Sijistānī, *Kitāb al-iftikhār*, ch. 7; also al-Kulīnī, *al-Uṣūl min al-kāfī*, ed. A. al-Ghaffārī, (Tehran, 1388/1968), i. 224.

[3] The literal meaning of *ta'wīl* is 'to cause something to return to its original state'. In the beginning it was synonymous with *tafsīr*, but in the course of time it became a technical term for the interpretation of the subject-matter, or for the exposition of the covert meaning. In this latter sense it formed a supplement to *tafsīr*, which meant expounding the narrative by making known the significations of the strange words or expressions and explaining the occasions on which the verses were revealed. Most of the sectarian groups, especially the Shīʿīs and the Ṣūfīs use *ta'wīl* on which to hang their own doctrines. See Lane, *Lexicon*, s.v. *a–w–l*; *EI*[1], '*ta'wīl*'.

[4] In his *al-Shawāhid wa'l-bayān* (MS: see M. Goriawala, *A Descriptive Catalogue*

The Ismā'īlī classification of religious sciences into two categories, the *ẓāhirī* sciences and the *bāṭinī* sciences, also reflects the above distinction. Accordingly, all branches of knowledge from philological to physical sciences and historical to juridical fall in the first category, while the other is comprised only of the *ta'wīl* and *ḥaqā'iq*.[5] Conspicuously absent from Ismā'īlī literature is the science of *tafsīr* (exegesis), classified as a branch of the *ẓāhirī* sciences.[6] Its absence implies that any *tafsīr* could be used for the external philological exposition of the Qur'ān and to explain the occasions on which the verses were revealed, but its inner, true meaning could be obtained only through the *ta'wīl* derived from the legitimate Imām. For this reason, the Imām is often called *Qur'ān-i nāṭiq* (the speaking Qur'ān), while the Book, since it needs an interpreter, is called *Qur'ān-i ṣāmit* (the silent Qur'ān).[7]

of the Fyzee Collection of Isma'ili Manuscripts (Bombay, 1965), 15, 209–10), Ja'far ibn Manṣūr al-Yaman states:

> The *bāṭin* does not stand up without the *ẓāhir*. The former is like the soul while the latter is like the body. Both taken together are the two roots, but one is not useful without the other. Each bears witness to the other. [The body] helps the soul in realizing its [potential] and thereby brings it back to life [i.e., the spiritual life with the acquisition of knowledge]. . . . The *ẓāhir* consists of performing the obligatory acts while the *bāṭin* is comprised of knowledge. Neither performing the obligatory acts without knowledge, nor the acquisition of knowledge without [performing] the obligatory acts, is useful. For example, body without soul is unfit for life, similarly [the existence of] soul cannot be proven without body.

See also al-Qāḍī al-Nu'mān, *Asās al-ta'wīl*, ed. A. Tāmir (Beirut, 1960), 28; Abū Ya'qūb al-Sijistānī, *Kitāb al-maqālīd*, MS Hamdani Collection, 63rd *iqlīd*; Ḥamīd al-Dīn al-Kirmānī, *Rāḥat al-'aql*, ed. M. Kāmil Ḥusayn and M. Ḥilmī, (Cairo, 1952), 16, 22, 27, 30–2. See also n. 31, below.

[5] The literal meaning of *ḥaqā'iq* is truth, reality. It represents the ultimate cosmological and eschatological system of the Ismā'īlī doctrine. 'Alī ibn Muḥammad ibn al-Walīd's book dealing with the Ismā'īlī doctrine is entitled *Kitāb al-dhakhīra fī'l-ḥaqīqa*, ed. M. al-A'ẓamī (Beirut, 1971). See also Zāhid 'Alī, *Ismā'īlī madhhab*, 395; and n. 6, below. In *Kitāb al-iftikhār*, al-Sijistānī refers to himself and his group as *ahl al-ḥaqq*.

[6] R. Strothmann's edition of *Mizāj al-tasnīm* by Ḍiyā'l-Dīn Ismā'īl ibn Hibat Allāh (d. 1184/1770) (Gottingen, 1944–55), under the title *Ismailitischer Koran-Kommentar*, is misleading. The word *tafsīr* is not mentioned by the author either in the title or in the introduction. The book deals with the *ta'wīl* of certain *sūras* and it is in the form of *majālis* (pl. of *majlis*, meaning 'gathering'—see M. Kāmil Ḥusayn, *Fī adab Miṣr al-Fāṭimīya* (Cairo, 1950), 33–41), selective audience, or students. Those tracts are collected and entitled by the prefix *ḥaqā'iq* added to the appellation of each *sūra*, such as *ḥaqā'iq sūrat al-naml*.

[7] Al-Kulīnī, *al-Uṣūl*, i. 246, reports a similar tradition which states: *inna al-Qur'ān laysa bi-naṭīq*^{in} *ya'muru wa yanhā, wa lākin li'l-Qur'ān ahl*^{un} *ya'murūna wa yanhawna*.

The following study deals with Ismā'īlī *ta'wīl* and its place within their overall system of thought. It also attempts to delineate general hermeneutical principles whereby the Qur'ān is interpreted. The research is based primarily on published and unpublished works of three major authors: al-Qāḍī al-Nu'mān (d. 363/947)[8] and his two lesser-known contemporaries, Ja'far ibn Manṣūr al-Yaman[9] and Abū Ya'qūb al-Sijistānī.[10] Their works, which exemplify three different trends of thought within the Ismā'īlī system, represent the earliest extant sources on the subject.

I

In his *Kitāb al-iftikhār*, al-Sijistānī, elucidating the source of *ta'wīl* from the Qur'ān, states:

The relationship of the [human] soul to the world of knowledge is more intimate than its [relationship] to the world of sensory perception. Indeed, the *nāṭiq*'s soul attains a high status of knowledge which his peers and likes are incapable of [reaching]. Hence, [the fact that] the *nāṭiq*'s revelations are expressions of the incorporeal world and its spiritual, luminous forms, cannot be denied. [This being the case], how could it be correct to translate

[8] For his life and works see Ismail K. Poonawala, *Biobibliography of Ismā'īlī Literature* (Malibu, 1977), 48–68.

[9] Ibid. 70–5. Al-Qāḍī al-Nu'mān faithfully served the first four Fatimid caliphs for half a century, and his sons and grandsons held the office of chief judge in the Fatimid empire for almost another half century. In addition to his pioneering works on jurisprudence and history, al-Nu'mān wrote some seminal works on the *ta'wīl*. Yet he is regarded mainly as an exponent of the *ẓāhirī* sciences. Ja'far ibn Manṣūr al-Yaman, representing the Yemenite school, on the other hand, is considered one of the leading exponents of the *ta'wīl*.

An interesting story narrated by the Yamanī *dā'ī*, Idrīs 'Imād al-Dīn (*'Uyūn al-akhbār*, MS Hamdani Collection, vi. 39–40), states that on a certain occasion, after al-Qāḍī al-Nu'mān had recovered from illness, he waited upon the Fatimid caliph, al-Mu'izz li-Dīn Allāh. The caliph inquired about the various dignitaries who had visited him during the illness. Al-Nu'mān replied that everyone came except Ja'far ibn Manṣūr al-Yaman. Al-Mu'izz, therefore, ordered certain books to be brought, gave them to al-Nu'mān for perusal, and asked for his opinion. After examining one of the books, al-Nu'mān replied: 'How can I comment on a work composed by you?' 'This is the work of your master Ja'far', replied al-Mu'izz. Al-Nu'mān, on hearing this, realized Ja'far's higher rank in the *da'wa* and went straight to him to pay his respects. Whether the story is authentic or not is another question, but it poignantly illustrates the lofty position of *bāṭinī* sciences over *ẓāhirī* sciences.

[10] Poonawala, *Biobibliography*, 82–9. Al-Sijistānī, who represents the Iranian school, was an original thinker and a distinguished author. He formulated a new synthesis of reason and revelation by adapting Ismā'īlī doctrine to Neoplatonic cosmology.

everything he transmitted to his *umma* [community] into physical, corporeal objects?. . . We affirm that the *nāṭiq* comes from [the spiritual] world; he is connected to it and derives [his knowledge] therefrom.[11]

The points made by al-Sijistānī are: (i) the prophet communicates with the higher, spiritual world, the fountain-head of his inspiration; (ii) the prophet's soul attains the highest attainable status of knowledge; (iii) revelations, being representations of the spiritual world in human language, cannot be taken literally.

In order to grasp the full purport of the author's statement, a brief outline of al-Sijistānī's theory of prophethood and the nature of revelation within the framework of his philosophical system is called for. According to al-Sijistānī, God is absolutely transcendent, beyond all thought and all being. His true being is neither conceivable nor knowable. All that is known about Him is His Command (*amr*) and His Munificence (*jūd*) as something united with the Intellect (*'aql*) originated (*abda'a*) by Him. The superstructure of the hierarchy of beings, thus, begins with the Intellect, the second hypostasis of the Neoplatonists. The descending order of al-Sijistānī's Neoplatonic cosmology consists of the Intellect, the Soul, Nature, the Spheres, the Elements (that is, fire, air, water, and earth), and the three Kingdoms of mineral, vegetable, and animal. Since all the species in the physical world are created in ascending order, man is the noblest of all creation. Man, by virtue of his position, is the central link in the long chain of being; below him is the animal kingdom and above him is the world of angels (or the spiritual world), and he is connected to both. Prophethood, therefore, is the highest spiritual rank a man can aspire to attain in this world.[12]

The basic notion in al-Sijistānī's theory of prophecy is that the prophet is the messenger of God to mankind, who brings with him revelation (or a scripture). He is called both a *nabī* (a prophet, that is, one who informs mankind or who is informed, respecting God and things unseen),[13] and a *rasūl* (a messenger, an apostle of God, that is, the relater, by consecutive progressions, of the tidings from God).[14] Both of the aforementioned terms not only stress his role as

[11] Al-Sijistānī, *Kitāb al-iftikhār*, ch. 12.

[12] See the following works of al-Sijistānī: *Kitāb al-iftikhār*; *Kitāb al-maqālīd*; *Kitāb al-yanābī'*, ed. H. Corbin, in *Trilogie Ismaelienne* (Tehran, 1961); *Ithbāt al-nubū'āt*, ed. A. Tāmir (Beirut, 1966).

[13] Lane, *Lexicon*, s.v. *n-b-'*.

[14] Ibid., s.v. *r-s-l*.

God's messenger to mankind, but they also imply that he is the knower of the 'unseen' and 'hidden'.

The prophet is further characterized as 'a pure man who is inspired (*al-mu'ayyad*) by the spirit of holiness'.[15] The key to the unravelling of the mystery of divine inspiration, or illumination, is the word *ta'yīd*. This term is derived from the Quranic usage of its verbal form *ayyada*.[16] Al-Sijistānī defines *al-mu'ayyad* as the one who attains full quiescence and one who receives benefits from the Intellect in a perfect way without mutation and interruption.[17] At another place he states that the prophet, by virtue of his pure soul, rises to the subtle, spiritual world and takes from it spiritual subtleties and luminous delights and conveys them to the world below.[18] The prophet is, therefore, an intermediary between the higher and the lower worlds, and it is through him that God bestows His bounties on the latter. Hence, he is described as 'the deputy of the Intellect in the physical world'.[19]

The soul, according to al-Sijistānī, is ordinarily divided into three parts: vegetative, animal, and rational. But the prophet has the fourth category called 'the sacred (*al-qudsīya*)', and because of it he is inspired and rises above the ordinary man.[20] In his *Kitāb al-yanābīʿ*, in the fourtieth *yanbūʿ* entitled 'The modality of receiving inspiration by the inspired ones in the physical world', al-Sijistānī explains the modality of inspiration as follows:

The promptings of inspiration are experienced when the inspired one is able to discover things without [passing through] sense perception, which is the normal way of inference from known to unknown things. Conversely, [the inspired one] finds himself abstemious to sensible things and desirous of abstract, intellectual things. The difference between the learned (*al-ʿālim*) and the inspired (*al-mu'ayyad*) is that the former is obliged to remember his learning and pronouncements on things perceptible through the senses, while the latter is able to dispense with it. The *mu'ayyad* conceives in his mind what the *ʿālim* would have been unable even to deduce by way of perceptible arguments. Probably the one who is

[15] Al-Sijistānī, *Ithbāt al-nubū'āt*, 119.

[16] The verb *ayyada* with *rūḥ al-quds* in regard to Jesus occurs three times in the Qur'ān; 2/87, 2/253, and 5/110. It means to strengthen, to aid, or to render victorious. Lane, *Lexicon*, s.v. *a-y-d*; al-Sijistānī, *Kitāb al-iftikhār*, ch. 5.

[17] Al-Sijistānī, *Kitāb al-yanābīʿ*, 36.

[18] Al-Sijistānī, *Ithbāt al-nubū'āt*, 144.

[19] Al-Sijistānī, *Kitāb al-yanābīʿ*, 72; id., *Ithbāt al-nubū'āt*, 127; Paul Walker, 'Abū Yaʿqūb al-Sijistānī and the Development of Ismāʿīlī Neoplatonism', Ph.D. dissertation (Univ. of Chicago, 1974), 166–79.

[20] Al-Sijistānī, *Ithbāt al-nubū'āt*, 13–48, 128, 152.

inspired conceives spiritual things without constructing syllogisms and expresses them in a perceptible language so that the people can perceive them.[21]

In his *Ithbāt al-nubū'āt*, al-Sijistānī suggests two possible modes through which the prophet receives inspiration: auditory or mental perception.[22] The former is ruled out because it involves intermediaries and is also corruptible. Mental perception, therefore, is the only mode of revelatory experience and is supported by the Qur'ān itself, wherein it is stated: 'The heart lied not [in seeing] what it saw' (Q. 53/11). Now, the question about the veracity of the prophet's mental perception as compared with that of others arises. The prophet's veracity, al-Sijistānī contends, is assured by the temperateness of his physical constitution and the purity of his soul. The Qur'ān states: 'It belongs not to any mortal that God should speak [that is, through an auditory mode] to him, except by revelation [that is, through mental/idea inspiration], or from behind a veil, or that He should send a messenger who reveals by God's permission whatever He wills' (Q. 42/51). In his *Ithbāt al-nubū'at*, in a section entitled 'The modality of God's speech', al-Sijistānī, commenting on the three modes of revelation as stated in the above verse, states:

Waḥy^{an} (by revelation) means *ta'yīd* from the Intellect; *min wara'i ḥijāb^{in}* [from behind a veil] means *ta'yīd* from the Intellect through the Soul, the latter being a veil between the Intellect and the Nature; and *aw yursila rasūl^{an}* [or that He should send a messenger] means that, when the *nāṭiq* attains his rank [i.e., receives the call], he is obliged to translate what has been brought down to his heart by the Trusted Spirit into his own tongue in order to convey it to his people.[23]

Thus the individual's mental perception is closely connected with his own speech pattern, and each prophet expresses his revelation in his own language. This is attested to by the Qur'ān wherein it is stated: 'We have made it [the Qur'ān] easy in thy tongue that thou mayest bear good tidings thereby to the godfearing, and warn a contentious people' (Q. 19/97).

Further elaborating on the various types of speech, al-Sijistānī states:

As for the speech [word] of God, when it became united with the first being

[21] Al-Sijistānī, *Kitāb al-yanābī'*, 95.
[22] pp. 147–9. [23] Al-Sijistānī, *Ithbāt al-nubū'āt*, 149.

[i.e., the Intellect] it did not have any sound (*ṣawt*) or print (*naqsh*), but this [knowledge] was shared by the Intellect and the Soul through the former's benefaction upon the latter. . . . As for the inspired speech (*al-kalām al-taʾyīdī*) emanating from the Intellect and connected with the *nāṭiq*, it is like spiritual dying of the *nāṭiq*'s soul. Each dye consists of an intellectual form which combines many psychic things and spiritual formations radiating into the receiver's soul with the knowledge of many things. . . . As for the compound speech (*al-kalām al-tarkībī*) emanating from the Soul and connected with the *nāṭiq*, it consists of psychic movements which manifest [in the movements of] the stars and the planets. . . . Only the *nāṭiq*, because he is inspired, is able to decipher this [compound speech] and how it is expressed in each epoch. . . . As for the *nāṭiq*'s own speech [sound-words], it possesses the forcefulness, elegance, and loftiness that those who speak the same language are unable to produce like unto it.[24]

Three spiritual forces, namely, *al-jadd*, *al-fatḥ*, and *al-khayāl*, emanating from the Intellect and the Soul are described as special prophetic gifts which form part of the prophet's *taʾyīd*.[25] Thus it is obvious that al-Sijistānī's theory of prophecy, like those of other Muslim thinkers such as al-Fārābī and Ibn Sīnā, is based upon Greek and Neoplatonic theories of the soul and its power of cognition.[26] To sum up the foregoing discussion, the following salient features should be noted. The prophet, unlike ordinary man, is endowed with a pure soul and extraordinary intellectual gifts. He does not need an external instructor, but his intellect develops by itself with the help of divine power prior to its final prophetic illumination (revelation) and, thereby, attains contact with the Intellect. The intelligibles thus bestowed upon the prophet by the Intellect are translated and expressed by him in symbolical and metaphorical language, since the commonalty cannot grasp purely spiritual things.[27]

[24] Ibid. 152–3.

[25] Al-Sijistānī, *Kitāb al-iftikhār*, ch. 4; al-Sijistānī, *Kitāb al-yanābīʿ*, 92.

[26] See Fazlur Rahman, *Prophecy in Islam* (London, 1958). For the Shīʿī theory of prophecy, see Henry Corbin, 'De la philosophie prophétique en Islam Shīʿite', *Eranos Jahrbuch*, 31 (1962), 49–116.

[27] According to the *Rasāʾil Ikhwān al-Ṣafāʾ* (Beirut, 1957), i. 76–8; ii. 210; iii. 344–5, the *taʾwīl* of the Qurʾān is indispensable. The Ikhwān's position is very similar to that of al-Sijistānī, see Ismail K. Poonawala, 'The Qurʾān in the Rasāʾil Ikhwān al-Ṣafāʾ', *International Congress for the Study of the Qurʾān* (Canberra, 1980), 51–67; also Yves Marquet, 'La Pensée d'Abū Yaʿqūb as-Sijistānī', *SI* 54 (1981), 95–128—Marquet has also pointed out some similarities between al-Sijistānī and the *Rasāʾil*.

II

In keeping with their basic distinction between the *ẓāhir* and the *bāṭin*, Ismāʿīlīs maintain the same distinction between the *tanzīl* (the divine message delivered by the Prophet in its literal form) and the *ta'wīl* (the hidden, spiritual meaning of the scripture explained by the Imām). In his *Kitāb al-maqālīd*, al-Sijistānī has devoted a separate *iqlīd* to elucidating the difference between the two. He states:

> The *tanzīl* is similar to the raw materials, while the *ta'wīl* resembles the manufactured goods. For example, nature produces various types of woods, but unless a craftsman works on them and gives them a specific shape, such as a door, a chest or a chair, the wood is not worth more than fuel [to be consumed] by the fire. The wood's worth and benefit become manifest only after it receives the craftsman's craftsmanship. The craftsmanship [is an art which] puts everything in its proper place. Likewise is the case of other raw materials, such as iron, gold, copper, and silver. Unless a craftsman works on them, their worth and utility remain hidden. . . . Similarly, the *tanzīl* consists of putting things together in words. Beneath those words lie the treasured meanings. It is the practitioner of the *ta'wīl* who extracts the intended meaning from each word and puts everything in its proper place. This is, then, the difference between the *tanzīl* and the *ta'wīl*.[28]

As the craftsman cannot practise his art without the raw materials, the function of *ta'wīl* comes after the *tanzīl*. Similarly, the rank of the practitioner of *ta'wīl* in the Ismāʿīlī hierarchy assigned to the *waṣī*, the deputy and successor of the prophet, comes after that of the *nāṭiq*. It is the *nāṭiq* who receives the *tanzīl* and promulgates the *sharīʿa*, while it is the *waṣī* who imparts the *ta'wīl*. It is worth noting that in the *daʿwa* organization, which corresponds to the spiritual hierarchy of the higher world, the religious offices of the *nāṭiq* and *waṣī* correspond to the Two Roots: the Intellect and the Soul. This correspondence between the two highest ranks of both the hierarchies is very revealing for the understanding of what follows. After his prophetic revelation, the prophet makes the *waṣī* privy to his illumination of the spiritual world so that the divine inspiration continues after his death. The *waṣī*, thus, is inspired from the heaven (*mu'ayyad min al-samā'*),

[28] Al-Sijistānī, *Kitāb al-maqālīd*, 52nd *iqlīd*.

and it is this role of imparting the *ta'wīl* which he passes on to his progeny, the Imāms.

It is repeatedly stressed that the *waṣī* is not only divinely inspired, but he is also divinely commissioned to impart the *ta'wīl*. In his *Kitāb al-iftikhār*, al-Sijistānī gives three reasons as to why it was incumbent on Muḥammad to appoint 'Alī as his *waṣī*:[29]

(i) People who accepted Islam during the lifetime of Muḥammad consisted of two groups: those who embraced Islam willingly and those who submitted out of fear, or for furthering their worldly interests. The latter group was waiting for Muḥammad's death to revert back to their old practices and declare their hostility to Islam. What prevented them from doing so was that they were awe-stricken by the prophet, as he was divinely inspired. Muḥammad, therefore, was instructed to select the most virtuous, the most noble, and the most learned person of his community and to make him privy to his illumination of the spiritual world so that the *ta'yīd* would continue after his death through the *waṣī*. This, in turn, would keep the insincere group awe-stricken and the nascent religion would take roots.

(ii) Muḥammad was sent to the Arabs who were surrounded by the Persians and the Greeks (Byzantines). Both these peoples were known for their shrewdness, discernment, acumen, and their mastery of fine sciences (*al-'ulūm al-laṭīfa*). As long as Muḥammad lived, they were unable to deceive the Muslims. The prophet, therefore, was instructed to designate his *waṣī*, who was divinely inspired (*mu'ayyad min al-samā'*), and to entrust him with the teaching of fine sciences and noble secrets (*al-asrār al-laṭīfa*) which would inspire awe among the Persians and the Greeks.

(iii) Had Muḥammad died suddenly without appointing his *waṣī* and entrusting him with the secrets of prophecy and teaching him the subtleties of wisdom and the intricacies of hermeneutics, the people would have thought that the prophethood was a temporary phenomenon which would cease with his death.

Such, then, is the importance of hermeneutics, according to al-Sijistānī. In another work entitled *Sullam al-najāt*, after stressing the importance of the *ta'wīl*, he poses a hypothetical question and states:

If it is said: Why did the prophet then not take upon himself to impart the

[29] Ch. 7.

ta'wīl? It should be said to him: Had the prophet done it himself, it would have weakened his call to follow the Qur'ān and the *sharīʿa*. Because, if he would have said that his [real] intention in performing the ritual purification by water was to purge the soul from doubt and perplexity and to purify it by knowledge, his community would have said: Since we have known the truth there was no need to perform the ritual purification. But the prophet's silence about the *ta'wīl* was to make the *sharīʿa* incumbent on the faithful and that they should seek the *ta'wīl* of the *mutashābihāt*.[30] Thus, the faithful would obtain goodness [success] both in this world and the hereafter.[31]

Both al-Qāḍī al-Nuʿmān and Jaʿfar ibn Manṣūr al-Yaman establish the necessity of *ta'wīl* by deducing evidence from the Qur'ān, the *sunna* (prophetic sayings and deeds in general), and the sayings of the Imāms.[32] Al-Nuʿmān states that God, the Creator, alone is One and unique, while every created thing in this universe consists of pairs. The Qur'ān states: 'And of everything We have created pairs, that you may reflect' (Q. 51/49). Although the individual is seemingly one person, he is composed of body and soul. Body is the external aspect, while soul is the internal aspect. The former is apparent, whereas the latter is hidden.[33]

Next, al-Nuʿmān justifies the usage of the term *bāṭin* by stating that it is mentioned several times in the Qur'ān. For example, the Qur'ān states: 'He has bestowed his favours upon you, both outwardly (*ẓāhirat*^{an}) and inwardly (*bāṭinat*^{an})' (Q. 31/20), and,

30 See Q. 3/7. *Mutashābihāt* verses mean those that are equivocal, or ambiguous. These verses are susceptible to different interpretations, see Lane, *Lexicon*, s.v. *sh-b-h*.

31 Al-Sijistānī, *Sullam al-najāt*, MS (M. Goriawala, p. 11). This passage clearly indicates that the *ẓāhir* and the *bāṭin* are two complementary aspects of religion. The former, which consists of following the injunctions of the *shariʿa*, is aptly called *al-ʿibāda al-ʿamalīya* (worship by performing prescribed acts of devotion), while the latter, which consists of seeking the *ta'wīl*, is called *al-ʿibāda al-ʿilmīya* (worship through knowledge).

32 Al-Qāḍī al-Nuʿmān, *Asās al-ta'wīl*, 23–32. Except for a brief introduction, the rest of the book deals with the *ta'wīl* of the tales of the prophets. In this introduction, the author states that he has dealt with the principles of *ta'wīl* in greater detail in another work entitled *Ḥudūd al-maʿrifa*. A. Tāmir, the editor of *Asās al-ta'wīl*, states that several copies of the latter are to be found in Maṣyāf, Syria, but I have not come across a copy of it in the private collections of Ismāʿīlī MSS accessible to me.

There is no systematic *exposé* of the necessity of *ta'wīl* by Jaʿfar ibn Manṣūr al-Yaman in his extant works, but his *al-Shawāhid wa'l-bayān* is very useful in this respect. He has collected in it all the typical evidences from the Qur'ān and the *sunna* generally cited by the Shīʿīs to support their claim that ʿAlī was nominated by the Prophet as his *waṣī* and that he was also commissioned to impart the *ta'wīl*.

33 See also Jaʿfar ibn Manṣūr al-Yaman, *al-Shawāhid wa'l-bayān*, 13–14.

'Forsake the outward sin, and the inward' (Q. 6/120). Thus it is implied that the faithful have to know what are the inward bounties and sins.

Furthering his claims, al-Nuʿmān adds that the Qur'ān states: 'It is He who sent down upon thee the Book, wherein are clearly formulated verses, those are the essence of the Book, and others ambiguous (*mutashābihāt*)' (Q. 3/7).[34] It is obvious, therefore, that those ambiguous verses stand in want of interpretation. The Qur'ān further states in the same passage: 'And none knows its interpretation (*ta'wīl*) save only God and those firmly rooted in knowledge.' 'Those firmly rooted in knowledge', al-Nuʿmān asserts, are the legitimate Imāms.'[35]

The Qur'ān also contains parables. It states: 'And those parables (*amthāl*) We coin them for the people, but none understands them save those who have knowledge' (Q. 29/43), and, 'Indeed We have coined in the Qur'ān every kind of parable (*mathal*) for the people, so that they may reflect' (Q. 39/27). Those parables need interpretation.[36] Moreover, the stories (*aḥādīth*) narrated in the Qur'ān call for an explanation, as it is stated in the story of Joseph: 'So will your Lord choose you, and teach you the interpretation of tales' (Q. 12/6), and, 'So We established Joseph in the land, and that We might teach him the interpretation of tales' (Q. 12/21).

The fact that the *ta'wīl* is indispensable is also stressed by Muḥammad. He is reported to have said: 'Not a single verse of the Qur'ān was revealed to me without it having the *ẓahr* and the *baṭn* [outer and inner dimensions].'[37] Muḥammad is also reported to have said to ʿAlī: 'O ʿAlī, I am the possessor of revelation while you

[34] See n. 30, above.

[35] See also al-Kulīnī, *al-Uṣūl*, i. 213, 221, 263, who reports a tradition which states:

> Gabriel brought two pomegranates to the Prophet. The Prophet ate one while the other he split into two halves; he ate half and gave ʿAlī the other half. Then he said to ʿAlī: 'Do you know what these two pomegranates mean?' 'No,' replied ʿAlī. He said, 'As for the first, it is the prophethood in which you do not have any share, but the other is knowledge and you are my associate in it.'

[36] See also Jaʿfar ibn Manṣūr al-Yaman, *al-Shawāhid wa'l-bayān*, 17–18.

[37] *Ẓāhir* and *bāṭin* are found as variant readings in some MSS of *Asās al-ta'wīl*. *Ẓahr*, the outer dimension of the Qur'ān is its apparent meaning, while *baṭn*, its inner dimension, is the meaning known to the elect few. The Qur'ān must be understood on both levels, exoteric and esoteric, and *ta'wīl* includes both. See also Muḥammad Ḥusayn al-Ṭabāṭabā'ī, *al-Mīzān fī tafsīr al-Qur'ān* (Beirut, 1973), i. 40; Muḥsin al-Amīn, *Aʿyān al-Shīʿa* (Beirut, 1960), iii. 22, 55, 65.

are the possessor of [its] hermeneutics. You will have to fight for the hermeneutics as I fought for the revelation.'[38] Yet another tradition states: 'I am leaving among you the two important things. If you will hold fast to them you will never be led astray. They are: the book of God and my family, and they will never be separated from each other until they arrive at the pond [in the hereafter].'[39] Referring to the *ta'wīl* of the Qur'ān, Ja'far al-Ṣādiq is reported to have stated: 'We can speak about a word in seven [different] ways.'[40] It is also well known in Arabic that a word might have one meaning outwardly and quite another inwardly. As the Quranic style and diction are celebrated for their *i'jāz* (inimitability, uniqueness), it is not surprising that the Qur'ān encompasses all those linguistic beauties. Its outward style and diction are Muḥammad's miracle, while the explication of its inner meaning is the Imām's miracle.

III

Since revelation is a symbolic expression in human language of the spiritual realities, it contains profounder spiritual meaning than that which lies on the surface. It is the *ta'wīl* which extracts this spiritual meaning. According to al-Sijistānī, two categories of verses stand in obvious need of the *ta'wīl*: (i) verses with physical objects, such as heaven, earth, mountains, rivers, animals, trees, and fruits; (ii) the *mutashābihāt* verses. The first category should be treated figuratively, especially when the literal meaning appears dubious. The second category, as mentioned in the Qur'ān itself, is defined by al-Sijistānī as follows:

When the listener hears the *mutashābihāt* verses, his intelligence disapproves of [their obvious meaning], and he becomes confused, because [their meaning] departs from [the accepted] norms and customs, such as the ant's speech to Solomon, the hoopoe's bringing the news about the personal religious beliefs of the Queen of Sheba, the cooling off of fire for Abraham,

[38] Ja'far ibn Manṣūr al-Yaman, *al-Shawāhid wa'l-bayān*, 74. See also al-Amīn, *A'yān al-Shī'a*, iii. 102; this tradition is transmitted both by al-Nisā'ī and al-Ḥākim in their *al-Khaṣā'iṣ* and *al-Mustadrak* respectively.

[39] Ibid. 91. For a slightly different version see al-Tabrīzī, *Mishkāt al-maṣābīh*, ed. M. al-Albānī (Damascus, 1961), iii. 255, English trans., James Robson, *Mishkat al-Masabih* (Lahore, 1975), ii. 1350. It is also reported in the *Ṣaḥīḥ* of Muslim.

[40] On this see further n. 69, below.

the gushing forth of twelve fountains when Moses struck his staff on a rock etc., in the stories of the apostles (*qiṣaṣ al-anbiyāʾ*). . . . When an intelligent person is presented with those *mutashābihāt* verses, his faith is not reassured, because he finds [those stories] surrounded by an element of impossibility.[41]

After a lengthy discussion of the problems involved in those *mutashābihāt* verses, al-Sijistānī raises some philosophical questions: why should one seek the *taʾwīl* of uncommon phenomena mentioned in those verses? Does not the seeking of the *taʾwīl* imply the denial of those occurrences and consequently infringe upon the Almighty God's omnipotence? Al-Sijistānī defends the use of the *taʾwīl* by stating that the literal interpretation of those unusual phenomena violates the law of nature. It further implies that God, who has willed the universe to function according to the laws of nature, could annul His own wisdom. Once this wisdom is nullified, then the whole creation is invalidated, which leads to *taʿṭīl al-khāliq* (denuding God of all content). Miracles that break the law of nature are therefore possible, but occur rarely.

The second argument advanced by al-Sijistānī in defence of the *taʾwīl* is based on 'the principle of disparity (*tafāwut*)', which is also his principal argument in defence of prophecy.[42] The basic postulate in this theory is that except for God and the Intellect, disparity prevails over everything in the universe. It is because of this disparity that the affairs of the two realms, the intelligible and the sensible, sustain their order. Creation (that is, emanation), according to al-Sijistānī, is in itself the principle and the order of Being. Accordingly, the higher is simpler, more subtle, and nobler than the lower. It is always the lower which receives the influence of the higher. The key to universal order, therefore, is the knowledge of each particular thing's proper place in the hierarchy to which it belongs. This is precisely what the *taʾwīl* accomplishes.

Next, al-Sijistānī outlines some general principles of hermeneutics, whereby the above-mentioned two categories of verses are to be interpreted:[43]

(i) Words could be interchanged when they resemble each other in

[41] Al-Sijistānī, *Kitāb al-maqālīd*, 54th *iqlīd*. Jaʿfar ibn Manṣūr al-Yaman, *Kitāb al-kashf*, ed. R. Strothmann (Bombay, 1952), 131–5; he gives the *taʾwīl* of the Q. 3/7 wherein *mutashābihāt* means antagonists of the Imāms.

[42] Al-Sijistānī, *Ithbāt al-nubūʾāt*, 13–48.

[43] Al-Sijistānī, *Kitāb al-iftikhār*, ch. 12.

meaning, for example, earth (*arḍ*) could be interchanged for knowledge (*'ilm*), as explained below.

(ii) Some words are used figuratively in order to achieve special meaning and effect, for example, Muḥammad's saying to Anjasha, the camel-driver: 'Gently, do not break the *qawārīr*.'[44] *Qawārīr* means glass vessels, or bottles. Muḥammad used this word figuratively to indicate the delicate nature of women. Anjasha had a sweet singing voice. His singing, therefore, would make the camels go quickly. As the women were riding the camels, Muḥammad told Anjasha not to make those beasts run so quickly. Certain verses of the Qur'ān, therefore, should be treated figuratively.

(iii) The stories of the apostles are to be interpreted allegorically, because the recitation of past stories does not benefit the reader if there is no moral to be learned and applied to a similar situation (either in the present or the future).

Whether interpreting an allegorical story, or words used metaphorically, Ismā'īlīs use special terms for the expounding of *ta'wīl*: *mathal* (likeness, example, model) and *mamthūl* (one who is exemplified).[45] In fact, hermeneutic principles are tied to this theory of *al-mathal wa'l-mamthūl*, which is based on establishing parallelism between the spiritual, physical, and religious hierarchies. For example, the noon prayer is *al-mathal* for Muḥammad, or, in other words, Muḥammad is the *mamthūl* of the noon prayer. Similarly, 'the blessed olive tree' stands for the Imām 'Alī Zayn al-'Ābidīn ibn al-Ḥusayn ibn 'Alī ibn Abī Ṭālib, or, in other words, the Imām is exemplified by that tree.[46]

IV

Let us now turn to some examples. First, we will deal with the verses wherein a certain physical object is mentioned. All of the following examples, unless stated otherwise, are taken from al-Sijistānī's *Kitāb al-iftikhār*, chapter 12.

[44] Al-Bukhārī, *al-Ṣaḥīḥ* (Beirut, 1978), iv. 82–3; Muslim, *al-Ṣaḥīḥ* (Cairo, 1334/1916), vii. 79; al-Tabrīzī, *Mishkāt al-maṣābīḥ*, ii. 576, English trans., James Robson, *Mishkat al-Masabih*, ii. 1004.

[45] These terms are borrowed from the Qur'ān (see Q. 29/43, 39/27).

[46] Al-Sijistānī, *Kitāb al-maqālīd*, 52nd *iqlīd*; Ja'far ibn Manṣūr al-Yaman, *al-Shawāhid wa'l-bayān*, 17–18; Zāhid 'Alī, *Ismā'īlī madhhab*, 398–9; Kāmil Ḥusayn, *Fī adab Miṣr al-Fāṭimīya*, 9–10; id., ed., *Dīwān al-Mu'ayyad* (Cairo, 1949), 106–8.

i. Earth

The Qur'ān states: 'When the word falls on them, We shall bring forth for them out of the earth a beast that shall speak to them' (Q. 27/82). A beast coming out of the earth, al-Sijistānī notes, has generated a lot of discussion among the commentators, but without any satisfactory explanation. The obvious meaning of 'earth' is that it is a coarse, motionless body, whereupon vegetation grows and the animals live. It is an abode of all 'generated beings' (*al-mawālīd al-tabīʿīya*), and they cannot exist without it. Likewise, the soul's subsistence and that of all 'the spiritually-generated beings' (*al-mawālīd al-rūḥānīya*) depend on true, spiritual knowledge. 'Earth', therefore, in *ta'wīl* means knowledge. The true meaning of the above verse, thus, reads as follows. 'When the word falls on them' means 'When the community is confronted with the proof', they will know that what they believed was falsehood. 'We shall bring forth for them out of the earth a beast' means 'God shall bring forth for them a leader who is well-versed in knowledge.' '[A beast] that shall speak to them' means 'who will deliver them from falsehood to guidance and from [the state of] doubt to that of certainty'. This, then, is the primary meaning of 'earth' in *ta'wīl*. In its secondary meaning, the earth is applied to the *waṣī*, the *asās*, since he is the source of the *ta'wīl* and the true sciences (*al-ʿulūm al-ḥaqīqīya*).[47]

Similarly, 'journey in the land', in Q. 29/20 and 22/46, means 'journey seeking knowledge from its rightful possessors'. Those who succeed in obtaining that knowledge would know how creation was originated. It is this knowledge which 'brings forth the second growth' of the soul and obtains success in the hereafter.

Commenting on Q. 50/7, 'And the earth We have stretched it forth, and have flung firm mountains therein, and have caused of every lovely pair to grow thereon', al-Sijistānī states:

> When a person reflects on the earth's stretching whose parts are piled up one upon the other, he will not be able to understand its meaning since the [act of] stretching comes after that of contraction. It is also not possible to think of [the earth's] contraction without its stretching. Casting of unshakable mountains therein is also not necessary, because one casts a thing into a thing [which is made] of a different thing. Mountains have sprung from the earth itself. . . . Its *ta'wīl* is realized when the word 'earth' is exchanged for 'knowledge,' or 'the one who is the source of knowledge.'

[47] Al-Sijistānī, *Kitāb al-iftikhār*, ch. 12; see also Ja'far ibn Manṣūr al-Yaman, *al-Shawāhid wa'l-bayān*, 39–40, 113.

Thus, the setting up of the *asās* and [his] promulgation of the *ta'wīl* is analogous with the earth's stretching, while the casting of firm mountains is similar to appointing religious dignitaries to disseminate knowledge among the deserving. 'Causing of every lovely pair to grow thereon,' means the growth of twofold knowledge, exoteric and esoteric.[48]

The following verses are interpreted likewise. 'Know that God revives the earth after its death' (Q. 57/17) means that God will revive knowledge after it has become extinct and that the *asās* will revive his authority by returning the power to his son. 'The she-camel of God', in the story of the prophet Ṣāliḥ (Q. 11/64) stands for the *asās*; obedience to him is obligatory on the faithful. 'Leave her that she may eat in God's earth' means that he should be left alone so that he will derive benefit from the divine knowledge and will confer it upon them. 'Touch her not with evil' means that they should neither deceive him nor conspire against him. 'Lest you be seized by a nigh chastisement', means that they would miss their good fortune, whereby their souls will perish. Also of interest is Q. 21/105: 'And verily We have written in the Psalms, after the reminder: My righteous servants shall inherit the earth.' The literal meaning of earth in this verse does not make any sense, because it is always inherited by the oppressors and seized by the tyrants. The true meaning reads: 'My righteous servants shall inherit the knowledge.'

ii. The Heavens

The word *samā'* (sky) is applied to a fine, rotating body studded with the stars. It is analogous with the *nāṭiq*, who forms 'the sky of religion'.[49] For example, the verse, 'He sends down water from the sky, so that valleys flow each in its measure' (Q. 13/17) means that God revealed the Qur'ān to Muḥammad's heart (literally, brought it out from the prophet's heart) so that the people would carry it, each according to his capacity and the purity of his soul. 'And the flood carries a swelling foam' means the differences and disputes that surfaced among the Muslim community with regard to the Quranic exegesis and hermeneutics. In the same verse, 'Then, as for the foam, it vanishes as jetsam, while, as for that which profits mankind, it remains in the earth' means that the differences and

[48] Al-Sijistānī, *Kitāb al-iftikhār*, ch. 12.

[49] See also Ja'far ibn Manṣūr al-Yaman, *al-Shawāhid wa'l-bayān*, 39–40, 60, 82.

disputes vanish, but that which is useful to mankind remains with the *asās*.

In its secondary meaning, the sky is applied to the *sharī'a*, promulgated by the *nāṭiq*. The verse, 'On the day when We shall roll up heaven as a scroll rolled up with the writings' (Q. 21/105), means the cancellation of the *sharī'a* and its abrogation.

Commenting on Q. 41/11–12, 'Then He lifted Himself to heaven when it was smoke, and said to it and to the earth: Come willingly, or unwillingly. They said: We come willingly. So, He ordained them as seven heavens in two days, and revealed its mandate in every heaven', al-Sijistānī states that God's address to the dead body (that is, the heaven and earth) can be understood either in the sense of an inspiration, or in the sense of (the) Creation. He then adds, how could a dead body, which does not have intelligence, be inspired? The second option, that is, discourse in the sense of their creation, is also impossible. The real meaning of the above verse is that the Soul looked at the administration of *dawr al-satr* (the epoch of concealment)[50] and the state of the leaders in that epoch. At first, it looked as if it were smoke. The furnishing of inspiration did not kindle any (human) soul who would rectify the situation. The Soul, therefore, realized that the remedy, that is, the administration of laws, could be provided by depositing the hidden, inner meaning underneath the outward meaning. 'And said to the heaven and to the earth: Come willingly, or unwillingly' means that the soul enjoined on the *nāṭiq* and the *asās* the necessity of setting up two *da'was*, voluntary and obligatory, where the former is for the *bāṭin* and the latter for the *ẓāhir*. 'They said: We come willingly' means that both the *nāṭiq* and the *asās* willingly accepted the call. 'He ordained them as seven heavens in two days' means that the Soul ordained seven leaders from the epoch of concealment in two distinct hierarchies: exterior and interior. 'Revealed its mandate in every heaven' means that each leader's share of God's Word was inspired to him individually. The words 'sky' and 'earth' in Q. 11/44 and 54/11–14 are to be interpreted similarly.

iii. Mountains

Firmly established mountains in the land serve as signposts whereby the travellers are guided and wherefrom streams gush

[50] Ismā'īlīs view history as a progressive cycle which develops through various epochs; see Poonawala, *Biobibliography*, 21–2.

forth. In *ta'wīl* they stand for the *ḥujaj*,[51] who are established in every region of the earth to guide the faithful with their knowledge. Streams gushing forth from the mountains are analogous with the fountains of wisdom and knowledge radiating from the *ḥujaj*. An example of this is David's subjection of the mountains and their singing God's glory with him in the following verse, 'And with David We subjected the mountains to give glory' (Q. 21/79). Taken literally, this verse does not make any sense. David was an *imām*, obedience to whom was obligatory. The mountains in the above verse, therefore, mean the *ḥujaj* and various *da'wa* dignitaries.[52] The passage Q. 34/10 is to be interpreted similarly.

The Qur'ān also states: 'And when Moses came to Our appointed time and his Lord spoke with him, he said: My Lord, show me, that I may behold Thee! He said: Thou shalt not see Me, but behold the mountain, if it stays fast in its place, then thou shalt see Me' (Q. 7/143). Commenting on the above verse, al-Sijistānī states that it is in obvious need of interpretation. How could God manifest Himself through an inanimate object, such as the mountain? How could a major lawgiver–prophet like Moses ask such an impossible question? The real meaning is that Moses thought that his intellect would be able to perceive the Creator's quiddity (*innīya*) and that he would be able to dispense, via negation, with affirming the *tawḥīd* (unity of God). When he realized that it was not possible, he repented and glorified his Lord by asserting *tanzīh* (dislodging all association from God). The mountain in the above verse means the Soul.[53]

Similarly, the mountain is mentioned in Q. 59/21, 'If We had sent down this Qur'ān upon a mountain, thou wouldst have seen it humbled, split asunder out of the fear of God.' The mountain here represents a learned, pious, and godfearing *mu'min* (faithful). Al-Sijistānī cites the following two verses to support this interpretation: 'Is it not time that the hearts of those who believe should

[51] The *ḥujja* (pl. *ḥujaj*) is a particular figure in the *da'wa* hierarchy who serves at a given time as an evidence, or a proof, among mankind, of God's will; it also means a rank following that of the Imām. Ismā'īlī doctrine divides the inhabited earth into twelve regions; each region's *da'wa* hierarchy is headed by a *ḥujja*. Zāhid 'Alī, *Ismā'īlī madhhab*, 305. See also al-Kulīnī, *Kitāb al-ḥujja*, in his *al-Uṣūl*, i. 168–74.

[52] See also al-Qāḍī al-Nu'mān, *Asās al-ta'wīl*, 253.

[53] See also Ja'far ibn Manṣūr al-Yaman, *al-Farā'iḍ wa ḥudūd al-dīn*, MS (Goriawala, p. 14), 229–30; his *ta'wīl* is different.

be humbled to the remembrance of God?' (Q. 57/16), and, 'Only those of His servants fear God who have knowledge' (Q. 35/28).

iv. Trees

Goodly trees mentioned in the Qur'ān are the righteous, godfearing, and virtuous people, while the corrupt trees, or those uprooted from the earth, are the debauched ones. 'The blessed olive tree' in Q. 24/35, therefore, stands for the Imām ʿAlī Zayn al-ʿĀbidīn ibn al-Ḥusayn,[54] while 'the accursed tree' in Q. 17/60 stands for the second Umayyad caliph, Yazīd ibn Muʿāwiya, who was responsible for Imām al-Ḥusayn's massacre at Karbalā'.[55]

These were, then, some examples of Ismāʿīlī *ta'wīl* of certain physical objects mentioned in the Qur'ān. Interpretation of the tales of the prophets is one of the major themes in Ismāʿīlī *ta'wīl* literature, especially with Jaʿfar ibn Manṣūr al-Yaman. The main purpose of those stories, as stated earlier, is to drive home a moral lesson; hence, they are interpreted allegorically. Even a cursory survey of all those stories is beyond the scope of the present study. As an illustration, I will confine myself to the story of Jonah, which is also selected by al-Sijistānī, because, according to him, it is in greater need of *ta'wīl* than any other story. Jonah was an *imām* and was entrusted with the task of upholding the *sharīʿa* of his epoch's *nāṭiq*. He lived under difficult circumstances and did not measure up to his task. Consequently, he was demoted, his knowledge faded away, and he was overwhelmed by a younger rival who was accomplished in exoteric knowledge. Jonah being swallowed by the whale (Q. 37/142) represents his falling into the abyss of ignorance and doubt. Then, his being thrown on a desert shore while he was sick (Q. 37/145) means that, when he confessed his wrongdoing, God flung him from the depth of ignorance to the spaciousness of knowledge. God's causing a tree of gourds to grow over him (Q. 37/146) signifies that God appointed a trustworthy, knowledgeable, and gentle person to treat the affliction into which Jonah had fallen so that he might be completely cured.[56] Most of the stories of

[54] See n. 46, above.

[55] Jaʿfar ibn Manṣūr al-Yaman, *al-Shawāhid wa'l-bayān*, 310; he states that the accursed tree stands for the Umayyads, in general, as well as the adherents of Mazdaism.

[56] See also al-Qāḍī al-Nuʿmān, *Asās al-ta'wīl*, 286–90; Jaʿfar ibn Manṣūr al-Yaman, *al-Shawāhid wa'l-bayān*, 569–74. There are some differences in their *ta'wīl*.

the prophets narrated in the Qur'ān are similarly interpreted.[57]

All of the aforementioned three authors, especially al-Sijistānī, use *ta'wīl* on which to hang the Neoplatonic cosmology and eschatology.[58] God's Command, described in the Qur'ān,[59] fits well into the Ismā'īlī scheme of creation, especially al-Sijistānī's doctrine of the Command (*amr*), or the Word (*al-kalima*),[60] namely, that there is one intermediary between the Originator/Innovator (*mubdi'*, that is, God) and the First Originated/Innovated (*al-mubda' al-awwal*, that is, the Intellect), and that is the Command, or the Word of the Originator.[61] The Quranic pairs of words, such as *al-kursī wa'l-'arsh* (royal seat and throne) (Q. 2/255, 39/75), *al-qalam wa'l-lawḥ* (pen and tablet) (Q. 96/4, 85/22), *al-shams wa'l-qamar* (sun and moon) (Q. *passim*), *al-qaḍā' wa'l-qadar* (fate and divine decree),[62] are equated with the Two Roots (*aṣlān*), that is, the Intellect and the Soul, in turn, corresponding to the *naṭiq* and the *asās*. Al-Sijistānī even takes great pains to interpret Q. 13/4, 13/28, 5/116, 39/21, 67/10, and 89/5 to establish that both the Intellect (*al-'aql*) and the Soul (*al-nafs*) are mentioned in the Qur'ān.[63]

The concept of the Last Judgement held by the commonalty, that it will be accompanied with complete upset of the cosmos, dislocation of the earth and the heaven, such as the splitting of the heaven, scattering of the stars, swarming over of the seas, etc., is ridiculed by al-Sijistānī. How could God, he argues, gather mankind and call them to account when the cosmos, which sustains

[57] For the tales of the prophets see al-Qāḍī al-Nu'mān, *Asās al-ta'wīl*; Ja'far ibn Manṣūr al-Yaman, *Asrār al-nuṭaqā'*, MS Hamdani Collection; id., *Sarā'ir al-nuṭaqā'*, MS in the possession of the late A. A. A. Fyzee; id., *al-Farā'iḍ wa ḥudūd al-dīn*.

[58] The terminology used by al-Sijistānī to describe creation is of Quranic origin, e.g., God is described as *al-khāliq*, *al-bāri'*, *al-muṣawwir*, *badī' al-samāwāt wa'l-arḍ*. Thus, those terms imply both temporal creation (in the religious sense) and real creation (in the philosophical sense of emanation). Q. 59/24; 2/117; Al-Sijistānī, *Kitāb al-maqālīd*, 14th *iqlīd*; P. Walker, pp. 133 ff.

[59] 'His command, when He desires a thing, is to say to it "Be," and it is', Q. 36/82.

[60] The Command is also called Will (*irāda*).

[61] Al-Sijistānī, *Kitāb al-iftikhār*, ch. 2; id., *Kitāb al-maqālīd*, 19th *iqlīd*.

[62] In theology, these words were taken to mean predestination and freewill. See Harry Wolfson, *The Philosophy of Kalam* (Cambridge, Mass., 1976), 601–24. The Qur'ān uses the word *qadar* in the sense of both power and measuring, see Fazlur Rahman, *Major Themes of the Qur'ān* (Chicago, 1980), 12, 65–8.

[63] Al-Sijistānī, *Kitāb al-iftikhār*, ch. 3.

human existence, is dislocated? Reward and punishment are similarly interpreted spiritually.[64]

Interpretation of the *sharīʿa* is another celebrated theme in Ismāʿīlī *taʾwīl*. Al-Sijistānī has devoted the last five chapters of his *Kitāb al-iftikhār* to expound the *taʾwīl* of the five pillars of Islam. A brief summary is in order. Ablution (*wuḍūʾ*), the minor ritual purification performed before prayer, implies disavowal of the imamate from those who claimed it unjustly. Water used for purification represents knowledge which purifies the soul from doubt and uncertainty. Prayers signify *walāya* (devotion) of the *awliyāʾ* (plural of *walī*, meaning saint, man close to God, that is, the Imāms). The five obligatory prayers correspond to the five *ḥudūd*: the Intellect, the Soul, the *nāṭiq*, the *asās*, and the Imām. The poor tax (*zakāt*) in *taʾwīl* means that those individuals who are rooted in knowledge should set up trustworthy mentors to guide the people. By so doing, that is, by setting up a hierarchy, the lower rank would become *zakāt* for the higher. Fasting (*ṣawm*) means observing silence and not revealing the secret to the uninitiated. Pilgrimage to Mecca, that is the house of God, symbolizes having an audience with the Imām, because he is the house wherein knowledge of God resides.[65]

Another interesting aspect of *taʾwīl* found in the works of al-Sijistānī is the technique of transposing the letters of certain verses to vindicate a particular Shīʿī tenet. *Sūra* 108, accordingly, is employed to demonstrate ʿAlī's *waṣāya* (the rank of plenipotentiary). First, al-Sijistānī explains the occasion of its revelation and states that when Muḥammad was informed about the future events which would take place in his community, especially that his grandsons would be persecuted by the Umayyads, he was overcome by grief. Subsequently, the *sūra* entitled 'Abundance' (that is, Q. 108) was revealed, giving him the good tidings concerning his offspring through his daughter Fāṭima and ʿAlī:

إِنَّا أَعْطَيْنَٰكَ ٱلْكَوْثَرَ فَصَلِّ لِرَبِّكَ وَٱنْحَرْ إِنَّ شَانِئَكَ هُوَ ٱلْأَبْتَرُ

'Surely we have given thee abundance; so pray unto thy Lord and sacrifice. Surely he that hates thee, he is the one cut off.' This

[64] Ibid., chs. 9–11.

[65] Ibid., chs. 13–17. See also al-Qāḍī al-Nuʿmān, *Taʾwīl al-daʿāʾim*, ed. M. al-Aʿẓamī (Cairo, n.d.); al-Nuʿmān's details differ from those of al-Sijistānī.

interpretation, al--Sijistānī contends, can be demonstrated by transposing the letters of the *sūra* to read:

ألا أنّ الكوثر الطاهر وصيّك علي إن تنحر فإن شانئك أبو بكر

The absence of letters *qāf* (indicating *'atīq*, that is, Abū Bakr[66]) and *mīm* (indicating 'Umar and 'Uthmān) from the *sūra* further indicates that the caliphate will not continue in the progeny of those three caliphs.[67] Similarly, Q. 17/60 is employed to demonstrate the imamate of al-Ḥusayn ibn 'Alī ibn Abī Ṭālib and the infidelity of the second Umayyad caliph, Yazīd.[68]

The fact that Ismā'īlis take great pride in their *ta'wīl* is obvious from the very title of al-Sijistānī's polemical work, *Kitāb al-iftikhār* ('The book of pride'). In this book, after refuting his opponents' arguments, al-Sijistānī expounds his own doctrine and then concludes by stating: 'What pride is greater than comprehension of the *ḥaqā'iq* and pursuing the [right] path?' This phrase, like a refrain, is repeated after each argument throughout the book.

Despite the Ismā'īlī claim that their *ta'wīl* is derived from the Imāms, numerous differences in interpretation are found in the works of the aforesaid three authors.[69] One example will suffice. The verse relating to light (Q. 24/35), interpreted by al-Sijistānī (= *Sij*) and Ja'far ibn Manṣūr al-Yaman (= *Jaf*), is selected; what follows is a brief summary.[70] The verse in question reads: 'God is the Light of the heavens and the earth, the likeness of His Light is as a niche wherein is a lamp, the lamp in a glass, the glass as it were a glittering star kindled from a blessed tree, an olive that is neither of the East nor of the West whose oil would almost glow forth, even if no fire touched it; Light upon Light; God guides to His Light whom He will.'

Light	*Sij*:	Light of knowledge radiating from the Command of God, and from the Intellect and the Soul
	Jaf:	*imām*

[66] 'Atīq was Abū Bakr's nickname; see al-Ṭabarī, *Ta'rīkh* (Cairo, 1962), iii. 424–5.

[67] Al-Sijistānī, *Kitāb al-iftikhār*, ch. 7.

[68] Ibid., ch. 8.

[69] Zāhid 'Alī, 399 ff.; he has dealt with this question at great length.

[70] Al-Sijistānī, *Kitāb al-maqālīd*, 52nd *iqlīd*; Ja'far ibn Manṣūr al-Yaman, *Kitāb al-kashf*, 7, 16–18 (his interpretation resembles that of al-Kulīnī, *al-Uṣūl*, i. 195). See also Henry Corbin, 'Epiphanie divine et naissance spirituelle dans la gnose Ismaélienne', *Eranos Jahrbuch*, 23 (1954), 141–249.

Niche	*Sij*: *nāṭiq*
	Jaf: Fāṭima (the Prophet's daughter)
Lamp	*Sij*: *asās*
	Jaf: Imām al-Ḥusayn
Glass	*Sij*: The first *mutimm*, i.e., the first Imām, al-Ḥasan
	Jaf: When al-Ḥusayn was in his mother's womb
A glittering star	*Sij*: Imām al-Ḥusayn
	Jaf: Fāṭima
The Blessed Olive Tree	*Sij*: Imām ʿAlī Zayn al-ʿĀbidīn
	Jaf: Abraham
Neither of the East nor of the West	*Sij*: It qualifies the tree, i.e., ʿAlī Zayn al-ʿĀbidīn
	Jaf: Abraham's religion, which was neither Judaism nor Christianity
Oil would almost glow forth	*Sij*: Imām Muḥammad al-Bāqir
	Jaf: Al-Ḥusayn might have spoken about his imamate while he was still in his mother's womb
Even if no fire touched it	*Sij*: Fire stands for Imām Jaʿfar al-Ṣādiq
	Jaf: Even though the (previous) Imām had not yet appointed al-Ḥusayn as his successor
Light upon light	*Sij*: Al-Qāʾim
	Jaf: (Text is not clear)

It is obvious, thus, that differences in interpretation of the same verse between the two authors are quite striking. In his *Asās al-taʾwīl*, al-Qāḍī al-Nuʿmān quotes a tradition from Imām Jaʿfar al-Ṣādiq. It states that one day the Imām, while he was explaining the *taʾwīl* of a certain verse, was confronted with a question from a listener saying that his *taʾwīl* on that particular day was different from the one given by him on a previous occasion. The Imām, thereupon, replied: 'We can speak about a word in seven different ways.' When the astounded questioner said, 'Seven!', the Imām retorted: 'Yes, even seventy. If you ask us more we can increase it even more.' Aspects of *taʾwīl*, that is, explanation and interpretation, therefore, al-Nuʿmān notes, depend on the rank (*ḥadd*) of its practitioner, the higher the rank, the higher the number of interpretations.[71] It is clear from the above tradition that differences in interpretation by various authors are glossed over.

[71] Al-Qāḍī al-Nuʿmān, *Asās al-taʾwīl*, 27.

Finally, exegesis, or interpretation of the Bible, has been used by both Jews and Christians throughout their histories for various purposes. The exigencies of particular historical situations, as well as polemical or apologetical conditions, very often dictate and anticipate the truth to be discovered from the sacred scripture. Quranic exegesis has also been exploited for different ends by different groups, Ismāʿīlīs consider *ta'wīl* as a science *par excellence* and cultivate it studiously. Al-Sijistānī divides knowledge, derived either through 'revelation' or '[Greek] wisdom',[72] into three categories: lower, middle, and higher. He then states that the knowledge of revelation consists of jurisprudence, *ʿilm al-kalām* (scholastic theology), and *ta'wīl*, and they are graded on an upward scale.[73] Al-Sijistānī further points out that both types of knowledge (that is, revelation and wisdom) do not conflict with each other. The growth and development of Ismāʿīlī *ta'wīl* can thus be seen as a reflection of the general concern of Muslims and of Islamic theology, which was being developed in the fourth/tenth century. In his numerous studies, Henry Corbin has rightly pointed out that it was the tension between the *sharīʿa* and the *ḥaqīqa* that led to esoterism, which, in turn, led to what he calls 'herméneutique spirituelle du Qorān'.[74] *Ta'wīl* plays an important role in the Ismāʿīlī formulation of a new synthesis of reason and revelation based on Neoplatonism and Shīʿī doctrine.

[72] *Ḥikma* (wisdom) is used loosely by Ismāʿīlī authors to signify philosophy. See *Rasā'il Ikhwān al-Ṣafā'*, iii. 345–7; both the *ḥukamā'* and the *ʿulamā'* are described as heirs to the prophets.

[73] Al-Sijistānī, *Ithbāt al-nubū'āt*, 122. *Rasā'il Ikhwān al-Safā'* (i. 321–3) classifies people into the following eight categories in ascending order: (i) the Qur'ān reciters and the scribes; (ii) the transmitters of the Prophet's biography as well as his traditions; (iii) the *fuqahā'* (jurists) and the *ʿulamā'* (scholars); (iv) *al-mufassirūn* (the Qur'ān commentators); (v) the warriors who defend Islam; (vi) the caliphs who uphold the *sharīʿa*; (vii) the *zuhhād wa'l-ʿubbād fī'l-masājid* (the ascetics and the devout worshippers); (viii) the possessors of *ta'wīl* (the Imāms).

[74] Henry Corbin, 'Pour une morphologie de la spiritualité Shīʿite', *Eranos Jahrbuch*, 29 (1960), 57–71; id., 'Le Combat Spirituel du Shīʿisme', *Eranos Jahrbuch*, 30 (1961), 69–125.

11

Interpretation as Revelation: The Qur'ān Commentary of Sayyid 'Alī Muḥammad Shīrāzī, the Bāb (1819–1850)

B. TODD LAWSON

THE writings of the Bāb are many; on his own estimate they exceed 500,000 verses.[1] In the past, these writings have been examined mainly for what they have to tell us about the history of the Bābī movement. The purpose of this discussion is to draw attention to the literature itself in order to begin an evaluation of what must surely be one of the most important questions to be raised not only by students of the Bābī and Bahā'ī religions, but also by those interested in the history of nineteenth-century Iran, upon which the dramatic events associated with the name of the Bāb made such a vivid mark. That question, how did the Bāb read the Holy Book of Islam, will automatically be of interest to those engaged in studying the history of the interpretation of the Qur'ān. It should be mentioned that *tafsīr* represents only one of several types of exposition to which the Bāb applied himself. That it should be regarded as among the most important types is clear from the mere fact that it comprises a large percentage of his extant work and that it was by means of a *tafsīr* that he first made his claims known.

It was the *Tafsīr surat Yūsuf*, also known as the *Qayyūm al-asmā'*, which the Bāb's earliest followers used to propagate his cause. It has been referred to by Bahā'u'llāh (1817–92) as 'the first, the greatest, and mightiest of all books', and by Shoghi Effendi (1897–1957) as being 'universally regarded, during almost the entire ministry of the Bāb, as the Qur'ān of the people of the Bayān'.[2] In addition to this work, there are three other major *tafsīr*s

[1] 'Alī Muḥammad Shīrāzī, *Bayān-i farsī* = *Le Béyan Persan*, trans. A.-L.-M. Nicolas (Paris, 1911–14), iii. 113. See also the discussion of the amount of the Bāb's work that has survived in Denis MacEoin, 'A Critical Survey of the Sources for Early Bābī Doctrine and History', unpublished thesis (Cambridge, 1976) (hereafter: MacEoin, 'Critical'), 8–10.

[2] Bahā'u'llāh, the title assumed by Mirzā Ḥusayn 'Alī-yi Nūrī, was the founder of

extant, and a series of shorter commentaries.[3] It appears that all of these belong to the earliest period of the Bāb's career and are, therefore, important in themselves as a source for his earliest thought.[4]

As will be seen, some of this material represents a distinct type of scriptural interpretation; this is particularly apparent in the *Tafsīr sūrat Yūsuf*, excerpts from which will appear below. That there are problems connected with the proper categorization of some of these writings is something which Browne suggested long ago; in speaking of the above-mentioned *tafsīr* he said: 'A *Commentary* in the strict sense of the word it is not, but rather a mystical and often unintelligible rhapsody.'[5]

In the following pages an attempt will be made to show some aspects of this work and one other of the Bāb's *tafāsīr* in an attempt to indicate, in however limited a form, some elements of the logic of structure and content of this important work while calling attention to the clear transformation of style and thought between it and the earlier *Tafsīr sūrat al-baqara*. Before proceeding directly to the texts, a brief outline of the life of the Bāb will help put the following discussion in perspective.

1. LIFE OF THE BĀB

The Bāb was born in Shīrāz on 20 October 1819 (1 Muḥarram

the Bahā'ī faith. This comment is found in his *Kitāb-i iqān* (Cairo, n.d.), 180 = *Kitāb-i-iqān: The Book of Certitude* (Wilmette, 1970), 231. The second statement is from Shoghi Effendi, great-grandson of Bahā'u'llāh and eventual Guardian of the Baha'ī Faith (*walī amru'llāh*), *God Passes By* (Wilmette, 1970), 23.

[3] All works of the Bāb referred to in this paper are, unless otherwise noted, still in MS. The following and the titles of his works which contain either the word *tafsīr* or *sharḥ* (the first four being in chronological order): (1) *Tafsīr sūrat al-baqara* (actually the first *juz'* of the Qur'ān); (2) *Tafsīr sūrat Yūsuf* (Q. 12); (3) *Tafsīr sūrat al-kawthar* (Q. 108); (4) *Tafsīr sūrat wa'l-aṣr* (Q. 103); (5) *Tafsīr sūrat al-ḥamd* (Q. 1) (distinct from (1) above, which includes *sūrat al-fātiḥa*); (6) *Tafsīr sūrat al-tawḥīd* (Q. 112); (7) *Tafsīr sūrat al-qadr* (Q. 97); (8) Tafsīr bismillāh; (9) *Tafsīr hā'* (commentary on the significances of the Arabic letter *hā'*, the 26th of the alphabet); (10) *Tafsīr āyat al-kursī* (Q. 2/255); (11) *Tafsīr āyat al-nūr* (Q. 24/35); (12) *Tafsīr ḥadīth Kumayl*; (13) *Tafsīr ḥadīth al-jārīya*; (14) *Tafsīr naḥnu wajhu'llāh*. Not all of these works concern Quranic material.

[4] E. G. Brown, 'Bāb, Bābīs', *Encyclopedia of Religion and Ethics* (New York, 1909), ii. 305a.

[5] E. G. Browne, 'Some Remarks on the Bābī Texts Edited by Baron Victor Rosen in Vols. I and VI of the *Collections scientifiques de l'Institut des langues Orientales de Saint Petersbourg*', *JRAS* 24 (1892), 261.

1235) into a family of fairly prosperous merchants. His father died when he was about 7 years old, and the responsibility for his upbringing devolved upon his uncle. His formal education consisted of six or seven years at a local *maktab* under the direction of one Shaykh 'Ābid, who happened to be an adherent of the then somewhat popular Shaykhī school. It appears that the Bāb, whose name was 'Alī Muḥammad, was not particularly fond of school, although, according to some reports, this antipathy was not the result of any intellectual incapacity. On the contrary, the few reports which exist tend to show the Bāb at this early stage as the owner of a precociously inquisitive and outspoken nature.[6]

At age 13 the Bāb left the *maktab* and two years later moved with his uncle to Būshihr to pursue the family business there. After about four years of working in partnership with his uncle, the Bāb became independent. There is disagreement about what the Bāb's attitude to trade was, but so far no compelling evidence has been brought to light to support the statement that this basic attitude was negative.[7] It was while the Bāb was in Būshihr that he began to write various religious works. Although it is not known exactly what these were, they probably included essays on various theological topics and eulogies of the Imāms. Some of these were apparently written at the request of certain of his fellow merchants. There is also an indication that even before voicing any particular claim to spiritual authority, the Bāb had aroused a certain amount of attention, and even ill will, by the production of these earliest works.[8]

In 1840, the Bāb closed his business and left Būshihr for the region of 'Atabāt (lit. 'thresholds', it refers to the holy cities of

[6] H. M. Balyuzi, *The Bāb, the Herald of the Day of Days* (Oxford, 1973), 34–9. Other treatments of the Bāb's life are: Amanat Abbas, 'The Early Years of the Bābī Movement: Background and Development', unpublished Ph.D. thesis (Oxford University, 1981), 100–47; now published, Cornell University Press. Denis MacEoin, 'From Shaykhīsm to Bābism: A Study in Charismatic Renewal in Shī'ī Islām', unpublished Ph.D. thesis (Cambridge University, 1979; available from University Microfilms, Ann Arbour) (hereafter: MacEoin, 'Charismatic'), 137–42. An important discussion of the problems associated with the biography of the Bāb is Stephen Lambden, 'An Episode in the Childhood of Sayyid Ali Muhammad the Bāb', in Peter Smith, ed., *In Iran: Studies in Bābī and Bahā'ī History*, iii (Los Angeles, 1986), 1–31.

[7] The Bāb's statement, cited by MacEoin, 'Charismatic', 138, that a dog belonging to a Jew is to be preferred to the people of the bazaar because of the latter's lack of religious devotion, must be seen as an indictment of the people themselves, not their occupation.

[8] See Balyuzi, p. 40; MacEoin, 'Charismatic', 138–9.

Karbalā' and Najaf), where he remained for nearly a year.[9] It was during this time that he attended lectures by Sayyid Kāẓim Rashtī, the undisputed successor of Shaykh Aḥmad, founder of the Shaykhī school. It seems that the Bāb's family did not approve of his preoccupation with things religious and that his marriage, in 1842, was arranged in the hope of inducing him to concentrate his attention more on the practicalities of existence. Prior to his marriage, while he was still in Karbalā', it is said that the Bāb became acquainted with and attracted a certain amount of attention from a number of Shaykhīs, some of whom later became his followers.[10] Even his arch-enemy, Muḥammad Karīm Kirmānī, says in his polemical *Izhāq al-bāṭil* that, although he himself never met the Bāb, it was true that he was held in respect in Karbalā' and that he did in fact meet and serve Sayyid Kāẓim.[11]

The picture that emerges, then, is of a pious young man, who, despite a lack of formal training in the higher religious sciences was nevertheless motivated to produce religious works, the nature of which was sufficiently impressive to win the respect of his readers. Indeed, it was undoubtedly the very fact of this lack of training, together with his status as a merchant, which called attention to his undeniable spiritual and literary gifts. Thus a variation on the Islamic theme of the 'unlettered prophet' begins to take shape. In this connection it is also interesting, and perhaps instructive with reference to the way in which Muḥammad's so-called illiteracy may be understood, to observe that the Bāb was manifestly not illiterate; in fact, many of his writings were produced before witnesses. That these works were written by one untutored, or at best self-taught, and perhaps even more convincingly, that they were written with astonishing speed and fluency, combined to present to some people at least an evidentiary miracle comparable, in every way, to the Qur'ān itself.[12]

In 1844, shortly after the death of Sayyid Kāẓim, the Bāb put forth his claim, in writing, to be in direct contact with the Hidden Imām and so a locus of tremendous spiritual authority. Mullā

[9] Opinion is divided on just how long the Bāb stayed in Karbalā', where Kāẓim Rashtī held his classes. The discussion appears rooted in polemic; sources favourable to the Bāb prefer a shorter length of time.

[10] See Peter Smith and Moojan Momen, 'The Bābī Movement: A Resource Mobilization Perspective', in P. Smith, *In Iran*, iii. 60 and references.

[11] Cited by MacEoin, 'Charismatic', 140.

[12] See, e.g., A.-L.-M. Nicolas, *Seyyed Alī Mohammed dit le Bāb* (Paris, 1905), 234.

Ḥusayn and seventeen other young Shaykhīs, including the famous poetess Ṭāhira, gave their allegiance to him, and the Bābī movement was born. Some months later the Bāb departed on his pilgrimage, returning to Shīrāz in March 1845. As a result of the activity of his followers, he was now arrested for the first time and shortly released. In 1846, the Bāb took up residence in Iṣfahān where he remained from September of that year until March 1847, shortly after his powerful protector, the *mu'tamid-i dawla*, Manuchir Khān, died on February 21. At this time he was arrested by government troops and escorted to the western frontier of Iran where he was to spend the rest of his life in secluded imprisonment.

During this last stage of his career, the Bāb continued to experience and record revelations. It was at this time that his Persian *Bayān* was written, together with many prayers, *ajwiba*, and other correspondence to his by now numerous following throughout Iran. According to Nabīl, the Bāb, during the nine months he was held in the castle at Māh-kū, produced no less than nine complete commentaries on the Qur'ān.[13]

As is well known, the Bāb's literary activity came to an end on 9 July 1850, when he was publicly executed in Tabrīz.[14]

2. THE SHAYKHĪ SCHOOL

In a 'Foreword' to his account of the first hundred years of the Bābī/Bahā'ī religion, Shoghi Effendi asserts the significance of the Shaykhīya in Bābī and Bahā'ī history:

> I shall seek to represent and correlate, in however cursory a manner, those momentous happenings which have insensibly, relentlessly, and under the very eyes of successive generations, perverse, indifferent or hostile, transformed a heterodox and seemingly negligible offshoot of the Shaykhī school of the Ithna-'Ashariyyih sect of Shi'ah Islam into a world religion.[15]

The 'seemingly neglible offshoot' here mentioned is of course the

[13] Mullā Muḥammad Zarāndī (Nabīl), *The Dawnbreakers: Nabīl's Narrative of the Early Days of the Bahā'ī Revelation*, trans. and ed. Shoghi Effendi (Wilmette, 1932) (hereafter: Nabīl), 31.

[14] There is some disagreement about the exact date; see Moojan Momen, ed., *The Bābī and Bahā'ī Religions, 1844–1944: Some Contemporary Western Accounts* (Oxford, 1981), 77–82.

[15] Shoghi Effendi, *God Passes By*, p. xii.

Bābī religion. It has already been mentioned that the Bāb's teacher, Shaykh 'Ābid, was a follower of this Shaykhī school. It is also known that several of the Bāb's merchant relatives were attracted to the teachings of this movement.[16] As was mentioned above, the Bāb himself attended the lectures of Sayyid Kāẓim Rashtī and in at least two works directly refers to him as 'my teacher' (*mu'allimī*).[17] It is therefore important that at least some brief statement on the history and teachings of the Shaykhī school be offered so that a better understanding may be gained of the context in which the Bāb wrote his Quranic commentaries.

The founder of the Shaykhīya, or the Kashfīya as its adherents preferred to be designated, was Shaykh Aḥmad ibn Zayn al-Dīn ibn Ibrāhīm ibn Ṣaqr ibn Ibrāhīm ibn Dāghir al-Aḥsā'ī. He was born in 1752 in a small village in Baḥrayn (namely al-Aḥsā) apparently of pure Arab lineage, and his family had been followers of the Shī'ī version of orthodoxy for five generations. From his early childhood, it was clear that Shaykh Aḥmad was strongly predisposed to the study of religious texts and traditions. By the age of 5 he could read the Qur'ān, and during the remainder of his primary education he studied Arabic grammar and became exposed to the mystical and theosophical expressions of Ibn 'Arabī (d. 638/1240) and the less well-known Ibn Abī Jumhūr (d. *c.* 901/1495–6), author of the *Kitāb al-mujlī*. In 1772, Shaykh Aḥmad left his home to pursue advanced religious studies in the area of the 'Atabāt in Iraq. He received his first *ijāza* from the renowned scholar Sayyid Muḥammad Mahdī Baḥr al-'Ulūm (d. 1797), and eventually six others from various recognized teachers.[18]

Shaykh Aḥmad remained away from Baḥrayn for about a year, and then returned to pursue his studies, presumably independently, for the next twenty-five years. As a result of the Wahhābī attack on his native al-Aḥsā, he travelled to Baṣra in 1797 and remained in the religious centres and other localities of Iraq and Iran until the

16 Nabīl, p. 30.

17 The two works are *Risālat al-sulūk* and *Tafsīr sūrat al-baqara*; they are, as it happens, probably the two earliest of the Bāb's works remaining to us.

18 The most recent detailed account of the Shaykhīya is: Vahid Rafati, 'The Development of Shaykhī Thought in Shī'ī Islam', unpublished Ph.D. thesis (UCLA, 1979). Other important discussions of this subject are: Said Amir Arjomand, *The Shadow of God and the Hidden Imam: Religion, Political Order, and Societal Change in Shi'ite Iran from the Beginning to 1890* (Chicago, 1984), see index, 'Shaykhism'; Mangol Bayat, *Mysticism and Dissent: Socioreligious Thought in Qajar Iran* (Syracuse, 1982), 37–58; Henri Corbin, *En Islam Iranien* (Paris, 1971–2), iv. 205–300.

end of his life. He died on pilgrimage to Mecca in 1825 and was buried in the famous Baqī' cemetery of Medina. The work of Shaykh Aḥmad was continued by his favourite student, Sayyid Kāẓim Rashtī (1798–1844). After the death of Sayyid Kāẓim, his students divided into several groups, one centred around the personality of Muḥammad Karīm Khān Kirmānī, another around Sayyid 'Alī Muḥammad, the Bāb.

3. Shaykhī teachings

The distinguishing features of this school, as is the case with most Muslim religious sects, are related to the manner in which spiritual authority was to be defined. At this time, the Shī'ī world was experiencing an active controversy carried on by the followers of two groups called the *uṣūlīya* and the *akhbārīya*. These terms refer to the way each group tended to support its statements on Islamic law and theology. The debate was based on the question of whether *ijtihād*, 'exerting individual effort to form an opinion', rather than wholesale acceptance of the guidance contained in the preserved statements (*akhbār*) of Muḥammad and the Imāms, was the best way to resolve the questions of religion, which would of course include questions of law. Finally the *uṣūlīya*, those in favour of *ijtihād*, won the day and for the last 200 years this basic attitude towards the written sources of the Islamic religion has held sway over most of the Shī'ī world.

Shaykh Aḥmad grew up in one of the last bastions of the *akhbārī* approach, and his synthesis may be seen as a radicalization of this method. By means of propounding a doctrine of the Perfect Shī'a, an obvious adaptation of the Ṣūfī idea of the Perfect Man (*al-insān al-kāmil*), Shaykh Aḥmad was able, at least in theory, to circumvent the restrictions imposed by either of the two above methods and arrive at a much less fettered and independent position *vis-à-vis* the reinterpretation of the raw material of the Islamic religion—the Qur'ān, the *sunna*, and the teachings of the Imāms which were preserved in the *akhbār*. In short, this doctrine held that the Perfect Shī'a was always present on earth as a direct link to the Hidden Imām, Muḥammad ibn al-Ḥasan, the twelfth Imām of the Shī'a, who disappeared from the public ken at the age of 6 after succeeding his late father as Imām, and whose occultation had now lasted nearly 1,000 years. While neither Shaykh Aḥmad nor Sayyid Kāẓim ever publicly claimed the rank of Perfect Shīʿī, it seems fairly certain that their followers considered them as such.

Shiʿism has traditionally based itself on five main principles: divine unity (*tawḥīd*) prophethood (*nubūwa*), return (*maʿād*), the imamate (*imāma*), and divine justice (*ʿadl*). Shaykh Aḥmad reduced these to three by combining 'justice' with 'unity' and placing the 'return' in the category of 'prophethood'. To these three, Unity, Prophethood, and the Imamate, was added the idea of the Perfect Shīʿa sometimes referred to by the Shaykhīs as the Fourth Support (*al-rukn al-rābiʿ*) of religion, an allusion, in parallel, to the four pillars of God's throne (*ʿarsh*, *kursī*).[19] Other distinguishing characteristics of the beliefs held by the Shaykhīs pertained to eschatology, in which a corporeal resurrection was denied in favour of a somewhat complex recourse to a separate reality in which a resurrection of one's spiritual or subtle (*laṭīf*) body underwent a process designated by the familiar terminology of *maʿād*, *qiyāma*, and so forth. Surely the emphasis here is on the denial of the scientifically untenable bodily resurrection which so many Muslim philosophers prior to Shaykh Aḥmad also found impossible to believe.[20] Shaykh Aḥmad's contribution on this matter is in the form of a sufficiently detailed and appealingly possible alternative—even the most hard-bitten sceptic would never completely deny the possibility of the totally spiritual process which Shaykh Aḥmad propounded. These three features, the doctrine of the Perfect Shīʿa, the extreme veneration of the Holy Family, and the denial of bodily resurrection are perhaps the most important with regard to the relationship of Babism to Shaykhism.

The doctrine of the Perfect Shīʿa was inseparable from the

[19] Concern with the doctrine of the Fourth Support is, therefore, one of the most convincing evidences that the Bāb was writing his first *tafsīr* in a Shaykhī milieu. Early in his commentary on *sūrat al-baqara* he says that the Fourth Support is, in fact, the main body of the Shīʿa. That the Bāb understood the Fourth Support in this way is also evidence that at this time he either did not harbour any claims to the special spiritual authority implied by other uses of this term, or he did not want to be perceived as doing so. Cf. the way in which later Shaykhīs were to eventually discuss the idea of the Fourth Support (viz., as *ecclesia spiritualis*), in Corbin, *En Islam Iranien*, iv. 274–86, esp. 285. Also see D. MacEoin, 'Early Shaykhī Reactions to the Bāb and his Claims', in M. Momen, *Studies in Bābī and Bahāī history*, i (Los Angeles, 1982), 1–42.

[20] See Oliver Leaman, *An Introduction to Medieval Islamic Philosophy* (Cambridge, 1985), 17.

Shaykhī apophatic theology and implied a virtual deification[21] of the Fourteen Pure Ones (*chehardeh ma'ṣūm*) of orthodoxy: Muḥammad, Fāṭima, 'Alī, al-Ḥasan, al-Ḥusayn, and the remaining Imāms of Twelver Shi'ism. God here is eternally unknowable (rather than remote), and makes His will known through various stages. Eternally crucial to this process is the twofold institution of prophecy/imamate, and whenever any positive statement about divinity is made, its proper reference is to this institution. The Prophet and Imāms are a different order of creation as mediators between God and humanity. The Perfect Shī'ī acts as mediator between the Imāms, represented by the twelfth, Muḥammad ibn al-Ḥasan, and humanity. Therefore when the Bāb claimed to have received the *Tafsīr sūrat Yūsuf* from the Imām (see below), even though he did not explicitly claim for himself the title of the Perfect Shī'ī, those Shaykhīs who were his first readers were already convinced of the necessity for such a link as a *bāb* ('gate'), even if they were not agreed as to who was best qualified to act as such, or, less important, what the exact name for such a link should be.

Before leaving the subject, it is important to point out that up until the period of time in which the Bāb wrote, the Shaykhīya were probably not yet seen as a separate sect of Twelver Shi'ism. According to Rafati:

> Although the terms 'Shaykhī,' 'Posht-i Sarī,' and 'Kashfīya' refer to a certain group of people, and were intended to distinguish them from the rest of the Shī'a, the group solidarity and identity of the Shaykhīs was in fact not so distinct as to sharply separate them from the rest of the Shī'ī community of Iran as an independent sect or even branch of Twelver Shī'a. The Shaykhīs considered themselves true Shī'a who thought and behaved in accordance with the teaching of the Shī'ī *imāms*; they did not consider themselves innovators. It is difficult to believe that during Shaykh Ahmad's lifetime he was considered the founder of a new school within the Shī'i framework. However, as time went on and the nature of his ideology received greater intellectual attention, a group of fundamentalist *'ulamā'* perceived a radical distinction between his views and the established doctrines of the Shī'a and increasingly differentiated themselves from the Shaykhīs. This Shaykhī school, then, gained more group solidarity as it

[21] This statement must be tempered by reference to the innumerable assertions of the servitude of Muḥammad and the Imāms to the essence of God. It would be misleading in the extreme to suggest incarnationism. See a characteristic statement on this question by the Bāb himself in his *Risalah-ye i'tiqādāt* in *Majmū'ah-yi athār-yi hazrat-i A'lā*, Iran National Baha'i Archives, Tehran, lxix (1976), 411–16.

developed historically, reacting as a group against the main body of the Shīʿa when it encountered social and intellectual opposition.[22]

4. *TAFSĪR* WORKS

Among the Bāb's writings there are numerous works of *tafsīr*.[23] Some of these are commentaries on such important traditions as the *ḥadīth al-jārīya* or the *ḥadīth Kumayl*. Most of the others are commentaries on either a complete *sūra* of the Qur'ān or one of the more notable verses, such as the light verse (Q. 24/35) or the throne verse (Q. 2/255). These commentaries present a broad range of ideas and exegetical techniques—to such a degree that any attempt to discuss all of them here would ultimately be meaningless. This is so in spite of the fact that they all seem to come from the same general period, usually referred to as early Babism.[24] Despite the astonishingly varied nature of the style and content of these commentaries, or more accurately because of it, they are of course extremely valuable for a study of the development of the Bāb's thought. Collectively they represent a unique individual corpus of Islamic scriptural commentary.

Of the numerous titles in this genre, however, four stand out as major works. In chronological order they are the commentaries on *al-baqara* (*sūra* 2), *Yūsuf* (*sūra* 12), *al-kawthar* (*sūra* 108), and *wa'l-ʿaṣr* (*sūra* 103). In the following discussion attention will be focused exclusively on the first two of these commentaries.[25]

[22] Rafati, pp. 48–9. For a helpful summary of the points which came to be regarded as representing the most important differences between the Shaykhīs and the Shīʿa, see Moojan Momen, *An Introduction to Shiʿi Islam: the History and Doctrines of Twelver Shiʿism* (Oxford and New Haven, 1985), 226–8; on the importance of the doctrine of the Perfect Shīʿī, see Browne, 'Bāb, Bābīs', in *Encyclopedia of Religion and Ethics*, ii. 300a–b.

[23] See n. 3, above.

[24] Browne, 'Bāb, Bābīs', *Encyclopedia of Religion and Ethics*, ii. 305a.

[25] The other two works deserve some brief mention at this time, inasmuch as they both exhibit one of the more distinctive exegetical procedures of the Bāb, and one which is not applied by him to the two *sūra*s under detailed discussion here. Both of *sūra*s 108 and 103, which are among the shortest chapters in the Qur'ān, are explained by the Bāb not verse by verse, or even word by word, but rather letter by letter. In this way, the Quranic material is 'exploded' by the commentator in an attempt to mine it for as much meaning as possible. See B. T. Lawson, 'Exploded Commentary', paper presented at the American Academy of Religion Annual Meeting, Anaheim, California, 1985, for a study of this method and its antecedents, *ḥurūfī*, *ṣūfī*, and others.

i. Tafsīr sūrat al-baqara

The Bāb was just under 25 when he completed the first volume of this work in Muḥarram 1259.[26] The work was therefore completed a few months before he made his momentous claim to Mullā Ḥusayn, the young Shaykhī, on the evening of 22 May 1844 (4 Jumāda I, 1260). In corroboration of this dating, Mullā Ḥusayn is reported to have noticed this *tafsīr* resting on a shelf in the Bāb house during the course of that very evening.[27] This earliest sustained religious work of the Bāb's includes a brief commentary on *al-fātiḥa* (*sūra* 1), which is prefaced, in some manuscript copies, by an introduction which is noteworthy for the reference it makes to the date on which composition was begun. Here the Bāb says that the night before he began the work, he had a dream in which the entire city of Karbalā' (*arḍ al-muqaddas*) rose bit by bit into the air and came to rest before his house in Shīrāz, whereupon he was informed of the approaching death of Sayyid Kāẓim Rashtī, the Shaykhī leader, to whom he here refers as his revered teacher.[28]

The way in which *sūrat al-fātiḥa* is treated is in some ways characteristic of the rest of the commentary. For the Bāb, meaning may be derived from the book chiefly by way of relating its contents to the Holy Family (Muḥammad, Fāṭima, and the twelve Imāms). To this end, each of the seven verses of the opening *sūra* is

[26] Numerous MSS of this work, which represents a commentary on the complete first *juz'* of the Qur'ān, exist; five copies have been consulted for this discussion: Cambridge, Browne F. 8; Teheran Bahā'ī Archives 6014 C (hereafter: TBA); the privately published limited edition, in xerox, found in *Majmū'ah-yi athār-yi hazrat-i A'lā*, Iran National Bahā'ī Archives, Teheran, lxix (1976), 157–410; two uncatalogued MSS in the Princeton University 'Bābī Collection'. Many thanks to Mr James Weinberger, curator of the Near Eastern Collection, Princeton University, for access to these last two items. All references in this paper are to TBA, which has been paginated in a xerox copy.

A word should also be said about the notorious vol. ii of the *Tafsīr sūrat al-baqara*. According to Nicolas (n. 12), this was among those works by the Bāb which were stolen from him during his pilgrimage (see pp. 45–6). However, MacEoin, 'Critical', 36, lists a MS of the Bibliothèque Nationale which he says may be this missing volume. An examination of BN Or.5805 indeed discloses that it is a commentary on the 2nd *juz'* of the Qur'ān. At this time, however, it is not possible to ascribe its authorship to the Bāb with complete confidence. The MS in the British Library (BL Or. 7845) is a similar case. Finally, a few pages of a commentary on this 2nd *juz'* are found in the *Majmū'a* (mentioned above), 377–410. There seem to be some important stylistic differences between this material and the preceding *tafsīr*, one example being a much more frequent use of the first person.

[27] See the *Tārīkh-i jadīd* as quoted by E. G. Browne, 'Catalogue and Description of 27 Bābī Manuscripts', *JRAS* 24 (1892), 496.

[28] TBA 6.

designated as a writing (*kitāb*) of one of these sacred figures. Beginning with Muḥammad, these include (in this order) ʻAlī, Fāṭima, al-Ḥasan, al-Ḥusayn, Jaʻfar (al-Ṣādiq), and finally Mūsā ibn Jaʻfar. As will be seen below, the number seven plays an important part throughout this work.[29] In this instance, the seven names represent the different names by which each of the fourteen Pure Ones are known. That is, each of the names Muḥammad, ʻAlī, al-Ḥasan, and al-Ḥusayn may be applied to more than one figure. The names Fāṭima, Jaʻfar, and Mūsā, however, may only be used once. The name Muḥammad is applicable not only to the prophet himself but also to Muḥammad al-Bāqir, the fifth Imām (d. 113/731–2), Muḥammad al-Jawād, the ninth Imām (d. 220/835), and Muḥammad ibn al-Ḥasan al-ʻAskarī, the twelfth Imām, also known as al-Mahdī (disappeared 260/873–4). The name ʻAlī may properly designate not only the first Imām (d. 40/661), but also his grandson the fourth Imām, ʻAlī ibn al-Husayn (d. 94/712–13), the eighth Imām, ʻAlī al-Riḍā (d. 202/817–18), and ʻAlī al-Hādī, the tenth Imām (d. 254/868). The name al-Ḥasan may be applied to both the second Imām (d. 50/670) and the eleventh (d. 260/873–4). The result is that although there are fourteen different personalities involved, it may be said that there are in reality only seven different names. That the Bāb has chosen to associate each verse with one of these seven names has, as will be seen, implications for the way in which he understood one of the more common names for this *sūra*, namely, *al-sabʻ al-mathānī* (cf. Q. 15/87), the meaning of which is

[29] The question, often raised, of Ismāʻīlī ('Seveners') influence on the Bāb is probably best answered by emphasizing the importance of Shaykhī influence on his writings (see Rafati, p. 167). The better question to ask would be about the Ismāʻīlī influences on the writings of Shaykh Aḥmad and the later elaboration of his school, especially by Sayyid Kāẓim Rashtī. Following Amanat, the Shaykhī movement may best be understood as a synthesis of 'three major trends of thought in post-Safavīd Shiʻism; the theosophic school of Isfahan (*hikmat-i ilāhī*), which itself benefited from the theoretical Sufism of Ibn ʻArabī and the "Oriental" theosophy (*hikmat-i ishrāq*) of Suhravardi, the Akhbārī "traditionalist" school of Bahrain which traced its chain of transmission to the early narrators of *hadīth* mostly by the way of "intuitive" perception and the Gnosticism which was diffused in the Shīʻī milieu and was strongly influenced by crypto-Ismāʻīlī ideas as well as other heterodoxies of southern and southwestern Iran' (Amanat, p. 29). It would appear that Browne's advice and hope, written nearly one hundred years ago, that 'a full and critical study of the Shaykhī doctrines would . . . form an indispensable preliminary to such a philosophical history of the Bābīs as must some day be written' (Browne, 'Bāb, Bābīs', *Encyclopedia of Religion and Ethics*, ii. 300b) remains to be completely acted upon.

disputed by the classical exegetes.[30] Later in the commentary, the Bāb states that one of the results of the process of creation is that seven becomes fourteen.[31] Thus this opening chapter, which is also known as the 'Mother of the Book' (*umm al-kitāb*) because in it is contained the essence of the entire Qur'ān, may be likened to the divine will which, in Shaykhī thought, is represented by the pleroma of the Holy Family, and may be understood as containing, *in potentia*, all creation.[32]

One of the main concerns of this *tafsīr* is in fact the propounding of this particular metaphysical notion. This, together with the method adopted for such—constant reference to the Holy Family as the principle of this process—is the most distinctive and distinguishing feature of the work and may be designated by the rather awkward term 'imamization'. It is unlikely that this represents, at the time and place it was written, a polemic in the context of an immediate Sunnī–Shī'ī debate.[33] Rather, it would seem that this method of interpretation is linked to at least two factors. The first is that it reflects the extreme veneration in which the Imāms were held by the Shaykhīs,[34] and, of course, the Shaykhī influence on the author of this work. But perhaps more importantly, especially for under-

[30] See below, p. 241; also see Mahmoud Ayoub, 'The Prayer of Islam: A Presentation of *sūrat al-fātiḥa* in Muslim Exegesis', *Journal of the American Academy of Religion, Thematic Issue*, 47 (1979), 635–47, esp. 638.

[31] TBA 112–13, *ad* Q. 2/29: 'It is He who created for you all that is in the earth, then He lifted Himself to heaven and levelled the seven heavens; and He has knowledge of everything.' The Bāb's Arabic is: *wa'l-sab' idhā karrarat fi'l-ibdā' wa'l-ikhtirā' ṣārat arb'a 'ashar*.

[32] For the idea of *tajallī* much used by the Shaykhīs, but which as a technical term in Muslim discussions of ontology and metaphysics has a much longer history, see Rafati, 69–101. For one of the major antecedents for this usage, see Toshihiko Tzutsu, *Sufism and Taoism: A Comparative Study of Key Philosophical Concepts* (Berkeley, 1984), 152–8.

[33] This 'imamization' is reflected in most *tafsīr* works of Akhbārī Shi'ism. See, e.g., Muḥsin Fayẓ al-Kāshānī (d. 1092/1680), *al-Ṣafī fī tafsīr kalām Allāh al-wāfī* (n.p., 1283), and Sayyid Hāshim al-Baḥrānī (d. 1107/1695), *Tafsīr al-burhān* (Tehran, 1334 Shamsī). On these authors and the Akhbārī hermeneutic, see Corbin, *En Islam Iranien*, i. chs. 4 and 5.

[34] See sect. 2, above. This veneration was one of the main reasons that the Shaykhīya ran foul of the more orthodox interpretations of Shi'ism, which did, in fact, denounce the group as extremists (*ghulāt*) on several occasions. In his *Tafsīr sūrat al-baqara* it is clear that the Bāb was sensitive to such charges. Very early on in the work he cites the following tradition from al-Bāqir, the fifth Imām: 'O concourse of the Shī'a . . . Be the true Shī'a—a middle position (*al-numraqat al-wusṭā*) so that even the extremist (*al-ghāli*), might return to you and the one who lags behind (*al-tālī*) might catch up to you.' See TBA 20.

standing the eventual development of the Bāb's teaching, it allows the Bāb to assert his complete independence from all others, including Shaykh Aḥmad and Sayyid Kāẓim (who are not mentioned in the main body of the *tafsīr*[35]), apart from the Holy Family, and, of course, the Qur'ān itself.

A ready example of this allegorical method is found at Q. 2/26: 'God is not ashamed to strike a similitude even of a gnat, or aught above it.'[36] Here the 'gnat' is explained as being 'Alī himself, while 'aught above it', *mā fawqahā*, is none other than Muḥammad. This interpretation is not new with the Bāb; it is found in at least three other well-known Shī'ī commentaries where it is ascribed to the sixth Imām, Ja'far al-Ṣādiq. Unlike his practice in similar instances in the commentary, the Bāb cites no authority here. The adoption of this interpretation must therefore be seen as an example of the abundantly attested and universally approved process of selection from the overall tradition (rather than 'creation') as a means of offering an 'original' interpretation, which is so characteristic of Muslim religious scholarship.[37] That the Bāb was creative in the modern sense as well will be seen in what follows.

A more extended allegory is found at Q. 2/49–51 in the Bāb's reading of the story of Moses in the wilderness with his troublesome retinue:

> (49) And when We delivered you from the folk of Pharoah who were visiting you with evil chastisement, slaughtering your sons, and sparing your women; and in that was a grievous trial from your Lord. (50) And when We divided for you the sea and delivered you, and drowned Pharoah's folk while you were beholding. (51) And when We appointed with Moses forty nights then you took to yourselves the Calf after him and you were evildoers.

The Bāb says the verse 49 is being addressed to (*mukhāṭabat^{an} li-*) Fāṭima, her husband, and her father.[38] 'Pharoah' stands for

[35] They are, however, referred to in the *Tafsīr sūrat Yūsuf*, as e.g., the 'two gates' (*bābayn*). It is just this kind of terminological association which, of course, represents a doctrinal or philosophical affinity that was so instrumental in the Bāb's winning to his cause a number of Shaykhīs.

[36] All translations of the Qur'ān are from A. J. Arberry, *The Koran Interpreted* (Oxford, 1964). In some cases the translation has been adapted slightly.

[37] Al-Baḥrānī, *al-Burhan*, i. 70; 'Abd 'Alī al-Ḥuwayzī, *Tafsīr nūr al-thaqalayn* (Qom, [1382–5/1962–5]) i. 37–8; al-Ṭabarsī, *Majma' al-bayān fī tafsīr al-Qur'ān* (Beirut, 1380/1961), i. 38.

[38] Two of the MSS add 'and her grandfather' (*jadd*), although this word is not quite so clear in TBA 179.

'Umar,[39] while his 'folk' stands for 'wherever *kufr*, *shirk* or *sharr* exist, because these are the various places where he appears (*maẓāhir nafsihi*)'. In this place the specific reference is to Yazīd, the Umayyad caliph responsible for the killing of Ḥusayn, while 'slaughtering of your sons' is a direct reference to 'the sons of the Messenger and their lord, Abū 'Abd Allāh al-Ḥusayn' (the third Imām).

At this point, the Bāb embarks upon a rather lengthy discussion to justify why God would allow such a heinous deed as the murder of one of the Holy Family to take place. During the course of this discussion, the Bāb compares the killing of Ḥusayn with the sin of Adam. The main point seems to be that this apparent victory of evil over goodness, the murder of an Imām, was not due to any weakness in Ḥusayn. On the contrary, the Imām, because of the strength of his perfect (*mu'tadil*: 'harmonious') body, would have been able to destroy the whole world had such been the divine purpose.

At verse 50 the 'sea' is the 'sea of divine power'. Those being addressed are the 'People of Infallibility' (*ahl al-'iṣma*), another name for the Holy Family. 'The meaning of the second "Pharoah"', says the Bāb, 'is the one who rejected the signs of 'Alī, upon him be peace, which exists in all things.' 'Moses,' at verse 51, 'according to the primary meaning (*fa'l-murād bi'l-ḥaqīqat al-awwalīya*) is Muḥammad.' 'Forty' is understood as referring to 'Alī and the ten proofs (*ḥujaj*) from his progeny. The Bāb explains as follows: 'Alī stands for thirty since he lived for thirty years after the death of Muḥammad. 'Forty' is arrived at when reference is made to the ten remaining Imāms (who were allowed to fulfil their mission, the mission of the last or twelfth Imām being at this time still incomplete and therefore the number 'ten' would not pertain to the length of time spent in the wilderness precisely because the *parousia* of the last Imām will signal the end of this spiritual banishment).[40] But 'nights' alludes to the concealment of the glory of the Imāms by the darkness of disbelief. One of the evidences of this disbelief was the choosing of the 'calf' which was actually Abū Bakr (*al-awwal*) as a legatee (*waṣī*). Therefore the 'evildoers' are those who gave their allegiance (*bay'a*) to him.

[39] The actual name in the text is *abū'l-shurūr*, 'father of iniquities', a way of referring to one who, in the estimation of the Shī'a, was one of the arch-villains of history. See Goldziher, *Richtungen*, 288, 298.

[40] Cf. Q. 7/142 where God extends the desert sojourn from 30 to 40 days.

This section is concluded with a reference to the *qā'im*, whose return will cause all that has been alluded to in the foregoing to appear.[41] This is an example of the idea that each divine manifestation (*ẓuhūr*) sets in motion a replay of the major events of a kind of primal sacred history. Later, in some of his other writings, the Bāb refers to his very first followers, the eighteen 'Letters of the Living', as the reappearance of the fourteen Pure Ones and the four *abwāb*—those leaders of the Shī'a who are believed to have been in contact with the Hidden Imām, Muḥammad ibn al-Ḥasan, during the so-called Lesser Occultation.[42]

In the course of this interpretation, the Bāb alludes to the metaphysics from which it ultimately springs. Repeated reference is made, for example, to the process of divine self-manifestation—*tajallī*. Once again, the commentary on *sūrat al-fātiḥa* provides a characteristic example. The third verse of the opening *sūra* is characterized by the Bāb as the 'book (*kitāb*) of Fāṭima'. He continues by saying that:

> God has put in it all that is hers and all that pertains to her. This verse is the Garden of Grace. God has provided its shade for whoever believes in her and loves her after he has properly recognized her—according to what she manifested to him (*li'l-'ārif*) by means of his own capacity for understanding. At this time this Garden will open to him.[43]

The operative phrase here is: *kamā tajallat li'l-'ārif lahu bihi*.[44] An interesting parallel to this usage is found in the *Fuṣūṣ al-ḥikām* of the great mystic Ibn 'Arabī. Here the author discusses *tajallī*, or the way in which God makes himself known to humanity, with these words: *fa-waṣafa nafsahu lanā binā*, 'He has described Himself to us by means of us', or, less concisely: 'He has described Himself to us by means of our own ability and willingness to perceive His description.'[45] It is not intended to go into great detail here on the relation of the Bāb's thought to that of Ibn 'Arabī, nor is it intended to go into great detail about the nature of the Bāb's thought *per se*; attention is drawn to this subject only by way of indicating the kinds of ideas which find expression during the task

[41] TBA 179–84.

[42] MacEoin, 'Charismatic', 146. See also Shoghi Effendi, *God Passes By*, 32.

[43] TBA 7–8. The Quranic verse thus explained is *al-raḥmān al-raḥīm*—'the Beneficent and Merciful'.

[44] My thanks to Dr Afnan for suggesting the above translation.

[45] Ibn al-'Arabī, *Fuṣūṣ al-ḥikam*, ed. Affifi (Cairo, 1946), i. 53.

the Bāb has set for himself (and which is the subject of this discussion), namely, the interpretation of the Qur'ān. Suffice it here to say that both the Bāb and Ibn 'Arabī appear to rely for the ultimate justification of such a view on Q. 41/53: 'We shall show them Our signs in the horizons and in themselves, till it is clear to them that this is the truth.' The frequency with which this idea is encountered in the *Tafsīr sūrat al-baqara* throws into sharp relief the curious fact that there seems to be no mention of it at all, at least in the above terms, in the *Tafsīr sūrat Yūsuf*.

This metaphysics is related also to ethical concerns in one interesting passage of the commentary on *sūrat al-baqara*, *ad* Q. 2/3: '[Those] who believe in the unseen, and perform the prayer, and expend of that We have provided them.' Here the Bāb chooses to comment on the significance of 'faith' (*imān*) represented in the above citation by the verb 'believe'. In his introductory remarks to this lengthy section he says the following:

> If man knew how God had created His creation, no one would ever blame another. This means that God has created mankind (*khalq*) according to the creature's already existing propensities for acceptance or rejection [of the truth]. The cause of rejection is the same as the cause of acceptance, namely, choice (*ikhtiyār*). God has given to each what he deserves according to his already existing propensity (*bi-mā huwa 'alayhi*). This divine knowledge is the knowledge of potentialities.[46]

The object of the discussion is an extended treatment of the problems surrounding the perennial puzzle posed by the ideas of an individual's freewill and God's role in determining a person's fate. Once again, statements of the Bāb appear to have much in common with the views of Ibn 'Arabī, in particular his notoriously difficult idea of *al-'ayān al-thābita*.[47] It is probably the case here, as in the above comparison with Ibn 'Arabī, that these coincidences are due more to the traces of Ibn 'Arabī's thought existing in the teaching of the Shaykhīs (which, as has been said, is acknowledged to be the single most formative influence on the way in which the Bāb expressed his ideas) than to any direct borrowing by the Bāb from Ibn 'Arabī himself. Indeed, in one of his later *tafāsīr*, the Bāb makes

[46] TBA 22.

[47] See, e.g., Izutsu, p. 159, where the author defines *al-'ayān al-thābita* as the 'eidetic realities' of possible things. A possible thing becomes actualized in the phenomenal world, each according to the requirements of its own personal archetype.

it clear that he does not agree with Ibn 'Arabī at all on at least one point.[48]

Continuing with the Bāb's commentary on this same verse, we are soon in the presence of another major pattern in the work. The importance of the number seven has already been mentioned and briefly illustrated; a few more brief examples are added here for emphasis.

In his discussion of *imān*, the Bāb speaks of seven different levels or grades (*marātib*). The first is applied to the people of the garden, or paradise, of the Divine Will (*ahl jannat al-mashīya*). The remaining six grades are respectively applicable to the people of the heaven of the Divine Purpose (*al-irāda*), the sea of the Divine Decree (*baḥr al-qadr*), Eden (*'adn*), Divine Permission (*idhn*), Eternity (*khuld*), and finally Refuge, or Repose (*ma'wā*). Other examples of this seven-fold structure of spirituality may be found in the *tafsīr* at Q. 2/1, where eight gardens, or paradises, and seven hells are described. Here, each hell is but the shadow of the heaven above it. The reason that there are only seven is because the highest heaven casts no shadow, in fact, it is completely isolated from the rest of the structure. The highest heaven represents the Absolute of this apophatic theological model.[49] At Q. 2/2 we are introduced to seven classes of people;[50] at Q. 2/5 we read of seven different grades of lordship (*rubūbīya*).[51] A final example is at Q. 2/22, where seven heavens and seven earths are enumerated.[52]

Another example of the Bāb's exegesis may be taken once again from Q. 2/3, which is divided into two parts for the purposes of the commentary: '[Those] who believe in the unseen, and perform the prayer.' *Ghayb* ('unseen') is interpreted the following way. The Bāb says that it represents Muḥammad because he is truly known only by himself and only God knows his true nature (*kunh*). The particular place (*wa maḥall tafṣīl hādhā'l-ghayb*[53]) is none other than the currently concealed *Qā'im*, Muḥammad ibn al-Ḥasan. The Bāb then quotes a tradition from the sixth Imām, Ja'far al-Ṣādiq, wherein several stages of *ghayb* are enumerated.[54] It has already been explained how for the Bāb, who at the time of writing this

[48] *Tafsīr sūrat wa'l-'aṣr*, MS Cambridge, Browne F. 9 (6), fo. 71ʳ.

[49] In the Bāb's words: *lā ḍidd lahā [al-jannat al-ulā] wa lā ẓill, bal fī'l-ḥaqīqa khalwa min al-jinān wa'l-jinān khalwa minhā; wa hiya jannat al-tawḥīd*. TBA 9.

[50] TBA 14. [51] TBA 38–40. [52] TBA 81–2.

[53] TBA 23 has *tafḍīl*, an obvious mistake. [54] TBA 23–4.

particular commentary was making use of the terminology and thought of the Shaykhīs,[55] the number seven represents the totality of the Holy Family. While it may be of some interest to try and determine other influences apart from the Shaykhī school, to insist on such would be to miss this most important point. One of the more pertinent lessons to be learned here, it would seem, is how the number seven can have importance for both the *Ithnā 'Asharīya* ('Twelvers') and the so-called *Sab'īya* ('Seveners'), or the Ismā'īlīya.[56]

To conclude this somewhat random sampling from this earliest of the Bāb's commentaries, attention will be paid to his reading of the word *ṣalāt* (prayer, divine service) in this same verse, Q. 2/3. First of all, its performance symbolizes obedience to Muḥammad and his legatees and progeny—which in turn represents absolute *walāya*. From the beginning to the end of its performance, it is the 'form of divine aloneness' (*ṣūrat al-tafrīd*), the shape of divine unity (*haykal al-tawḥīd*), and the 'outward representation of love or allegiance' (*shabaḥ al-walāya*). However, none but Muḥammad and his Family performs it properly, because *ṣalāt* is the foremost station of distinction between the lover and the Beloved (God). The Holy Family is the collective bearer of this love and as such is the object of the famous *ḥadīth qudsī*, 'I was a hidden treasure and desired to be known, therefore I created mankind [*khalq* here refers specifically to the Imāms, according to the Bāb's interpretation] in order to be known.' Thus it is through the Imām that 'lordship' (*rubūbīya*) appeared and 'servitude' (*marbūbīya*) was perfected. The perfect performance of *ṣalāt* by the Imāms is therefore an ability or quality directly from God (*waṣf Allāh*) which they have been endowed with by means of their own innate capacities (*lahum bihim*), while in the case of others who perform the *ṣalāt*, this ability comes from the Imāms. This is a perfect example of the Shaykhī imamology referred to above.[57]

The Bāb then states that the Imāms are in fact the seven *mathānī*. This becomes clear when the worshipper recites the *fātiḥa*, in each

[55] See, e.g., the description of Shaykh Aḥmad's ontology and his 'absolute distinction between Possible Being and Necessary Being', which is illustrated by a seven-stage hierarchy, Rafati, pp. 103–4.

[56] See, e.g., one of the four Shī'ī canonical books of *ḥadīth*, al-Kulīnī (d. 328/939 or 329/940), *al-Uṣūl min al-kāfī* (Tehran, n.d.), i. 149, no. 27; one of its chapters is headed: *bāb fī annahu lā yakūn shay' fī'l-samā' wa'l-arḍ illā bi-sab'a*.

[57] See sect. 2, above.

verse of which God has described one of the Holy Family by means of the tongue of the servant, who, in the course of two prostrations, will have uttered the seven verses of the *fātiḥa* twice, which is, of course, an affirmation of the sanctity of the Fourteen Pure Ones. If the prayer is performed in this spirit, then the worshipper has succeeded in performing it as properly as he can. The prayer has then become a meeting with the Beloved and the Face of the worshipped One—a true means of spiritual elevation, *mi'rāj*, for the individual believer.[58]

Having briefly examined this very early work of the Bāb, which, it must be remembered, was written before his declaration in which he claimed special spiritual authority and is therefore concerned more with the Shī'ī tradition than with any new system, we will now turn to a *tafsīr* of a very different order.

ii. Tafsīr sūrat Yūsuf

Approximately four months after the completion of the commentary on *sūra* 2, the Bāb began his commentary on the Quranic story of Joseph (*sūra* 12). This *tafsīr* is utterly different in all of its aspects from the *Tafsīr sūrat al-baqara*. Unlike the previous commentary, this work contains no direct references to doctrinal discussions on such important Shaykhī topics as the Fourth Support, and no architectonic metaphysical representations.[59] Although allegory and typological exegesis are still among the chief methods of the actual interpretation, they are of a somewhat different character. Indeed, direct interpretation of the verses represents only a portion of the material. In one way, the work is much more structured, taking as its model the Qur'ān in its use of *sūra* divisions, and in another way it is much less 'logical', in that it is difficult many times to see just how the text is tied to the Quranic material itself. It is

[58] TBA 26. The use of the word *mi'rāj* here brings an association with another distinctive aspect of Shaykhī theology. While the mainstream of both 'orthodoxies', Sunnī and Shī'ī, interpret the account of Muḥammad's ascent, *mi'rāj*, through the seven heavens as an actual journey, the Shaykhī school taught that the story should be taken rather more figuratively. Therefore the journey was indeed accomplished, but in the spiritual realm of *hūrqalyā* and not in the world of mundane experience; see Rafati, p. 115. On the Shaykhī understanding of worship, see Corbin, *En Islam Iranien*, i. 194.

[59] There are on occasion lists of 'spiritual types' such as are found in the *Tafsīr sūrat al-baqara*. See, e.g., the Haifa MS, *Tafsīr sūrat Yūsuf*, 226, where nine types are detailed. Oblique reference to the 'Fourth Support' may also be found, e.g., p. 107.

also a very long work and one in which a variety of concerns, images, terminology, laws, exhortations, and prayers are presented. Interestingly, there seem to be no *ḥadīth*. What is offered in the next few pages is merely a very brief description of the work. The intention is to give some idea of the kinds of problems which the *tafsīr* presents to the student of the history of Qur'ān commentary, to point out the dramatic difference between the two works which are the subject of this discussion, and to make some very general conclusions.

The *Tafsīr sūrat Yūsuf*, also known widely as the *Qayyūm al-asmā'*[60] and the *Aḥsan al-qaṣaṣ*, which is of course the name which the Qur'ān gives to the *sūra* of Joseph (Q. 12/3), was described in some detail by Rosen in 1877, and discussed by Browne in 1889 and again in 1892.[61] Since then, it has received a certain amount of attention from scholars concerned chiefly with the social history of the Bābī movement.[62] Several manuscripts of the work exist, two of which have been consulted for the purposes of this study.[63] The older of the two, and perhaps therefore the most reliable, was transcribed in 1261/1845 and differs from the later manuscript in many details. The work itself is quite long, the manuscript of 1261 running to 234 pages, with each 9.5 × 17.5 cm.[64] page bearing 25 lines of closely written text; this copy is today found in Haifa.

The text is modelled after the Qur'ān, with its use of disconnected introductory letters, *sūra* divisions, and verse divisions. In fact, the older Haifa manuscript, in imitation of the *sajdat al-tilāwa* tradition in the Qur'ān, carries the instruction *sajda wājiba* at various places on the margin of the text where the word *sajada* or some derivative occurs, to indicate that a prostration should be

[60] 'Colui che s'erge sugli Attributi', as translated by Alessandro Bausani, *Persia Religiosa, da Zaratustra a Bahā'u'llāh* (Milan, 1959), 460.

[61] In the study cited above, n. 5. For the 1889 discussion see Browne, *JRAS* 21 (1889), 904–6.

[62] Moojan Momen, 'The Trial of Mulla 'Ali Bastami: A Combined Sunni-Shī'ī Fatwa against the Bab', *Iran* 20 (1982), 113–43. This important article contains the translation of several excerpts from the *Tafsīr*. See also Amanat, pp. 204–7 and *passim*; MacEoin, 'Charismatic', 157–62.

[63] For a fairly complete list of MSS see MacEoin, 'Critical', 46. The two used by me are xerox copies of the Cambridge, Browne F. 11 (9), dated 1891, and the Haifa copy, dated 1261, which according to MacEoin, 'Critical', p. xxxviii n. 213, was discovered only recently. An addition to MacEoin's list would be the Princeton University 'Bābī Collection', no. 55 (uncatalogued). All further references are to pages of a xerox of the Haifa MS, hereafter cited as *QA*.

[64] Dimensions are of the area covered by the text, not the actual size of the page.

performed while reading the particular verse. In addition, the Haifa manuscript supplies at the head of the 111 *sūras* (each chapter of the commentary is called a *sūra* by the Bāb) the number of verses, which in this manuscript is invariably forty-two and the Cambridge manuscript, where the verses number forty, indicates the place of revelation, which is invariably Shīrāz.[65] The number of verses is thought to represent the *abjad* value of the word *balā*, which according to the Qur'ān, was the word used to convey man's assent to the primordial divine covenant (Q. 7/172).[66]

Immediately following this comparatively technical information comes the standard Islamic *basmala*: 'In the name of God, the Merciful, the Compassionate'. This occurs without exception at the beginning of each chapter and is followed by the verse from the Qur'ān which is to be the subject of the commentary. However, the first *sūra* of the *Tafsīr* does not contain such a citation, and is anyway of a slightly different order from the rest, being something of an introduction.

Continuing this imitation of the form of the Qur'ān, the Bāb has placed between the *āya* to be commented upon the main text of each *sūra* (except four[67]), a series of disconnected letters, some of which are Quranic. Thus chapter 3, *sūrat al-imān*, bears the two letters *ṭā'-hā'*, while the *sūra* immediately following, *al-madīna*, carries the un-Quranic *alif-lām-mīm-ṭā'-hā'*. While the vast majority of these sets of letters must remain at this stage somewhat mysterious, it is interesting to note that at the head of *sūras* 108 and 109, the following combinations occur: *'ayn-lām-yā'* and *mīm-ḥā'-mīm-dāl*, giving the names 'Alī and Muḥammad. The titles of these two *sūras* are respectively *al-dhikr* and *al-'abd*, both of which represent titles assumed by the Bāb in the course of his commentary.[68]

[65] Thus a typical chapter heading in the Cambridge MS would appear as follows: *Sūrat al-imān, wa hiya Shīrāzīya, wa hiya arba'ūn āya.*

[66] Dr Muhammad Afnan, personal communication. Concerning the Cambridge MS, Browne notes in 'Some Remarks', *JRAS* 24 (1892), 262, that the *abjad* value of the Quranic *lī*, 'to me' or 'before me', is 40. The prepositional phrase refers of course to the dream of Joseph: 'Father, I saw eleven stars, and the sun and the moon: I saw them bowing down before me (*lī*)' (Q. 12/4). In either case, the number of verses is taken to be symbolic of either the acceptance, or the assertion, of spiritual authority.

[67] *Sūras* 1, 2, 52, and 95 in *QA*. Incidentally, there are many blank spaces at the heading of the *suwar* in the Cambridge MS. It appears that the scribe intended to insert rubrications in these blanks which would carry such information as the number of verses, and so on.

[68] *QA* 223 and 225, respectively.

It is likely, therefore that these two names pertain first of all to the Bāb himself (Sayyid 'Alī Muḥammad) and indirectly to the first Imam and the Prophet Muḥammad. Needless to say, the ambiguity was no accident.

Following the disconnected letters there are usually one or perhaps two verses (terminations of which are marked in *QA* by the typical Quranic verse-marker, an independent *hā' 'marbūṭa*, and in the Cambridge manuscript by means of a space), which offer some variation on the frequent Quranic introductory formula: *dhālika al-kitāb* . . . (Q. 2/2), or *kitab*^un^ *unzila ilayka* . . . (Q. 7/2), which has been shown to be one of the common elements shared by those *suwar* which bear disconnected letters.[69] A few examples will serve as illustrations.

Sūra 1, *al-mulk*, begins after the title material described above and the respective Quranic verse as follows:

> (1) *al-ḥamdu li-llāh alladhī nazzala al-kitāb 'alā 'abdihi bi'l-ḥaqq li-yakūna li'l-'ālamīn sirāj*^an^ *wahhāj*^an^.[70]
>
> *Sūra* 2, *al-'ulamā'*: (1) *alif lām mīm, dhālika al-kitāb min 'indi Allāh, al-ḥaqq fī shān al-dhikr qad kāna bi'l-ḥaqq ḥawl al-nār manzūl*^an^; (2) *wa inna naḥnu qad ja'alnā'l-āyāt fī dhālika'l-kitāb mubīn*^an^ [*sic*].[71]
>
> *Sūra* 3, *al-imān*: (1) *ṭā' hā'*; (2) *Allāh qad anzala al-Qur'ān 'alā 'abdihi li-ya'lama al-nās anna Allāh qad kāna 'alā kulli shay' qadīr*^an^.[72]
>
> *Sūra* 37, *al-ta'bīr*: (1) *fā' 'ayn sīn nūn*; (2) *al-ḥamdu li-llāh alladhī anzala 'alā 'abdihi al-kitāb li-yakūna 'alā'l-'alamīn bi'l-kalimat al-'alī shahīd*^an^ [73]

The slightly variant *sūra* 59, *al-af'ida*, just as one example has the following, which is however still concerned with the way God communicates to mankind:

> (1) *kāf hā' 'ayn ṣād*; (2) *Allāh qad akhbara'l-'ibād bi'l-ism al-akbar: an lā ilāh illā huwa al-ḥayy al-qayyūm*.[74]

Finally, the example of *sūra* 111, *al-mu'minin*, is offered by way of emphasizing the more or less standard pattern which obtains throughout the work:

> (1) *alif lām mīm*; (2) *innā naḥnu qad ja'alnā baynakum wa bayna al-qurā'l-mubāraka min ba'd al-bāb hādhā unās*^un^ *ṭāhirīn yad'ūna al-nās ilā dīn Allāh al-akbar wa lā yakhāfūna min dūn Allāh al-ḥaqq 'an shay'*,

[69] Alford Welch, 'al-Ḳur'ān, *EI*² v. 414a.
[70] *QA* 3. [71] *QA* 5. [72] *QA* 6.
[73] *QA* 67. [74] *QA* 116.

ulā'ika hum qad kānū aṣḥāb al-riḍwān fī umm al-kitāb maktūb^{an}; (3) *wa innā naḥnu qad ja'alnā hādhā'l-kitāb āyāt li-ulī al-albāb alladhīna yusabbiḥūna al-layl wa'l-nahār wa lā yafturūna* [cf. Q. 21/20] *min amr Allāh al-ḥaqq min laday al-bāb 'alā dharra min ba'ḍ al-shay' qiṭmīr^{an}*.[75]

This then gives some idea of the Bāb's conscious desire to make his *Tafsīr* structurally resemble or 'imitate' the Qur'ān. It is doubtful whether one of the reasons *sūra* 12 was chosen was because the number of its verses closely approximates the total number of Quranic *suwar*,[76] although the effect of this coincidence was undoubtedly not lost upon the readers of the commentary. The Quranic story of Joseph is a favourite among Muslims because it contains within the confines of a single sustained narrative many subjects of importance to Islam including its link with past religions.[77] The *sūra* had also been the subject of earlier commentaries and elaborations; thus, the renowned Abū Ḥāmid al-Ghazzālī (d. 505/1111) composed a somewhat mystical *tafsīr* on this *sūra*.[78]

The great mystic, Ibn 'Arabī also took up the Quranic Joseph in his *Fuṣūṣ al-ḥikam* as a basis for his discussion of the spiritual imagination.[79] It would seem also that the choice of the *sūrat Yūsuf* as the subject of this commentary of the Bāb's is connected with a long tradition which reveres the story of Joseph as representing the spiritual mystery of *taqīya*, or cautious concealment, which is so important to Shī'ī religiosity in general,[80] and Shaykhī religious thinking in particular. According to Nabīl, Mullā Ḥusayn, the young Shaykhī who was the first to accept the Bāb's claim, had once asked the Shaykhī leader, Sayyid Kāẓim Rashtī, to write a commentary on *sūrat Yūsuf*. His teacher responded that such a task

75 *QA* 231.

76 *Sūra* has 112 verses, while 17 and 12 both have 111. No *sūra* has 114 verses, the number which corresponds exactly to the total number of *suwar* in the Qur'ān.

77 According to al-Tha'labī (d. 437/1036), *Qiṣaṣ al-anbiyā'*, the story of Joseph is the most beautiful (*aḥsan*) 'because of the lesson concealed in it, on account of Yūsuf's generosity and its wealth of matter, in which prophets, angels, devils, jinn, men, animals, birds, rulers and subjects play a part'. See B. Heller, 'Yūsuf ibn Ya'qub', *EI*^{2}, *ad loc.*

78 Abū Ḥāmid al-Ghazzālī, *Tafsīr sūrat Yūsuf* (Tehran, 1895). The work has virtually nothing in common with the Bāb's, except of course the Quranic citations from the *sūra* of Joseph.

79 Ibn al-'Arabī, *Fuṣūṣ*, i. 99–106.

80 As when Jacob warns Joseph not to tell his dream to his brothers (Q. 12/5). The concealment (*ghayba*) of the Imām is considered a kind of *taqīya*. See R. Strothmann, '*Taḳīya*', *EI*^{1}, ad loc.

was beyond his abilities, but that the 'great One, who comes after me will, unasked, reveal it for you. That commentary will constitute one of the weightiest testimonies of His truth, and one of the clearest evidences of the loftiness of His position.'[81] Rashtī's response here would appear to be conditioned by numerous *ḥadīth*s which say that the *qā'im* will resemble Joseph in several respects.[82] Throughout the Bāb's commentary it seems clear that he is seeing himself as Joseph, in that the Quranic story is read as a prefigurement, however allegorical, of the Bāb's own mission.

After the disconnected letters and the above-mentioned introductory verses which claim divine revelation, the next section of a given *sūra* begins. It is this section which is most difficult to characterize because of the variety of concerns which may appear in it. Generally speaking, the last section of a *sūra* is where the Bāb turns his attention directly to the verse of the Qur'ān under which his commentary is written. The method of exegesis, then, is usually simple paraphrase of the Qur'ān in which the Bāb makes various substitutions with words which give a meaning much more specific to his own claims and situation. In the course of his exegesis, there is never recourse to the usual markers of an interpretative statement such as *ay* or *ya'nī* ('that is'), or *aqūlu* ('I say'). Rather, the exegetical equivalences are offered by the Bāb as much closer to the Quranic material than would be the case if the above words, along with the semantic distance to be travelled that their use implies, were used.[83] Before giving examples of this kind of commentary, it may be of interest to discuss in some detail the first *sūra* of the *Tafsīr*.

The *sūrat al-mulk*, which is in fact the part of the work which was written in the presence of Mullā Ḥusayn on the night of 22 May 1844, forms a kind of introduction to the whole, and is unusual in that it is not written under a verse of Qur'ān *sūra* 12.

[81] Nabīl, 59.

[82] Muḥammad ibn 'Alī al-Qummī ibn Bābūya, *Ikmāl al-dīn wa itmām al-ni'ma fī ithbāt al-raj'a* (Najaf, 1369/1970), 18.

[83] This method may be a reflex of the idea contained in the famous Shī'ī *hadith* which quotes the Imām al-Bāqir as: 'It is we who are the meanings (*ma'ānī*). We are the Hand of God, His vicinity, His tongue, His command, His decision, His knowledge, His truth. We are the Face of God which is turned toward the terrestrial world in your midst. He who recognizes us has certitude for an *imām*. He who rejects us has Hell as an *imām*'; cited in Corbin, *En Islam Iranien*, i. 194. The interesting statement 'we are the meanings', among other things, takes for granted the absolute spiritual authority implied in the act of paraphrase.

Evidence that it is indeed part of a commentary on the Qur'ān does not occur until well into the text, where the following statement is found:

God hath decreed that this book, in explanation (*fī tafsīr*) of the 'best of stories' . . . should come forth from Muḥammad, son of Ḥasan, son of 'Alī, son of Mūsā, son of Ja'far, son of Muḥammad, son of 'Alī, son of Ḥusayn, son of 'Alī, son of Abū Ṭālib, unto his servant [the Bāb] that it may be a proof of God on the part of the Remembrance (*dhikr*) reaching the two worlds.[84]

The title of this *sūra* is related to the fact that the entire chapter, rather than dealing with subjects connected to an understanding of the twelfth chapter of the Qur'ān, is a sustained and impassioned challenge first to Muḥammad Shāh, the reigning monarch of Iran at that time, and then to his Prime Minister, Ḥājī Mīrzā Aqāsī, to submit to the command of the Remembrance (*dhikr*, that is, the Bāb). In the course of this *sūra* we see several elements which are, however, characteristic of the whole book. The first of these is the proclamation of the Bāb's spiritual rank, either as *bāb* or *dhikr*, to name only two of the several different designations which are used throughout the text.[85] Then there are the fluent paraphrase of the Qur'ān, the call to absolute obedience, the summons to the world beyond Iran, the reference to laws (*aḥkām*), the language, and the imagery which is striking in the extreme. An example of this last is the Bāb's juxtaposition of opposites. In the *sūrat al-mulk*, one reads, for example: *inna al-nār fī nuqṭati'l-mā' li'llāh al-ḥaqq sājid*[an] *'alā'l-arḍ* ('the fire which is in the drop of water is itself prostrate upon the earth before God, the Reality').[86] This may, of course, be a simple case of an echo of basic alchemical imagery, particularly in this instance; in later *suwar*, however, this combining of opposites appears to take on original characteristics which seem to somehow designate the source of the Bāb's inspiration.[87]

84 Trans. Browne, *JRAS* 21 (1889), 908.

85 Some others are the word (*kalima*), *qā'im* of the year one thousand, the blessed tree in Sinai, and the resurrection. For a discussion of these and other designations of spiritual authority, see M. Afnan and W. S. Hatcher, 'Western Islamic Scholarship and Bahā'ī Origins', *Religion*, 15 (1985), 29–51.

86 In this same *sūra* the following statement occurs: *wa inna qad sayyarnā'l-jibāl 'alā'l-arḍ* (cf. Q. 18/47) *wa'l-nujūm 'alā'l-'arsh ḥawl al-nār fī quṭb al-mā' min ladā'l-dhikr bi-llāh al-ḥaqq* ('We have set the mountains in motion upon the earth, and the stars upon the Throne around the fire which is in the point [lit. axis] of water in the presence of the Remembrance in God (*bi-llāh*), the Reality').

87 Another more dramatic example of this 'figure' is: 'We have apportioned

This third section of a given *sūra* may also consist of a running exegetical paraphrase of extended sections of the Qur'ān. For example, chapters 52 and 53, *al-faḍl* and *al-ṣabr*,[88] present a detailed rewriting of the first fifty or so verses of the second *sūra* of the Qur'ān, *al-baqara*.

At Q. 2/2–5, for example, we have:

Qur'ān	*Bāb*
That is the book wherein there is no doubt, a guidance to the godfearing who believe in the Unseen, and perform the prayer, and expend of that We have provided them; who believe in what has been sent down to thee and what has been sent down before thee, and have faith in the Hereafter; those are upon guidance from their Lord, those are the ones who prosper.	By thy Lord! Thou [the Hidden Imām, and by implication, the Bāb himself] art the Book wherein there is no doubt, and thou art praiseworthy in the estimation of God. Those who believe in the Remembrance of God, in his *ghayba*, and rule among mankind with truth by means of his verses, we will, in very truth,[89] bestow upon them, as a blessing from Our side, a great reward. Those are upon a guidance with the Remembrance of God, and those are the ones who hastened first, in truth, in the Book of God.[90]

Another more extended example of this running paraphrase may be found in *sūras* 80 to 95 inclusive,[91] which treat most of the Quranic material from Q. 10/57 up to the first few verses of Q. 17. A random example is the Bāb's rewriting of Q. 10/87.

Qur'ān	*Bāb*
And We revealed unto Moses and his brother, 'Take you, for your people, in Egypt certain houses;	And We revealed to Moses and his brother, 'Take you, [or "set aside"] in the Egypt of the hearts, for the

mountains on the earth, and placed the earth upon the water, and the musky air [we have caused to come forth] from under the hot coldness (*al-ḥarr al-bard*)', *QA* 137. Numerous other examples could be cited. The coincidence of opposites is a frequent topos in this work; the Bāb's use of it is undoubtedly influenced by such important traditions as the *khutbat al-tatanjīya*. For a fuller discussion see B. T. Lawson, 'The Qur'ān Commentary of the Bāb', Ph.D. thesis, McGill University (1987).

88 *QA* 100–5.

89 'In very truth' translates a frequent 'refrain' throughout this work: *'alā'l-ḥaqq bi'l-ḥaqq*. The translation does not carry the all-important allusion to God, *al-ḥaqq*, 'The Truth' *par excellence*.

90 *QA* 100.

91 *QA* 160–95.

Qur'ān	*Bāb*
make your houses a direction for men to pray to; and perform the prayer; and do thou give good tidings to the believers.	people of the earth, houses consecrated to the exclusive unity (*aḥadīya*) of the Most Great Remembrance of God, the Living, and He is God, the Knowing, the Judge. And verily God made them [houses] a direction for men to pray to, and to perform all the prayers in, so give good tidings to the sincere servants of God'.[92]

As mentioned above, the fourth section of a given *sūra* usually returns to the verse of the Qur'ān under which it is written. The method again is paraphrase, of which the last two of the following three examples are characteristic. The second chapter, *sūrat al-'ulamā'*, is written under Qur'ān 12/1, '*alif-lām-rā'*; these are the verses of the Manifest Book'. The passage thus ends with a commentary on these three disconnected letters. The Bāb says that God created the letter *alif* to represent that servant of His [the Bāb himself?] who is strong in the divine cause (*amr*). The letter *lām* signifies the ascendancy of his rule over the rule of the book [the Qur'ān?]. The letter *rā'* was made by God for the spreading (*inbisāṭ*) of His cause according to the way it has been ordained in the Mother of the Book.

Sūra 71, *al-qalam*, is written under Qur'ān 12/70: 'And when he had equipped them with their equipment, he put his drinking-cup into the saddlebag of his brother. Then a herald proclaimed, "Ho, camel-riders, you are robbers"!' The Bāb's paraphrase of the verse is as follows:

> Verily, We command the angels to place the drinking-cup of the Remembrance in the saddlebag of the believers, by the leave of God, the Exalted, and God is Knower of all things. O crier (*al-mu'adhdhin*), cry out! O camel-riders, you are robbers. Indeed the cup of the Remembrance is concealed from you in the highest station, in very truth. And God is the Preserver of all things. And God is powerful over all things.[93]

The metaphors in the above commentary (drinking-cup/Remembrance; saddlebag/believers) are similar to the previously cited 'Egypt of the hearts'. In this instance, however, they refer to a

[92] *QA* 161. [93] *QA* 145.

subject raised in the *Tafsīr sūrat al-baqara*, namely one's innate, and in a sense predetermined, capacity for accepting or rejecting the Imām as the locus of divinity, in this case represented by the Bāb. The believers are therefore privileged to be so because they hold within themselves the 'signs' of the Remembrance, here represented by 'drinking-cup'. Likewise, the 'robbers' are prevented from accepting the truth because these signs have been withheld from them.[94]

The *sūrat al-ḥajj*, number 103, is written under Qur'ān 12/102: 'This is of the tidings of the Unseen that We reveal to thee; thou wast not with them when they agreed upon their plan, devising.' The Bāb's paraphrase is as follows:

> This (*dhālika*) *tafsīr* is of the tidings of *al-'amā*, written upon the leaf of the heart by the permission of God, the Exalted, in the vicinity of the sacred fire. Verily, God has revealed to you the tidings of the Unseen while you were the most Great Truth, when their word conflicted, lying. God is, in very truth, Witness over you.[95]

5. CONCLUSIONS

> In order to account for the triggering of the interpretative process, we must assume at the outset that the production and reception of discourse . . . obey a very general rule of pertinence, according to which if a discourse exists there must be a reason for it. So that when at first glance a given discourse does not obey this rule, the receiver's spontaneous reaction is to determine whether the discourse might not reveal its pertinence through some particular manipulation. 'Interpretation' . . . is what we call this manipulation.[96]

The examples of the textual concerns of *Tafsīr sūrat Yūsuf* which have been provided here, along with the general description of the work, are sufficient to make possible a few very general observations. While it is clear that the work is most unusual *vis-à-vis* the *tafsīr* tradition, or for that matter any other genre of Arabic literature, it

94 On this idea see Corbin's discussion of *isomorphisme* in *En Islam Iranien*, iv. 286–300.

95 *QA* 212. *Al-'amā* is a frequent term in this work. For a treatment of its spiritual significance, see Stephen Lambden, 'An Early Poem of Mīrzā Ḥusayn 'Alī Bahā'u'llāh: The Sprinkling of the Cloud of Unknowing (Rashḥ-i 'Amā)', *Bahā'ī Studies Bulletin*, 3, no. 2, pp. 4–114, esp. 42 to end.

96 Tzvetan Todorov, *Symbolism and Interpretation*, trans. Catherine Porter, (Ithaca, 1982), 28.

would appear that by categorizing the work as *tafsīr* the author wished it to be read and judged in this context. This, of course, raises the question of what in fact distinguishes *tafsīr* from other types of literature. It should not be assumed that since the Bāb was not a typical religious scholar that he was therefore unaware of the standard works of *tafsīr*,[97] or that he thought this work of his should be received as a continuation of that tradition. Rather, the contrary would seem to be the case, particularly in view of the earlier *Tafsīr sūrat al-baqara*, which, however different from the main sources of orthodox Shī'ī Qur'ān commentary it may be, exhibits many of the usual approaches and methods found in those works. In composing the later commentary, the Bāb was attempting a break with a tradition which he perceived as moribund, particularly so in the context of the advent of a new order of which he himself claimed to be the herald. In addition, as was noted earlier, there seems to have been a certain amount of eschatalogical expectation centred on the appearance of one who would produce a commentary on the twelfth *sūra* of the Qur'ān.

Browne's statements that the work is inappropriately titled notwithstanding, it is abundantly clear that not only does it offer interpretative statements on the *sūra* of Joseph, but comments on a large portion of the rest of the Qur'ān in the process, albeit usually by means of paraphrase. Unusual, there is no doubt. To say that it is not interpretative, or that it does not make clear what the Qur'ān meant, at least to the Bāb, is either not to have read it, or to have imposed upon it too rigid a notion about what constitutes *tafsīr*, which is after all fundamentally only 'explanation'. Given the method of allegorical and typological exegesis which is fluently and ceaselessly expressed in the constant use of such rhetorical devices as metaphor and simile, in addition to the 'heresy of paraphrase' and the exploitation of ambiguity—all of which have been cast in an unabashed imitation of the Qur'ān[98]—the work is clearly one of

[97] e.g., one of the few mentions of any but an Imām in the *Tafsīr sūrat al-baqara* is a reference to 'the author of *al-Ṣāfī*', i.e., Muḥsin Fayḍ Kāshānī, author of the *Tafsīr al-ṣāfī*. The reference itself is not flattering; see *Majmū'a*, 402. Kāshānī is criticized for his purely superficial (*qishr maḥḍ*) interpretation of Q. 2/143. In addition, the Bāb says that he has not referred to the *tafsīr* of the '*ulamā*' because 'such is not worthy of the purpose of this book'. It must be noted that this reference comes in the course of the commentary on the second *juz*' of the Qur'ān, the authorship of which is open to debate.

[98] The Bāb repeatedly asserts that the work is in fact the *same* Qur'ān that was

interpretation. The work itself is the result of a re-ordering of the basic elements of the scripture of Islam which have been fully internalized and finally transformed by the apparently opposite processes of imitation and inspiration to become finally an original 'act' of literature. Taken as a whole, this remarkable work of the 25 year-old merchant from Shīrāz, representing as it does a text within a text which strives to interpret itself, offers a concrete and literary example of a singularly heroic attempt to transform what became known much later, and in a culture quite alien to his own, as the hermeneutic circle,[99] into a hermeneutic spiral.

By comparing these two works, which were written at about the same time, we see how differently the act of interpretation, yet springing from the same mind, is capable of expressing itself. And with the second work, not only do we have a new example for the history of *tafsīr*, but because the work itself is a call to action, we also have the rather startling example of *tafsīr* directly affecting history—in a sense, becoming history.[100]

revealed to Muḥammad; see, e.g., Adib Taherzadeh, *et al.*, *Selections from the Writings of the Bāb* (Haifa, 1978), 67.

[99] Cf. Mohammed Arkoun, 'Lecture de la Fātiḥa', in his *Lectures du Coran* (Paris, 1982), 41–67, esp. 49. Here the author, who appears to be speaking from a Sunnī standpoint, makes a reference to Ricoeur's definition of the 'cercle herméneutique' in setting forth what he considers to be the eight principles, either explicit or implicit, of classical exegesis. I stress the Sunnī nature of the schema because in it he presents his seventh principle in the following terms: 'La disparition du prophète a enfermé tous les croyants dans un cercle herméneutique: chacun est confronté, désormais, au texte qui *re*-présent la Parole; chacun doit "croire pour comprendre et comprendre pour croire".' By comparison, it would appear that the same thing occurred within Twelver Shīʿī Islam, or at least was perceived later to have occurred, with the disappearance of the twelfth Imām.

[100] I am grateful to Prof. H. Landolt, McGill University, for his interest, encouragement, and assistance with this paper.

PART IV

MODERN TRENDS IN *TAFSĪR*

12

Quranic Exegesis in the Malay World: In Search of a Profile

ANTHONY H. JOHNS

SOUTH-EAST Asia is the home today of almost one-quarter of the world's Muslims. In the Malay peninsula, Sumatra, and Java in particular, there is abundant testimony to six centuries of Islamization. Social structures, laws, and systems of government have been modified by Islamic influences, a rich stratum of Arabic loan words is established in the major languages of the region such as Malay and Javanese, and up to modern times, an adapted form of the Arabic script is widely used. As well, a significant if not large corpus of belles-lettres and religious works deriving from or inspired by Arabic and to a lesser extent Persian sources is extant.

Malay has a special role in the Islamization of the area, where it has been widely known and used as a lingua franca since at least the fifteenth century. Malay manuscript sources alone, however, give an inadequate and uneven picture of the transmission and development of the traditional disciplines by which the Muslim community lives, disciplines such as *tafsīr*, *ḥadīth*, and *fiqh*. Diverse works relating to these disciplines are to be found at various centres throughout the archipelago, yet none of them in any place adds up to a critical mass of material such as might normally be expected to command the undivided attention of a scholar, or serve as a benchmark for a study of the pursuit of Islamic learning in the region. This lack of materials to sustain a continuing tradition of scholarship in any one place is among the reasons why Muslim intellectual life remains largely an unexplored field, and why Malay has not yet become the vehicle for an Islamic literary culture in its own right.

Yet this is not the whole story. Such sources as exist are intractable and incomplete. These difficulties are compounded by the fact that the survival of manuscripts in a tropical region in which centres of political power are unstable is largely a matter of chance. The collection of materials for a documentary study of Islamic intellectual history in this part of the world did not begin until the end of the sixteenth century, when the first European ships entering the area began to take manuscripts home to Europe. Inevitably, chance played a major role in the materials that they collected, which were thereby preserved and subsequently became available in libraries. Thus, they are not necessarily representative of the distributions of schools and tendencies within their provenance and are by no means exhaustive. As if this were not problematic enough, the cataloguing of extant manuscripts is inadequate. Van Ronkel, for example, one of the principal cataloguers of Malay manuscripts, did not regard provenance as important,[1] and his descriptions were brief, often to the point of being uninformative. There is a further factor that needs to be taken into account: the dominance of the oral tradition in the regions under discussion. This has a direct relation to the paucity of manuscripts, but is reflected in another circumstance. Arabic was the language of the basic texts used for religious instruction—the translations of and commentaries on these texts being given orally in Malay and rarely written down. Thus, from the very beginnings of Islamization, a tradition of *diglossia* was established: Arabic as the authoritative language of learning, Malay as that of popular exposition. This broad generalization is not without its exceptions; in fact, the vernacularization of Islam in the region, although uneven, has some striking achievements as early as the sixteenth century.

In view of such difficulties, no single approach can treat the extant material satisfactorily. The skills of the philologist can only occasionally be used to full effect; any attempt to establish a chronology for the study of one or another of the Islamic disciplines has to accept that many gaps must long remain unfilled; and substantial case studies based upon the work of outstanding individuals are only occasionally possible. In this, as in other areas of historical investigation, the sources available for a study of Indonesia's past, as Bastin has cogently argued, do not provide evidence that makes for a strong personality base.[2]

[1] G. W. G. Drewes, *Directions for Travellers on the Mystic Path* (The Hague, 1977), 198.

[2] John Bastin, 'Problems of Personality in the Reinterpretation of Modern Malayan History', in J. Bastin, R. Roolvink, eds., *Malayan and Indonesian Studies* (Oxford, 1964), 141–53, esp. 152–3.

Thus, in attempting a historical approach to *tafsīr* in the Malay world, this essay does not hope to achieve more that to seek a profile on the basis of some of the extant material, and suggest approaches for further study that may be fruitful. My method, then, is eclectic. It takes something from various approaches, but is able fully to exploit none. There is, however, one basic premiss that must be accepted whatever approach is adopted and whatever field of Islamic learning is investigated. The study of Islam in the territories that now comprise Indonesia and Malaysia must be locally based; the primary focus of the historian's attention is the urban settlements and port-city states which were the first centres for the establishment of Islamic learning and the further diffusion of the religion. These were the places where the core Islamic disciplines were first taught and studied to meet the needs of a growing Muslim community, and among these disciplines, Quranic exegesis, *tafsīr*, surely held a pride of place.

I

The earliest Islamic political entities in the Malay region are to be found on the north and east coasts of Sumatra. Their existence and the names of their rulers are attested by tombstones, but little evidence of their cultural life remains. For this we have to wait until the period of Malacca, 1400–1511.

Unfortunately, although there is a chronicle, known in English as the *Malay Annals*,[3] which purports to give information of life at the court from its foundation until its destruction by the Portuguese, there are no direct indications of religious life and thought in the period from supporting texts. In the *Malay Annals* itself, there are occasional references to religious personalities who are presented as eccentric, ill-tempered, or cowardly. One is enraged by the small boys who fly kites over his house, and he shoots the objects down with a sling; another is made fun of by a tipsy court official because he cannot pronounce Malay words correctly, a third goes out to battle against the Portuguese accompanying the Sultan who is mounted on an elephant, and amid the cannon-shot urges his master to return to the palace with the words: 'This is no place to

[3] C. C. Brown, 'Sejarah Melayu or "Malay Annals." A Translation of Raffles MS 18', *JMBRAS* 25 (1952), esp. 55–171.

discuss the mystical union.'[4] What religious intellectual life is to be discovered behind such references is difficult to determine.

A successor state to Malacca that was to become a major power in the region emerged in the mid-sixteenth century. This was Aceh, situated at the north of Sumatra. In dealing with it, thanks to the greater availability of sources, we are on much firmer ground than we were with Malacca, but this is only relative. It is possible to identify an author who lived between 1550 and 1599, Ḥamza Pansūrī,[5] an Acehnese. Only a few facts are known of his life. He is known to have visited Thailand and Java, and to have made the pilgrimage to Mecca. More important is the fact that some of the writings attributed to him have survived until today. They include a number of poems devoted to mystical topics, and various prose works which are expositions in Malay of the mystical philosophy that infuses and structures the poems. His theosophy is that of the Ibn 'Arabī tradition, although he was a member of the Qādirīya *ṭarīqa*. No work of *tafsīr* as such is attributed to him, but, in both his prose and poetry, he renders into fluent Malay numerous verses of the Qur'ān—many of them the favourites of mystics—to which he gives the mystical interpretation of the Ibn 'Arabī tradition. Equally striking is the skill with which he integrates Quranic verses into his poetry. A marvellous example is his treatment in one of his quatrains of Q. 112, *sūrat al-ikhlāṣ*:

laut itulah yang bernama aḥad
terlalu lengkap pada asy'uṣ-ṣamad
olehnya itulah lam yalid wa lam yūlad
wa lam yakun lahu kufu$^{'an}$ *aḥad.*

It is that ocean of being that is called *aḥad*.
The One besought of all is present in all things.
This is why He neither begets nor is begotten.
And nothing is equal to Him.[6]

The combination of words and phrases from Arabic and Malay—languages totally unrelated—is so fluent, and the exposition of the mystical and theosophical ideas so lucid, that Ḥamza's writings can only reflect a long period of association between the two languages

[4] Brown, 'Annals', 131, 153, and 168 respectively.

[5] J. Doorenbos, *De Geshcriften van Hamzah Pansoeri* (Leiden, 1933); a new edition of the poems is now provided by G. W. J. Drewes and L. F. Brakel, *The Poems of Hamzah Pansuri* (Leiden, 1986).

[6] Doorenbos, *Hamzah Fansoeri*, 94.

as Islam put down its roots. In any case, such a vernacularization of the Ibn 'Arabī tradition could not have occurred at the beginning of Islamization. There is no direct evidence of the length of the period in question, nor of its modality. It is certain, however, that peoples of Malay stock had made the pilgrimage to Mecca before Ḥamza, and there are records of Malays crossing the Indian Ocean—to Surat, to Zanzibar, and one may be sure, to the Ḥijāz—before him. The skill that he demonstrates, and the religious passion that he expresses has the hallmark of great literature; it could not have appeared fully formed immediately, yet the tradition from which it emerged and of which it is a high point no longer exists. Nor does it have any successor. The fact remains that Ḥamza's writing includes the earliest extant rendering into Malay of Quranic verses. The reason for the survival of these poems is twofold. They were written by a master-mystic for a spiritual élite, and it was due to the special value that this élite placed on the poems that they survived, despite the efforts of the representative of a rival school to have them destroyed; this is apart from the fact that some of them found their way back to Holland. Although his writings are not *tafsīr*, they are evidence, albeit occasional, of the presence of a particular tradition of *tafsīr* in his circle.

The next piece of evidence, however, is a fragment of a *tafsīr* work. It is a manuscript that dates from before 1620 which was taken to Holland by a Dutch ship. It is a rendering into Malay of a commentary on *sūra* 18, *al-kahf*.[7] The language is fluent and idiomatic, and bears relatively little trace of a calque type of translation. It, too, clearly belongs to a tradition of Qur'ān study which was already well established and which, no less than that of Ḥamza, had already reached a high standard. Although no author is indicated, it has been established that it is in fact a close translation of al-Khāzin's[8] (d. 741/1340) treatment of this *sūra*. Now, al-Khāzin is far removed from the mystical tradition of Qur'ān exegesis. Essentially his work is concerned with the meaning of the Arabic words, filling out the narrative of Quranic stories, and providing appropriate *asbāb al-nuzūl*. This fragment

[7] P. S. Van Ronkel, 'An Account of Six Malay Manuscripts of the Cambridge University Library', *Bijdragen tot de koninklijk instituut voor taal- land- en volkenkunde*, 46 (1896), 2 ff.

[8] 'Alā' al-Dīn 'Alī ibn Muḥammad ibn Ibrahim al-Baghdādī al-Khāzin, *Lubāb al-ta'wīl fī ma'ānī al-tanzīl* (Beirut, n.d.).

reflects a very different kind of treatment of the text, and a very different kind of spiritual world, to that of Ḥamza Pansūrī. Either it was prepared for students of a different level of understanding, or else it represented a different tradition of Islamic learning, deriving from a different teacher and a different school. One can do no more than speculate, but one thing is sure: it is unwise to assume uniformity in Islam even in one cultural region in one period—it is perilous to formulate hypotheses on the basis of an absence of evidence.

Ḥamza Pansūrī had a number of students who now draw our attention. Among them was a fellow Sumatran, Shams al-Dīn,[9] a man who was to become an outstanding *'ālim* at the court of Sultan Iskandar Muda who ruled Aceh from 1605 to 1636. By the beginning of this period, Aceh had become a power on the international stage. Iskandar Muda maintained relations with the Ottoman and Mughal empires as ruler of a great Muslim principality in the region. Indeed, there are accounts by foreign visitors to Aceh of the imposing scale on which the court celebrated the two major festivals of the Islamic calendar, that of the ending of the fast, and of the sacrifice. It was visited regularly by *'ulama'* from South Asia and the Middle East, and had gained a reputation throughout the archipelago as the gateway to Mecca.[10] Although no direct evidence survives, it must have been a region in which *madrasas* flourished.

At the court of Aceh, Shams al-Dīn combined the roles of scholar, foreign minister, and personal adviser to the ruler. He was a Naqshbandī, and inducted the Sultan into that *ṭarīqa*. The sources refer to him by the title *Shaykh al-Islām*. He wrote on theosophical topics, and he is the first Malay author we know by name who wrote in Arabic.[11] He, too, belongs to the Ibn 'Arabī school, apparently to a north Indian offshoot of that tradition.

The existence of his works in Arabic and Malay, the more scholarly ones in Arabic, more popular expositions of certain

[9] A full account of his writings and background is given in C. A. O. van Nieuwenhuize, *Samsu'l-Din van Pasai Bijdragen tot de kennis der Sumatraansche Mystiek* (Leiden, 1945).

[10] Snouck Hurgronje, *The Achehnese*, trans. A. W. S. O'Sullivan (Leiden, 1906). See esp. ii. chs. 1 and 4.

[11] An edition of his major Arabic work, *Jawhar al-ḥaqā'iq*, is included in van Nieuwenhuize, *Samsu'l-Din*, 245–66.

features of his theosophical doctrines in Malay, are another illustration of the tradition of *diglossia* already referred to.

None of the surviving works of Shams al-Dīn includes a Quranic commentary. As in the case of Ḥamza, however, renderings of Quranic verses and phrases stud his works, many of them verses beloved of the mystics and interpreted in a mystical sense.

The period between 1607 and 1636 was one of considerable creativity and promise in the intellectual life of Islam in Aceh. Unfortunately, upon the death of Iskander Muda in 1636, there broke out a struggle for power between representatives of two rival schools of religious thought, a struggle that involved both executions and the burning of books, and that lasted until 1642. How many books were destroyed cannot be guessed, but it is certain that the number included many of the works of Ḥamza and Shams al-Dīn, possibly along with commentaries on the Qur'ān.

The situation stabilized with a change of ruler in 1642.[12] This was the year in which the first Sumatran scholar who spent a long period of study in Arabia can be identified, 'Abd al-Ra'ūf of Singkel. He left for Arabia around 1640 and returned to Sumatra in 1661 with an *ijāza* to propagate the Shaṭṭarīya order in Aceh, from whence it spread widely throughout the islands. He secured the patronage of the ruler of Aceh at that time, the Sultana Ṣafīya al-Dīn Tāj al-'Ālam (1641–1675), and during the remainder of his long life, he prepared a commentary on the Qur'ān with the title *Tarjumān al-mustafīd*,[13] of which several manuscripts still exist. The *tafsīr* was published in Istanbul around the 1880's and is still regularly reprinted and widely used. It has not been closely studied and for many years there was some doubt as to the nature and character of the work.

For many years this *tafsīr* has been referred to as a rendering into Malay of al-Bayḍāwī's (d. 685/1286) *Anwār al-tanzīl*. A recent study, however, has made it clear that this attribution is mistaken; the certificate of three scholars at Mecca that the work neither adds to, subtracts from, nor alters by translation anything of the text of al-Bayḍāwī cannot be accepted at face value. Likewise, Snouck Hurgronje's description of it as a rendering of *Anwār al-tanzīl* appears to have been derived from a too hasty reading of the text. It is, in fact, a rendering into Malay of the *Tafsīr al-Jalālayn*,

12 See "Abd al-Ra'ūf al-Sinkilī', *EI*[2] i. 88.

13 'Abd al-Ra'ūf al-Singkeli, *Tarjumān al-mustafīḍ* (Singapore, 1951/1370).

supplemented by a few citations from al-Bayḍāwī, extensive pericopes from al-Khāzin's treatment of *sūrat al-kahf* into Malay referred to earlier), principally of anecdotal material relevant to *asbāb al-nuzūl*, and finally scattered pericopes consisting of *qirā'āt* which derive neither from *Tafsīr al-Jalālayn*, nor for that matter from al-Bayḍāwī.[14] The identification is important for several reasons. One is that it demonstrates how far the work stands from the mystical tradition of exegesis espoused by Ḥamza and Shams al-Dīn. Perhaps more important, however, is the choice of the work. The *Tafsīr al-Jalālayn* of Jalāl al-Dīn al-Maḥallī (d. 864/1459) and Jalāl al-Dīn al-Suyūṭī (d. 911/1505) is often dismissed out of hand as contributing little to the development of the tradition of *tafsīr*. In fact, it is a masterly word by word exegesis of the Qur'ān, both lucid and succinct, including relevant *asbāb al-nuzūl* alongside selected *qirā'āt* and the alternative significances that they involve. As a first recourse in the study of the text of the Qur'ān, especially for Muslims (and scholars) whose native language is not Arabic, it is of very great value. Thus, 'Abd al-Ra'ūf's rendering of it is to his credit as a teacher and is evidence of his modesty and dedication. For obvious reasons, the work of al-Bayḍāwī with its condensed presentation and frequent elipses would have been quite unsuitable for his purposes.

This choice gains further significance when seen in relation to the listings of the holdings of Arabic manuscripts in the Indonesian National Museum in Jakarta, where there is a large number of manuscripts of *Tafsīr al-Jalālayn*, making it by far the most popular work of *tafsīr*.[15] These Arabic holdings have not yet been adequately studied. Although they cover various Islamic disciplines and were collected from various parts of the archipelago, the distribution of the holdings is uneven and they display various traditions, interests, and emphases. Only a few manuscripts are older than the eighteenth century, and they are not particularly rich in *tafsīr*. There is, however, a copy of al-Bayhaqī (d. 494/1101), *Kitāb al-tahdhīb fī tafsīr al-Qur'ān*, ḍating from 1652 (the date is significant when we consider that we are looking not only at *tafsīr*

[14] P. Riddell, 'The Sources of 'Abd al-Ra'uf's *Tarjuman al-mustafid*', *JMBRAS* 57 (1984), 198.

[15] P. S. van Ronkel, *Supplement to the Catalogue of the Arabic Manuscripts Preserved in the Museum of the Batavia Society of Arts and Science* (Batavia, 1913), 17–29.

writing in the region, but at the types of *tafsīr* that were known there), and an undated fragment of the mystical *tafsīr*, *Taṣdīq al-ma'ārif*.

Other questions apart, on the basis of holdings in this museum, the popularity of *Tafsīr al-Jalālayn*, at least, needs no arguing. It is more than likely that it was well known before 'Abd al-Ra'ūf made his rendering and that his rendering was made in response to a need. It needs stressing that *tafsīr* is not primarily a theoretical discipline, but one of teaching, inspired by a passion to explain the revealed word clearly and accurately.

Another point is that 'Abd al-Ra'ūf's rendering is a classic example of an interlinear calque translation. In this, it differs markedly from the renderings of individual verses by Ḥamza and the anonymous translation of al-Khāzin's treatment of *sūrat al-kahf*. This feature has been studied closely by Dr Riddell, and he has shown how closely even the forms of the Arabic verb have been imitated, the Malay subject being placed in a pre-verb position for the Arabic *muḍāri'*, and in post-verb position for *al-māḍī*.[16] Although the rendering is not exactly computer-like, and human inconsistencies—sometimes to the improvement of the style—show through, the result is a strikingly reliable guide to *Tafsīr al-Jalālayn*, a study aid that, for a Malay speaker, is a useful stepping stone to the Arabic text of the *Tafsīr* as a student makes progress in the original language. One might even suggest a reconstruction of the circumstances in which the rendering came to be made; first, the reading-out of Arabic phrases from the original text, each phrase followed by an oral equivalent in Malay, a practice which over the years suggested the value of a full Malay version. Although the calque translation is not always easy to understand on the printed page, the intonation of the spoken word in many cases makes intelligible what is obscure, as an explanation is followed by an explanation of the explanation, followed by a further synonym for the word or phrase to be clarified. The work has never been repeated; for its purpose it could hardly be improved upon. This accounts for its continued popularity in local religious schools. The fact that the translation is so close to the original renders it easy to turn back into Arabic, and this renders it invaluable for teaching purposes.

[16] P. Riddell, "Abd al-Ra'ūf's *Tarjumān at Mustafīḍ*', Ph.D. thesis (Australian National University, Canberra, 1984), 104–6.

It may be observed that *Tafsīr al-Jalālayn* retains its role in Islamic education up to the present. Abdul Kahhar Muzakkir, a distinguished Indonesian Islamic educationalist who studied in Cairo for eleven years between 1925 and 1935 and included among his teachers Rashīd Riḍā and al-Maraghī, as recently as 1959 noted that the study of the Qur'ān in Muhammadiyya schools—the largest and best-organized Islamic school system in the country—was based on the work *Tafsīr al-Jalālayn*.[17]

'Abd al-Ra'uf's rendering of the *Tafsīr al-Jalālayn*, then, is in more than one way a landmark in the history of Islamic learning in Malay. It is a significant achievement in its own right; it is a full rendering of the Qur'ān in Malay, and in addition it lays the foundation for a bridge between *tarjama* and *tafsīr*. It had no immediate successors, but it established a reference-point, if not a tradition. It must not be seen as existing in isolation; rather, it must be stressed that a written work, particularly in this region of the world in this period, is exceptional, and that alongside it, the oral tradition of instruction continued to flourish, and that the well-springs of *tafsīr*, and the forms and emphases that it takes, derive from a teaching tradition that does not leave tangible records.

From the seventeenth century on there are increasing numbers of locally written works, both in Arabic and Malay, which contribute to the richness and diversity of Islamic discourse in the Malay world. The prime movers in this enrichment were Jāwīs (Jāwī being the term used in Arabic to designate pilgrims or scholars from anywhere in the Malay archipelago) who settled for many years (as had 'Abd al-Ra'ūf), and in some cases permanently, in the Ḥijāz, who taught and wrote in both Arabic and Malay for their compatriots there, and who kept in contact with their kinsfolk and fellow villagers at home through returning pilgrims who brought family news and advice, both by word of mouth and by the letters and manuscripts that they carried.

A highpoint in this process was an eighteenth-century rendering into Malay of *Lubāb Iḥyā' 'ulūm al-din*, an abridgement of al-Ghazzālī's (d. 505/1111) major work, probably authored by his brother Aḥmad. This translation was made by 'Abd al-Ṣamad of Palembang, who prepared it in al-Ṭā'if between 1760 and 1780, and gave it the title *Sayr al-sālikīn*.[18] 'Abd al-Ṣamad followed the

[17] Mustafa Baisa, *al-Abroor—Tafsīr Djuz' 'Amma* (Surabaya, n.d.), 9.
[18] Drewes, *Path*, 222.

example of 'Abd al-Ra'ūf and many others as a modest and dedicated teacher. He made no contribution to the study of *tafsīr* as such, yet, of course, the number of Quranic citations and *ḥadīth* included in this work is very great; an investigation of what may be called the secondary *tafsīr* in his work will certainly add to our knowledge of what *tafsīr* was known at this time, for 'Abd al-Ṣamad's work, while purporting to be a translation of that of al-Ghazzālī, in fact contains extracts of various, much later compositions. It may also be noted that despite his absence from his homeland, there is evidence of 'Abd al-Ṣamad's interest in political concerns related to the exercise of Dutch power there.

II

It is not until the last quarter of the nineteenth century that we find a contribution to *tafsīr* by a Jāwī of the same stature as that of 'Abd al-Ra'ūf. This is a large, two-volume work in Arabic compiled in Mecca by a man named al-Nawawī (1815–98) from the village of Tanara in Banten, West Java, who settled permanently in Mecca after 1835.[19] That the work is written in Arabic demonstrates once again the tradition of *diglossia* in the teaching of Islam in the Malay world. The work is of special importance not only because it was published in the Middle East, but because it has established itself as a basic work of *tafsīr* in its own right, perhaps the only Arabic work by a Jāwī to do so. It is still used widely as a middle-level work (*mutawassiṭ*) in Malaysia and Indonesia. Equally significantly, it is an extension and enrichment of the type of commentary found in *Tafsīr al-Jalālayn*.

Al-Nawawī's background is typical of many unknown Jāwī scholars, although not many equalled his learning. We are fortunate in that Snouck Hurgronje met him in Mecca in 1884, and in the second volume of his work *Mekka*, he gives an exquisite thumb-nail sketch of his personality.[20] Snouck mentions that, when they met, al-Nawawī was leader of the Jāwī community, and had

[19] A. H. Johns, 'Islam in the Malay World: An Exploratory Survey with Some Reference to Quranic Exegesis', in A. H. Johns and R. Israeli, *Islam in Asia*, ii. *Southeast and East Asia* (Jerusalem, 1984), 131–2.

[20] Snouck Hurgronje, *Mekka in the Latter Part of the 19th Century* (Leiden, 1931), 268–72.

studied and taught in Mecca for 30 years. For the previous fifteen years he had largely withdrawn from teaching and devoted most of his time to writing. Snouck adds that he inspired increasing numbers of Malays, Javanese, and Sundanese to the thorough study of Islam. At the time Snouck met him (and spoke with him extensively), al-Nawawī had already published a large number of books, many of them in Cairo, between 1880 and 1886, including, in 1881, *Fatḥ al-mujīb*, a commentary on a work by one of his teachers, al-Nahrawī, entitled *al-Durr al-farīd*; in the same year he published a commentary on *Ajrumīya* (a grammatical work), on *Lubāb al-bayān* (style), and, in 1886, *Dharī'a al-yaqīn*, a commentary on a well-known work of al-Sanūsī (d. 892/1486).

Most important for our purposes, however, is Snouck's remark that al-Nawawī had just published a large commentary on the Qur'ān with the then newly established Mekkan Press.[21] If al-Nawawī sent it to the press around 1884 and had devoted himself to writing about fifteen years earlier, then we may think of his having begun it towards the end of the 1860s. It was subsequently reprinted by Ḥalabī in Cairo, a work in two volumes of around 500 pages each, with al-Wāḥidī's (d. 468/1076) *Kitāb al-wajīz fī tafsīr al-Qur'ān al-'azīz* on the margin.[22]

Al-Nawawī called his work *Marāḥ Labīd*. He gives the conventional reason for commencing the work, that some of his friends urged it upon him; he also gives an account of his hesitations—thinking of the saying of Muḥammad reproving those who interpret the Qur'ān according to personal opinion—thus he follows the example of the ancestors in writing to preserve knowledge, not to add to it. He points out that every age is in need of a renewal of knowledge, and concludes his exordium by saying: 'May undertaking this work be a help to me, and to those deficient such as me.' Concerning the authorities he has drawn on, he lists *al-Futūḥāt al-ilāhīya*, *Mafātīḥ al-ghayb*, *al-Sirāj al-munīr*, *Tanwīr al-miqbās*, and the *tafsīr* of Abū'l-Su'ūd.[23].

The *Mafātīḥ al-ghayb* of Fakhr al-Dīn al-Rāzī (d. 606/1209), and *Tanwīr al-miqbās* attributed to Ibn 'Abbās (d. 68/687) need no introduction here, although the use of al-Rāzī's work as a principal source by a Jāwī scholar is a fact of some significance. The *Futūḥāt*

[21] Hurgronje, *Mekka*, 271.
[22] al-Nawawī, *Marāḥ Labīd: Tafsīr al-Nawawī* (Cairo, n.d.).
[23] Ibid. 2.

al-ilāhīya is not so well known. It is a massive commentary on *Tafsīr al-Jalālayn* by Sulaymān ibn 'Umar al-'Ujaylī al-Azharī, known as al-Jamal, an Egyptian who died in 1205/1790.[24] *Al-Sirāj al-munīr* is likewise relatively unknown.[25] It was written by Muḥammad ibn Muḥammad al-Khāṭib al-Shirbīnī, also an Egyptian, who died in 977/1570. Al-Nawawī had, or was guided to, some special interest in this author, for he wrote a commentary on his work on the pilgrimage, *Manāsik al-ḥajj*.[26] Abū'l-Su'ūd was a Turkish scholar who lived from 898/1492 to 982/1574. The full title of his work is *Irshād al-'aql al-salīm ilā mazāya'l-Qur'ān al-karīm*.[27] All these works are available in print, although they are not always easy to find. Manuscripts of all of them, however, were available in Cairo and other Middle East centres. Obviously al-Nawawī had access to them.

There are various issues that need to be considered in analysing al-Nawawī's *tafsīr*: how did he use these sources, and precisely what did he look for in each? Does any one of them, rather than another, have a central role? Where he quotes a variety of sources other than those he cites by name, are they cited directly or only quoted second hand? All these points are of interest, for they have to do with the man's scholarship and the technical aspects of his work. Rather more important from a human point of view, however, is to uncover his principles of selection, to discover what his choice of material reveals of his personality and his personal

[24] The full title of the work is *al-Futūḥāt al-ilāhīya bi tawḍīḥ tafsīr al-Jalālayn li'l-daqā'iq al-khafīya*. It was first published by Būlāq in 1275/1858, and there is a 4-vol. edition, Cairo, 1318/1900. Brockelmann (*GAL*, ii. 353) gives a dozen or so references to al-Jamal and his work, describing him as a traditionalist and member of a group that developed the use of tradition to counter the use of personal opinion in religious matters. For further information he refers to al-Jabartī, who notes that he was distinguished for his piety and asceticism (he remained celibate), that he became a *khalīfa* of the Khalwatīya *ṭarīqa*, and that he taught *tafsīr*, *ḥadīth*, and *fiqh* at the famous Ashrafīya school founded by Sultān al-Malik al-Ashraf Barsbay in 1423.

[25] The full title of the work is *al-Sirāj al-munīr fī'l-i'āna 'alā ma'ārif ba'ḍ ma'ānī kalām rabbina'l-ḥakīm al-khabīr*. There are at least two printed editions, each in 4 vols.: al-Khayrīya, Cairo 1311/1893, and Būlāq, 1285/1868. Biographical information about him is not prolific. There are a few notes in Brockelmann (*GAL* ii. 320; S ii. 441) and a paragraph in al-Dhahabī's extensive treatment of his work in *al-Tafsīr wa'l-mufassirūn* (Cairo, 1976), i. 338–45.

[26] Hurgronje, *Mekka*, 271.

[27] His full name is Abū'l-Su'ūd Muḥammad ibn Muḥammad al-Amadī. His dates are 898/1492–951/1544. According to al-Dhahabī (*al-Tafsīr*, i. 345), he has a very high reputation. See also *GAL* ii. 438. His *tafsīr* was first published by Būlāq in 1275/1858 and is also available in a 5-vol. print, Cairo, 1347/1928.

concerns as a teacher, what kind of intellectual and spiritual conformation he wished to give to the students from West Java and elsewhere in the Indies who came to him for over forty years in the Ḥijāz, not to mention those Indonesian and Malaysian students of today for whom his work is still a basic text. In what direction did he envisage these students developing? All the time it must be kept in mind, however, that he avowedly did not wish to add anything to the deposit of knowledge, but only wished to give a new presentation of it.

It is not possible, at this stage, to make a thorough analysis of al-Nawawī's treatment of the Qur'ān as a whole in order to assess the scope and character of his *tafsīr*, and there is no guarantee that a random sample of the treatment of particular *sūra*s will produce results true for the Qur'ān as a whole. In preparing this essay it has been possible only to examine the treatment of few *sūra*s. A study of *sūrat al-ḍuḥā* (Q. 93) and *sūrat al-tīn* (Q. 95) suggests that al-Nawawī's working method may have been something like this. He used *Tafsīr al-Jalālayn* as his first resource to find synonyms for Quranic words. He read that work in conjunction with *al-Futūḥāt al-ilāhīya*. He used al-Shirbīnī's *al-Sirāj al-munīr* as an additional source for synonyms and explanations of words and phrases. It is also clear, however, that he placed considerable reliance on the *Mafātīḥ* of Fakhr al-Dīn al-Rāzī and made direct and copious use of this work.

The grounds for this view—still provisional—may be summarized as follows. As far as Q. 93 and 95 are concerned, al-Jamal, al-Shirbīnī, and Abū'l-Su'ūd present material that is to be found more richly developed and better structured in al-Rāzī; when they repeat this material they often use variant wording. Al-Nawawī, however, even though he too selects, summarizes, and simplifies, is likely to use the wording of al-Rāzī, and occasionally he uses phrases that occur in al-Rāzī but not in the later commentators that he consults.

The opening lines of his treatment of *sūra* 95 give some idea of al-Nawawī's style. He uses the definition of *tīn* (and *zaytūn*) found in *Tafsīr al-Jalālayn*, and then gives an account of the uses of these two fruits as food and medicine. The other three commentators do the same. Al-Jamal (commenting on a commentary) is prolix and repetitive, while al-Nawawī is condensed but lucid. He writes:

wa'l-tīn wa'l-zaytūn. They are both well-known fruits and God swears by them both because of their good qualities and uses. The fig is a wholesome fruit, it has no stone. It is a light meal, easily digested, and a medicine of many uses; it makes mild the disposition, it eases the throat (*bulʿum*), adds weight to the body, opens blockages of the liver and the spleen, and prevents haemorrhoids. The olive is a fruit, something to eat with bread, and a medicine.[28]

It might, at first, be thought that this rationalism was indicative of contact with Muḥammad ʿAbduh (1849–1905), since their careers, in part, overlapped. In fact, this rationalist emphasis is already established in al-Rāzī, who opens his discussion of the *sūra* by raising the question as to why God should swear by these two things. His answer is that if the words are used literally and not metaphorically, it is because of their numerous benefits to humanity.[29]

Al-Nawawī's presentation lacks the sweep of al-Rāzī's, and omits many of the points and arguments that the latter develops. It is, however, lucid and limpid. He has a clear, rather than a speculative or philosophical, mind. His work, in fact, reflects the personality that Snouck Hurgronje attributed to him. Yet he had his own mind. For example, there is a difference of opinion among the commentators as to the meaning of words occurring in Q. 38/33, *fa ṭafiqa masḥ*^{an} *bi'l-sūq wa'l-aʿnāq*, which describe Solomon's reaction after horses have been paraded before him. Al-Jamal, al-Shirbīnī, and Abū'l-Suʿūd give prominence to the view that Solomon sacrificed the horses because, on one interpretation, their beauty had distracted him from his prayers. Al-Rāzī, however, argues passionately that the words mean that he patted their necks and legs warmly and appreciatively.[30] Al-Nawawī accepts this interpretation, and remains silent on the other possibility, perhaps because he found the slaying of horses distasteful.[31]

At first sight it might seem that there is little of intrinsic interest in the work. But al-Nawawī was a teacher dedicated to the interests of his fellow countrymen; he understood their needs when they came to Mecca to study, and he wrote in a way that they would understand, and he prepared his book in such a way that, from it, they could gain the skills and confidence necessary to explore more complex works. His work, in fact, provides a foundation for the

28 Al-Nawawī, *Marāḥ* ii. 453.
29 Fakhr al-Dīn al-Rāzī, *al-Tafsīr al-Kabīr* (Teheran, n.d.), xxxii. 8.
30 Al-Rāzī, *Tafsīr*, xxvi. 203–4.
31 Al-Nawawī, *Marāḥ*, ii. 230.

study of his authorities, and develops the necessary skills to learn from any one of them, and others, at first hand.

But this was not the limit of al-Nawawī's goal, or his achievement, nor did he restrict his sources to the works mentioned by name or author in his introduction. On the *ḥāmish* of the Ḥalabī edition of *Marāḥ Labīd* is printed the *Kitāb al-wajīz* of al-Wāḥidī, which is frequently paraphrased or cited in al-Nawawī's own work. Perhaps it was placed in the margin at his request. Al-Wāḥidī's work is a terse and simple *tafsīr*, thus one well suited to the kind of audience for whom al-Nawawī was writing. Al-Wāḥidī, however, is better known for his work on *asbāb al-nuzūl* than for his *tafsīr*, and his interest in this field of learning is reflected in his *tafsīr* and was drawn upon by al-Nawawī. The contextualization provided by the *sabab* frequently serves to set particular pericopes into a human frame of reference and to enhance a human dimension of Muḥammad. Al-Nawawī also has an awareness that words, especially particles, have a meaning according to context. Thus he sees fit, in the context of the *asbāb* he adduces, to make clear, for example, whether an expression such as *kallā* simply means *ḥaqq*^{an}, whether it refers to something within the text itself, or whether it refers to an event—an objection, a challenge, or assertion—outside the text.[32]

Some of the printed editions of al-Nawawī's works ascribe to him the *nisba* al-Qādirī. Snouck Hurgronje, in his meeting with him, reported him as saying that he was not personally affiliated to a *ṭarīqa*, that he did not recommend to his students that they join a *ṭarīqa*, but that neither did he discourage them from doing so.[33] There is no evidence from the *tafsīr* that he was concerned with speculative theosophy of the Naqshbandī, derived from Ibn ʿArabī, and expressed in a system of grades of being. Nevertheless, it is clear that al-Nawawī was a spiritual man, and there are various places where he shows a level of spiritual awareness that may be described, in the tradition of al-Ghazzālī, as ethical mysticism. Thus while it is difficult to discover in this work anything denoting a characteristically Indonesian environment, it clearly reflects emphases that were regarded as normative for those students and pilgrims from the Indies who came to him. It represents an elaboration of the tradition of *Tafsīr al-Jalālayn* that

[32] Ibid. ii. 455.
[33] Hurgronje, *Mekka*, 271.

Abdul Kahar Muzakkir, as cited earlier, remarked as dominant in 1959.[34] It also served to expunge the Ibn 'Arabī tradition of exegesis from the Indonesian context; it was ideally suited to oral exposition in Malay, and it prepared the ground for the study of more advanced works.

The paradox is that although in many respects al-Nawawī's *tafsīr* is traditional, not to say old-fashioned—it takes for granted a Ptolemaic astronomy, for example—its approach is consistent with Reformist ideas, and it perhaps helped pave the way for them, characterized as it is by the three strands of rationalism, frequent reference to the life of Muḥammad—the best of creation—in the elucidation of the text of the Qur'ān, and the 'sober' mysticism or spirituality that infuses this and his other works.

All in all, al-Nawawī's work provides a convenient summary of a traditional understanding of the Qur'ān, and brings into focus something of late medieval Quranic exegesis, of which little is known; yet, at the same time, thanks to the rational elements it brings from the Rāzī tradition, it stands alongside the emergence of a new order, that of the Reformist tradition pioneered by Muḥammad 'Abduh and Jamāl al-Dīn al-Afghānī (1838–97).

III

The Jāwīs in Cairo participated eagerly in the Reformist movement, no doubt stirred by its political as well as its educational and religious dimensions, and it established itself early in the Malay world. In fact, letters written in Arabic from Java, Sumatra, Singapore, and Borneo began to appear in 'Abduh's journal *al-Manār* from the first year of issue, 1898. These letters dealt with various topics. One expressed the desire of Muslims in Java to acquire Ottoman citizenship and the reaction of the Dutch to this aspiration, which was to have Ottoman consulates withdraw from the colony (1898); another (1899) concerned Dutch aggression against the Acehnese, and the rights of the Acehnese to Ottoman citizenship (the Aceh war against the Dutch lasted from 1873 to 1910). Yet another concerned the pretensions of the Sayyids, and a letter from Singapore (1905) requested a legal opinion concerning

[34] Baisa, *al-Abroor*, 9.

the marriage in Singapore of a male Indian commoner with a *sharīfa*.[35]

The responses to the movement were wide-ranging. Students from both the British- and Dutch-ruled territories in South-east Asia who were studying in the Middle East were inspired by the new movement, and began to make their mark in their homelands on their return, laying emphasis on the Qur'ān and the *sunna* as the foundations for independent judgement, reforming instruction in religious schools from the *ḥalaqa* to the *ṣaff* method of instruction, and preparing graded textbooks on religious instruction. There was a move to simplify the exposition of the Qur'ān, including reducing the excess baggage of the *isrā'īlīyāt*, and the numbers of *qirā'āt*, which were, in any case, to become of less significance with the increasing acceptance of the Ḥafṣ recitation, culminating in the official Egyptian edition of the Qur'ān in 1929. In addition, there was a stress on *asbāb al-nuzūl*, *ḥadīth*, the personality of Muḥammad, and the Qur'ān itself, in the interpretation of the Qur'ān, and a renewed emphasis on Islam as a religion of reason along with an appeal to the uses of reason enunciated in the arguments of the Qur'ān which had been put forth to convince the Jews and pagan Meccans of the truth of Muḥammad's claims.

Despite all this activity, documentation of the development of *tafsīr* itself remains inadequate. Abdul Kahar Muzakkir, however, in the work referred to earlier, gives a useful summary of twentieth-century Egyptian exegetes whose works became known in the Dutch East Indies/Indonesia. First among them he puts Muḥammad 'Abduh, and lays stress on his exile by the British to Lebanon, where he wrote *Risālat al-tawḥīd*, and then on his stay in Paris where he published *al-'Urwa al-wuthqā*, thereby spreading political awareness throughout the world of Islam. He adds that Ṭanṭāwī Jawharī (d. 1940) had a considerable interest in Islam in Indonesia, and that 'Abd al-Azīz Jawis (d. 1928) had similar concerns, and was instrumental in opening the doors of Egyptian government schools to students from Indonesia (including himself); he also notes that he himself was a student for two years of al-Maraghī (d. 1945) at the *Dār al-'ulūm* during the period that the Maraghī *tafsīr* was being published.[36]

[35] J. Bluhm, 'A Preliminary Statement on the Dialogue Established between the Reform Magazine *al-Manar* and the Malayo-Indonesian World', *Indonesia Circle*, Nov. 1983, 35–42.

[36] Baisa, *al-Abroor*, 13–15.

These remarks, interesting though they are, are little more than points of departure for further research. Even if Abdul Kahar Muzakkir does not give much attention to the intellectual content or methodology of such works, he makes abundantly clear how strong the political current was that flowed through them. He does regret the scant attention given to the writing and collecting of books on religious matters in Indonesia, attributing the reason to the continuing strength of the oral tradition. He points out, however, that useful works may be gleaned from libraries and private collections in Malaysia, Thailand, and the Philipines, as well as in Mecca, Medina, and Cairo.[37]

A component in the development of *tafsīr* in Indonesia easily overlooked and difficult to quantify is the role played by members of Arab families resident in that country. By virtue of their Arab ancestry they were able in particular cases to exercise a leadership as by right, and to contribute to Islamic life by pioneering work in the founding of schools, by writing, and by lecturing in study-clubs and associations in Arabic with the aid of interpreters. Even at this point, *diglossia* still had a role to play.

An important representative of this group is Ahmad Soorkatie, who established himself as a teacher in Batavia in 1908. He was instrumental in the founding of schools, he pioneered the Reformist ideas of Muḥammad ʻAbduh, and, although a Sayyid himself, he wrote vigorously against the claims that the Sayyids made for themselves in the region. He lectured widely, speaking in Arabic, accompanied by an interpreter. Many of his lectures were recorded by his brother, and written up in a manuscript of several hundred pages, much of it biographical in character.[38] This manuscript includes a series of lectures on the Qur'ān in the manner of a commentary. His treatment of Q. 1, *al-fātiḥa*, in a lecture given on 25 July 1937 at the Jamʻiyya club in Batavia provides an example both of his exegetical techniques and of at least one aspect of Islamic intellectual life in Indonesia during the 1930s.

The Almighty says *bismi'llāh al-raḥmān al-raḥīm*. Allāh, in Arabic, is a proper name belonging to the Creator of the world and its Originator from

[37] Ibid. 16.

[38] Miss Bluhm (see n. 35), currently writing a Ph.D. thesis on contacts between the *Manār* group and Indonesia *'ulamā'*, uncovered this material in the course of fieldwork in Jakarta in 1983 when she met members of the Soorkatie family. She has made it available to me on a personal basis, for which I am most grateful.

non-being. It means the Divinity worshipped by right, i.e., one in authority who deserves submission to his command in everything without choice and without resentment by his creatures. The meaning of *bismi'llāh* here is 'at His command,' i.e., He recites to you the commands, the prohibitions, the exhortations, the wise sayings, the laws, the good tidings, the warnings in this book [the Qur'ān] at the command of Allāh, *al-raḥmān al-raḥīm*.

The meaning of *al-raḥmān* is 'great of mercy,' the one whose mercy and grace has no limit, the bestower of every great favour, and every one of His favours is great.

The meaning of *al-raḥīm* is the one who makes mercy continuous, i.e., the one who constantly bestows; the one whose mercy and righteousness has no interruption and no end.

In the expression *al-raḥmān al-raḥīm* there is proof that there was no call on Him for the revelation of His book on the tongue of this prophet, nor for these commands and prohibitions, nor for this favour upon this man other than mercy on the sons of Adam [mankind] who desire good for themselves and to ward off evil, because from every possible standpoint He has no need of the worlds.

As for those who make themselves the losers, who refuse the guidance of their Lord, and turn aside from His injunctions, this mercy is turned against them as a proof of His [justice], as He says, 'By it He leads astray many, and by it He guides many, but He leads astray by it only the wicked' (Q. 2/27) and 'Say: to those who believe, it is guidance and healing. But those who do not believe, in their ears is deafness, and to them it is blindness' (Q. 41/45).

After examining each word of Q. 1/1–2, Soorkatie then digresses in order to develop, on the basis of the text of the Qur'ān, certain key ideas of the reformers.

When Islam came, it addressed itself to reason, arousing it and alerting it to modes of proof for the existence of God and His attributes, condemning inflexibility and the blind imitation of fathers and forefathers in this regard. Thus God in His book directs His address constantly to those endowed with intelligence who understand, and the learned who are pure from the defilements of passion, as for example in His words, 'In this indeed are signs for a people who understand' (Q. 30/25), and His words, 'We have made clear signs for a people who understand' (Q. 6/99) and His words, 'None realize it except those with intelligence' (Q. 3/8) and His words, 'In this indeed is a *dhikrā* to one who has a heart, and gives to it a hearing and is observant' (Q. 50/37), and His words, 'God testifies that there is no god but He, and so do the angels and those with knowledge, and upholds justice—there is no god but He, the Mighty the Wise' (Q. 3/18). This is why it is said that Islam is the religion of the intelligent and the generous, not the religion of the stupid and avaricious, because the stupid cannot draw conclusions from the principle of reason and cannot follow the path of knowledge when God opens it; and the avaricious do not recognize what may be understood or known due to passion or sickness in the soul. These two [i.e. the foolish and the avaricious] do not deserve to be addressed on this matter.

Now, there is a group of people who yearn to understand these signs, but the [limits of] their understanding and their innate disposition prevents this. Yet these, if they believe by will and intention, if they abandon delusion and obstinacy and fear God in what He commands and prohibits, then God has promised that He will illumine their sight, and bring them to what will put their hearts at rest. He says, 'O you who believe, if you fear God, He will set you apart, free you from your evil deeds and forgive you. God is of great mercy' (Q. 8/30). He also says, 'Those who strive in Our path, We will guide them in our ways. God indeed is with the righteous' (Q. 29/69). 'And fear God. He will teach you—God knows all things' (Q. 2/282).

As for a second group, it is those who do not wish to reflect on the Book of God, or to consider the signs of creation, or to turn whole-heartedly to God by making use of their gifts to seek guidance from Him, or to persevere in good works and devotion and to strive in His path. These are the party of hell of whom God says, 'We have destined for hell many of the *jinn* and of mankind. They have hearts, and do not understand with them; they have eyes, and do not see with them, they have ears, and do not hear with them. These are like beasts—but more errant than they, these are the heedless' (Q. 7/179). He also says, 'The worst of creatures to God are the deaf and the dumb, those who do not use their minds. Had God known of any good in them, He would have made them to hear, yet had He made them to hear, they would have turned aside; even now they are turning away' (Q. 8/23–4), and He says, 'What is it in them that they are turning away from the warning as though they were frightened donkeys fleeing from a lion' (Q. 75/50–3).

There is yet another group that pretends to profess Islam, and they claim that they are the cream of the believers. Indeed, they claim to love God and his messenger more than others. They serve God in ways for which God has not revealed any authority, and they worship through innovations and superstitions they have made up. They are guilty of polytheism, either knowingly or unknowingly by following teachers of evil who make licit for them what God has forbidden, and forbid them what God has declared permitted. They think that they are correct, but they have no share in Islam. They make gods of their whims. They use in their worship of God the beating of drums, singing to the sound of pipes, dancing in the mosques and clapping their hands like the polytheists of whom God says, 'Their prayer at the house is nothing but whistling and clapping of hands' (Q. 8/35).

This is sufficient to indicate the character of the lecture and the spirit behind Soorkatie's explanation of the Qur'ān. Although the manner of presentation inevitably has the character of a sermon, the basic principles are clear. There is a sweep and even a passion in the organization of the material that is reminiscent of 'Abduh: the insistence that God revealed the Qur'ān as an act of will, not simply because it was His nature to do so, reflects the rationalist emphasis of the Reformist tradition, which is made even more explicit by Soorkatie's appeal to the role of reason—the Qur'ān provided the intellectual tools for people to discover God by the use of reason. Every point of the argument is supported by Quranic quotation only. But this is not really interpreting the Qur'ān by the Qur'ān. Rather, he is using the Qur'ān to support ideas and teachings that are close to his heart as a Reformist, and he uses his further quotations to support the ideas he elicits from his base text.

Legitimate questions to raise concern the degree to which this kind of exegesis was understood by the audience. How much of the sense did the interpreter manage to convey? How much rhetorical force was used in the presentation? How many people were in attendance at the lecture for ritual purposes rather than as an educational act?

The questions cannot be answered with precision. In any case, at this level, it is not so much the understanding by individuals of each point of the argument that is crucial, but rather their participation in the atmosphere in which, as it were, ideas of this kind were swimming. This apart, it has already been stressed that the use of two languages is part of a time-honoured tradition. Arabic was the language which conferred authority on religious teaching; only when this authority had been established was the teaching passed on to those who did not know Arabic by an interpreter who explained and glossed what had been presented. During this period, it may be remarked, it was still a matter of debate as to whether the Friday sermon in the mosque should be delivered in Arabic or in a local vernacular.

IV

In 1928, the incipient nationalist movement in Indonesia formulated the ideal of a national language. At a Youth Congress held in

Batavia in October of that year, a resolution was passed pledging allegiance to one country and one language. The language was Malay, which under the new name and with the new *persona* of Bahasa Indonesia was to be the language of national unity in a region of more than 300 languages and ethnic groups. There was no dramatic, instantaneous response to this pledge, but a new course had been set towards the creation of a modern, independent state, and towards the development of Malay as a language of the modern world. This was a move away from the diversity and primacy of regional cultures and was a move towards the creation of a momentum of movement from an oral towards a written tradition for the language. As efforts were made to develop Bahasa Indonesia into a stable vehicle of a modern secular literary culture, so too there were efforts to enrich it as a language of the religious tradition, for which, in fact, the soil had been well laid.

From the late 1920s on, a number of *tarjama* of individual *juz'* of the Qur'ān and even of the whole scripture began to appear.[39] This process accelerated after the achievement of independence in 1945. Today, an Indonesian rendering of the Qur'ān published by the Ministry of Religion has considerable authority.[40] There is, in addition, a so-styled literary version by a noted literary critic not trained in Arabic, which is very popular.[41] *Tafsīr* works in the proper sense of the word, however, are still few. There is a ten-volume work issued under the auspices of the Ministry of Religion,[42] and also one by a noted *'ālim*, Hamka, with the symbolically chosen title, *Tafsīr al-Azhar*.[43] Commentaries on popular *sūra*s, and in particular of the *juz' 'amma*,[44] are numerous. Although these texts are generally lucid, the techniques by which the language expresses the nuances of Arabic, the technical terms of its grammar, and its philosophical ideas, are not yet fully developed and socialized. Indonesia does not yet have the resources of a language such as Persian, for example, which can bring a dimension of its own to the understanding of the text.

[39] A pioneering work was that of Mahmud Junus, *Tafsir Qurān Karim* (Jakarta, commenced in 1922 and first published as a whole in 1938).

[40] *Al-Quraan dan Terjemahnya* (Jakarta, 1980).

[41] H. B. Jassin, *al-Quranu'l-Karim—Bacaan Mulia* (2nd edn., Jakarta, 1982).

[42] *Al-Quran dan Tafsirnya* (Jakarta, 1975).

[43] Hamka, *Tafsīr al-Azhar* (Jakarta, 1982).

[44] In addition to the two works to be discussed, books by T. M. Hasbī Ash-Shiddieqy (Jakarta, 1964) and Adnan Lubis (Islamyah Medan, 1949) may also be noted.

These modern works differ in quality and perceptiveness, and usually follow the order of the format text (*muṣḥaf*) providing a literal translation, the meaning of individual words and sentences, and a commentary.

A popular work is *al-Abroor* by Mustafa Baisa, published in 1959. The following is a literal rendering of his interpretation of Q. 1.

1. In the name of Allāh, the generous, the compassionate.
2. All devotion and praise are directed to the God of all the worlds.
3. The loving and compassionate.
4. The sovereign power on the day of requittal.
5. It is only to You that we give homage, and to You that we ask for help.
6. Show us the straight path.
7. The path of those to whom You give blessings, not the path of those smitten by Your anger, and not that of those who are astray.

The explanatory notes that the author adds include the following points:

1. A *ḥadīth* saying that no prayer is valid without the recitation of *al-fātiḥa*;
2. A definition of *al-ḥamd*. Praise for a good act; the crown of gratitude for all the goodness of God; a word which may not be used or directed except in respect of or to God;
3. Definition of *rabb*—the nurturer, the guide, the creator, the teacher and the perfector of everything in creation; a word that can be used generally—*rabb al-ibil*, *rabb al-bayt*;
4. Definition of *'ālamīn*—a plural, the singular is *'ālam*, it means, here, all the worlds; it is used for the world of man, the world of animals, the world of plants, but is not used for the world of stones and the like.[45]

To these observations are added a number of devotional and ethical aspects. A few of these may be mentioned. In discussing verse 4, 'The sovereign power on the day of requittal', as the author renders it, he says: 'He [God] alone can change those who are arrogant and who will not hear the cry of the poor. His punishment for those who will not change is not in the world to come alone. The proofs of this are many; consider the imperialist races that have been expelled by the peoples of Asia.'

Concerning verse 5, 'It is only to You that we give homage', he notes that God is closer than our pulse, so whoever asks blessing,

[45] Baisa, *al-Abroor*, 20.

guidance, or requests (the conception of) a child, a job, a cure, and the like from holy (righteous) men, graves, or statues, is disobeying God's command.[46]

In the comments on verse 4 we can see an aspect of the political dimension to *tafsīr* by the reference to the achievement of Indonesian independence, and perhaps as well a covert reference to near-contemporary events in Indonesia: the poor showing of the Muslim parties in the 1955 general elections, the centralization of authority in the hands of Soekarno, and the increasing power of the Communist party. In the comments on verse 5, there is one of the leitmotifs of the reformists, also evident in Soorkatie's lecture, that is, the continuing campaign against *ṭarīqa* and traditional cult practices.

Interestingly, there is an irenic touch in the explanation of *maghdūb 'alayhim* and *ḍāllīn* occurring in verse 7. Baisa makes no explicit reference to Jews or Christians, to whom the words are widely held to apply. The treatment ends with a traditional expression of devotion by citing a tradition from Abū Hurayra which states, 'When the *imām* recites *ghayr al-maghdūb 'alayhim*, begin to recite *āmīn*, for whoever recites *āmīn* together with the *imām*, will have their past sins forgiven.'[47]

With the treatment of *sūrat al-fātiḥa*, the author is barely getting into his stride. His treatment of the *juz' 'amma* is rich and diverse. A few points give some further idea as to his personality and emphases. One example is the treatment of Q. 113/4, referring to the evil of women who blow upon knots. Baisa stresses that reports suggesting that Muḥammad was ever influenced other than physically by black magic were spread by polytheists. Thus he acknowledges, and affirms that the Qur'ān recognizes, the existence of black magic, and he interprets the verse as referring to the way in which black magic can separate friends or husband and wife.[48]

Another example is his manner of presenting scientific information. For example, *sūrat al-shams* (Q. 91) is introduced with a scientific statement about the sun being a mixture of gases with temperatures between 3,000 and 3,200 degrees, and the relative distances and length of orbit of the various planets, with illustrations of what life forms on Venus and Pluto might be like.[49] When he

[46] Ibid. 21. [47] Ibid. 23.
[48] Ibid. 29–31; cf. the treatment of Muḥammad 'Abduh, *Tafsīr al-Qur'ān al-karīm, juz' 'amma* (Cairo, 1341), 181–2. [49] Ibid. 110.

comes to the phrase, much beloved by mystics, *al-nafs al-muṭma'inna* in Q. 89/27, he uses it as an occasion to set out a diagram of basic instincts, aspects, inclinations, and emotions based on a popular psychology textbook in which to locate or contextualize the emotion named by the Qur'ān.[50] This is not *tafsīr 'ilmī*, but an attempt to place phenomena named by the Qur'ān in a scientific framework in order to highlight the authority with which it speaks. He makes no reference to the mystical understanding of the phrase.

Another volume devoted to the *juz' 'amma* was published in Malaysia in 1975.[51] It too includes a treatment of Q. 1. In methodology it is more traditionally scholastic than the preceding example, and it does not include any parenthetic scientific knowledge. The author adopts a verse by verse approach, explaining each one, then setting out the lessons to be learnt from it.

He understands Q. 1, *al-fātiḥa*, as follows:

1. All praise belongs to Allāh, the God of all creatures.
2. The Generous, the Loving.
3. Who possesses the day of requittal.
4. It is You we serve, and You of whom we ask aid.
5. Lead us along the straight path,
6. the path of those on whom You bestow Your favour.
7. with whom You are not angry, and who do not go astray.[52]

A few individual points may be noted. He does not regard the *bismillāh* as part of *al-fātiḥa*; he arrives at seven verses for the *sūra* by breaking into two the more usually accepted single verse 7, treating the first part as verse 6, and the portion beginning *ghayr al-maghḍūb* as verse 7. In doing so, he has chosen an alternative reading of the syntax, resulting in the sense, 'the path of those on whom You bestow Your favour, with whom You are not angry, and who do not go astray', recognized as canonical, but less usual.[53]

The explanations that he offers as to the meanings of the formulaic *basmala* may serve to illustrate his style.

[50] Ibid. 122; also J. M. S. Baljon, *Modern Muslim Koran Interpretation* (Leiden, 1968), 5.

[51] A. Hassan, *al-Hidayah Tafsiir Juz 'Amma* (Penerbit Kelantan, 1975).

[52] Ibid. 7–16.

[53] Ibid. 16.

1. I recite this *sūra* at the command of Allāh [A sense of *bismillāh* given by Soorkatie];
2. I recite this *sūra* with the help of Allāh;
3. This *sūra* is revealed at the command of Allāh;
4. This *sūra* is revealed by the Mercy of Allāh;
5. You are to begin the recitation of this *sūra* by mentioning the name of Allāh.

He adds that there are other meanings depending on the context.[54] The author then outlines the lesson to be derived from the use of the formula, the richness of its meaning, and the merit recitation of it brings.

For *al-ḥamdu li-llāh*, he gives four possible meanings in Malay:

1. The praise of Allāh to Himself;
2. The praise of Allāh for His creatures;
3. The praise of the creature for Allāh;
4. The praise of the creature for the creature.

He derives from these meanings the conclusion that all praise belongs to, derives from, and returns to God.[55]

The phrase *iyyāka naʿbudu*, 'It is you we worship' (verse 4 in his reading) he explains as follows. To worship something means to obey any order it gives or to perform devotions to it. Obedience may be given to two things: to God and to creatures. The orders of God are to be obeyed in all circumstances; the orders of humanity are laws which God commands or approves that we obey in worldly matters; they are not issued in the name of religion, but they are not opposed to the law of God. *Ḥarām* and *ḥalāl*, however, depend entirely on the book of God.

He then explains the meaning of God's exclusive claim to worship. Worship of other than God is of two kinds. One is that which is outward, such as the worship of Jesus, Mary, idols, fire, and the like. The other is that which is inward. This, he continues, may be of three kinds:

1. the performance of religious duties out of a desire for praise.
2. the abandonment of religious duties out of fear.
3. the acceptance solely on the word of a teacher of what is *ḥalāl* and what is *ḥarām*.[56]

It may be noted that this *tafsīr* is more given to polemic than the

[54] Ibid. 5–6. [55] Ibid. 7. [56] Ibid. 11.

former. It differs from the former also in its treatment of Q. 113/4, where it may be noted that the information supplied in the circumstance of revelation, the knotted cord placed in the well by the evil women, is not even mentioned.[57]

Both of the preceeding texts, despite their differences in nuance, reflect the Reformist tradition. In these works there is no listing of *qirā'āt*, and no reference to authorities other than the Qur'ān and tradition as far as the text is concerned.

Other types of *tafsīr*, however, are known in Indonesia. Maurice Bucaille's book, *The Bible, the Qur'ān and Science*, has been translated into Indonesian, and has a fair degree of popularity. In its wake, a few works have appeared propagating the ideas of *tafsīr 'ilmī*. There is also a range of selections from foreign *tafsīrs* by authors such as Sayyid Quṭb (1906–66) and Mawdūdī (1903–79). These may be regarded as mainstream contributions.

Outside this mainstream tradition, however, in the Javanese *primbon* literature, there are adaptations and uses of Javanese theosophical ideas to elaborate and multiply worlds of meaning to be discovered in the Qur'ān. These theosophical ideas are eclectic and include some notions that may ultimately derive from old Javanese and Indian traditions. Numerology is sometimes used with breath-taking ingenuity.

The Islamic periodical *Kiblat* recently published an article inspired by such notions, designed as a technical self-help for readers to discover the oceans of meaning concealed in Q. 1, *sūrat al-fātiḥa*.[58] The author takes as an example the phrase *bismillāh al-raḥmān al-raḥīm*. He points out that it contains 19 letters. The number 19 is 1 and 9. God is 1, there are 9 levels to the macrocosmos—above the 7 heavens is *al-kursī*, and then *al-'arsh*. There is 1 sun and 9 planets; a human child is carried in the womb 9 months and 9 days; Muḥammad lived 63 years (6 + 3 = 9). The total number of letters in the Qur'ān is 36 octilion (27 zeros), which may be arithmetically expressed 3 + 6 = 9 and 2 + 7 = 9. He sees the letters of the Qur'ān serving to outline the human body, with the 33 vertebrae of the backbone. As an illustration he takes Q. 36/82, *innamā amruhu* . . ., and discovers in it 32 letters which correspond to the 33 nodes of the backbone less one, *al-ṣulbī*, the

[57] Ibid. 27–8.

[58] Mpu Wesi Geni, 'Samudera al Fatikhah', *Kiblat*, 30, no. 23 (20 Apr.–5 May 1983), 40–1.

first to be created, and from which the body will be re-created at the resurrection.

He then turns to *sūrat al-fātiḥa* itself. It has, he says, 7 verses; therefore, it is a sign of the secret knowledge of the 7 heavens and the 7 levels of the earth. The outer world then is complete, made up to the number 9 by *al-kursī* and *al-'arsh*. Since the *basmala* is the first verse of *sūrat al-fātiḥa*, reciting it at the commencement of any other part of the Qur'ān means that one is reciting *sūrat al-fātiḥa* in miniature.

He then observes that if the first verse, *bismi'llāh al-raḥmān al-raḥīm*, is removed from the *sūrat al-fātiḥa*, the remaining verses comprise 111 letters. In the first verse there are 3 *alifs*, which, since the numerical value of *alif* is 1, designate the number 111. Then he draws attention to the fact that the most frequently occurring letters in *sūrat al-fātiḥa* are *yā'*, occurring 14 times, *mīm*, 15 times, *nūn*, 11 times, and *alif*, 19 times. Rearranged, these read *āmīn*.

In addition, each of these letters signifies a particular cosmological level:

Alif	God's creative word *kun*
Mīm	Dāwud
Yā'	Muḥammad
Nūn	Sulaymān

Thus, he continues, *amīn* signifies Muḥammad, the messenger of God who brings religion springing from the inspiration of Allāh, and occupying the golden mean between harshness of David, the king wielding authority over the earth, and the secret knowledge of Solomon. Further, each signifies a different part or organ of the body, all of which are thereby called upon to pray to God:

Alif	the brain
Mīm	the kidney
Yā'	the heart
Nūn	the gallbladder

V

This paper has attempted to outline with a broad brush some manifestations of *tafsīr* as it is to be found in the area that is now Indonesia. The survey began with the time when a tradition of

Islamic learning was established, when the use of the Arabic script was the norm for writing Malay, and Arabic loan words were already an important stratum in the language. It then demonstrated the existence of a tradition of *diglossia*: Arabic for the learned, Malay for largely oral popularizations.

It then set out suggested reference-points in the unfolding of the history of *tafsīr*, including the rendering of *Tafsīr al-Jalālayn* in Malay, the translation of the *Sayr al-sālikīn* into Malay, and then the Arabic commentary *Marāḥ Labīd*. It then referred to the new stream of ideas brought into Islam in the region by the Reformist movement, generating renewed activity in preparing a *tarjama* of the Qur'ān, and the preparation of more scholarly works in Malay, *pari passu* with the emergence of a higher educated public concerned with a better understanding of things Islamic. It was then noted that in this more vital understanding of Islam, there was a strong political thread. It attempted to lift a corner on the wonderworld or fantasy land of traditional Javanese thinking about the Qur'ān. Javanese Muslim writing, it was pointed out, is represented by a vast corpus of manuscripts still to be explored, whether *qiṣaṣ* material (the number of manuscripts on the Yūsuf story alone is very great) or theosophy.

It is not wise at this stage to attempt to draw conclusions from the material surveyed. It is possible, however, to isolate themes that have been highlighted and which merit further exploration.

One theme is the variety of traditions that characterize the development of Islam in the area now known as Indonesia from very early times; another is the intellectual modesty and dedication, and alongside it the measure of political commitment, that characterize so many of the local scholars of Islam; yet another is the illustration of the modalities by which the centre and periphery of the Islamic world are held in close embrace. Although attention has frequently been drawn to the role of the Ḥijāz in the religious training of the Jāwī, very much under-investigated is the role of Egypt in the education of students from South-east Asia.

There are two other points. One is the transition from a largely oral, non-literate tradition in Malay to a literary one. The transition is not yet complete, nor is it progressing evenly. Indonesian is still young as a language of intellectual discourse, and, as it grows in range and capacity, and as its roots extend deeper into the soil of history, its role as a language of religious learning will expand. The phenomenon of *diglossia* in religious matters then may well be modified.

Finally, and perhaps from the standpoint of Islamology as a discipline most interestingly of all, attention is inevitably drawn to the late medieval tradition of Quranic exegesis. Although neglected by European scholars as the product of a period of decadence, it is of continuing importance in the Muslim world.[59]

[59] The greater part of the research for this paper and the first draft of it were prepared during my tenure of a fellowship at the institute of Advanced Studies, Hebrew University in Jerusalem, in 1985. I am most appreciative of the facilities and resources made available to me during this period.

13

Qur'ān Recitation Training in Indonesia: A Survey of Contexts and Handbooks

FREDERICK M. DENNY

1. GENERAL OVERVIEW

Islam was spread in the Malay-Indonesian archipelago by Arab, Persian, and Indian traders and merchants.[1] The missionary work was gradual and non-aggressive. Ṣūfī sensibilities and personal styles deeply informed the ways in which Java, especially, became Islamized. On that most populous island of the archipelago, many elements of the Javanese and the Hindu-Buddhist past were woven into the preaching of Islam.[2] The recitation of the Qur'ān has for long been a fundamental part of the piety of Indonesian Muslims, and at least in Central Java, early cultivation possibly included use of Javanese stories and melodies, with the former expressed in shadow-puppet plays, known as *wayang kulit*.[3]

[1] A brief introduction is the article, 'Indonesia', *EI*[2] iii. 1218–21. The history of the Islamization of the Malay-Indonesian archipelago is enormously complex and elusive. Three good recent assessments of the state of scholarship are: A. H. Johns, 'Islam in Southeast Asia: Reflections and New Directions', *Indonesia*, 19 (Apr. 1975), 33–55; M. C. Ricklefs, 'Six Centuries of Islamization in Java', in Nehemia Levtzion, ed., *Conversion to Islam* (New York, 1979), 100–28; and M. B. Hooker, 'The Translation of Islam into South-East Asia', in M. B. Hooker, ed., *Islam in South-East Asia* (Leiden, 1983), 1–22. An older survey, which must be used with care, but which is useful and readable, is T. W. Arnold, *The Preaching of Islam* (London, 1896), ch. 12, 'The Spread of Islam in the Malay Archipelago'.

[2] Sunan Kalijaga, one of the legendary *wali songo*, 'nine Saints', who brought Islam to Java, is said to have used traditional *wayang* theatre in his preaching. The earliest Javanese mosques of which we know resembled Hindu-Buddhist religious structures and had a multi-tiered roof, reflecting the symbolism of the Buddhist world mountain, Meru.

[3] There is a Quranic school (*pondok pesantren*) in the hills near Magetan, East Java, whose *kiai* teaches Quranic recitation using Javanese translation and traditional Javanese melodies, in addition to the standard recitation in Arabic according to the rules of *tajwīd*. This *kiai* believes that the singing of the translated Qur'ān was the manner by which the Qur'ān was introduced in his part of Java. I have recorded examples of the recitation of one of the *kiai*'s students and can testify that the sound is very beautiful and could be imagined to have engaged the attention of listeners attuned to indigenous Javanese songs when Islam was first appearing on the island.

By the nineteenth century at least, more scripturalist forms of Islam gained ground, and increased numbers of Muslims, known as *santris*, were exhibiting a Muslim piety that would have been considered orthodox across the Muslim world. *Santris*[4] are strict Sunni Muslims who strive to learn Arabic, to observe all the canonical observances (*'ibādāt*), to go on *ḥajj*, and especially to dissociate themselves from practices of pre-Islamic times in Indonesia, such as attending *wayang* performances (which feature Hindu epics), listening to traditional gamelan music, and participating in magical rituals connected with local demons and deities.

Among *santri* Muslims the proper recitation of the Qur'ān has been a central means of purifying the faith and transmitting it intact from generation to generation. In the last century, and even more in the current one, many Quranic schools were established in Indonesia, particularly in Java. As in the classical Middle-Eastern *kuttāb*, instruction centres on learning to read and write Arabic, with the Qur'ān text serving as a source of exercises. *Kiais*,[5] religious teachers (cf. *shaykh*) of more or less formal Islamic learning but recognized piety and forcefulness, have been the nucleus of such schools, known as *pesantrens* (from *santri*). Such *pesantrens* have been associated with mosques and neighbourhoods where they have functioned like day schools. In recent decades, as universal public education has spread in Indonesia, such schools have been convened in the hours after the end of the public school day, like Hebrew schools in Jewish neighbourhoods in the West. But the most influential type of Qur'ān school is a boarding school called a *pondok pesantren*,[6] the word *pondok* being from the

[4] The tripartite division of Javanese society into *santri* (orthoprax Sunni), *abangan* (village culture, made up of traditional animistic and Islamic beliefs), and *priyayi* (bureaucratic class, redolent of earlier ruling-class ideals and Hinduistic views) was presented in an influential manner by Clifford Geertz in *The Religion of Java* (New York, 1960). Since the appearance of this book, this neat division has come under increasing criticism, but the general denomination *santri* still figured as a prominent aspect of Muslims' self-perception in my conversations with Javanese Muslims. Ricklefs has provided a useful discussion of the Geertzian classification and its critics in 'Six Centuries of Islamization in Java', 118–27.

[5] See Clifford Geertz, 'The Javanese Kijaji: The Changing Role of a Cultural Broker', *Comparative Studies in Society and History*, ii (1960), 228–49.

[6] Geertz provides a vivid description of *pesantren* life in ibid. 231–9. A more recent and much more detailed study is Karel Adriaan Steenbrink, *Pesantren, Madrasah, Sekolah: Recente Ontwikkelingen in Indonesisch Islamonderricht*, Proefschrift, University of Nijmegen (Krips Repro Meppel [Holland], 1974), in Dutch, with English summary on pp. 356–62.

Arabic *funduq*, meaning hostelry or hotel. Certain *pondok*s have become famous, drawing students from all over Java and Sumatra and beyond. There are *pondok pesantren*s for both sexes.

The most famous twentieth-century *pondok* is the Pondok Modern at Gontor, a few miles south of Madiun in East Java. Founded in the 1920s, and run by one *kiai* and his family until recently, Gontor is innovative in that it has a modern curriculum and many extracurricular activities for the nearly 2,000 boys and young men who are enrolled (aged 8 to mid-20s). Arabic is the language of instruction for Qur'ān and religion courses, English for English courses, and Bahasa Indonesia for all others. In social life on campus, only Arabic and English are permitted. Violations are punished in various ways, but the worst punishment seems to be having the hair cut short. Gontor emphasizes the interpretation of the Qur'ān more than its ritual recitation, and so graduates generally do not emphasize training in readings and recitation when they become teachers. Exceptions are Gontor graduates who attended a traditional *pesantren* in their early years, where they may have memorized the Qur'ān or a large part of it, but such boys rarely get to go to Gontor, because their *kiai*s discourage such a modern education or because the boys are simply not well-enough prepared, knowing only the Qur'ān and religious subjects. Graduates of Gontor have risen to high positions in the government and in educational institutions all over Indonesia and beyond. Many go on to advanced studies in Mecca, Medina, Cairo, and other Middle-Eastern locales.

The vast majority of *pondok pesantren*s, however, are traditionalist. Most are tucked away in villages. East Java has the largest number of *pondok*s, from the ultra-modern Gontor to the very traditionalist large one in Situbondo, on the highway halfway between Surabaya and Bali. One *pondok* on East Java's north coast is for small children aged 5 to 7. There, hundreds of students are taught elementary Arabic and recitation, emphasizing memorization. A large proportion of the children are from families of religious scholars and teachers. It is thought by many of the parents that an early start living away from home in a regimented Islamic environment will develop strong piety and a sense of social co-operation. It is also thought that this early preparation will enable the children to enter a top *pondok* at age 8 or so. The north Javan institute is a kind of pre-*pondok*. There is great difference of opinion among Indonesian educators about the effects of such an early boarding school experience. Many modern Muslim educators disapprove of it, because it takes the children away from their parents and family too early. Supporters remind me of Hannah, Samuel's mother, who dedicated her little boy to the sanctuary at Shiloh at a tender age.[7]

Another *pondok*[8] is in Singosari, East Java, near Malang, about 50 miles south of Surabaya. It is exclusively for Quranic studies, but goes beyond recitation into advanced Arabic grammar and rhetoric, exegesis, and readings and recitation, highly demanding technical fields which are found mostly in Middle-Eastern Islamic countries where Arabic is spoken as the native language. The Singosari institute was founded and is run by a native Javanese man trained in Cairo. He is one of the leading experts on recitation in South-east Asia and a frequent judge at regional, national, and international competitions in recitation. The boys, about 200, attend the public school in the town for secular subjects, but live at the *pondok*, where they share in its maintenance and governance, the older boys exerting leadership and setting good examples. The students even cook their own meals. This self-governance idea is central to *pondok* education and instils in the students both a strong sense of Islamic life and traditional Javanese values of co-operation and consensus-seeking.[9]

In recent years there have been a large number of textbooks produced concerning recitation of the Qur'ān. The *kiai* at Gontor published one quite a few years ago.[10] Then other *kiai*s began writing their own versions and publishing them, at least locally. There would seem to be a certain sense of prestige connected with publishing one's own handbook. Although the fieldwork for this research was focused on East Java, I was able to purchase recitation books there that were published in Bandung (West Java), Jakarta

[7] 1 Sam. 1: 11–28.

[8] The name of this *pondok* is *Ma'had al-Dirāsa al-Qur'ānīya*, and its *kiai* is H. M. Basori Alwi.

[9] It is noteworthy that the *kiai* and the older boys convene a Qur'ān recitation class for townspeople—both men and women—each week. When I visited the *pondok* during one of these sessions, at least 500 adults had gathered for instruction, which was conducted in a rote manner with all reciting together after the leader, whose quality of *tajwīd* and beauty of voice were as excellent as I had ever heard anywhere.

[10] I. Zarkasyi, *Pelajaran Tajwid* (Gontor Ponorogo, East Java, 1955; 22nd printing, 1983).

(also West Java) and Semarang (Central Java); two or three examples published in North Sumatra (Medan) were also obtained. The majority of the books surveyed, however, are from Surabaya, East Java, and environs. The most scholarly and well-produced handbooks come from Jakarta and Bandung, both of which are more sophisticated cities than Surabaya (which is a large industrial port and the main Indonesian naval base).

The handbooks which have been consulted are all practical. Some are more traditional in method than others, but all have resulted from actual teaching experience based on models that can be traced back to the first three centuries of Islam, when the principles and practices of recitation were developed and perfected. Most of the handbooks are rather brief, 40 to 60 pages. Several are simply reprints of old method books which are also to be found in Cairo and other Middle-Eastern cities. These are printed in Arabic script,[11] with Arabic text and, sometimes, also an interlinear Javanese or Indonesian translation, either in the Roman alphabet or, in the older ones, Jāwī script, based on Arabic. There are a fair number of more modern handbooks, written in Indonesian in the Roman alphabet, with extensive quotation of the Qur'ān, *ḥadīth*, and other classical texts in Arabic script, with translations. Several of these will be described in the second section of this essay. Such books follow traditional procedures in explaining the phonetics of Qur'ān recitation, known by the technical term *'ilm al-tajwīd*. These more thorough treatments sometimes have bibliographies, but it has not been possible to locate a truly comprehensive scholarly bibliography of recitation and readings produced in Indonesia.[12] There is one quite modern attempt at introducing

[11] e.g., *Matn al-Jazarīya [fī fann al-tajwīd]*, a classic handbook in brief compass, comprising the Arabic text of Ibn al-Jazarī's (d. 843/1429) rhymed prose work together with an Arabic commentary (Surabaya, n.d.) in 55 pp. Another widely used handbook is *Hidāyat al-mustafīd fī aḥkām al-tajwīd*, by the Syrian recitation teacher of the late 19th century known as Abū Rīma. This handbook is in question-and-answer form, and numbers, in the Indonesian edition I found, 32 pp. (Surabaya, 1969). Still another Arabic handbook is *Tuḥfat al-aṭfāl* (Semarang, 1381/1962), a popular, brief manual by the Egyptian, Sulaymān al-Jamzūrī (b. *c.* 1160s/1750s).

[12] I cannot say that I have found one in Egypt, either. See the discussion of bibliographies below. For an accurately selected bibliography, which lacks several available works, but is nevertheless the best I have seen in print otherwise, see Kristina Nelson, *The Art of Reciting the Qur'an* (Austin, 1985), 225–34. Nelson's work is an epoch-making study, making available for the first time the whole range of Quranic recitation material in a Western language, with special emphasis on performance.

Qur'ān recitation training using recent methods of teaching language and reading, based on UNESCO publications of William S. Gray (*The Teaching of Reading and Writing: An International Survey* (Chicago, 1956)) and Frank C. Laubach (*Teaching the World to Read: A Handbook for Literacy Campaigns* (New York, 1947), and with Robert F. Laubach, *Towards World Literacy: The 'Each One–Teach One' Way* (Syracuse, 1960)).[13]

The last point highlights the importance of basic Arabic instruction for Indonesians, whose native language is far removed from Semitic languages, although there are very many words of Arabic origin, due to Islamization. That is, the students must learn the Arabic alphabet and phonetics at the same time that they are learning the recitation of the Qur'ān text. Teachers often confessed to me that most students learn only the sounds of Arabic, and few comprehend what they recite. This is the main reason why Gontor emphasizes exegesis rather than recitation. But many Muslims believe that God's grace falls on anyone who recites the Qur'ān excellently, with or without understanding.[14]

The best handbooks which it has been possible to examine include explications of traditional *tajwīd* practices within a larger framework of the philosophy of Qur'ān recitation in the religious life of individuals and the community. Such books feature chapters on ritual acts (for example, prostration, 'seeking refuge', saying the *takbīr*) associated with recitation, and the etiquette (Arabic, *ādāb*) of reciting and listening to reciting. Al-Nawawī, the thirteenth-century Syrian *ḥadīth* scholar and Shafi'ite legist, is frequently the

[13] M. T. Fatahuddin, *Belajar Membaca dan Menulis Al Qur-an* ('Learn to Read and Write the Qur'ān') 5 vols. (Jakarta, 1982). The pamphlet-length volumes (*c.* 60 pp. each) appear to have been prepared by a team for a curriculum project sponsored by the Department of Religion, Republic of Indonesia. The work does not engage in *tajwīd* training, but limits itself to Arabic language training as a preliminary.

[14] S. Soebardi and C. P. Woodcroft-Lee have related the experience of the modern Indonesian writer, Muhammad Rajab, who, in his biography, *Semasa Kecil di Kampung* ('A Village Childhood'), recalled 'how when he was twelve, he was sent to study the *Qur'an* along with other boys of his village [in the Minangkabau region of west central Sumatra]. Rajab recalls that he actually recited the *Qur'an* seven times without any idea that, if it were translated into his own native tongue, it might become something meaningful for his own life. Although he was told it was the word of God, "God never said anything which I was able to understand". On the other hand, the students were extremely careful with their pronunciation of the Arabic text, and strove to recite it as well as they could for the teacher had made it clear that he who mispronounced an Arabic letter had slight chance of entering heaven.' See 'Islam in Indonesia', in Raphael Israeli, ed., *The Crescent in the East: Islam in Asia Major* (London and Dublin, 1982), 185.

source of such sections, which are based on his unique *al-Tibyān fī ādāb ḥamalat al-Qur'ān*,[15] which has been translated into Indonesian.

One book which was examined concerned musical chanting of the Qur'ān, written by a leading Egyptian scholar, Labīb al-Sa'īd, whose major Arabic work, *al-Muṣḥaf al-murattal*, has had considerable influence on recent thinking about Quranic recitation and its recording for mass distribution. Al-Sa'īd's *al-Taghannī bi'l-Qur'ān* (1970) has been translated as *Melagukan al-Qur'ān*[16] ('Chanting the Qur'ān') and is the only treatise which has been found in Indonesian that concentrates on chanting as such.

At this point we must distinguish recitation from reading, that is, *qirā'a* as live performance (*tilāwa*) from *qirā'āt* as textual variants, 'readings'.[17] The former is regulated by the rules of *tajwīd*, whereas the latter is a much more difficult text-critical matter. The two are of course related, because the *qāri'*, or reciter, must recite the text perfectly within whatever reading is chosen. (For all practical purposes, there is only one reading that is nearly universally recited these days, that of Ḥafṣ.) However, the *qāri'* does not need to have mastered the history of the reading of the text. The one who does that is called a *muqri'*. Such a specialist is also a *qāri'*. But he is much more, in the sense that he is qualified and licensed (by an *ijāza*) to teach recitation and readings. The *muqri'* is to Quranic readings and recitation what the *'ālim* is to jurisprudence.

During two field research periods in Indonesia, a month in 1980 and nearly nine months in 1984–5, I failed to meet a single native *muqri'* in the strictest sense. *Qāri'*s abound, and some of them are also *ḥuffāẓ*, meaning they have memorized the entire Qur'ān. Many

[15] For an analysis of this work, see Frederick M. Denny, 'The *ādāb* of Qur'an Recitation: Text and Context', in A. H. Johns and Syed Husain M. Jafri, eds., *International Congress for the Study of the Qur'an*, Series I (Canberra, 1980), 143–60.

[16] Labieb Saied [Labīb al-Sa'īd], *Melagukan Al Qur'an: Tinjauan Historis Jurisprudensi*, trans. into Indonesian by Jamaluddin Kafie (Surabaya, n.d.). *Al-Muṣḥaf al-murattal* was published originally in Cairo, 1387/1967. An abridged and edited translation was published under the title *The Recited Koran: A History of the First Recorded Version*, trans. and adapted by Bernard Weiss, M. A. Rauf, and Morroe Berger (Princeton, NJ, 1975).

[17] For a brief review of the two fields, see Frederick M. Denny, 'Exegesis and Recitation: Their Development as Classical Forms of Qur'anic Piety', in Frank Reynolds and Theodor Ludwig, eds., *Transitions and Transformations in the History of Religions: Essays in Honor of Joseph M. Kitagawa* (Leiden, 1980), 91–123. A detailed and fairly technical survey is contained in *The Recited Koran*.

have also reached a high scholarly plane in the very traditional field of readings, where there are to be found seven canonical variants, sometimes expanded in number to ten and even to fourteen. I was introduced to a well-known reciter and teacher of recitation in North Sumatra and I asked him if he considered himself a *muqri'*. He answered 'Yes', but when I asked him what the curriculum and training for *muqri'*s in Indonesia consists of, he then said that he did not think there are any *muqri'*s in Indonesia. He himself had been trained in Mecca and Cairo, where there are indeed full-fledged *muqri'*s in the sense of scholars of high degree and with proper licences certifying that they had been prepared in the requisite texts and examined. I also questioned a prominent and influential recitation teacher in East Java, one who has written a leading recitation handbook and is founder and principal *kiai* of a Quranic school. This person thought for a while and concluded that he is not a real *muqri'* either. Modesty must also be considered a factor in my informants' answers.

I do not wish to disparage Qur'ān recitation training in Indonesia by these observations, but the most advanced education in the field is still scarce in Indonesia, which nevertheless has the largest national population of Muslims in the world, 90 per cent of 175 million. The most advanced recitation authorities still receive their training in the Middle East. I am informed that in the ancient Islamic city of Kudus in the north of Central Java, east of Semarang, is a special Qur'ān institute with bona fide *muqri'*s. In any event, there is nothing wrong with Qur'ān recitation in Indonesia. It is world class in the performance sense, if not in related scholarship.

Every two years Indonesia holds a national level Qur'ān chanting tournament. The contestants come from all twenty-six provinces and include boys, girls, men, and women, divided by sex for purposes of judging, but all reciting on the same programme at times. Blind reciters also make up a category for judging, which includes evaluation of memory. The *Musabaqah Tilawatil Qur'an* (= MTQ, 'Competition in the Recitation of the Qur'ān') is widely hailed by Indonesians as a *disiplin nasional*. Local, regional, and provincial levels hold preliminary competitions, a process that takes up all the time between national contests. The last MTQ was held in May 1985 in Pontianak, West Kalimantan (Borneo). It went on for ten days and was reported on television every night and in the daily papers all over Indonesia.[18]

The types of competition in the MTQ are beginning to be reflected in the contents of the handbooks.[19] In addition to recitation, school-age contestants also participate in quiz shows, with three teams of three students each (mixed sexes), who are asked questions about the Qur'ān, about recitation, and even about the system of Quranic education in the Republic of Indonesia. A male and a female reciter are on hand to demonstrate styles and musical modes. Answers, which must snap forth quickly, are graded on a scale from 1 to 100 and points are totalled on an electronic scoreboard. Large audiences shout and applaud when their favourite team scores highly, and there is wholesome rivalry between regions. The overall winners in 1985 were the team from East Java, my own research area. Many of the team had received their training in traditional *pondok*s, both for boys and girls. These champions will probably become recitation and religion teachers and go on to write handbooks of their own.

Times are changing, however, in that more and more Quranically literate people are also receiving advanced training in other Islamic fields. A leading *qāri'a*, Dra.[20] Maria Ulfa, went to a *pondok* as a young girl, but then she studied at one of the newer state Islamic institutes, where she majored in *sharī'a*. After that she went on to a unique institute near Jakarta that trains women in advanced Quranic sciences, such as *tafsīr* and readings, as well as Arabic studies. Maria Ulfa won the international reciting competition in Kuala Lumpur a few years ago and was acclaimed as the leading woman reciter in the world. She served as a reciter at the quiz show in the Musabaqah in 1985, demonstrating styles of recitation and melodic modes for identification by the contestants.

[18] For a general description, in a popular vein, see Frederick M. Denny, 'The Great Indonesian Qur'an Chanting Tournament', *William and Mary Magazine* (Summer, 1985), 33–7, illustrated. Reprinted in slightly revised form in *The World and I*, 6 (1986), 216–23.

[19] One such is *Bahan Training Centre Menghadapi M.T.Q.*, compiled by H. Abubakar Ya'qub (Medan, 1396/1976). The title, loosely translated, means 'Materials for a Training Centre for Preparing for the Competition in the Recitation of the Qur'ān'. The 64-page booklet is actually a fairly typical *tajwīd* manual, with added sections on MTQ judging categories, a short history of the Qur'ān text (for the quiz show), a brief review of melodic modes permissible in *mujawwad* recitation, and two poems about the MTQ.

[20] Drs. and Dra. are abbreviations of the degree Doktorandis (male)/Doktoranda (female), a graduate degree between the master's and the doctorate.

It seems likely that increasingly centralized regulation of Quranic training in the Ministry of Religion, coupled with increased literacy and educational differentiation, will enable Indonesian Muslims to maintain their high standards of recitation while entering increasingly into the modern world. The mosques were full of young people in all the cities and towns I visited during my fieldwork. Activities such as reciting competitions provide enjoyment as well as edification.

The latest development in Qur'ān education is tape cassettes which teach proper recitation practices. Although they will never take the place of a live professional teacher, they have opened up the field to many more Indonesians who use tapes in connection with handbooks, whether in private study or in classes.[21]

2. DESCRIPTIVE ANALYSIS OF SELECTED HANDBOOKS

Three levels of difficulty and thoroughness in Indonesian-medium recitation handbooks may be discerned. The most elementary is the kind of manual that introduces the Arabic alphabet and concentrates on learning the pronunciation of the words prior to studying recitation proper. An example is the optimistically titled *Belajar Membaca al-Quran dalam 10 Jam* ('Learn to read the Qur'ān in ten hours'),[22] whose 98 pages proceed with Romanized Indonesian pronunciation approximations juxtaposed with Arabic letters at first, and then, later, with whole phrases. The final sections contain characteristic Arabic Quranic terms and brief phrases to be mastered. Another elementary manual[23] introduces the Arabic alphabet and the pronunciation of words and brief phrases, and then proceeds immediately to whole short *sūra*s of the Qur'ān. This book of 52 pages is exceedingly terse and absolutely requires a live teacher to introduce it and guide the student. The cover has a

[21] One such set is the 2-cassette *Tuntunan Lagu Lagu: Al-Qur'an*, compiled by M. Thoha Hasan, under the auspices of the East Java province of the *Lembaga Pengembangan Tilawatil Qur-an*, the major national Qur'ān recitation organization in Indonesia. The teacher–reciters on the cassettes are H. M. Bashori Alwi (the same H. M. Basori Alwi who is *kiai* of the Singosari *pondok*) and his close associate, the distinguished teacher of musical modes in recitation, H. M. Ahmad Damanhuri, of Malang, East Java.

[22] Compiled and written by J. Amiery (Surabaya, n.d.).

[23] S. Marzuki, *Sistim Cepat Belajar Membaca al Qur'an* ('A Speedy System for Learning to Read the Qur'ān') (Sala [Solo], 1979).

drawing of a mother teaching her two children how to read the Qur'ān.

The second level of handbooks introduces technical *tajwīd* terminology and concepts and provides examples for study and practice. Even at this level, though, the manuals tends to be laconic, presupposing an instructor to explain matters and provide detailed explanations. One such handbook is *Pelajaran Tajwid* ('A course in *tajwīd*'), by Minan Zuhri.[24] This 44-page book with 21 chapters, has six review exercises distributed throughout the work. A clear and concise handbook, it requires a basic reading knowledge of Arabic to be able to follow it. It could serve as a good review of *tajwīd* rules for one who has already received basic instruction. In order to convey some idea of the manual's directness and conciseness, the entire introduction is provided here in English translation:

The Science of *tajwīd*

The science of *tajwīd* is the science whose purpose is to make known the place[s] of the articulation of the letter[s], and their characteristics when reading [aloud].

The Goal of the Science of *tajwīd*

The goal in the diligent study of the science of *tajwīd* is to make it possible for one to read verses of the Qur'ān with fluency [brightly and clearly] and exactness, according to the teachings of Prophet Muḥammad (may God bless him and grant him salvation), [and] with the capacity to guard one's tongue from mistakes when reading the Qur'ān.

The Legal Status of Studying the Science of *tajwīd*

The study of the science of *tajwīd* is a sufficient duty [i.e., in Islamic law, incumbent on a representative number of believers, but not on all]. But the practice of the science of *tajwīd* is an individual duty [i.e., required of all] for a Muslim, whether male or female.

The table of contents of *Pelajaran Tajwid* is quite comprehensive for such a short book. Notice that some Arabic technical *tajwīd* terms are used.

1. *Bab Nun mati dan Tanwin* ('Chapter of vowel-less [lit. 'dead', = Arabic *sākina*] *nūn* and nunnation')

The chapter details various matters, like nasalization (*ghunna*);

[24] Kudus, 1401/1981. This handbook states that it is intended for elementary-level religious schools (*madrasah ibtidaiyah*).

assimilation (*idghām*); transformation of *nūn* into *mīm*, as pronounced, when followed by *bā'*: as in *layunbadhanna*, which would be pronounced *layumbadhanna* (this procedure is known in Arabic as *iqlāb*). Numerous examples are provided covering all points introduced in the chapter.

2. *Latihan I* ('Exercise I')

Ten questions for study and review, e.g., 'What is the science of *tajwīd*?', 'From where does a person learn about the places of articulation of the letters?', 'Find the five types of pronunciation mentioned above in the following verses.'

3. *Bab Mim Sakinah* ('Chapter about vowel-less *mīm*')
4. *Bab Mim dan Nun yang bertasydid* ('Chapter concerning doubled *mīm* and *nūn*')

Requires nasalization.

5. *Bab Al Ta'rif* ('Chapter concerning the definite article *al-* [*ta'rīf*]')

Covers the 'sun' and 'moon' letters.

6. *Latihan II* ('Exercise II')

Thorough review.

7. *Bab Idgham* ('Chapter about assimilation')

Covers the lesser and greater forms of assimilation or contraction of letter sounds, under six headings. This is a critically important aspect of *tajwīd* and requires considerable application for a non-native Arabic speaker to master.

8. *Bab Lam Jalalah* ('Chapter about the *lām* of majesty [*jalāla*]')

The *lām* in *Allāh* is pronounced emphatically (*tafkhīm*) when in a phrase like *qul huwa Allāhu aḥad* ('Say: He is God, one'), and softly (*tarqīq*) in a phrase like *bismi-llāhi* ('In the name of God').

9. *Latihan III* ('Exercise III')

Among other tasks, the student is asked to examine a lengthy Qur'ān passage and divide all the *lām jalālas* into *tafkhīm* and *tarqīq*.

10. *Bab Ra'* ('Chapter about *rā'*')

Both *tafkhīm* and *tarqīq* forms.

11. *Bab huruf Qalqalah* ('Chapter concerning the 'concussive' [*qalqala*] letters')

This section concerns the neutral vowel sound (schwa) that follows certain unvowelled letters (*qāf*, *ṭā'*, *bā'*, *jīm*, and *dāl*).

12. *Latihan IV* ('Exercise IV')

Mostly on *qalqala*, with a long Qur'ān passage to master in the application of the greater and lesser forms.

13. *Bab Mad* ('Chapter concerning drawing out the voice over long vowels [*madd*]')

This is the longest chapter with 7 pages. It is usually the longest in *tajwīd* manuals.

14. *Latihan V* ('Exercise V')

Covers *madd* only.

15. *Bab Saktah* ('Chapter on silence')

Sakta is pausing briefly between two words, without breathing. There are four places in the Qur'ān where this is required, according to the rules of *tajwīd*.

16. *Bab Makhraj* ('Chapter about the places [*makhārij*] of articulation')

Divided into five parts of the vocal anatomy: the hollow of the mouth, the larynx, the tongue, the lips, and the nose.

17. *Bab Takbir* ('Chapter about reciting *Allāhu akbar*')

It is recommended (*sunna*) that the *takbīr* be said upon completion of the recitation of the Qur'ān, and at certain other points during the recitation.

18. *Bab Bacaan-bacaan* ('Chapter concerning phrases [lit., "readings"]')

Three examples of extra-Quranic pious phrases that may be uttered at specified places in the text: for instance, after reciting Q. 88/23–4, 'But whosoever turns away and disbelieves, God will bring down on him the greatest punishment', the reciter may say, 'My Lord, protect me from your punishment.'

19. *Latihan VI* ('Exercise VI')

20. *Sujud Tilawah* ('The prostration of recitation')

Gives the 15 places in the text where a prostration is recommended or required.

21. *Penutup* ('Conclusion')

Several pious sayings about Qur'ān recitation culled from the *ḥadīth*, e.g., 'There are many who recite the Qur'ān who will be cursed by the Qur'ān', or 'The best service of my community is the recitation of the Qur'ān.'

Pelajaran Tajwid is not a scholarly treatise on recitation, obviously, nor does it provide anything beyond the bare minimum in what it does cover. Yet, there is enough matter to provide a sufficient grounding in the rules governing the proper recitation of the Qur'ān. A person who masters this handbook, under a qualified instructor, will be at a level of proficiency and self-confidence to go further in the field of *tajwīd*. For that person, there are excellent handbooks available in Indonesian to satisfy a desire for higher study.

Among the *tajwīd* manuals which were collected are four which are both quite comprehensive in coverage and advanced both as to phonetics and required knowledge of Arabic. The most well-rounded treatment, in my view, is *Tajwid Qur'anulkarim: Pelajaran Tajwid al-Qur'an—dengan secara: Praktis, Populer, dan Sistimatis* ('Recitation of the Noble Qur'ān: A course in *tajwīd* of the Qur'ān, with an approach [that is] Practical, Popular, and Systematic'), by Ismail Tekan.[25]

Tekan's book is 183 pages long, divided into nine sections of twenty-six lessons, plus appendices on the divisions of the text, the early readers of the Qur'ān, some prominent scholars in text and *tafsīr*, the history of the text, the revelation of the Qur'ān, its collection, and a selection of *ḥadīth*s about Qur'ān recitation, with Indonesian translations. A bibliography of five titles ends the work.

Every aspect of this book is much more detailed than the handbook described above. In addition, there are topics not mentioned in the earlier work, such as 'seeking refuge' (*isti'ādha*) before reciting the Qur'ān; saying the *basmala*; 'stops and starts' (*al-waqf wa'l-ibtidā'*), which amount to Quranic punctuation; and a long section on the *ādāb*, etiquette and proper procedures connected with recitation. The topics mentioned in the appendices

[25] Jakarta, 1388/1967; 4th printing, 1983.

are also absent from the earlier handbook, as well as most others.

The *ādāb* of recitation are treated in about half of the Indonesian *tajwīd* manuals examined, but the extent varies considerably. Ismail Tekan is very concerned with the subject, which also appears in this book in places other than the chapter devoted to it, without the label *ādāb*. An example is a chapter on matters that are forbidden in recitation, such as dancing, making the voice quaver (*tar'īd*), and phonetic distortion (*táḥrīf*).

One unusual feature of Tekan's handbook is its graphic thoroughness concerning precise pronunciation of the Arabic alphabet. It is common for manuals to contain at least one diagram of the vocal anatomy, usually in schematic form, showing by arrows or letters the articulation places in the nose, mouth cavity, throat, teeth, palate, and lips. Tekan provides sixteen detailed illustrations, accompanied in each instance by the letters to be articulated. The drawings of wide open mouths, tongue positions, and lip and teeth movements, are very well realized, so that one may form all the letters and recite the examples of Quranic words by following the author's instructions precisely. It is unlikely, however, that a person with no Arabic language training would be able to do very much with the phonetic graphic aids, but they would probably be helpful to someone learning the alphabet and practising it alone, after having first heard a competent Arabic speaker demonstrate the sounds. Figure 1 reproduces an example of Tekan's drawings, one that shows the places of articulation of *qāf* and *kāf*. The explanation is provided in Indonesian, while the recitation examples are in Quranic Arabic script.

Perhaps it would be better to characterize Ismail Tekan's handbook as comprehensive rather than advanced, because it is not any more difficult, conceptually, than the briefer manual of Minan Zuhri, described earlier. There is simply much more to learn in Tekan's book. Another handbook that may be classified at the advanced level is *Pedoman Membaca al-Qur'an* (*Ilmu Tajwid*) ('A Manual for Reading the Qur'ān: The Science of *tajwid*'), by Drs. H. A. Nawawi Ali.[26] This work of 206 pages is divided into seven sections, with a total of forty-four chapters. Like other recitation manuals, this one has prefaces by prominent authorities. Among the books examined, this one seems to have the most influential

[26] Jakarta, 1983.

—PADA "LIDAH"—

5. *Makhraj PANGKAL-LIDAH DENGAN LANGIT-LANGIT,* adalah tempat keluarnya 1 (satu) huruf, yaitu: QAF (ق)

Misal:

قَاتَلَ - مُقَرَّبُوْنَ - مُتَّقِيْنَ - يَعْقُوْبُ - اِقْرَأْ .

dan lain-lain.

6. *Makhraj DIMUKA SEDIKIT DARI PANGKAL-LIDAH DENGAN LANGIT-LANGIT* (*dimuka-Makhraj QAF*), adalah tempat keluarnya 1 (satu) huruf, yaitu: KAF (ک)

Misal:

اِيَّاكَ - فِى الْكِتَابِ - لَكُمْ - كُنْ فَيَكُوْنُ - اَكْبَرُ .

dan lain-lain.

1. Diagram to show the Articulation of *qāf* and *kāf*, from Ismail Tekan's *Tajwid Qur'anulkarim*.

official and semi-official backing in the form of statements of directors of three institutes of Quranic studies, including the national-level organization, *Lembaga Pengembangan Tilawātil*

Qur-an, which unites efforts from the local levels of training and recitation on up to the all-Indonesian recitation tournament described earlier in this essay. The prefaces serve as imprimaturs.

Pedoman Membaca al-Qur'an is an authentic scholarly treatise and could serve as an introduction to Quranic studies as well as a detailed and authoritative survey of recitation practice. It would make a good college-level text for persons studying to be teachers of Islam in Indonesia. The author is obviously much more than a village *kiai* who has privately published his own tried and true methods of training locals in basic recitation. There is an above-average display of knowledge of the classical Arabic literature of readings, recitation, *ḥadīth* concerning the subject, and related matters. Interestingly, there is less use of Arabic script examples than in Tekan's book, and much more explanation and illustration in Indonesian, with frequent transliteration of Arabic terms into the Roman alphabet.

Pedoman Membaca al-Qur'an does not contain a section on the *ādāb* of recitation, but sticks to the main subject of technical *tajwīd* and the closely related matter of variant readings of the text. This absence of an *ādāb* chapter is puzzling in a work of this scope. Even very brief manuals on recitation generally have at least a page devoted to the *ādāb* of *tilāwa*. Possibly Nawawi Ali considers his book to be for readers who are already fully acquainted with the *ādāb* of recitation. Another of the handbooks[27] which can be grouped in this third, advanced category, but which has not been described here, opens with a four-page chapter on *Adab Membaca al-Qur'an*, reminiscent of *fiqh* handbooks, which always open with a disquisition on *ṭahāra*, ritual purification, before describing the *ṣalāt* prayer service. In any case, *Pedoman Membaca al-Qur'an* provides a great deal of solid material pertaining to *tajwīd* and a high-level treatment of it for educated Indonesian readers who can also read Arabic script.

In the first section of this essay it was remarked that the books on recitation which have been examined have little in the way of bibliographies. Scholarly bibliographies are, of course, not really appropriate for brief instructional manuals. Even relatively advanced treatments, like *Pedoman Membaca al-Qur'an*, however, display

[27] H. Abdurrahman Thaha, compiler–author, *Seluk Beluk Hukum Membaca al-Quran* ('The Fine Points of the Law of Reading/Reciting the Qur'ān') (Bandung, 1399/1979).

little evidence of wide exposure to classical recitation and readings literature. *Pedoman*, for example, lists the following recitation titles in its bibliography: Muḥammad Makkī Naṣr's *Nihāyat al-qawl al-mufīd fī 'ilm al-tajwīd*, first published in Cairo in 1349/1930 and, its title notwithstanding, an extremely competent and helpful treatise containing practically everything that had ever been written about the subject, including around thirty pages on *ādāb al-tilāwa* (out of a total of 259 pages); Muḥammad al-Ṣādiq Qamhāwī's recent work of 44 pages, *al-Burhān fī tajwīd al-Qur'ān*;[28] and the classic compendium of Quranic sciences down to its author's day, *al-Itqān fī 'ulūm al-Qur'ān* by Jalāl al-Dīn al-Suyūṭī (d. 911/1505), which has a substantial section on readings and recitation. Other titles cited in *Pedoman* include traditional Arabic works such as the *tafsīrs* of Ibn Kathīr (d. 774/1373) and al-Qurṭubī (d. 671/1272), al-Bukhārī (d. 256/870), *al-Ṣaḥīḥ*, and al-Asqalānī (d. 852/1449), *Fatḥ al-Bārī'*, as well as four modern works, three in Indonesian, including Ismail Tekan's *Tajwid Qur'anulkarim*, described above.

Tekan's bibliography contains five titles, all of which are on *tajwīd*, including one on the difficult sub-field of *al-waqf wa'l-ibtidā'*. Tekan apparently assumes that his readers know something about the field of *tajwīd* literature, because at the end of his brief listing he wrote: *dan lain-lain*, 'and so forth'. A balanced view of this business of bibliographies appended to *tajwīd* treatises requires the observation that most manuals published in Arabic (at least in Egypt, the Muslim scholarly centre I know best) contain little, either, and often nothing at all, in the way of bibliographies or 'sources consulted'. This is not to imply that *tajwīd* handbooks are not documented or carefully written. It is simply to acknowledge that they tend to be unselfconscious, utilitarian aids and not academic discourses.

Finally, there is very little treatment of actual chanting of the Qur'ān in any of the works that I surveyed. *Pedoman* does provide the standard description of the three tempos of recitation: slow (*taḥqīq*), medium-speed (*tadwīr*), fast (*ḥadr*), and the unadorned, rhythmic recitation known as *tartīl*, which can be said to apply to both slow and medium tempos, if they are not accompanied with melodies. Melodic recitation, which none of the handbooks treat, is known as *mujawwad* style. There does exist, however, an

[28] Cairo, 1971–2 (10th printing).

excellent set of audio cassettes in which the recitation teacher fully discusses and demonstrates the various musical modes (*maqām*). The musical dimension of Qur'ān recitation is very important, but it cannot be learned from books, obviously. The recitation tournaments that Indonesian Muslims love so much include the musical dimension, called *lagu-lagu*, 'melodies', as one of the main judging categories, along with *tajwīd*, meaning the technical phonetics of recitation, and *ādāb*, the etiquette of recitation and the proper comportment of reciters. Modern musical notation is not acceptable in the teaching of melodic recitation of the Qur'ān, partly because of its associations with popular and art music, which are considered to be different in every way from acceptable *mujawwad* chanting. One of the handbooks, however, does contain something very close to Western musical notation, namely the do-re-mi-fa-sol-la-ti-do scale, written without the staff.[29]

This has been only a preliminary survey of recitation handbooks available in Indonesia. Potentially fruitful areas for further research include braille instruction books, the increasing numbers of sound cassettes, and unpublished recitation guides of limited circulation such as may be found in *pondok pesantren*s. Although my field research was conducted in East Java, I have noted many similarities with other regions that I visited. The well-developed system of recitation contests, including especially the national level MTQ, will doubtless ensure more nearly uniform standards and styles of recitation in the future. Handbooks devoted specifically to the MTQ phenomenon can also be expected to proliferate in increasing numbers.[30]

[29] H. Dt. Tombak Alam, *Ilmu Tajwid Populer 17 X Pandai* (Jakarta, 1979; 4th printing, 1984). Solfeggio is introduced on p. 16, using associated numbers 1 to 7, but the device is not developed further in the text.

[30] For making possible the writing of this chapter, I wish to make grateful acknowledgement to the following institutions: the Council on International Exchange of Scholars and the Fulbright Program, for an Islamic Civilization Research Grant in 1984–5 for field research in East Java; the Council on Research and Creative Work of the University of Colorado, Boulder, for a Faculty Fellowship and Grant-in-Aid for the same period; the Rektor and Faculty of the State Islamic Institute of Religion (IAIN) of Sunan Ampel, Surabaya, and its Centre for Middle Eastern Studies, for sponsorship and research assistance during my months in Indonesia; and finally, the Lembaga Ilmu Pengetahuan Indonesia (LIPI), for its gracious permission to conduct research.

14

Abū'l-A'lā Mawdūdī's *Tafhīm al-Qur'ān*

CHARLES J. ADAMS

AMONG the numerous writings of the well-known Indo-Pakistani religious leader, publicist, and political figure, Abū'l-A'lā Mawdūdī (1903–79),[1] is a *tafsīr* of the Qur'ān with the title *Tafhīm al-Qur'ān*. In its original Urdu version, the first part of which was published in Lahore in 1951, it comprises six large volumes of Arabic text, Urdu translation, and commentary. Preparation of the *tafsīr* was begun in 1942 while Mawdūdī was living with the small community he had created in Dār al-Islām near Pathankot in East Panjab and continued for some time until the distraction of the events surrounding partition brought the work to a halt with the end of *sūrat Yūsuf*. Free time to progress with the work, revise it, and to see the initial portions through the press was afforded only by Mawdūdī's arrest under the Public Safety Act in August 1948, following a much-discussed incident in the great mosque of Peshawar. The commentary thus owes much to Mawdūdī's incarceration in the Multan Jail. The completion of the full commentary was a project of more than thirty years' duration.

From indications on the reverse side of the title-page it appears that an illegal, pirated edition of the *tafsīr* was issued by some unidentified person shortly after its publication, causing the publisher to take steps to protect his interests and to guarantee the genuineness of his remaining stock. To this end, each set of the *tafsīr* is numbered by hand and signed by both the author and the publisher.

1 For a bibliography of Mawdūdī's works and scholarship on him, see Qazi Zulqadr Siddiqi, S. M. Aslam, and M. M. Ahsan, 'A Bibliography of Writings by and about Mawlānā Sayyid Abul A'lā Mawdūdī', in Khurshid Ahmad and Zafar Ishaq Ansari (eds.), *Islamic Perspectives: Studies in Honour of Mawlānā Sayyid Abul A'lā Mawdūdī* (Leicester, 1979), 3–14. Further information about the life and work of Mawdūdī may be found in Kalim Bahadur, *The Jama'at-i-Islami of Pakistan* (Lahore, 1978); Charles J. Adams, 'The Ideology of Mawlana Mawdudi', in Donald Smith, ed., *South Asian Politics and Religion* (Princeton, 1966), 371–97; id., 'Mawdudi and the Islamic State', in John Esposito, ed., *Voices of Resurgent Islam* (New York, 1983), 99–133.

An incomplete English translation, which had reached twelve medium-sized volumes in 1984, began to appear in 1967.[2] The portions of the English translation printed to date cover the first 46 *sūras*, that is, up to and including *sūrat al-aḥqāf*. This English version is by no means a straightforward and faithful translation of the Urdu. While the general sense is the same, there is both some simplification and some rearrangement of the material.

In the Preface to the *tafsīr*, Mawdūdī explains his aim in preparing the work to have been an explanation of the Qur'ān for the purposes of the ordinary educated Indian Muslim who thirsts for greater knowledge of the Holy Book. There were, he believed, many individuals without knowledge of Arabic or acquaintance with the Quranic sciences whose desire for more knowledge was strong and real. There is no need, he said, for more technical works on the Qur'ān in Urdu, since a great abundance of such studies is already available. To prepare another would be a work of supererogation. With this intended audience in mind, his desire was to expound the teachings of the Qur'ān with force and clarity in those passages where there is no doubt of the meaning, and to answer questions that might arise in the mind in connection with other passages. Since the work does not aim at contributing to the expertise of Quranic scholars, it does not utilize the full panoply of scholarly sources and devices that might otherwise be employed, but refers only to materials appropriate for its intended readers.

Somewhat similar considerations govern the style of the translation. Mawdūdī explains that he has abandoned the traditional mode of literal word-for-word, interlinear translation in order to adopt a freer style. The choice was not made because of any lack of appreciation for the traditional approach which allows one to understand with precision the meaning of each individual word in the text, but rather because of the conviction that he had nothing to add to the prior efforts along these lines of such men as Shāh Walī Ullāh, Shāh 'Abd al-Qādir, Mawlānā Maḥmūd al-Ḥasan, and Mawlānā Ashraf 'Alī Thanawī. Moreover, his purposes were different from theirs. In spite of the undoubted virtues of literal translations, they also have certain shortcomings. For one thing they cannot convey the force and eloquence of the original to one who does not know Arabic. In its original divine form, the Qur'ān,

[2] All references in this paper are to this translation published under the title *The Meaning of the Qur'ān*, trans. Muhammad Akbar (Lahore, 197-).

when recited, can cause one's hair to stand on end, but literal translations have no such power. Neither can they stir the emotions in the same way as the original nor convey its literary excellence. If these things are lacking, much of importance about the Qur'ān will have been missed, and there will be no possibility of understanding how and why the book had such a transforming effect on the Arabs and, indeed, on much of the world. Another defect in interlinear translations, or those arranged in the modern fashion with the Arabic and the translation in side-by-side columns, Mawdūdī believed to lie in the way in which they destroy the flow of the argument and prevent the teaching from being understood as a whole. This is a particular defect of English translations where scholars divide the verses from one another, giving each a number, and then treating them as individual entities rather than as a connected whole. Furthermore, English translators tend to employ the language of the Bible for their renderings of the Qur'ān with the result that they make the Muslim scripture unintelligible.

Still another shortcoming of literal translations lies in their inability to reproduce or even hint at the nature of the original Quranic communications. It must be remembered that the Qur'ān came as a recitation, an oral communication, that it was spoken not written. Mawdūdī lays much emphasis on the difference between spoken and written language, insisting that the meaning of written language can be made clear only by the use of still more words, while the meaning implicit in spoken discourse can often be indicated by inflection, emphasis, facial expression, and so on. If one thinks of the Qur'ān in terms of the words of a literal translation, there must be a serious failure to grasp the quality—and meaning—of the original.

A further failure of literal translations is likely to arise from the special Quranic use of language. Though the Qur'ān is sent down in 'plain Arabic', it often employs words in a technical way in senses other than the customary ones. It may also use one and the same word in different senses according to the demands of the context. One who concentrates attention upon a literal word-by-word rendering is, therefore, in Mawdūdī's opinion, likely to do grave injury to the meaning of the message. As an instance he cites the Quranic use of the word *kufr*,[3] which, he says, differs sharply from

[3] i. 10.

the meaning given to it by the *mutakallimūn* and the *fuqahā'* of the community, who tend to circumscribe its significance quite sharply. By contrast, in the Qur'ān it is used to convey several things. It may mean the general state of being without faith; at other times, it means denial of faith; at still others, its sense is that of ingratitude; while in yet others it may signify the failure to perform those duties required by faith in God.

Rather than a literal translation, therefore, Mawdūdī prefers to treat the text with considerable freedom so that its sense can be properly conveyed. While he affirms the intention to translate plain Arabic into plain Urdu, he is concerned that his reader, the common person, should understand, and understand correctly.

In addition to the Preface, the *tafsīr* also has a long introduction which Mawdūdī says is intended to make the reader aware of matters necessary for understanding the Qur'ān and to answer beforehand certain questions that are likely to arise. The issues then discussed have to do with some of the problems that have most occupied critical scholars of the Qur'ān in modern times, namely: the reasons for the order of the materials in the text, the process of the formation of the text, the variant readings, and the authenticity of the received text. Mawdūdī acknowledges[4] that the Qur'ān is likely to puzzle one who comes to it for the first time, because it is not organized like other books, exhibits no evident literary form, does not group its materials for a systematic presentation of doctrines, is repetitious, and so on. Questions about all of these matters arise, however, only because people fail to grasp the uniqueness of the Qur'ān, the fact that it is a book like no other and cannot, therefore, he expected to conform to the criteria for a normal book. All preconceived ideas of what a book is or should be must be given over and the Qur'ān taken on its own terms for the singular reality that it is. The Qur'ān is a divine guidance sent to people, one whose central object is to invite them to the 'Right Way' that brings success in worldly life and felicity in the hereafter. Fastening the gaze firmly on the central aim, one will find no confusion or incongruity in the organization of the Qur'ān, for every word in it supports the achievement of that aim.[5] The variations in the Quranic style are explained in much the same way. For the central aim to be properly impressed upon the consciousness

[4] i. 7–8. [5] i. 13.

of different people in a variety of situations, it was necessary that at some times the mode of address should be emotional and ecstatic, and at others, more rational or legalistic. The prophet was the founder of a movement—a key notion for Mawdūdī in connection with his political and reform activities—and the revelations had to be adapted to the different requirements of the movement as it passed through successive stages. Thus, it was necessary to speak sometimes in one way and sometimes in another, and often to repeat the basic creedal statements and moral formulas.[6] In short, the problem of the alleged disorderliness of the Qur'ān does not exist at all except in the minds of those who have not come to terms with the nature of the scripture and what it is trying to do.

Mawdūdī explains the compilation of the Quranic text by combining elements of the traditional stories. It was, he says, written down on various materials under Muḥammad's direction, piece by piece, immediately as it was revealed, and the pieces gathered into a bag. Thus, the prophet was responsible under divine inspiration for the order of the *sūra*s and their internal arrangement, as well as for the collection process itself. The order of the Quranic material was most clearly indicated in his recitations of the complete scripture, an act which he performed in the presence of Gabriel. In answer to the question why the order of the sūras does not preserve their chronological sequence, Mawdūdī replies that the requirements of a developing community are different from those of a community already well established. The revelations in their chronological order served the needs of the new community as it slowly emerged, but the Qur'ān is a book for all times, not simply for seventh-century Arabia. The later community needed to have the teachings presented in another manner to ensure its ongoing religious life. It is for this reason that such long *sūra*s as *al-baqara* with their detailed instructions for practice are placed at the beginning of the Qur'ān. The later community needed more than anything else to know precisely how it should behave.

The collection of the Qur'ān was achieved as follows. Under 'Umar's prodding, Abū Bakr caused Zayd ibn Thābit to compile a connected book, and this official copy was put into the safekeeping of Ḥafsa bint 'Umar for all who might want to consult it.[7] 'Uthmān's function was to protect the purity of the Qurayshī

[6] i. 20. [7] i. 2–3.

dialect of the Qur'ān by having all other versions burned and distributing a number of copies of the official version. To assure that the correct pronunciation was observed and in view of the imperfections of the Arabic script at the time, 'Uthmān is also said to have sent a *qāri'* along with each official copy of the Qur'ān that went to distant places.[8] The complete authenticity of the received Qur'ān is guaranteed according to Mawdūdī by the fact that there is no difference of any kind between the oldest manuscripts and the printed book of our day, as well as by the fact that a Qur'ān purchased in Algeria is identical to the last vowel point with one purchased in Java.

Although some of the major problems that have occupied critical students of the Qur'ān are touched upon in the Introduction, especially those that might rouse doubt in a sensitive Muslim mind, they are treated in a cursory and relatively superficial way. It is to Mawdūdī's credit that he was aware of these issues, but he cannot be said to have made a significant contribution towards resolving them. Given the audience he intended to address and the fact that he was writing in Urdu, which was little likely to be read outside the Indian subcontinent, his stance is not surprising. He was preaching to the converted and not writing for the critics. From time to time in the text of the *tafsīr*, however, he does return to some of these problems in more detail. One that appears to have troubled him especially is that of the internal structure of individual *sūra*s. How is one to explain their abrupt changes of subject or their repetition of matters treated elsewhere, and so on? These questions arise, he thinks, when individual *āya*s or groups of *āya*s are considered in themselves in isolation from their context. The answers are to be found in the logic of the *sūra*s as wholes. The basic unit of Quranic communication is the *sūra*, each of which is an integral entity with its own central theme and purpose. Each, therefore, has its own logic into which the various *āya*s and subjects discussed neatly fit. Mawdūdī constantly emphasizes the need to discern the logic of whatever *sūra* may be under discussion, and the need to respect the flow of the argument which it contains. Nothing is accidental or out of order if one grasps the spirit and thrust of what is being said. To reinforce this point, every *sūra* is provided with an introduction that sets out its theme and basic aim, and the explanatory notes

[8] i. 26.

often make the same point when they deal with abrupt transitions in the text. This aspect of the *tafsīr* undoubtedly serves an apologetic purpose *vis-à-vis* certain critics of the Qur'ān. At the same time it makes a broad point about the rationality of the Qur'ān and of Islamic teaching more generally. This theme is central to much of Mawdūdī's other work; indeed, he held that the uncompromising rationality of Islam was among its strongest features and a proof of its validity and truth. In terms of methods for interpreting the Qur'ān, the concern for rational structure also signifies his rejection of the proof-text approach. He neither followed nor approved of the practice of drawing broad consequences from a single word or phrase in isolation. Quranic passages were always to be put into the larger framework of *sūra*s and the argument being pursued; only then would they be properly understood and their relationship to other parts of the *sūra* be appreciated.

We may now turn to some of the principal characteristics of the *tafsīr*. We shall abjure the method of seizing upon passages of particular interest or verses that have been controversial in the writings of the classical commentators. While these may be interesting in themselves, they do not necessarily help us to establish the general orientation of the commentary or to locate it with respect to the development of the genre.

To begin with, we may point to Mawdūdī's use of *ḥadīth* in the *tafsīr*. At numerous places in his writings he lays emphasis upon the importance of the *sunna* of Muḥammad as a source of guidance second only to the Qur'ān itself. Divine revelation though it may be, the Qur'ān is not sufficient in itself in Mawdūdī's view to provide guidance for the community. Not infrequently, the Quranic treatment of important matters is brief, abstract, or incomplete, and there is the need for more concrete and practical direction to the community. 'The actual work of building the Islamic way of life, in accordance with the instructions contained in the Book, was entrusted to the Holy Prophet. . . .'[9] From this perspective the study of *sunna* would seem essential to the interpretation of the Qur'ān. As a corollary of this position there is an implicit refusal of the view that the Qur'ān is self-interpreting, the notion that a passage may be expounded only by reference to another part of the book. It must

[9] i. 31.

be remembered that India has a long tradition of the kind of interpreters of the Qur'ān known as *ahl-i Qur'ān*, going back at least to early parts of the nineteenth century.[10] Mawdūdī knew the opinions of these people well; in fact, after the establishment of Pakistan one such group, the followers of Ghulām Aḥmad Parvēz, were numbered among his principal ideological opponents. Appeal to tradition, therefore, was not perfunctory but represented a substantial principle for Mawdūdī.

Now, in these circumstances one would expect a frequent, indeed constant, resort to *ḥadīth* as a resource for understanding the Quranic message. In fact, however, the method in the *tafsīr* is not one of primary dependence upon *ḥadīth* materials. There is little kinship between Mawdūdī's interpretation of the Qur'ān, which is decidedly responsive to modern considerations, and those of the classical commentators whom we know as traditionalists. Mawdūdī belongs with the large group of Muslim reformists and revivalists who considered themselves *ghayr maqallad* with respect to the medieval schools of law. Most of these people, like Mawdūdī, make Qur'ān and *sunna* the exclusive authorities in religion as a way of gaining more freedom for the adaptation of Muslim thought and practice to modern conditions. While in legal matters he did assign some significance to the opinions of the *fuqahā'* of previous times and believed it important for modern Muslims to acquaint themselves with their opinions, for him their views have no final validity. The modern Muslim is not bound by the opinions of his predecessors, but is free to interpret the Qur'ān and the *sunna* for himself, provided only that he has the proper qualifications. The real key to Mawdūdī's manner of expounding the Qur'ān lies in this claim to freedom of the exercise of the intellect within the limits and on the basis of the materials provided by the Qur'ān and *sunna*. The procedure that he actually follows in the commentary is one of paraphrase, or recasting the Quranic message in his own words, and, when appropriate, supplying reasonable arguments to uphold its validity. More often than not, when explanations of technical

[10] For a history of the *ahl-i Qur'ān* in India see Raja F. M. Majid, 'Ghulām Jīlānī Barq: A Study in Muslim Rationalism', unpublished MA thesis (McGill University, 1962), and C. J. Adams, 'The Authority of the Prophetic *ḥadīth* in the Eyes of Some Modern Muslims', in D. P. Little, ed., *Essays on Islamic Civilization* (Leiden, 1976), 25–47. For a treatment of Mawdūdī's exegesis in the general context of Indian modernism see J. M. S. Baljon, *Modern Muslim Koran Interpretation (1880–1960)* Leiden, 1968), *passim*.

terms or Quranic allusions are offered, no authority for the explanation is cited. Only from time to time is a *ḥadīth* quoted, but no concern is evidenced consistently to buttress the commentary with such authoritative material. What is said apparently stands on its own authority. There is one significant exception to this general tendency, however, and to that we may now turn.

The exception is seen vividly in connection with those passages of the Qur'ān that deal with the details of legal matters. As examples we may point to the commentary on *sūra* 22,[11] where rules for the ownership, rent, and sale of land in Mecca are discussed, and the commentary on *sūra* 24, which deals with rules for the relations between the sexes. In each instance the commentary goes far beyond what is said in the Qur'ān itself and ultimately becomes a systematic exploration of the rules that pertain to the matter at issue with their specifications, exceptions, implications, and so on, as worked out by the Muslim lawyers. That is to say that the commentary becomes the vehicle of an essentially *fiqhī* exercise. In these instances and others like them, *ḥadīth* are quoted liberally. There is also a certain amount of criticism of *ḥadīth* that Mawdūdī judges to be weak or unacceptable for the purpose. In these cases there is no lack of traditional scholarly paraphernalia and erudite technical argument. Mawdūdī's general statement about *sunna* emphasized that it was to spell out the practical implications of the general principles stated in the Qur'ān, and this is precisely the way in which he employs *ḥadīth* to expand upon the legal passages in the Qur'ān. Furthermore, the debates of the *fuqahā'* around these points are also reproduced and the varying perspectives of major jurists set forth. Such portions of the commentary are impressive for the learning they evidence and for the depth and breadth of acquaintance with the relevant Islamic literature that they exhibit. In this respect they stand in marked contrast to the approach in much of the rest of the *tafsīr*. Further, the comments on these 'legal' portions of the Qur'ān are much longer, by a wide margin, than those on other portions of the scripture.

From the disproportionate interest lavished on these legal matters, it is evident that the commentary here approaches issues that were very dear to Mawdūdī's heart. Indeed, taking into account his other works and his long years of activity in

[11] vii. 195 n. 43.

organization and Islamic *da'wa* along with the *tafsīr*, we may say that the emphasis on legal teachings is a true expression of his perception of Islam. For Mawdūdī the fundamental message of the Qur'ān was the obligation laid upon people to render obedience and homage to their sovereign Creator and Lord. He understood the basis of religion to be a specified set of commands and prohibitions which all men are free either to neglect or observe with commensurate results for both their this-wordly and their other-worldly destinies. There is nothing vague or indefinite about the duties of men relative to God and to each other. The very essence of true homage or worship for him is strict obedience to what God has commanded. In the simplest of terms, Islam has to do with the difference between right and wrong in human conduct; it is moralistic to the core, even puritanical. It should not be surprising, then, that Mawdūdī dwells with minute detail on those portions of the Qur'ān that he sees as giving clearest expression to the guidance that men should follow.

This aspect of the *tafsīr* is also important for what it excludes. In its legalistic and moralistic approach to the human situation, it lays great weight upon the distance between God and His creatures, and on the subservience of the latter to the former. While God is to be respected, obeyed, held in awe, and feared, as is appropriate to the attitude of a servant, very little of the *fascinans* aspect of the divine nature emerges from the *tafsīr*. It would be very difficult, indeed, to find a ground for mysticism or for any effort to cultivate intimacy with the divine in Mawdūdī's *tafsīr*. Those verses which emphasize the nearness of God or His ubiquitous presence and accessibility ('Wherever you turn your faces', etc.) are taken by Mawdūdī to refer to the surveillance of the stern judge who sees all that we do and who will one day call us to the reckoning. This aspect of the *tafsīr* is paralleled by the views expressed in such books as *Iḥyā'ō tajdīd al-dīn*, where the true meaning of Sufism is equated with purity of heart and life in the strictly moralistic sense. For most of what we know as Sufism, Mawdūdī has little respect, and this fact is reflected both negatively and positively in the *tafsīr*, negatively in an interpretation that provides no place for the mystical quest, and positively in the attacks on adoration of saints, prayers addressed to holy men, reverence paid to tombs, and the like.

The *tafsīr* is also little concerned with other matters that are often characteristic of works of the genre. There is, for example, almost no attention paid to the *i'jāz* of the Qur'ān beyond merely asserting that it exists. In connection with those verses which challenge the Arabs to 'produce a *sūra* like it', Mawdūdī mentions the miraculousness of the Qur'ān's literary qualities and argues that these were a necessary element of the prophet's attraction for his followers. Part of the prophetic gift lay in Muḥammad's capacity to charm those who heard him. The fascination which he exercised over his audiences was constituted, on the one hand, by his personality, but also, on the other, by the perfection and beauty of the revelations that were delivered through his mouth. There is, however, no analysis of the literary composition and appeal of the Qur'ān, none of the dissection of the rhetorical structure of the text that so much fascinated other *mufassirūn*. Likewise, little attention is bestowed on strictly linguistic considerations with respect to the text. Very occasionally only is there some explanation of a feature of Quranic expression, for instance, a comment on why a word is plural rather than singular. Philological problems and issues of grammar or syntax fall very far down on the list of matters dealt with in this *tafsīr*. There is one of the rare exceptions to this broad statement in the commentary on Q. 20/85 and 95, where the man who led the Israelites to worship the golden calf is identified as al-sāmirī. Mawdūdī does not accept this designation as a proper name but as a *nisba* indicating the person's race or place of origin, and he supports his view by a brief discussion of the *yā'* of the *nisba* and the use of the definite article in Arabic. A similar disinterest is accorded to the approach to the Qur'ān which seeks to explain the meaning through reference to other literature, particularly to the poetry of the pre-Islamic and early Islamic periods. The absence of such discussions may perhaps be attributed to Mawdūdī's focus on the common person who would be neither equipped nor disposed to pursue such technicalities, but it accords also with his insistence upon making the Quranic message in its integrity and wholeness the centre of attention. Too much attention to detail would have defeated his purpose. His aim was a *tafhīm* of the Qur'ān, a persuasive and comprehensive exposition of its central themes, that would leave no doubt of its claims upon human life. The *Tafhīm al-Qur'ān* is, thus, a variety of preaching, at once the basis and an instrument of the vigorous movement of Islamic resurgence that Mawdūdī sought to launch.

Another striking feature of the *tafsīr* is its citation and use of materials from the Bible, both the Hebrew and the Christian Bibles. While it may be generally true that modern Muslims and Indian Muslims in particular have shown little inclination to study the Bible closely or to deal with it in terms of what it actually says, Mawdūdī exhibits a close acquaintance with the text. In connection with certain Quranic verses he quotes the Bible *in extenso*, the quoted passages being sometimes several pages in length. For example, in relation to the story of the birth of John the Baptist as told in the first part of *sūra* 19, the explanatory notes reproduce the whole of Luke 1: 5–22. In this instance, attention is called to the difference between the Quranic and Biblical accounts by material added in parentheses. The Quranic story makes Zechariah's affliction with dumbness one of the signs of God, while Luke characterizes it as a punishment which God inflicted on Zechariah for his initial doubt about the announced birth of a son; there is also some difference in the duration of the dumbness in the two stories.

The generous quotation of Biblical material is in itself striking, but the use to which it is put in this and a number of other instances is even more so. In the explanatory note on Q. 19/13–15, Mawdūdī urges the usefulness of the Gospels for achieving a broader and more detailed understanding of the life of John the Baptist.[12] To this end he quotes from all four of the Gospels in a lengthy exposition of the activities, career, and eventual fate of John. In these examples and elsewhere, the Bible is thus used to confirm the Qur'ān and is explicitly recognized as giving even more authentic information about some matters than the Quranic revelations can afford. In other cases, however, the Bible is quoted and the text compared with the Qur'ān as a means of showing the superiority of the Qur'ān over the Bible. Mawdūdī says at one point that merely reading the two side by side and noting the differences between them is sufficient to demonstrate the greater authenticity and the truth of the Qur'ān. He concludes a long comment on the story of Adam and Eve in *sūra* 20, in which the Bible story is also given, by saying:

> It is obvious that the Bible has not done justice to Adam and Eve, nay, even to God Himself. On the other hand the account given in the Qur'ān is in itself a clear proof that the stories in it have not been copied from the Bible;

[12] vi. 66 n. 12.

for the Qur'ān not only corroborates those parts of the Bible which remain untampered but also corrects its wrong statements.[13]

This assertion is made boldly without any further discussion or substantiation.

The Biblical material just referred to was taken from the Hebrew Bible. Indeed, there is a much greater use in the *tafsīr* of material from the Jewish Bible and the Talmud than of that from the New Testament. That it should be so is readily understandable, since the Qur'ān devotes much more attention to the Jews, their history, and their prophets than it does to Christians and their concerns. One brief example of the many appeals to the Jewish Bible will suffice to illustrate the method of the *tafsīr*. The personage mentioned above, *al-sāmirī*, is told by Moses in Q. 20/97, 'Then go! And lo! In this life it is for thee to say: Touch me not!' For the explanation Mawdūdī goes to the Book of Leviticus (13: 45–6), where rules are laid down for lepers who must cry out to everyone they may encounter warning of their unclean and outcaste status. Mawdūdī concludes that *al-sāmirī* was perhaps actually afflicted with leprosy as punishment for his misdoing, or if not, that he was to be treated in this extreme way because of his 'moral leprosy'.[14] Another instance of a more wide-ranging reference to the Bible (Psalms, Isaiah, Jeremiah, and Ezekiel, as well as Matthew and Luke) may be seen in the note on Q. 17/4.[15]

Reference to the Talmud and long quotations from it are offered in the commentary on the story of Abraham in *sūra* 21. In this case there is a kind of ambiguity in Mawdūdī's assessment of the value of these Jewish materials, an element both of approval and of disapproval. On the one hand the Talmud seems to corroborate many aspects of the Abraham story as given in the Qur'ān, especially the events of his life in Iraq such as his conflict with his father and his being cast into the fire, elements of the story that are not mentioned at all in the Bible. However, 'one can clearly feel that the account given in the Talmud is full of heterogeneous and hypothetical things while the one given in the Qur'ān is most clear and contains nothing unworthy of Prophet Abraham'. Again the differences between the Qur'ān and the Talmudic version of the story are taken as prima-facie evidence that the Qur'ān has no literary dependence on Biblical or other Jewish literature.[16] The

[13] vii 131 n. 106.
[14] vii. 120 n. 74.
[15] vi. 117 n. 6.
[16] vi. 160 n. 66.

Talmud has authority and usefulness, but they are clearly limited, and no indication is given of the point at which the line must be drawn.

Another way of locating Mawdūdī's *tafsīr* in the spectrum of interpretations of the Qur'ān, at least in the Indian subcontinent, is to consider the attitude adopted towards miracles and other overt manifestations of the supernatural. In the late nineteenth century, Sayyid Aḥmad Khān had attracted much attention with his dictum that 'the Word of God cannot contradict the Work of God'.[17] This view issued in a thorough-going naturalistic commentary on the Qur'ān that sought explanations for allegedly supernatural events in natural phenomena, in the metaphorical use of language, and the like. Many of the Muslim modernists after Sayyid Aḥmad also adopted this perspective as part of their apologetic for the rational character of Quranic and Islamic teaching. Their approach was intended to allay some of the doubts that might arise for Muslims in coming to terms with the 'enlightenment' of the modern age. Although Mawdūdī shares the apologetic aims of these thinkers and also upholds their emphasis upon rationality, he is not reluctant to affirm the existence of the supernatural and the miraculous nor to recognize their operation in the affairs of men. Many examples could be cited, an outstanding one being the interpretation of Muḥammad's *mi'rāj*. The Qur'ān gives a very brief account of the famous night journey, and Mawdūdī fleshes out the bare bones with details taken from *ḥadīth*. He does not, however, insist that one must accept every detail supplied by the traditions. He also recognizes that some individuals believe the *mi'rāj* to have been either a dream or a mystical vision, in any case less than a tangibly real event. In Mawdūdī's view, the prophet was actually taken physically through the seven heavens and into the presence of God where the veils were lifted and he literally saw with his bodily eyes the unseen realities. The physical nature of the occurrence is proven, Mawdūdī says, by the language which the Qur'ān uses. There is no discussion of the reports such as that from Muḥammad's aunt and others which describe the night journey as a

[17] On this point and Sir Sayyid's exegetical principles in general, see Daud Rahbar, 'Sir Sayyid Ahmad Khan's Principles of Exegesis, translated from his Taḥrīr fī uṣūl al-tafsīr', *MW* 46 (1956), 104–12, 324–35, esp. 'The Fourteenth Principle', 325. See also Aziz Ahmad, *Islamic Modernism in India and Pakistan, 1857–1964* (Oxford, 1967), 31 ff and, in even greater detail, Christian Troll, *Sayyid Ahmad Khan: A Reinterpretation of Muslim Theology* (New Delhi, 1978).

dream. Mawdūdī finds it unreasonable and strange that anyone could question whether such an event were possible. Questions of possibility and impossibility arise only in respect to people and never to God, whose power and capabilities are unlimited. How is it, he asked, that one should ask about God's ability to perform miracles when mere people have been able to reach the moon?[18] The resolution to the problem posed for some people by miracles is thus found in the nature of God as all-powerful and unlimited divine being. By definition, God can do anything; and if one believes in God, one must not doubt the infinite divine capacity. Such, he says, was the stance which Muḥammad and the Qur'ān had taken towards those disbelievers who challenged the possibility of resurrection from the dead. The Quranic response had called attention to the creative power of God in first bringing men into existence, and had demanded to know why such a powerful being should not again raise men from their graves. It is interesting that the *mi'rāj* story, probably the most evocative single passage in the entire Qur'ān for those with a mystical temperament, serves for Mawdūdī only to prove the possibility of miracles.

But once again, as in many other things, the position adopted is not entirely unequivocal. Mawdūdī does in several instances show a tendency similar to that of modernists by interpreting in a naturalistic way a Quranic allusion which has traditionally been taken as referring to miraculous happenings. In *sūra* 15, for example, reference is made to the punishment visited upon the people of Lot in the form of stones of baked clay that were rained down upon them. Mawdūdī understands the 'stones' in this case to have been either a shower of meteorites or a fall of volcanic ash and lava.[19] The latter interpretation would seem justified by the reference to their habitations being turned upside down (possibly in an earthquake?) and the reference to the stones having been baked or heated. In the same *sūra* Mawdūdī translates verse 16, *wa laqad ja'alnā fī al-samā'i burūj wa zayyināhā lil-nāẓirīn*, as: 'And We divided the heavens into many fortified spheres for the sake of administration.'[20] He then goes on to explain the fortified spheres in terms of a large group of meteorites surrounding the various

[18] vi. 115 n. 1. This comment has an additional interest because of the refusal of some members of the religious class in Pakistan to believe that men had actually walked on the moon.

[19] vi. 47 n. 41.

[20] vi. 34 n. 12.

heavenly bodies in such a way as to protect them from still other meteorites or debris from space that might otherwise do them harm. We cannot see them, but there they are, he asserts, invisible walls that keep each sphere distinct from the others and guard against their destruction. The spheres are, thus, somewhat of the nature of natural law.

As a final point we may consider the political dimension or implications of the *tafsīr*. As is well known, Mawdūdī is among the foremost of those modern Muslim thinkers who have insisted that true Islam involves overt political activity and must issue in the emergence of an Islamic state controlled by sincerely religious men who are determined that both their own lives and the life of society generally shall conform to the Islamic system. His views on the nature of Islam and what it demands may be taken almost as a definition of Islamic resurgence, since they conform so closely with the opinions of similar leaders in other parts of the Muslim world, many of whom profess great admiration for Mawdūdī.[21] It would be reasonable, therefore, to expect to find a great emphasis upon the political side of Islamic teaching in Mawdūdī's interpretation of the Qur'ān. Yet, astonishingly, the political element does not have prominence in the *tafsīr*. Far from being a thread that runs through the whole, issues that might be considered to be specifically political or to have political implications arise only very occasionally. If one were to characterize the central issues that arise from the commentary, they appear to be theological and moral. In so far as morality may be seen to have relationship to law, and law to the state, an argument could perhaps be mounted to claim specifically political significance for all the passages which take up moral issues as well as for those which contain definite prescriptions and proscriptions. But even if this argument were to be granted, the treatment of strictly political problems would still be secondary, conducted by implication through the attention given immediately to other matters.

There are passages, though few, where the nature of the state figures explicitly. *Sūra* 17 is said to be 'a sort of Manifesto of the intended Islamic state which had been proclaimed a year before its actual establishment'.[22] In the commentary on the *sūra* he says of a certain verse, 'This is a clear proof that according to Islam, political

[21] See C. J. Adams, 'Mawdudi and the Islamic State'.
[22] vi. 111–12.

power is also required to introduce reform. . . . It is not only lawful but desirable to acquire power, and those who consider this to be a worldly thing are obviously in the wrong.' The desirability of power, however, is yet a long way from its necessity; there is in other words a certain reserve about the attitude to power in his reading of the Qur'ān. It should be kept in mind that Mawdūdī never found in Islam that driving and overriding need for power that would precipitate revolutionary action.

The most often-repeated emphasis of a theme with political overtones is that upon the sovereignty of God. This teaching, which was a pillar of Mawdūdī's theology and world view, is returned to and underlined constantly throughout the *tafsīr*. But seldom, however, is the exposition of the theme linked to the nature of a polity or the conduct of state. Most often the context is theological, dealing with such things as monotheism, the powerlessness of the pagan deities, or the arrogance of the pagan Arabs for thinking that they would be able to escape the divine retribution. Were one not acquainted with Mawdūdī's attitudes and his political activities from other sources, it is not at all certain that any strong impulse would emerge from the *tafsīr* clearly to identify him with the resurgence perspective, at least in my opinion. On the contrary, the general impression that it leaves is one of a conservative, largely traditional approach to the Qur'ān, though one that shows the marks of certain strictly modern influences.

GENERAL INDEX

INDEX OF QURANIC CITATIONS